Springer Texts in Education

Springer Texts in Education delivers high-quality instructional content for graduates and advanced graduates in all areas of Education and Educational Research. The textbook series is comprised of self-contained books with a broad and comprehensive coverage that are suitable for class as well as for individual self-study. All texts are authored by established experts in their fields and offer a solid methodological background, accompanied by pedagogical materials to serve students such as practical examples, exercises, case studies etc. Textbooks published in the Springer Texts in Education series are addressed to graduate and advanced graduate students, but also to researchers as important resources for their education, knowledge and teaching. Please contact Natalie Rieborn at textbooks.education@springer.com or your regular editorial contact person for queries or to submit your book proposal.

More information about this series at https://link.springer.com/bookseries/13812

E. Leslie Cameron • Douglas A. Bernstein

Illustrating Concepts and Phenomena in Psychology

A Teacher-Friendly Compendium of Examples

E. Leslie Cameron
Department of Psychological Science
Carthage College
Kenosha, WI, USA

Douglas A. Bernstein
Department of Psychology
University of South Florida
Tampa, FL, USA

ISSN 2366-7672 ISSN 2366-7680 (electronic)
Springer Texts in Education
ISBN 978-3-030-85649-6 ISBN 978-3-030-85650-2 (eBook)
https://doi.org/10.1007/978-3-030-85650-2

© Springer Nature Switzerland AG 2022

This work is subject to copyright. All rights are reserved by the Publisher, whether the whole or part of the material is concerned, specifically the rights of translation, reprinting, reuse of illustrations, recitation, broadcasting, reproduction on microfilms or in any other physical way, and transmission or information storage and retrieval, electronic adaptation, computer software, or by similar or dissimilar methodology now known or hereafter developed.

The use of general descriptive names, registered names, trademarks, service marks, etc. in this publication does not imply, even in the absence of a specific statement, that such names are exempt from the relevant protective laws and regulations and therefore free for general use.

The publisher, the authors and the editors are safe to assume that the advice and information in this book are believed to be true and accurate at the date of publication. Neither the publisher nor the authors or the editors give a warranty, expressed or implied, with respect to the material contained herein or for any errors or omissions that may have been made. The publisher remains neutral with regard to jurisdictional claims in published maps and institutional affiliations.

This Springer imprint is published by the registered company Springer Nature Switzerland AG
The registered company address is: Gewerbestrasse 11, 6330 Cham, Switzerland

Foreword

I often talk to students after my classes and a particular group of them who lived in the same residence hall stands out in my memory. One member of the group was doing really well on the exams, much to her friends' bewilderment. She did not study as long and hard for exams as her friends did, nor did she have a background in psychology, but she was at the top of the class. In class, this student would sit in rapt attention, but would not take extensive notes like other students. One time I was talking with her and I asked her what she liked about the class. "I like the examples you give," she said, "I think about them a lot outside of class." She did not consider this studying because it did not involve notecards or highlighting. Based on what we know about the power of good examples to facilitate learning, however, this was actually a powerful form of studying (Chiu & Chi, 2014).

  This book is intended to help you harness the power of good examples in your teaching. There are multiple and diverse examples for virtually every concept in psychology. Your job is to select the best ones for your teaching, which can be more difficult than you might think. The effectiveness of an example depends on the academic context. Factors such as the students' prior knowledge, their cultural backgrounds, and how they process the examples all influence effectiveness (cf. Chew & Cerbin, 2020). An example that is effective at a large, open enrollment, public university might not be effective at a small, selective historically black college or university. What is effective at a two-year community college focused on vocational training may not be effective at a small liberal arts college. Teachers must determine which examples work best for their students.

  There are two basic truths about examples, one of which is generally acknowledged but the other of which is generally ignored. The truth we acknowledge, and the reason for this book, is that examples can be powerful tools to enhance student learning. No pedagogical approach, be it traditional lecture or technology-enhanced collaborative group learning, discounts the usefulness and importance of good examples. Pedagogical research overwhelmingly supports the usefulness of examples. The truth we generally ignore is that using examples effectively is neither simple nor straightforward (Chew, 2007). Poor examples are not just ineffective, they can actually hurt learning. Too often, teachers come up with examples that are intuitively clear to them, but what is clear to an expert with years of training may not be clear to students learning psychology for the first time. Many years ago, I had both teachers and students of psychology rate a set of examples for their clarity and effectiveness. I found good agreement among teachers about what was a good example, and good agreement among students, but little agreement between teachers and students. This book provides you with a pool of examples to try out in your classes. The best examples may not be the ones you expect.

Research has also found that students, especially weaker students, typically do not make the best use of examples (Chiu & Chi, 2014). Good students reflect on them and map the components of the example onto the critical aspects of the concept, as in the case of my student above. Weaker students tend to memorize the example, thinking that if they remember the example, then they understand the concept. Alternatively, they may focus on the superficial elements of an example rather than its key structural elements. They may learn about Pavlov and classical conditioning and think it only applies to dogs and food. They do not see classical conditioning as a fundamental form of learning that applies to a wide array of situations, such as drug addiction and prejudice. When teaching with examples, it is always a good idea to prompt students to reflect on examples and think about how the example relates to the concept.

When you teach a course multiple times, it is always a good idea to refine your teaching methods and activities to make the course better. This book will help you to refine the examples you use and how you use them. Good teachers have "tried and true" examples for every concept that they teach, but they also have Plan B and Plan C examples as well. No single example is going to be effective for everyone in the class, and this book will provide you with multiple, diverse examples.

Examples are powerful because they can be used to achieve multiple learning goals. They can be used as part of formative assessments to give students feedback about their level of understanding. They can be used to address the common misconceptions students often have about psychology. They can be used to promote good learning habits, like spaced practice, interleaving, and retrieval practice. They can help students see the relevance of what they are learning beyond the class itself and promote the transfer of knowledge. But to do all of these things, you have to start with a set of good examples. You have that in this book. To use an analogy (which is a form of example), you are like a chef with a wide assortment of fine ingredients. What you can create with them is limited only by your creativity.

Stephen L. Chew
Samford University
Birmingham, AL, USA

References

Chew, S. L. (2007). Designing effective examples and problems for teaching statistics. In D. S. Dunn, R. A. Smith, & B. Beins (Eds.), *Best practices for teaching statistics and research methods in the behavioral sciences* (pp. 73–91), Mahwah, NJ: Erlbaum.

Chew, S. L., & Cerbin, W. J. (2020). The cognitive challenges of effective teaching. *The Journal of Economic Education*, https://doi.org/10.1080/00220485.2020.1845256.

Chiu, J. L., & Chi, M. T. H. (2014). Supporting self-explanation in the classroom. In V. A. Benassi, C. E. Overson, & C. M. Hakala (Eds.), *Applying science of learning in education: Infusing psychological science in the curriculum* (pp. 91–103). Society for the Teaching of Psychology. https://teachpsych.org/ebooks/asle2014/index.php.

Preface

Like other professors who teach psychology, we are perpetually seeking ever-better examples of the concepts, theories, and phenomena that we introduce in class. It is important to have these examples because, as we know from research in cognitive psychology and from long experience in teaching, they help make course material more interesting and they help students understand, learn, and remember it (e.g., Craik & Lockhart, 1972). This is particularly true if the examples are clear, vivid, offbeat, funny, or relevant to students' life experiences (Bernstein, Franz, & Chew, 2020; Rogers, Kuiper & Kirker, 1977).

For psychology teachers in the USA, a reminder of the importance of giving good examples is contained in the latest edition of the American Psychological Association's *Guidelines for the Undergraduate Psychology Major* (version 2.0; APA, 2013). Specifically, Outcome 1.3a (p. 21) states that students completing a psychology major should ideally be able to describe examples of relevant and practical applications of psychological principles. The value of this outcome lies in assuring that students can recognize how those principles apply to everyday life.

To help them do so, teachers must be ready with plenty of examples. The problem is that psychology teachers are generally on their own when it comes to finding the most useful and compelling examples to illustrate and animate the vast array of material included in most psychology courses, especially introductory psychology. They have to search for (or stumble upon) those gems of examples that are scattered far and wide in scholarly books, journal articles, textbooks, instructors' manuals, test banks, discussion group threads, teaching conference presentations, blogs, and YouTube videos, among other places. As a result, many teachers of psychology—particularly those who are new to teaching or are teaching a course for the first time—find that good, useful examples are in short supply, especially when, as so often happens in the introductory course, they are teaching material that is outside their own area of specialization. Generating examples on the fly in class is difficult, and finding good, accurate, and error-free examples in advance takes a lot of time—as we can attest after having created this compendium. Asking students for examples in class is risky; the results can range from the surprisingly good to the stunningly incorrect, inappropriate, or bizarre, leading to confusion at best and awkward or embarrassing moments at worst.

To illustrate the problem, imagine that you are an industrial/organizational psychologist teaching your first introductory psychology course, and today's class is on the basic principles of classical conditioning, including the concept of negative reinforcement. You introduce this widely misunderstood phenomenon by saying that it involves strengthening a behavior by removing a negative reinforcer after the behavior occurs. You have correctly described the process, but many of your students will not have a clue as to what you mean. To help them understand, you offer the example of a rat in a cage whose floor is electrified and is delivering a continuous, uncomfortable shock that will stop when the rat presses a button. If the rat learns to press the button, it will have done so via negative reinforcement; button-pressing was strengthened by the removal of the shock. Got it? Five percent of your students will understand, while the rest will probably just write down what you said and hope that it will not be on the test (it will be). Some of them might ask for clarification, but you might not be able to offer much beyond what you already said. If you then move on to the next topic, the majority of your class will either have to figure out the negative reinforcement principle on their own or to simply fail to understand it, thus helping to perpetuate the widely held misconception that negative reinforcement is the same as punishment.

Worse yet, you will not look forward to trying to teach this difficult concept in the future. Experiences like this are among the factors that create teaching anxiety, impair relationships with students, and reduce some teachers' motivation to try to improve their courses (Bernstein, 1983; Bernstein, Frantz, & Chew, 2020). What you need are more and better examples, including those available on YouTube, in cartoons, in clinical case studies, or scenarios such as these:

1. We learn to push our TV's mute button through negative reinforcement; pressing it eliminates the sounds of a commercial or a commentator that we cannot stand.
2. We learn to take pain relievers through negative reinforcement because after doing so, our pain disappears.
3. We learn to get out of unpleasant social situations through negative reinforcement, as when we end a boring date early after complaining of an imaginary headache.
4. Our fear of spiders can be solidified through negative reinforcement when we escape anxiety by changing the channel when a spider appears on a nature show.
5. We learn to fasten our seat belts through negative reinforcement because doing so stops that annoying reminder chime.

Adding a few of these examples would probably have helped students to better understand the concept of negative reinforcement.

What This Book Is and What It Isn't

This book is the result of our efforts to gather examples of the most important and most commonly taught topics in undergraduate psychology courses. We have organized those topics roughly in the order that they appear in the tables of contents of most introductory psychology textbooks, but our goal was to find examples that will be useful to teachers of all psychology courses. You can quickly find the topics you are looking for either by electronically searching the e-book file or consulting the index of the print book.

Our first criterion for selecting topics was that they appear frequently in the glossaries of many kinds of psychology textbooks. A secondary criterion, though not always employed, was that students might find the topics difficult to understand and that faculty might find them difficult to teach (e.g., Cassidy et al., 2019; Park, 2007; Peck et al., 2006). We arrived at the final set of topics by first creating a master list based on the glossaries of many textbooks and the literature on common course topics (e.g., Gurung & Landrum, 2013; Landrum, 1993; Proctor & Williams, 2006; Quereshi, 1993). After reviewing that list independently, we compared notes, resolved any differences of opinion, and eventually agreed on the topics that our 72 collective years of teaching experience told us are most in need of good examples. Our choice of topics, and some of our examples, were also shaped by the advice of the many colleagues listed in the acknowledgements section below.

We hope that the examples offered here will not only help your students to better understand the concepts and phenomena of psychological science but will in some cases also help you to debunk the many myths and misconceptions that students bring with them to psychology courses at all levels (Bernstein, 2017).

What You Will Find Here

We present our examples in many forms. Some are just lists of short, simple illustrations based on textbook content and our own teaching notes. Others are anecdotes or brief stories, because storytelling, when done well, can be memorable and meaningful (e.g., Brakke & Houska, 2015; Goodfriend & Heinzen, 2020; Green, 2004). Still other examples are case studies or descriptions of research results published by psychological scientists around the world. Some topics are presented in pairs to more easily clarify contrasting elements, to create connections with related topics, or to indicate what the topic is NOT. So, for example, the topics of punishment and reinforcement are presented together in the learning chapter to promote an understanding of their similarities and differences.

Throughout, you will find hundreds of links to relevant websites or videos. They appear as hyperlinks for those who are reading the digital version of the book and scannable QR codes through which readers of the print book can reach those materials on a mobile device. We also found many cartoons that offer humorous examples of psychological topics but the high cost of permission to reproduce them led us to simply describe them and provide a hyperlink and QR code that will allow you to take a look and decide which ones to use in your classes.

A word of caution: Over the many months that we spent searching for links to the best online examples for this book, we ran across materials whose titles suggested that they would be useful and appropriate, but upon closer inspection turned out to be inappropriate for classroom use or, worse, to be poor, oversimplified, or even incorrect examples. This was especially the case for videos, so when you follow the video links that we provide, be aware that we are recommending only the video on the page where you land. Others listed in the margin of that page may or may not be equally useful.

Be aware, too, that some of the video examples in this book will be found in a *Databrary* volume entitled "Illustrating Concepts and Phenomena in Psychology: A Teacher-Friendly Compendium of Examples" (https://nyu.databrary.org/volume/1269). *Databrary* is a specialized data repository for storing, streaming, and sharing video and audio data for purposes of research and documentation. Videos that are shared on the repository for teaching and presentation purposes have received permission from participants to be shown to audiences outside of a research laboratory setting; typically, such non-research uses do not require approval from an institutional review board.

All the Databrary videos we identify are freely available to both teachers and students to view, download, and reuse. To access these videos, you must become an "authorized user" by registering for a free Databrary account at https://nyu.databrary.org/user/register and accepting the Databrary Access Agreement at https://databrary.org/about/agreement.html. This agreement is a legal contract between you, your institution, and Databrary's host institution, New York University. After you register for an account and your institution approves the agreement, you will have open access to all shared data on Databrary. As an "authorized user," you can also give your students, staff, and trainees access to the shared data on the repository. These arrangements are necessary because as of 2021 the repository held an additional 72,000+ hours of shared video from 1265 authorized researchers from 622 institutions worldwide. With its mission to support data sharing among researchers and educators in the behavioral, social, educational, developmental, neural, and computer sciences, Databrary restricts access to all *non-public* data.

What You Will NOT Find Here

We created this book for psychology teachers, not students, and we assume that our readers have at least some familiarity with the topics for which we offer examples. We have therefore not provided definitions for terms and concepts—except in cases where we think there may be some difference of opinion among instructors. (If you need to brush up on information about any of the topics to be covered in courses outside your main area of expertise, we recommend taking a look at a recent textbook on introductory psychology, an advanced textbook for the course, and/or the APA Dictionary of Psychology at https://dictionary.apa.org/).

Accordingly, we have focused on providing *examples* of topics, not *explanations* of them. This is neither a textbook nor an instructor's manual, so in the chapter on Biological Aspects of Psychology, for example, though we include descriptions, illustrations, and cases of disorders that can result from damage to various brain regions and structures, we do not explain where they are, what they normally do, and how they do it. Our goal in that chapter, as in all the others, is to provide you with illustrative material that will enhance your own explanations, and though we occasionally offer suggestions based on our experience, we assume that you are the best judge of how, when, and where to use each example.

We hope that our examples will be helpful to you, either as we have written them, or as you modify them to fit your course, your students, and your teaching style. We hope, too, that you and your students will enjoy having more examples included in your class sessions even if presenting those examples slows the pace of your lectures. We believe that presenting somewhat less material in a more memorable way can motivate students to learn on their own, including by completing assigned readings.

An Invitation to Contribute

We know that links to websites can be unstable, so when you find a broken link, we hope you will let us know, either by contacting us at our email addresses below, or by leaving a comment on the feedback page of the book's website at www.psychexamples.com. We also invite you to comment on our examples and to propose examples of your own for posting on the website and for inclusion in a future edition of the book. Finally, we invite you to subscribe to our blog at www.psychexamples.com so that you will be notified whenever new examples are posted.

We look forward to hearing from you, and we wish you all the best in your teaching.

Kenosha, WI, USA E. Leslie Cameron
lcameron@carthage.edu

Tampa, FL, USA Douglas A. Bernstein
douglas.bernstein@comcast.net

References

American Psychological Association (2013). *APA guidelines for the undergraduate psychology major: Version 2.0.* Retrieved from http://www.apa.org/ed/precollege/undergrad/index.aspx.

Bernstein, D. A. (1983). Dealing with teaching anxiety. *Journal of the National Association of Colleges and Teachers of Agriculture, 27,* 4–7.

Bernstein, D. A. (2017). Bye-bye intro: A proposal for transforming introductory psychology. *Scholarship of Teaching and Learning in Psychology, 3,* 191–197.

Bernstein, D. A., Frantz, S., & Chew, S. (2020). *Teaching psychology: A step by step guide.* (3rd ed.). New York: Taylor & Francis.

Brakke, K., & Houska, J. A. (2015). *Telling stories: The art and science of storytelling as an instructional strategy.* Retrieved from the Society for the Teaching of Psychology website: http://teachpsych.org/ebooks/tellingstories.html.

Cassidy, S. A., Dimova, R., Giguère, B., Spence, J. R., & Stanley, D. J. (2019). Failing grade: 89% of introduction-to-psychology textbooks that define or explain statistical significance do so incorrectly. *Advances in Methods and Practices in Psychological Science,* 233–239. https://doi.org/10.1177/2515245919858072.

Craik, F. I. M., & Lockhart, R. F. (1972). Levels of processing: A framework for memory research, *Journal of Verbal Learning and Verbal Behavior, 11,* 671–684.

Goodfriend, W., & Heinzen, T. (2020). Nazis, wizards, & superheroes: Using case studies to bolster class effectiveness. Retrieved from http://teachpsych.org/E-xcellence-in-Teaching-Blog/8790051.

Green, M. (2004). https://www.psychologicalscience.org/observer/storytelling-in-teaching.

Gurung, R. A. R., & Landrum, R. E. (2013). Bottleneck concepts in psychology: Exploratory first steps. *Psychology Learning & Teaching, 12*(3), 236–245. http://dx.doi.org/10.2304/plat.2013.12.3.236.

Landrum, R. E. (1993). Identifying core concepts in introductory psychology. *Psychological Reports, 72*(2), 659–666. https://doi.org/10.2466/pr0.1993.72.2.659.

Park, J. H. (2007). Persistent misunderstandings of inclusive fitness and kin selection: Their ubiquitous appearance in social psychology textbooks. *Evolutionary Psychology.* https://doi.org/10.1177/147470490700500414.

Peck, A. C., Ali, R. A., Matchock, R. L., & Levine, M. E. (2006). Introductory psychology topics and student performance: Where's the challenge? *Teaching of Psychology, 33,* 167–170.

Proctor, D. L., & Williams, A. M. E. (2006). *Frequently cited concepts in current introduction to psychology textbooks.* Society for the Teaching of Psychology Office of Teaching Resources in Psychology. http://teachpsych.org/resources/Documents/otrp/resources/proctor06.pdf.

Quereshi, M. Y. (1993). The contents of introductory psychology textbooks: A follow-up. *Teaching of Psychology, 20*(4), 218–222. https://doi.org/10.1207/s15328023top2004_4.

Rogers, T. B., Kuiper, N. A., & Kirker, W. S. (1977). Self-reference and the encoding of personal information. *Journal of Personality and Social Psychology, 35,* 677–688.

Acknowledgements

We wish to acknowledge the following psychology teacher colleagues who took time to read drafts of one or more chapters in this compendium, to offer comments, and to suggest additional examples. We are deeply grateful for their advice and guidance, but we take full responsibility for any inaccuracies or examples that you do not find useful!

Tony Barnhart
Brian Burke
Catherine Ann Cameron
Elaine Cassel
Stephen Chew
David Daniel
Lisa Dierker
Regan Gurung
Claudia Jorgensen
Maya Khanna
Caroline Brown Kramer
Robert Maleske
April McGrath
David Myers
Nora Nickels
Louis Penner
Nastassia Savage
Jason Spiegelman
Caroline Stanley
Wolfgang Stroebe
Bethany Teachman
Adriana Uruena-Agnes
Vanessa Woods

Contents

1	**Research Methods and Statistics**	1
	Science Versus Pseudoscience	1
	Scientific Method	3
	Experimental Design	9
	Case Studies	20
	Naturalistic Observation	20
	Correlational Research	22
	Survey and Questionnaire Research	24
	Cross Sectional and Longitudinal Research	26
	Meta-Analysis	27
	Research Measures	28
2	**Biological Aspects of Psychology: Functions and Dysfunctions**	35
	Biological Bases of Behavior	35
	The Central Nervous System	36
	Syndromes of Neuropsychological Disorder	57
	Assessment of Neuropsychological Disorders	73
	The Peripheral Nervous System	74
	Endocrine System Functions and Dysfunctions	77
3	**Sensation and Perception**	81
	Sensory Systems	81
	Psychophysical Measurements	90
	Perceptual Processes	100
	Failures of Perception	102
	Perceptual Constancies	105
	Depth Perception	106
	Perceiving Biological Motion	112
	Visual Search	113
	Attention and Perception	114
	Subliminal Perception and Subliminal Messaging	118
	Bottom-Up Perceptual Processes	119
	Top-Down Influences on Perception	120

	Examples of Useful Classroom Demonstrations	123
4	**Learning**	125
	Classical Conditioning	125
	Applications of Classical Conditioning	131
	Operant Conditioning	133
	Applications of Operant Conditioning	148
	Observational Learning	150
	Non-associative Learning	152
5	**Memory**	155
	Memory Storage	155
	Short-Term (Working) Memory	158
	Long-Term Memory	160
	Encoding and Levels of Processing	167
	Retrieval	178
	Memory Failure and Its Consequences	183
	Schemas	190
	Biological Bases of Memory	192
6	**Thinking and Cognitive Abilities**	195
	The Functions of Thinking	195
	Mental Representations	202
	Thinking and Reasoning	205
	Problem Solving	215
	Obstacles to Problem Solving	222
	Decision Making	229
	Biases and Flaws in Decision Making	230
	Cognitive Abilities	232
	Tests of Cognitive Abilities	234
7	**Consciousness**	239
	Studying Consciousness	239
	Levels of Mental Processing	240
	Biological Rhythms	245
	Sleep Disorders	246
	Sleep Deprivation	260
	Dreams and Dreaming	261
	Hypnotic Phenomena and Applications	263
8	**Motivation and Emotion**	269
	Sources of Motivation	269
	Theories of Motivation	272

　　　　Maslow's Hierarchy of Needs 275
　　　　Intrinsic Motivation.. 278
　　　　Extrinsic Motivation 279
　　　　Achievement Motivation 282
　　　　Eating Behavior 283
　　　　Sexual Behavior 285
　　　　Links Between Motivation and Emotion........................ 286
　　　　The Nature of Emotion 289
　　　　Facial Expressions of Emotion............................... 291
　　　　The Biology of Emotion 293

9　　**Development** 295
　　　　Critical/Sensitive Periods.................................. 295
　　　　Maturation 299
　　　　Teratogens 299
　　　　Cognitive Development....................................... 300
　　　　Language 305
　　　　Language Development/Acquisition 309
　　　　Social Development 312
　　　　Child-Rearing and Parenting Styles 313
　　　　Moral Development 318

10　**Health, Stress, and Coping** 319
　　　　Stressors... 319
　　　　Stress Responses.. 321
　　　　Stress Response Mediators 323
　　　　Burnout 329
　　　　Posttraumatic Stress Disorder (PTSD) 331
　　　　Other Stress-Related Mental Health Problems................. 333
　　　　Health Promotion and Disease Prevention 333

11　**Personality** 335
　　　　Freudian/Psychodynamic Personality Structures 335
　　　　Ego Defense Mechanisms 337
　　　　Psychosexual Stages 342
　　　　Erickson's Psychosocial Stages of Development............... 344
　　　　Trait Theories of Personality 348
　　　　Big Five Personality Dimensions 349
　　　　Humanistic Theories of Personality 354
　　　　Social Cognitive Theory 357
　　　　Projective Personality Tests................................ 359
　　　　Nonprojective Personality Tests............................. 360

12	**Psychological Disorders**	361
	Defining Abnormality	361
	Diagnostic Manuals	362
	Examples of Psychological Disorders	365
	Insanity and Competency to Stand Trial	379
13	**Treatment of Psychological Disorders**	383
	Psychoanalytic/Psychodynamic Therapy	383
	Behavior Therapy	387
	Cognitive and Cognitive-Behavior Therapy	393
	Humanistic Therapy	400
	Medical Treatments	401
14	**Social Psychology**	405
	Identity Theory	405
	First Impressions	406
	Self-fulfilling Prophecies	406
	Attribution and Attributional Errors	408
	Cognitive Dissonance	411
	Ingroups and Outgroups	412
	Stereotypes, Prejudice, and Discrimination	413
	Interpersonal Attraction	414
	Social Norms	418
	Social Loafing	424
	Social Facilitation and Interference	424
	Conformity	428
	Compliance	429
	Obedience	433
	Aggression	434
	Helping	436
15	**Industrial/Organizational Psychology**	439
	Job Analysis	439
	Testing Employee Characteristics	439
	Employee Assessment Interviews	442
	Assessment Centers	444
	Assessing Job Performance	446
	Recruiting Employees	449
	Training Employees	450
	Employee Motivation	452
	Job Satisfaction	455
	Occupational Health Psychology	458
	Work Groups and Work Teams	461
	Leadership	462
Index		465

Research Methods and Statistics

We open this chapter with examples of pseudoscience that can help to start a conversation with students about ways in which psychological scientists use scientific method to study human behavior and mental processes. This is an excellent opportunity to introduce some of the **myths and intuitions** that people hold about human behavior and mental processes. Here is a video from Dan Simons and Chris Chabris in which Simons ask students about a number of these myths and intuitions, including whether or not they can tell if someone is staring at the back of their head. The students overwhelmingly endorse the myths and Simons busts one of those myths by having the students turn around and discover to their surprise that a person has been standing behind them and staring at the back of their head while dressed in a gorilla costume. The rest of the chapter provides examples of a wide range of scientific research methods and statistical analyses that we hope will stimulate your students' interest in these topics and lead to better comprehension of them.

Science Versus Pseudoscience

Most of the examples presented in this compendium focus on teaching about scientific thinking and science-based psychological knowledge, though to help your students understand what is and is not science, you may wish to provide some of the following examples of pseudoscientific disciplines:

1. *Phrenology* is perhaps the most widely used example of pseudoscience. A short, somewhat silly, video about phrenology can be found here.
2. A description of the history of phrenology can be found here.

© Springer Nature Switzerland AG 2022
E. L. Cameron and D. A. Bernstein, *Illustrating Concepts and Phenomena in Psychology*, Springer Texts in Education, https://doi.org/10.1007/978-3-030-85650-2_1

3. *Chiropractic medicine* is considered by many to be pseudoscientific. An interesting effort by chiropractors to clarify that some chiropractic claims are pseudoscientific is evident in this recent paper.
Reference: Côté, P., Bussières, A., Cassidy, J. D., Hartvigsen, J., Kawchuk, G. N., Leboeuf-Yde, C., ... & Schneider, M. (2020). A united statement of the global chiropractic research community against the pseudoscientific claim that chiropractic care boosts immunity. *Chiropractic & Manual Therapies*, 28(1), 1–5.
4. *Acupuncture.* An interesting short article with varying opinions on acupuncture can be found here.
5. *Graphology* is an example of pseudoscience that is still widely used by companies to analyze job candidates' "fit" when hiring.
A short article about graphology can be found here.

6. *Astrology.* A critique of astrology can be found here.

- Esteemed personality theorist Hans Eysenck was originally attracted to astrology and thought he'd found experimental evidence to support it. However, he discovered a flaw in his experimental design, and subsequently disavowed his earlier statements about the potential value of astrology. The history of his involvement can be found here.
  Additional reference: Thagard, P. R. (1978). Why astrology is a pseudoscience. *PSA: Proceedings of the Biennial Meeting of the Philosophy of Science Association*, 1, 223–234.
  The article ends with this statement

  My concern is social: society faces the twin problems of lack of public concern with the advancement of science, and lack of public concern with the important ethical issues now arising in science and technology, for example around the topic of genetic engineering. One reason for this dual lack of concern is the wide popularity of pseudoscience and the occult among the general public. Elucidation of how science differs from pseudoscience is the philosophical side of an attempt to overcome public neglect of genuine science.

7. The "Amazin Brain" pills website, found here can be used as an example of pseudoscientific evidence and an opportunity for critical thinking, as described in the next section.
8. Lilienfeld et al. (2012) offered ten warning signs of pseudoscience:

    Lack of falsifiability and overuse of ad hoc hypotheses
    Lack of self-correction
    Emphasis on confirmation
    Evasion of peer review
    Overreliance on testimonial and anecdotal evidence
    Absence of connectivity
    Extraordinary claims

Ad antequitem fallacy
Use of hypertechnical language
Absence of boundary conditions
[Source: Lilienfeld, S. O., Ammirati, R., & David, M. (2012). Distinguishing science from pseudoscience in school psychology: Science and scientific thinking as safeguards against human error. *Journal of School Psychology*, 50(1), 7–36.]

Scientific Method

1. There are many examples of diagrams/flow charts to illustrate the scientific method, such as this one and this one.
2. Here is an example that attempts to consolidate a number of such diagrams:

3. A description of the scientific method is given in this podcast. The main discussion and a summary of the scientific method begins at around minute 30. The overview is complete in about 6 min.

4. This video describes the scientific method, with simple examples.
[Note: In the context of discussing the scientific method, it might be useful to discuss confirmation bias, examples of which are provided in the chapter on thinking and cognitive ability.]
5. For historical context, you might want to show all or part of this 7-min video that provides examples of introspection as Wundt and Titchener used them.
6. The following example showing that the analysis of data can result in a range of conclusions, illustrates the fact that doing science is not easy, and that the outcome of any given scientific research project can be affected by the features of its design and the analytical tools used.
We suggest that you point out to your students that this example does not suggest that science is untrustworthy, but that reaching conclusions is best done by evaluating a body of evidence rather than the results of any single study.
7. Many textbooks present steps for *critical thinking* that frame the scientific method. For example, one introductory psychology textbook (Bernstein, 2019) asks student to address five critical thinking questions for particular research findings:

   1. What am I being asked to believe?
   2. What evidence is available to support the assertion?
   3. Are there alternative ways of interpreting the evidence?
   4. What additional evidence would help to evaluate the alternatives?
   5. What conclusions are most reasonable?

   [Source: Bernstein, D.A. (2019). *Essentials of Psychology* (7th ed.). Belmont, CA: Wadsworth Cengage Learning.]
8. Here is an example of critical thinking (adapted from Bernstein, 2019) focused on the question "are there drugs that make you smarter?"
It relates to claims on the Amazin Brain website, mentioned above.

   - *What am I being asked to believe?*
     The Amazin Brain website claims to have a "Revolutionary Clinically Designed Smart Pill" that will allow you to:
     Think Faster—Be Smarter
     Remember EVERYTHING
     Focus Clearly and Boost Energy
     Eliminate "Brain Fog Syndrome"
     Supercharge Success
     And you can find other claims on their website, such as "You will be limitless!" and this:

     Amazin Brain is a 100% natural water-soluble supplement that quickly enters the brain, to protect neurons, improve signal transmission, and support brain function and learning processes. It stimulates brain function so you can actually build new neurons and neural pathways.

Adequate functioning of neurotransmitter synthesis is essential in maintaining a healthy cognitive state that will supercharge your thinking capacity and lead to your ultimate success in anything that requires SUPERIOR BRAIN POWER.

- *What evidence is available to support the assertion?*
  The website indicates that the pill contains a substance whose "scientific term" is a "nootropic". They use terms such as "clinically proven" and "doctor-trusted" (note graphic). They offer three testimonials from "very satisfied, real customers." In the case of this particular website there is only anecdotal evidence to support the claims.
- *Are there alternative ways of interpreting the evidence?*
  One alternative explanation for evidence for a nootropic effect could be that the pill serves as a *placebo* and that people's belief in its efficacy could lead to improvement. In evaluating the literature, one would also want to carefully review the experimental methods (e.g., sample sizes) and effect sizes (these could be statistically but not clinically significant) in each study. Finally, any positive effects of these drugs should be evaluated in the context of any negative side-effects.
- *What additional evidence would help to evaluate the alternatives?*
  One could imagine designing a controlled scientific experiment to test the claims, which would involve using the scientific method. One would begin by reviewing the literature on the effect of "nootropics" on memory and cognition, a critical step in the scientific method. Even a cursory search would lead to the conclusion that there is not unequivocal evidence to support such claims. It would also lead to considering what variables and operational definitions might be most appropriate to test the claims. In addition to designing one's own study on the effect of nootropics on cognitive enhancement, one would want to continue to evaluate all of the evidence as it emerges. Each published study contributes to the literature and an expanding understanding of the effects of nootropics on cognitive enhancement.
- *What conclusions are most reasonable?*
  Finally, as in any scientific field, each published study must be evaluated and considered within the context of a developing theory. Considering the entire literature would likely lead to the conclusion that further study is needed.

9. Examples of the role of parsimony in drawing conclusions about data:

- If you hear a dog barking nearby and you own a dog, the explanation most likely to be correct is that your dog is barking. It is possible that it is someone else's dog, but the simplest explanation is that it is yours.
- If you flip a light switch and your light turns off, it could be because the FBI just happened to disable the light at that instant, but the most parsimonious, and most likely correct, explanation is that the switch controls the light.
- Magic tricks could be due to magic, but there are other more likely explanations.

- Some abstract and concrete examples of parsimony can be found here.
- *Zebra principle*—"when you hear hoofbeats, think of horses, not zebras".
- See also Occam's Razor, some good examples of which are found here.

Hypotheses

Note: Definitions and understanding of hypotheses vary in important ways. Some definitions suggest that a hypothesis is a testable (if...then...) statement, prediction or "educated guess" about the outcome of a study. Others define a hypothesis as a tentative explanation of a phenomenon, a point of view, or a proposition that has yet to be tested.

See also "hypothesis testing" in the section below on statistical significance.

1. Examples of hypotheses as predictions:

    - People will be less likely to help a stranger if there are other people around.
    - Exercise will relieve depression.
    - Extending the example of nootropics given in the critical thinking section above, one could hypothesize (predict) that, compared to a control group, taking the Amazin Brain pill will result in better memory (see examples of dependent variables and operational definitions below).
    - Students will learn more if they use retrieval practice rather than elaboration with concept maps.
    Source: Karpicke, J., & Blunt, J. (2011). Retrieval practice produces more learning than elaborative studying with concept mapping. *Science, 331*, 772–775.
    - You design a study to test the hypothesis that "smell training" (daily sniffing of a set of odors) improves smell function in people who lost their sense of smell due to Covid-19. Your hypothesis is that smell training will improve performance on a standard scratch and sniff test of odor identification.
    - You create a lesson plan on quantitative reasoning that you expect will improve student learning. You measure students' understanding with a short quiz before and after the lesson. Your hypothesis is that test scores will be higher after the lesson compared to prior to the lesson.
    - In a study that examined performance in a "risky" video game called "Chicken" in adolescents, young adults, and adults, either alone or in groups, Gardner and Steinberg (2005) explicitly stated three predictive hypotheses (p. 626):

        Hypothesis 1. Risk taking, risk preference, and risky decision making will decrease with age.
        Hypothesis 2. On average, individuals will demonstrate more risk taking, greater risk preference, and more risky decision making when in the company of their peers than when alone.

Hypothesis 3. The difference between levels of risk taking, risk preference, and risky decision making with and without the presence of peers will decrease with age. That is, group effects on risk orientation will be greater among adolescents than among youths, and greater among youths than among adults.
[Source: Gardner, M., & Steinberg, L. (2005). Peer influence on risk taking, risk preferences, and risky decision making in adolescence and adulthood: An experimental study. *Developmental Psychology, 41*, 625–635.]

2. Examples of hypotheses as explanations:

- People are less likely to help a stranger if there are other people around because there is a diffusion of responsibility (i.e., making the assumption that someone else will take action to help; see the chapter on social psychology).
- Exercise relieves depression because it causes release of endorphins, which help you feel better and more positive.
- Extending the example of nootropics (see example of predictive hypotheses above), one could hypothesize that, compared to a control group, people taking the Amazin Brain pill would show better memory simply because doing so increases blood flow to the brain.
- Students will learn more by using retrieval practice than elaboration (with concept maps) because reconstructing knowledge itself enhances learning.
  [Source: Karpicke, J., & Blunt, J. (2011). Retrieval practice produces more learning than elaborative studying with concept mapping. *Science, 331*, 772–775.]
- Smell training improves performance by increasing the rate of olfactory nerve cell regeneration. (Note: Evidence for this hypothesis is lacking; its validity is currently being tested and debated by researchers in the olfactory science community.)
- You create a lesson plan on quantitative reasoning that you expect will improve student learning. You measure students' understanding with a short quiz before and after the lesson. Your hypothesis is that test scores will be higher after the lesson compared to prior to the lesson because the lesson made explicit an aspect of quantitative reasoning that instructors wouldn't necessarily make explicit.
- A meta-analysis (see examples in a later section of this chapter) examined the effect of digital media on well-being and offered these hypotheses:
  Hypothesis 1: Telephone conversations and texting are positively linked to well-being because they are primarily used for contact with close relationship partners.
  Hypothesis 2: IM [instant messaging], SNS [social network sites] activity, and online gaming are negatively related to well-being, because they mainly feature interactions with strangers and acquaintances, which displace interactions with close relationship partners.

[Source: Liu, D., Baumeister, R. F., Yang, C. C., & Hu, B. (2019). Digital communication media use and psychological well-being: A meta-analysis. *Journal of Computer-Mediated Communication*, 24(5), 259–273.]

3. Additional examples of hypotheses:

   - Students are strongly interested in the idea of individual learning styles, so the following example of a hypothesis as an explanation may resonate with them: "The most common—but not the only—hypothesis about the instructional relevance of learning styles is the *meshing hypothesis*, according to which instruction is best provided in a format that matches the preferences of the learner (e.g., for a "visual learner," emphasizing visual presentation of information)." (Pashler et al., 2008, abstract)
   [Source: Pashler, H., McDaniel, M., Rohrer, D., & Bjork, R. (2008). Learning styles: Concepts and evidence. *Psychological Science in the Public Interest*, 9(3), 105–119.]
   - Some other definitions and examples of hypotheses can be found here here and here.

Theories

1. Major theories (models) in psychology are explanations of behavior, the mind, and mental processes from a variety of perspectives. Examples include those

   - at the level of the genetic or neural mechanisms (*biological* theories).
   - from a *psychoanalytic* perspective in which human behavior is thought to be deterministic and governed by the unconscious.
   - that focus uniquely on behavior with an emphasis on the role of the environment (*behaviorist* or *learning* theory).
   - that draw inferences about and explain mental processes by using a rigorous experimental approach (*cognitive* theories).
   - that explore and explain gender inequity (*feminist* theory).
   - that focus on freedom to act with a rational mind (*humanistic* theory).
   - that focus on psychological wellness and mental disorders by taking into consideration the interconnections between the biological, psychological and socio-environmental factors (*biopsychosocial* model).
   - that view mind, brain and behavior as a result of our evolutionary past and reflect adaptations and the process of natural selection (*evolutionary* theory).

2. Other prominent psychological theories include

   - *Bowlby's theory of attachment*—that attachment is key to psychological health and is adaptive (see evolutionary theory).
   - *Piaget's theory of cognitive development*—that children pass through a series of stages on their way to developing abstract thinking.
   - *Vygotsky's theory of learning*—that learning depends upon the social environment.
   - *Bandura's social learning theory*—that people learn primarily though observation, imitation and modeling.
   - *Terror management theory*—that humans are the only creatures capable of thinking about the future and realizing that they will all eventually die. Terror management theory suggests that humans cope with anxiety, including the terror that thoughts about death might bring, by developing a variety of self-protective psychological strategies, including engaging in escapism and efforts to increase the sense of self-esteem.
   - *Level of processing theory/model*—an alternative to the modal model of memory in which memory is thought to be better for material that is processed at a deeper level than material that is processed at a shallower level (see also the chapter on memory).

Experimental Design

Experiment Versus Non-experiment

Note: Additional examples in the sections below on dependent and independent variables and operational definitions might also be helpful in distinguishing between experiments and non-experiments.

1. A social psychologist conducts a study in which someone drops a bag of groceries in a public place, and then compares how often passersby offer to help when the person who dropped the bag is male or female, young or old, and does or does not have one arm in a sling. This study is an experiment because the researcher manipulated an independent variable (the characteristics of the person who dropped the bag) and measured its impact on a dependent variable (helping).
2. A social psychologist studies whether the physical characteristics of a person determines how likely they are to get help. In a bookstore, she rigs a magazine display so that when a customer picks up a magazine, the rest of the magazines tumble onto the floor. In the first study, she watches as customers pick up a magazine and cause the "accident," and records whether bystanders help that person pick up the magazines. She analyzes the data to see if people with certain characteristics (e.g., race/ethnicity, sex, age, etc.) are more likely to get help than others. In the second study, she arranges for a research assistant to trigger the

magazine "accident" when customers are nearby. The assistant has his arm in a sling on half of the trials. The researcher records and compares the number of bystanders who help pick up the magazines in the sling versus no-sling conditions. The first study was a non-experiment (an observational study) because no variables were manipulated. The second study, with its programmed event and manipulation of assistant characteristics, was an experiment.
3. You wonder how many people in your town wear seat belts while driving, so you conduct three days of observations at a busy intersection. You count the number of drivers who are and are not wearing seat belts, calculate the percentage who are wearing them, and then compare the percentages for each day of your study. This study is not an experiment because you did not manipulate an independent variable; you simply observed a sample of behavior and summarized it using descriptive statistics.
4. Mental health professionals wondered if legalizing recreational marijuana use leads users to begin trying other, still-illegal drugs such as cocaine. One research team studied this question by asking marijuana users in all U.S. states where recreational use is legal whether they also used cocaine. They compared the overall strength of the relationship between marijuana use and cocaine use in each state and then compared the strength of the relationship in three age groups: adolescents, young adults, and older adults. Finally, they conducted between-groups statistical analyses to see if the size of the marijuana-cocaine relationship differed by sex and across various ethnic and racial groups. This study was not an experiment. The researchers did not manipulate any variable; they simply analyzed self-reports coming from a survey.
5. Your psychology teacher wants to evaluate the possible beneficial effects on midterm grades of giving weekly quizzes in class. She gives the quizzes each week in her 8am class, but not in her 9am class, and then tests the size of the difference across the two sections' average midterm exam scores. This study is an experiment because the teacher manipulated a variable (weekly quizzes) and looked for its potential impact on a dependent variable (midterm exam scores).
6. A researcher was interested in the effect that writing letters of gratitude might have on mental health. Participants in psychotherapy were randomly assigned to one of three groups: those who received psychotherapy alone, psychotherapy plus an expressive writing task (i.e., they wrote about "their deepest thoughts and feelings about stressful experiences") or psychotherapy plus a task in which they wrote letters expressing gratitude to others. One and three months after the writing interventions, those in the gratitude writing condition reported significantly better mental health than those in the other two conditions, which did not differ from each other. This was an experiment because there was random assignment to groups, manipulation of an independent variable, and measurement of a dependent variable.
This study is described in this New York Times article https://www.nytimes.com/2021/02/27/at-home/how-to-write-a-gratitude-letter.html.
[Reference: Wong, Y. J., Owen, J., Gabana, N. T., Brown, J. W., McInnis, S., Toth, P., & Gilman, L. (2018). Does gratitude writing improve the mental health

of psychotherapy clients? Evidence from a randomized controlled trial. *Psychotherapy Research, 28*(2), 192–202.]

7. Here is part of the abstract of an article that will be of particular interest to students who use laptops in class:

"In this direct replication of Mueller and Oppenheimer's (2014) Study 1, participants watched a lecture while taking notes with a laptop (n = 74) or longhand (n = 68). After a brief distraction and without the opportunity to study, they took a quiz. As in the original study, laptop participants took notes containing more words spoken verbatim by the lecturer and more words overall than did longhand participants. However, laptop participants did not perform better than longhand participants on the quiz. Exploratory meta-analyses of eight similar studies echoed this pattern.. Overall, results do not support the idea that longhand note taking improves immediate learning via better encoding of information."

This was an experiment because students were assigned to different note-taking conditions (laptop vs. longhand) whose effects on dependent variables (kinds of notes taken and quiz performance) were measured.

[Reference: Urry, H. L., Crittle, C. S., Floerke, V. A., Leonard, M. Z., Perry, C. S., Akdilek, N., Albert, E. R , Block, A. J., Bollinger, C. A., Bowers, E. M., Brody, R. S., Burk, K. C., Burnstein, A., Chan, A. K., Chan, P. C., Chang, L. J., Chen, E., Chiarawongse, C. P , Chin, G., … Zarrow, J. E. (2021). Don't ditch the laptop just yet: A direct replication of Mueller and Oppenheimer's (2014) study 1 plus mini meta-analyses across similar studies. *Psychological Science, 32*(3), 326–339.]

Note: The previous example comes from Beth Morling's website where you can find more such examples.

Note: You might want to distinguish between experiments and quasi-experiments. Quasi-experiments include any case in which the "independent" variable of interest is a characteristic of the participants that cannot be manipulated by the experimenter. For example, sex, gender, age, height, weight, BMI, pregnancy status, employment status, GPA, level of depression or any other mental or physical health diagnosis would all be quasi-independent variables. Quasi-experiments are also distinguished by the fact that participants are not randomly assigned to conditions. Several examples of the distinction between experimental and quasi-experimental designs are presented at this website.

Experimental and Control Groups. *See examples provided in the previous section, the next section, and in a later section on confounding variables.*

Dependent and Independent Variables

Note: See also the Table of Levels of Measurement below for examples of other decontextualized variables.

1. A researcher measures children's reading skill after they take either a special reading class or a standard reading class. Those in the special reading class would be the *experimental group* and those in the standard reading class would be in the *control group*. (Reading skill is the DV; type of class is the IV).
2. College students' memory of the German vocabulary words they learned yesterday is tested after a normal night's sleep (i.e., the *control group*) or a night of repeatedly interrupted sleep (i.e., the *experimental group*). (Vocabulary test score is the DV; type of sleep is the IV).
3. You are about to read an article called "The effect of a daily versus weekly walking program on elderly people's lung capacity." (Lung capacity is the DV; walking frequency is the IV).
4. People's ability to drive safely (i.e., accident free) in a driving simulator is tested before, during, and after talking on a cell phone. [Driving performance (e.g., number of errors or accidents) is the DV; time of testing is the IV].
5. How quickly people can press a button (manual reaction time) to indicate that they have found a target (e.g., a green square) is measured in the context of varying numbers of distractor stimuli (e.g., red squares) presented on a computer screen. (Reaction time is the DV; number of distractors is the IV.) Note: If the experimenter also measures accuracy (number of correct target detections), that would be a second dependent variable.
6. A researcher measures memory for a list of 20 words when tested either 10 s (short delay) or 10 min (long delay) after hearing the list. (Number/percent of words remembered is the DV; length of delay is the IV.)
7. In the Stroop Effect, people have to read a list of color words as quickly as possible. Sometimes the color word and font color are the same/congruent and sometimes they are different/incongruent. The researcher measures reaction time under these two conditions. (RT is the DV; congruency/incongruency is the IV.)
8. To examine the effect of Fluoxetine, commonly known as Prozac, on depression, a researcher randomly assigns a group of patients to receive either the drug (i.e., the *experimental group*) or a placebo (*control group*). Students' level of depression is measured with the Beck Depression Inventory before treatment and 6 weeks after treatment. [Score on the BDI is the DV; drug (Prozac vs. placebo) and assessment times are the IVs.]
9. A high school principal decides to start the school's schedule 25 min later than usual. Before and after the change takes place, a researcher asks the students to report on their caffeine intake, the amount of sleep they get each night, and the amount of daytime sleepiness and depressed mood they experience. (Amount of

sleep, daytime sleepiness, depressed mood and caffeine intake are all DVs; school start time—regular or delayed—is the IV.)
[Reference: Boergers, J., Gable, C. J., & Owens, J. A. (2014). Later school start time is associated with improved sleep and daytime functioning in adolescents. *Journal of Developmental & Behavioral Pediatrics, 35*(1), 11–17.]

Definitions and examples of independent and dependent variables, including a discussion of differentiating and graphing these variables can also be found at this website.

Operational Definitions

1. Any of the DV/IV examples provided in the section above could be used as examples of how to operationally define variables, such as:

    - In this scenario: A researcher measures children's reading skill after they take either a special reading class or a standard reading class (reading skill is the DV; type of class is the IV). Neither of the variables are operationalized. An example of operational definitions could be: Reading skill could be measured as the number of errors a child made in a 15-word passage. All of the particular teaching methods used in the "special reading class" would constitute the operationalization of that variable.
    - In this scenario: A researcher measures memory for a list of 20 words when tested either 10 s (short delay) or 10 min (long delay) after hearing the list. Number of words remembered (percent correct, accuracy) is the DV; length of delay is the IV. The operationalization of "memory" (the DV) would be number of words remembered from a list of 20 and the operationalization of "time/delay" would be the delay in seconds/minutes.

2. Other examples:

    - Suppose you want to conduct an experiment to evaluate the effects of "Treatment X" for reducing anxiety about past experiences. The treatment requires patients to think about bad memories while focusing their eyes on the therapist's finger as it moves back and forth in front of their faces. You would want to test a hypothesis such as "Treatment X causes a significant reduction in anxiety," but in order to do so you would have to establish operational definitions of "Treatment X," "anxiety," and "significant reduction." "Treatment X" might be operationally defined as a specific number of back-and-forth eye movements per some unit of time. "Anxiety" might be defined as self-report ratings, or perhaps scores on a paper-and-pencil anxiety test, and "significant reduction in anxiety" might be operationally defined as a reduction of at least ten points on the anxiety measures being used.

- A group of researchers (Hyman et al., 2009) studied inattentional blindness in a real-world setting (see the chapter on sensation and perception). They examined the effect of divided attention during walking by observing people walk across a campus quadrangle (nicknamed "Red Square" because of its red brick surface) under four naturally-occurring conditions (quasi-IV): (a) talking on a cell phone, (b) listening to an MP3 player, (c) alone with no electronics or (d) with a partner. Here is how they operationally defined their dependent variables:

  > The observers also recorded several outcome measures for each individual. These measures included: the time it took each individual to cross Red Square, if the individual stopped while crossing, the number of direction changes (defined as an instance when the observer thought the individual was moving towards one exit from Red Square and changed direction enough so that the observer believed the individual was moving towards a different exit), whether the individual weaved while crossing, whether the individual tripped or stumbled, if the individual was involved in a collision or near-collision, and if the individual explicitly acknowledged other people by waving, nodding or talking (the size of Red Square precluded observations of eye contact and facial expressions).

  This an example of multiple DVs/outcome measures and includes some additional operationalization (e.g., what they coded as "change direction").

  In a second study, the experimenters observed participants walk across the quadrangle under the same four conditions, but this time a unicycling clown was riding around. The dependent variables included walkers' answers to two questions: First, whether they had "seen anything unusual while crossing Red Square" and second whether they had noticed the unicycling clown."

  [Source: Hyman Jr, I. E., Boss, S. M., Wise, B. M., McKenzie, K. E., & Caggiano, J. M. (2010). Did you see the unicycling clown? Inattentional blindness while walking and talking on a cell phone. *Applied Cognitive Psychology, 24*(5), 597–607. https://doi.org/10.1002/acp.1638]

3. Here are two examples of the fact that the operational definitions chosen by experimenters can affect conclusions about whatever they are studying:

   - Cultural standards about acceptable activity levels in children vary, so a child who is considered "hyperactive" by the operational definition prevalent in one culture might be considered merely "active" by the definition used in another culture. So, when mental health professionals from four cultures used the same rating scale to judge hyperactivity in a videotaped sample of children's behavior, the Chinese and Indonesians rated the children as significantly more hyperactive than did their U.S. and Japanese colleagues. As a result of differing definitional standards, children might or might not be diagnosed with ADHD, depending on where they were raised.

   (*Note:* This study is a better example of why reliable operational definitions are needed than of an operational definition itself. The scores on the rating scale operationally defined hyperactivity, but it wasn't reliable across cultures.)

[Reference: Jacobson, K. (2002). ADHD in cross-cultural perspective: Some empirical results. *American Anthropologist, 104*, 283–286.]

- A recent study found that practicing yoga was less effective than either cognitive-behavior therapy (CBT) or a stress education control condition in the treatment of generalized anxiety disorder. However, because the operational definition of *practicing yoga* was practicing a specific version called "Kundalini yoga," the conclusion should have been that that practicing *Kundalini yoga* was not as effective as CBT.
[Reference: Simon, N. M., Hofmann, S. G., Rosenfield, D., Hoeppner, S. S., Hoge, E. A., Bui, E., & Khalsa, S. B. S. (2021). Efficacy of yoga vs cognitive behavioral therapy vs stress education for the treatment of generalized anxiety disorder: a randomized clinical trial. *JAMA psychiatry, 78*(1), 13–20.]

Confounding Variables

Note: Many students assume that any variable other than the IV that could affect results is a confounding variable. Our challenge as teachers is to help them differentiate among three possible influences on the dependent variables: (1) random variables that add "noise" or variability to the data, (2) the presence of multiple IVs and (3) the presence of variables that might exert a systematic effect that confounds our ability to draw cause-effect conclusions about the relationship between IVs and DVs. These confounding variables can be more insidious and difficult to detect than the relatively obvious examples provided here, but the current examples provide a good starting point.

1. In an experiment in which the effect of exercise on depression is being studied, if the *experimental group* (those who exercise) were all also on antidepressant medication while no members of a no-exercise *control group* were on medication, then the differential presence of the medication could be a confounding variable.
2. In a study examining whether retrieval practice results in better learning than elaboration with concept maps, if all the highest-achieving students were in the "retrieval practice" condition (i.e., the *experimental group*), then achievement level could be a confounding variable.
3. In a study examining whether retrieval practice results in better learning than elaboration with concept maps, if all the students in the "retrieval practice" condition were tested in the morning and those in the "elaboration with concept maps" condition were tested in the afternoon, then time of day could be a confound.
4. In a study examining whether retrieval practice results in better learning than elaboration with concept maps, if those in the "retrieval practice" condition were senior psychology majors and those in the "elaboration with concept maps" condition were first year math majors, then age, school year, and academic major could all be confounding variables.

5. In an experiment on the effect of biological sex on odor sensitivity, if one group was tested after they had just eaten, and the other group was tested while fasting, satiety state could be a confounding variable.
6. In an experiment on the effect of smoking on odor sensitivity, if the group of smokers were also older than the group of non-smokers, age could be a confounding variable.
7. In an experiment examining the effect of massed versus distributed study schedules on exam performance, if students in the massed condition (studying in extended blocks) also spent the entire night before the exam "cramming" whereas those in the distributed group slept 8 h the night before the exam, lack of sleep could be a confounding variable.
8. In an experiment in which the effect of a daily versus weekly walking program on elderly people's lung capacity is assessed, if all of the people in the daily exercise condition were males and all of those in the weekly walking program were females, then sex/gender could be a confounding variable.
9. Placebo effects constitute an important potential confounding variable that is especially important in research designed to evaluate behavior change programs such as psychotherapy.

- This website describes the placebo effect and provides three examples of studies that have tested and demonstrated the effectiveness of placebos.
- Although placebos are typically thought of as synonymous with "sugar pills," other possible placebo treatments include acupuncture, nootropics, vitamins/supplements, and the attention of a psychotherapist or physician.
- In one study, participants were assigned to a condition in which they were either told that they had had a lot of REM sleep or only a little REM sleep. Their assigned condition affected their performance on some (but not all) cognitive tasks more than their actual sleep quality.
  [Reference: Draganich, C., & Erdal, K. (2014). Placebo sleep affects cognitive functioning. *Journal of Experimental Psychology: Learning, Memory, and Cognition, 40*(3), 857–864. https://doi.org/10.1037/a0035546]
- Here is an example of using a placebo-control condition to compare the extent to which the results of a smoking cessation treatment were caused by an experimental treatment versus a placebo effect. In this study, participants in the placebo group were given sugar pills described by the experimenter as "fast-acting tranquilizers" that would help them learn to endure the stress of giving up cigarettes. These people did far better at quitting than those who got no treatment; in fact, they did as well as participants in the experimental group, who received extensive treatment. These results suggested that the success of the experimental group may have been due largely to the participants' expectations, not to the treatment methods.
  [Reference: Bernstein, D. A. (1970). The modification of smoking behavior: A search for effective variables. *Behaviour Research and Therapy, 8,* 133–146.]

10. Here are some examples of double-blind designs aimed at eliminating confounds caused by experimenters' expectations of results.

    - One of your authors had a friend in graduate school named Fred who liked to volunteer for studies to support scientists and to make a little bit of money. One summer Fred participated in a study designed to assess whether Prozac could reduce uric acid levels (in the hope that it could be used to treat gout). The researchers assigned the participants to either a placebo control group or an experimental group (which received Prozac). Because coded labels were used on the genuine and placebo medication bottles, neither Fred nor the experimenters knew which group he was in until the experiment was over. Thus, this was a double-blind study.
    - This short video describes a double-blind vaccine trial.

    - This short news article and accompanying video describe a double-blind study that tested the efficacy of remdesivir in treating patients with Covid-19.

Random Assignment to Groups

The first minute or so of this short video provides an example of random assignment to groups. It also outlines the importance of randomization and provides some tools for randomization.

Samples/Sampling

Random assignment and random sampling are often confused in students' minds, so we recommend presenting the soup example and others listed below in conjunction with examples of random assignment to experimental and control groups.

1. Testing the taste and/or temperature of soup by taking a spoonful from the pot is a nice example of sampling. It can be extended to address issues in sampling such as when sampling for temperature, but the temperature is not uniform as the soup is warming up.
2. If you are interested in studying all college students in the United States and you study 100 students from your own institution, the 100 students would be considered to be a sample, and in this case a *convenience sample*.
3. If you are interested in studying people who have depression or anxiety, have had Covid-19, or have taken a college exam, you would select, or sample, a subset of people with those characteristics.
4. A description and examples of *random sampling* are shown in this video.

Hypothesis Testing

1. An experiment that tests the effect of exercise on depression would start with the null hypothesis that exercise has no effect on depression or that participants in experimental (exercise) and control (no exercise) groups would not differ in their depression scores after the experiment. An alternative hypothesis would be that depression scores would be lower after the exercise intervention. (Note: this is a directional prediction. A non-directional prediction would be that there would be a difference (either an increase or decrease in depression scores) after exercise.)
2. A study on the effect of a drug to decrease depression would start with the null hypothesis that the drug would have no effect on depression. An alternative hypothesis would be that the drug would improve depression. (Note: This is a directional prediction. A non-directional prediction would be that there would be a difference (either an increase or decrease in depression scores) after taking the drug.)
3. A study of an educational intervention would start with a null hypothesis that there would be no change in children's learning as a result of the intervention and an alternative hypothesis would be that there *would* be an improvement in learning following the intervention. (Note: This is a directional prediction. A non-directional prediction would be that there would be a difference (either increased or decreased learning) after the educational intervention.)
4. An example of hypothesis testing, working through the research question "Does exercise make people happy?" is described at this website.
5. Some nice graphics and examples of null hypotheses can we found here and a definition and examples of the null hypothesis can be found here.
6. A funny and memorable example of *Type I and II errors* is illustrated by this picture that shows a doctor telling an elderly man that he is pregnant (a Type I error) and an obviously pregnant woman that she is not pregnant (a Type II error).
7. This website walks the reader through Type 1 and Type 2 errors in the criminal justice system.

Experimental Design

Statistical Versus Practical/Clinical Significance of Results

1. An experiment that measures the effect of exercise on depression could lead to a statistically significant result even if the decrease in depression for the exercise group was so small (e.g., 1%) as to be of no clinical significance (i.e., clients are still noticeably different from non-depressed individuals).
2. A study on the effect of a drug to decrease depression could show a statistically significant effect that doesn't result in a meaningful change in the clinical picture (i.e. treated clients continue to experience disruptive symptoms of depression).
3. An educational intervention for children that, compared to a standard teaching regime, results in a statistically significant improvement in classroom test scores, but the difference is too small to be educationally significant.
4. The following excerpt from a 1990 *American Psychologist* article provides a detailed example of the difference between statistical and practical significance (and also offers an opportunity to highlight the difference between correlation and causation): "In 1986, there appeared in the *New York Times* a UPI dispatch under the headline 'Children's Height Linked to Test Scores.' The article described a study of nearly 14,000 children 6 to 17 years of age that reported a definite link between height (age- and sex-adjusted) and scores on tests of both intelligence and achievement. The relationship was described as significant and persisting, even after controlling for other factors, including socioeconomic status, birth order, family size, and physical maturity. The authors noted that the effect was small, but significant, and that it didn't warrant giving children growth hormone to make them taller and thus brighter. They speculated that the effect might be due to treating shorter children as less mature, but that there were alternative biological explanations. Now this was a newspaper story, the fruit of the ever-inquiring mind of a science reporter, not a journal article, so perhaps it is understandable that there was no effort to deal with the actual size of this small effect. But it got me to wondering about how small this significant relationship might be. Well, if we take significant to mean $p < 0.001$ (in the interest of scientific tough-mindedness), it turns out that a correlation of 0.0278 is significant for 14,000 cases. But I've found that when dealing with variables expressed in units whose magnitude we understand, the effect size in linear relationships is better comprehended with regression than with correlation coefficients. So, accepting the authors' implicit causal model, it works out that raising a child's IQ from 100 to 130 would require giving the child enough growth hormone to increase his or her height by 14 ft (more or less). If the causality goes the other way, and one wanted to create basketball players, a 4-in. increase in height would require raising the IQ about 900 points. Well, they said it was a small effect. (When I later checked the journal article that described this research, it turned out that the correlation was much larger than 0.0278. It was actually about 0.11, so that for a 30-point increase in IQ it would take only enough growth hormone to produce a 3.5-ft increase in height, or with the causality reversed, a 4-in. increase in height would require an increase of only 233 IQ points.)" (Cohen, 1990, p. 1309)
[Reference: Cohen, J. (1990). Things I have learned (so far). *American Psychologist, 45*(12), 1304–1312. https://doi.org/10.1037/0003-066X.45.12.1304]

Case Studies

The examples of case studies below are just a start. Many others can be found elsewhere in this book, including—but not limited to—chapters on biological aspects of psychology, development, memory, consciousness, personality, and psychological disorders.

1. Brief descriptions of seven of the most famous cases of the well-known neurologist, Oliver Sacks, are described in this magazine article.
2. Here is a description of one of the most famous of Sacks' cases, and the one for which one of his books was titled:

   "Dr. P.," came to see neurologist Oliver Sacks because, for one thing, when he looked at familiar people or objects, could no longer recognize them. So, while he and his wife were getting ready to leave Dr. Sacks' office, Dr. P. tried to lift off his wife's head as if it were a hat and put it on his own head. He could not name common objects that were in front of him, but he could describe what they looked like. When shown a glove, he said, "A continuous surface, infolded on itself. It appears to have ... five outpouchings, if this is the word ... a container of some sort." Only later, when he put it on his hand, did he exclaim, "My God, it's a glove!" (Sacks, 1985, p. 13).

   You can point out to your students that, using case studies such as this one, neuropsychologists have been able to describe the symptoms that commonly occur in association with different kinds of brain damage or disease. Eventually, neuropsychologists were able to tie specific disorders to specific causes. In Dr. P.'s case, a large brain tumor caused his symptoms.

   [Source: Sacks, O. (1985). *The man who mistook his wife for a hat.* New York: Summit Books.]

Naturalistic Observation

1. The Nurses Observation Scale for Inpatient Evaluation (NOSIE) is an observational coding system that allows nursing staff and other health professionals to measure the nature and frequency of specific behaviors seen in hospitalized patients, including behaviors that reflect depression, irritability, and psychotic disorders.

   [Reference: McGill, A. C., Jones, N. T., Boss, A. R., & Sheitman, B. (2017). Enhancing evidence-based clinical assessment in a large, public psychiatric hospital: Using behavior data collected by direct care nursing staff. *Worldviews on Evidence-Based Nursing, 14,* 246–248.]

2. Hospital and clinic staff also use observational coding systems to evaluate the developing skills of trainees who are learning to conduct interviews and other assessments.
3. School observation systems focus on children's behavior in the classroom or on the playground. They often concentrate on measuring behaviors associated with ADHD, including being off-task, disruptive, out-of-seat, or noncompliant, and to monitor changes in such behavior following the use of medication or other treatment. The results of these observations can be plotted in a graph like this one:

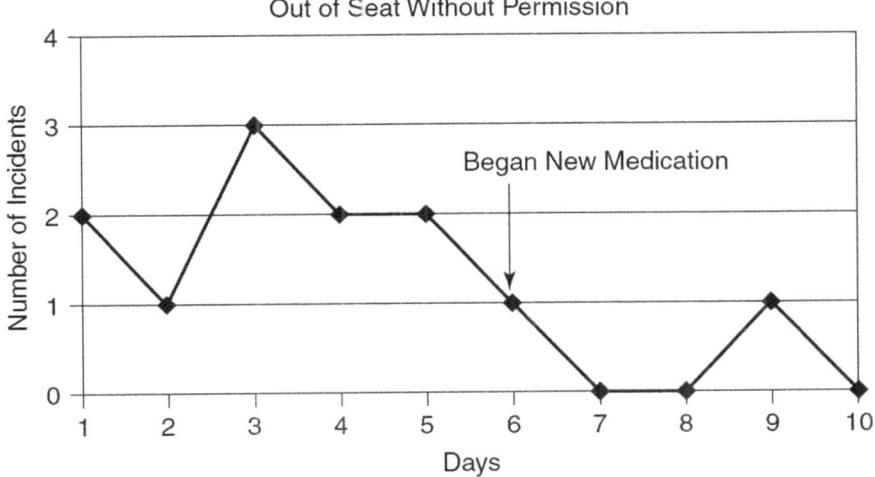

[*Source:* Brown, R. T., Carpenter, L. A., & Simerly, E. (2005). *Mental health medications for children: A primer* (p. 89). New York, NY: Guilford.]

4. Naturalistic observations can occur in remote locations, such when Margaret Mead observed people in the South Pacific or Jane Goodall observed great apes in Africa, but it can also occur in any social or organizational setting such as offices, schools, bars, prisons, dorm rooms, online message boards, or just about any other place where people can be observed as pointed out at this website.
5. A 3-min video clip of some early observations by Jane Goodall can be found here.
6. A poll conducted for the American Society for Microbiology (ASM) found that 92 percent of U.S. adults said that they always wash their hands after using public toilet facilities. However, an observational study, in which observers watched thousands of people in public restrooms across the United States, revealed that the figure is closer to 77 percent.
[Reference: Harris Interactive (2007). Handwashing survey fact sheet. Retrieved January 22, 2009, from http://www.asm.org/ASM.]

7. Observational studies found here, and here, have revealed that consumers and food service workers, too, wash their hands far less often than they should when preparing meals.

8. In the late 1960s, the manager of a car dealership in Chicago wanted to have some idea of which radio stations were most popular among his customers so that he could decide where to air his new-car commercials. Rather than sending customers a survey, he asked his mechanics to turn on the radio of each car that was brought in for service and to make a note of which station it was tuned to. Because these observations were not affected by customers' memories or by their possible desire to create any particular impression about their listening habits, this form of naturalistic observation is known as *unobtrusive*, or *nonreactive* measures.
9. Unobtrusive measures are sometimes used in clinical research to test theories about the causes of behavior problems. In one study aimed at identifying the precursors of schizophrenia, researchers reviewed videos that parents had made of their children as the children were growing up. Trained observers used a coding system to compare behaviors seen in videos of individuals who later developed schizophrenia as well as of their same-sex siblings who did not. The results revealed that long before they were diagnosed, those who developed schizophrenia showed significantly more negative facial expressions than did those who did not develop disorder. Some of the differences appeared before the children were 4 years old. A similar study used information contained in high-school yearbook profiles to link social isolation in adolescence with schizophrenia in adulthood.
[References: Barthell, C. N., & Holmes, D. S. (1968). High school yearbooks: A nonreactive measure of social isolation in graduates who later became schizophrenic. *Journal of Abnormal Psychology, 73*, 313–316.
Walker, E. F., Grimes, K. E., Davis, D. M., & Smith, A. J. (1993). Childhood precursors of schizophrenia: Facial expressions of emotion. *American Journal of Psychiatry, 150*, 1654–1660.]
10. Another example of a naturalistic observation is described here in which a group of engineers analyzed the walking patterns of people who were distracted (e.g., on their phones) or not. They found that one third of pedestrians were distracted and that their walking patterns were impacted.

Correlational Research

Researchers can measure and examine the relationship between any two measures as part of a correlational study. Here are some examples of variables that tend to be correlated:

1. Positive correlations (correlation coefficient >0)

   - Height and weight
   - Intracranial size and height
   - Years of education and income
   - Sense of humor and life expectancy
   - Amount of time studying for a class and grade
   - Score on the Beck Depression Inventory and performance on a smell test
   - Oil prices and airline ticket prices
   - Amount of money in a savings account and accrued interest
   - Hours worked and money earned (on an hourly rate)
   - Outside temperature and ice cream sales

2. Negative correlations (correlational coefficient <0)

   - Amount of sleep and caffeine consumption
   - Age and amount of time spent playing video games
   - Class absences and class performance
   - Outside temperature and heating bills
   - Length of a hike and hiking pace
   - Amount of exercise and body fat content
   - Amount of exercise and likelihood of heart attack
   - Brick-and-mortar retailers' stock and Amazon's stock

3. Some examples of graphs with positive, negative and zero correlations are shown in this 2-min video. The first minute includes the examples and the second provides correlation coefficient formulas.
4. Some studies have suggested a relationship between depression and olfactory function. Given that neither variable can be directly manipulated, these studies are necessarily correlational.
   [Reference: Schablitzky, S., & Pause, B. M. (2014). Sadness might isolate you in a non-smelling world: Olfactory perception and depression. *Frontiers in Psychology, 5*, 45].
5. A study examined the relationship between attire (specifically, wearing pajamas) on productivity and mental health during the Covid-19 pandemic. Because these variables were measured with a survey and there was no manipulation of conditions, the study is correlational.
   [Reference: Chapman, D. G. & Thamrin, C. (2020). Scientists in pyjamas: Characterising the working arrangements and productivity of Australian medical researchers during the COVID-19 pandemic. *Medical Journal of Australia, 213* (11), 516–520.]

6. Another study examined the association between going to a museum or attending a music concert and mortality rates. Again, because there was no random assignment to groups nor manipulation of conditions, this is a correlational study.
[Reference: Fancourt, D., & Steptoe, A. (2019). The art of life and death: 14 year follow-up analyses of associations between arts engagement and mortality in the English Longitudinal Study of Ageing. *BMJ, 367*.]
7. Here is a study that found a correlation between misogynist tweets and violence against women in 400 regions in the U.S.
[Reference: Blake, K. R., O'Dean, S. M., Lian, J., & Denson, T. F. (2021). Misogynistic tweets correlate with violence against women. *Psychological science, 32*(3), 315–325. https://journals.sagepub.com/doi/full/10.1177/0956797620968529].
8. Here are several sources that provide examples of **spurious correlations**:

- SPC for Excel

- TylerVigen.com

- Ionica Smeets at TEDxDelft

    At this website there is an interactive tool (see "Hack Your Way To Scientific Glory") to demonstrate correlations between the U.S. economy and which political party is in control. This is useful to demonstrate correlations, statistical significance, and the *many* involved in asking such a question.

Survey and Questionnaire Research

1. There are numerous free psychological tests/surveys/questionnaires that can be scored online (including some listed below). You can find them here.

(*Note: If you show or recommend any of these online versions to your students, be sure to caution them that your goal is only to familiarize them with test formats and sample items. If they fill out any of the online tests of personality or psychological disorders, any results they receive are not to be taken as valid clinical assessments. In fact, you should use the availability of such tests online as a springboard for raising and discussing the importance of standardized testing conditions and expert analysis of results in order to the maximize reliability and validity of tests of personality and psychological disorders.*)

2. Beck Depression Inventory (BDI) is a widely employed self-score scale of depression). Here is the scoring key.

3. Estimated Daily Intake Scale for Sugar (EDIS-S, a tool for estimating liking of sugar) includes these 11 items:
   1. I tend to eat cereals that have sugar in them.
   2. I tend to put a lot of syrup on my pancakes or waffles.
   3. I often eat candy to snack on when I am hungry.
   4. I tend to crave foods that are high in sugar.
   5. I tend to snack on healthier food options.
   6. I tend to consume a low sugar diet.
   7. I often snack on sugary foods when I am hungry.
   8. When I crave a snack, I typically seek out sweet-tasting foods.
   9. I tend to eat foods that are most convenient, even if they contain a lot of sugar.
   10. I like consuming sweet-tasting foods and drinks each day.
   11. I tend to avoid consuming a high sugar diet.
   [Source: Privitera, G. J., & Wallace, M. (2011). An assessment of liking for sugars using the estimated daily intake scale. *Appetite, 56*(3), 713–718.]

4. The IPIP-NEO (International Personality Item Pool Representation of the NEO PI-R™) is a measure of personality.

5. 24-hour Pregnancy-Unique Quantification of Emesis (PUQE-24) is a scale used to measure nausea and vomiting in pregnant women.

6. The Odor Awareness Scale is a scale the measures self-reported awareness of odors in daily life.
   [Reference: Smeets, M. A., Schifferstein, H. N., Boelema, S. R., & Lensvelt-Mulders, G. (2008). The Odor Awareness Scale: A new scale for measuring positive and negative odor awareness. *Chemical senses, 33*(8), 725–734.]

7. Generalized Anxiety Disorder-7 (GAD-7) is a short questionnaire that measures anxiety.

8. Hamilton Anxiety Rating Scale is a survey of anxiety.

9. Patient Health Questionnaire (PHQ-9), the 9-item depression screening tool from The Patient Health Questionnaire.

Cross Sectional and Longitudinal Research

1. One of your authors has studied changes in the sense of smell in children aged 4–18, using a "scratch and sniff" odor identification test. In order to complete the study within a reasonable timeframe, she opted for a cross sectional research design in which each child and young adult was tested once. Thus the study was completed within one year and involved analysis of differences across age levels to estimate how the sense of smell changes. To actully measure those changes, the researchers would have had to test a group of 4 year-olds every year for 14 years!
   [Reference: Cameron, E.L. & Doty, R.L. (2013). Odor identification testing in children and young adults using the smell wheel. *International Journal of Pediatric Otorhinolaryngology*, 77(3), 346–350. https://doi.org/10.1016/j.ijporl.2012.11.022].

2. One of your authors has conducted two studies of the sense of smell in pregnant women. In one study she used a cross-sectional design in which she tested each woman once, in either the first, second or third trimester of pregnancy, or in the postpartum period. She also tested some women who served as a nonpregnant control group.
   [Reference: Cameron, E.L. (2007). Measures of human olfactory perception during pregnancy. *Chemical Senses*, 32, 775–782. https://doi.org/10.1093/chemse/bjm045].
   In a second study, she used a longitudinal research design in which she followed a group of women throughout pregnancy, testing each of them in the first, second and third trimester of pregnancy and comparing their performance to that of nonpregnant control participants who were also tested three times. Data collection took considerably longer in this study than in a cross-sectional study.
   [Reference: Cameron, E.L. (2014). Pregnancy does not affect human olfactory detection thresholds. *Chemical Senses, 39*(2), 143–150. https://doi.org/10.1093/chemse/bjt063].

3. Another example of a longitudinal design can be found in the documentary series "Seven Up" in which a relatively small group of people were followed for several decades starting at the age of 7.
   A short preview of Seven Up (original, 1964) shows 20 seven-year-old British children from a variety of socio-economic backgrounds. 63 Up (most recent, 2019) is a 50-min video of 11 or 12 of the original 20 children.

   A review of the series can be found here.

Meta-Analysis

1. Quoted here are examples of recent meta-analyses taken from this website.

- Fictitious Example

    Do individuals who wear sunscreen have fewer cases of melanoma than those who do not wear sunscreen? A MEDLINE search was conducted using the terms melanoma, sunscreening agents, and zinc oxide, resulting in 8 randomized controlled studies, each with between 100 and 120 subjects. All of the studies showed a positive effect between wearing sunscreen and reducing the likelihood of melanoma. The subjects from all eight studies (total: 860 subjects) were pooled and statistically analyzed to determine the effect of the relationship between wearing sunscreen and melanoma. This meta-analysis showed a 50% reduction in melanoma diagnosis among sunscreen-wearers.

- Real Examples

    This meta-analysis was designed to determine whether obesity affects the outcome of spinal surgery. Some previous studies have shown higher perioperative morbidity in patients with obesity while other studies have not shown this effect. This study looked at surgical outcomes including "blood loss, operative time, length of stay, complication and reoperation rates and functional outcomes" between patients with and without obesity. A meta-analysis of 32 studies (23,415 patients) was conducted. There were no significant differences for patients undergoing minimally invasive surgery, but patients with obesity who had open surgery had experienced higher blood loss and longer operative times (not clinically meaningful) as well as higher complication and reoperation rates. Further research is needed to explore this issue in patients with morbid obesity.

    [Source: Goyal, A., Elminawy, M., Kerezoudis, P., Lu, V., Yolcu, Y., Alvi, M., & Bydon, M. (2019). Impact of obesity on outcomes following lumbar spine surgery: A systematic review and meta-analysis. *Clinical Neurology and Neurosurgery, 177*, 27–36. https://doi.org/10.1016/j.clineuro.2018.12.012].

    This meta-analysis explored whether physical activity during pregnancy prevents postpartum depression. Seventeen studies were included (93,676 women) and analysis showed a "significant reduction in postpartum depression scores in women who were physically active during their pregnancies when compared with inactive women." Possible limitations or moderators of this effect include intensity and frequency of physical activity, type of physical activity, and timepoint in pregnancy (e.g. trimester).

    [Source: Nakamura, A., van Der Waerden, J., Melchior, M., Bolze, C., El-Khoury, F., & Pryor, L. (2019). Physical activity during pregnancy and postpartum depression: Systematic review and meta-analysis. *Journal of Affective Disorders, 246*, 29–41. https://doi.org/10.1016/j.jad.2018.12.009].

2. This website provides examples of other accessible meta-analyses.
3. An example of a recent meta-analysis that may be of particular interest to students examined the effect on well-being of using various digital media, namely phone calls and texting versus social networking sites and online games. The meta-analysis included 124 studies and found phone calls and texting were positively correlated with well-being, whereas online gaming was negatively associated with well-being. Furthermore, the relationship between digital media use and well-being was also contingent upon the way the technology was used.
[Source: Liu, D., Baumeister, R. F., Yang, C. C., & Hu, B. (2019). Digital communication media use and psychological well-being: A meta-analysis. *Journal of Computer-Mediated Communication, 24*(5), 259–273. https://doi.org/10.1093/jcmc/zmz013].
4. Here is a meta-analysis of the impact of exercise on depression.

5. A description of several meta-analyses on the health effects of caffeine can be found here.

Research Measures

Scales of Measurement

Here is a table of examples of the four main types of measurement scales:

Nominal	Ordinal ("order")
• ZIP code	• Ranking of
• License plate number	– students in a class/cohort
• Credit card number	– favorite movie
• Country code	– favorite beverage
• Phone number	– favorite class
• Social Security number	– top psychology programs
• ID number	– colleges or universities
• Basketball jersey number	• Class standing
• Number on a pool ball	• Year in school
• Eye color	• Birth order
• Hair color	• Top 10 songs on iTunes
• Race	• Ranking in a talent show
• Gender	• Letter grade (A,B,C,D,F)
• Nationality	• Difficulty level of a task: hard-medium-easy
• Sexual orientation	• Order of finishing a race (1st place, 2nd place, 3rd place)
• Blood type	• Medals (gold, silver, bronze)
• Handedness	• Hottest to coldest
• Political party affiliation	• Richest to poorest
• Favorite season	• Lightest to heaviest
• Season of birth	

(continued)

Research Measures

- Marital status
- Relationship status
- Type of breakfast eaten

- Customer Service Scale: dissatisfied to satisfied
- Happiness: very unhappy to very happy
- Likert scale: strongly agree to strongly disagree

Interval
- Intelligence Quotient (IQ) score
- Scores on ACT/SAT/GRE/MCAT
- Temperature in Fahrenheit or Celsius (not in Kelvin)
- Body temperature in degrees Celsius
- Rating (e.g., 1–7) of
  - self-confidence
  - performance on a task
  - pleasantness of an odor
  - job satisfaction
  - happiness
- Measurements of latitude and longitude
- pH level
- Credit score
- Time on a clock with hands
- Calendar year
- Scores on psychological inventories
  - Beck Depression Inventory
  - Raven's Progressive Matrices
  - Big Five Personality Trait Test
  - Perceived Stress Scale

Ratio
- Height
- Weight
- Pulse rate
- Reaction time
- Speed
- Duration
- Time to run 100 m
- Number of minutes in a commute
- Accuracy
- Percent/proportion correct
- Test score
- Battery life on a cell phone
- Number of errors
- Number of hours of sleep per night
- Number of times a parent spanks a child per week
- Number of times one has to get up early per week
- Number of times a rat pushes a lever
- Number of fruits or vegetables consumed per day
- Probability
- Number of clients seen in a month

- A cartoon video example of the difference between nominal, ordinal and interval-ratio variables in the context of coffee can be found here.

Reliability

1. Test–retest Reliability

   - You weigh yourself twice in rapid succession. If your weight is the same both times, the scale you are using has high test–retest reliability.

   - Each time Connie takes the Wechsler Adult Intelligence Scale (WAIS) she scores at the mean for her age group, which demonstrates good test–retest reliability.

   - You took an intelligence test last January and again 6 months later. If your second score was much lower or much higher the second time, and nothing significant had occurred between test sessions—such as a head injury or a severe illness—that could have affected your cognitive ability, you would suspect that the test has low test–retest reliability.

- You are evaluating a new computer program that is designed to teach children to speak and read a foreign language. After they have used the program for 6 months you test their foreign language ability and discover that their scores are much higher than children who were learning the same language without using the program. You then you try the same program again with a new group of children. If the same results occur again, you will have demonstrated that your original results showed test–retest reliability (in this case, you can say that the results were repeatable, or replicable.)

2. Split-Half Reliability (Internal Consistency)

- Dr. Miller wants to evaluate the reliability of the final exam she gives to her developmental psychology students. She can only give it to the same students once, so she compares their scores on all the even-numbered test items with their scores on all the odd-numbered items. If there is a high and positive correlation between scores on the odd items and the even items, she can say that the test shows good split-half reliability, or internal consistency. That is, the test shows about the same level of difficulty throughout.
- Dr. Matthews wants to evaluate the reliability of the midterm exam he gives to his social psychology students. He can only give it to the same students once, so he compares their scores on items in the first half of the test with their scores on items in the second half. If he finds that there is almost no correlation between the two sets of scores he knows that the test shows poor split-half reliability. That is, it is not internally consistent. There is something different about the level of difficulty of items in each half of the test.

3. Interrater Reliability

- Three psychologists watch a video showing a diagnostic interview with a patient at a mental health clinic. Using the criteria included in the DSM-5 diagnostic system, all three psychologists diagnose the patient as having the same disorder. This result suggests that using the decision rules contained in the DSM-5 results in high interrater reliability.
- Four undergraduate research assistants are using a behavioral observational system designed to measure ADHD in children. After watching 10 children engaged in a 30-min free-play session, the observers make a list of which children displayed ADHD. Their lists show no agreement; each observer identified a different set of children as displaying ADHD. This observational system would appear to have very low interrater reliability. Note, however, that the problem might be due to inadequate training for the observers. Before discarding the observation system, you would have to evaluate the

quality of the training, including periodic calibration sessions to avoid observational "drift."
- A hiring committee at a computer company is looking for a new head of the accounting department. After a series of written tests identified the three top candidates, the six committee members meet with each candidate individually, using a standard rating scale to compare the various candidates and decide which one should be offered the job. After all interviews are complete, each candidate receives two votes. The fact that there was so little agreement among the committee members suggests that the rating scale has very low interrater reliability.
- You ask each of two physicians to look at the results of a patient's medical tests and, without consulting with each other, say what disease they think the patient has. If both doctors reach the same conclusion, you can say that they interpreted the test results with a high degree of interrater reliability.

Validity

1. Face Validity

   - An IQ test would be said to have face validity if it contains items—such as doing math problems, remembering word lists, and putting a series of pictures in a meaningful order—that are assumed to be part of what most people see as intelligence. Its face validity would be low if the test evaluated participants' ability to do pushups or dig a hole in the ground.
   - A depression survey would be said to have face validity if it asks questions about the subject's mood, happiness, motivation for work, energy level, and sleep quality, but not if it asked about the birthplaces of movie stars or the history of washing machines.
   - Giving definitions of a list of words is a valid test of vocabulary but may not be a valid test of intelligence.

2. Construct Validity

   - You want to know if your new test of people's current state of anxiety is really measuring the construct of anxiety. If it is, scores on your test should be significantly higher among people who are waiting to hear the results of a medical test for cancer than among people who have no health problems and are listening to pleasant music. If the scores of both groups of people are about the same, then your test would show low construct validity.
   - A researcher has developed a video game that is supposed to detect potential aggressiveness in adolescents. If the game is capable of measuring the construct of aggressiveness, adolescents who have been accused of bullying should show significantly higher signs of aggressiveness when playing the

game than those who have never shown any aggressive or violent actions. If this is the case, the video game appears to have some construct validity.
- Scores on a test of achievement motivation should be higher among people who have overcome great difficulties to become successful than among those with a history of giving up when faced with obstacles.
- People who are rated by peers as being sociable and outgoing should score higher on tests of extraversion than those whose peers describe them as shy and uncomfortable in social situations.
- If a teacher tests student learning in an introduction to psychology class using only fact-and definition multiple-choice questions rather than a mixture of definitional and applied multiple-choice questions, short-answer items, term papers, and class research projects, the outcome may not reflect all aspects of the learning construct, and could also have been affected by other factors such as test anxiety or stress on exam days.

3. Content Validity

- You want to develop a new interview protocol for identifying depression, so you include lots of questions about sad feelings. However, if you do not include any questions about other key features of depression, such as lack of concentration, feelings of guilt, worthlessness, or fatigue, the interview protocol might be valid for measuring sadness, but would have low content validity for measuring depression because it does not address all the important aspects of the disorder.
- State A's driver's license test includes a road test that requires candidates to show that they can safely steer, turn, and park a car, and also to pass a written test on the rules of the road. State B requires only the rules of the road test. State A's testing program has higher content validity than State B's because State A's test covers a wider range of the content associated with good driving ability.
- A test of what introductory psychology students know about the field would have lower content validity if it covers only items about social, personality, and developmental psychology than if it asks questions from all chapters in the textbook.
- A test of creativity would have higher content validity if it measured creativity through samples of people's writing, problem-solving, computer-programming, or other activities than if it measured only people's skill at, say, oil-painting.
- To have reasonable content validity, a comprehensive personality test should measure many traits or trait dimensions, such as openness, conscientiousness, extraversion, agreeableness, and neuroticism, rather than focusing on just one trait, such as extraversion.

4. Concurrent (Convergent) Validity

   - You have written a brief new self-report test for diagnosing depression that you hope will be quicker and easier to use than traditional, but longer, self-report tests of depression. Your test would have high concurrent validity if people's scores on your new test correlate highly with their scores on those longer tests.
   - To evaluate the concurrent validity of a structured interview designed to measure a person's level of moral development, a researcher compares scores derived from the interview with scores on previously established paper-and-pencil tests of moral development. If the two sets of scores are not strongly correlated, the interview's concurrent validity would be low.
   - Scores on a fill-in-the-blanks test of knowledge of office management procedures correlate strongly with scores on a two-day test of job candidates' ability to actually perform those procedures. In this case, the concurrent validity of the written test might be considered high enough that the more extensive test could be abandoned.
   - Since both blood pressure and cholesterol level are predictive of heart disease, they have convergent validity for heart disease risk.

5. Discriminant (Divergent) Validity

   - A researcher discovers that scores on a new test of anxiety show high and positive correlation with scores on other anxiety tests, but also with scores on tests of psychopathy and schizophrenic thinking. So, the new anxiety test appears to have low discriminant validity because it is probably not measuring anxiety alone.
   - An intelligence test would be said to have high discriminant validity if people's scores on the test show high and positive correlations with academic achievement, but almost no correlation with scores on tests of relatively unrelated targets such as anxiety or self-esteem.
   - A test designed to measure affection would appear to have high discriminant validity if scores on a test predict long-term commitment in a relationship, but are unrelated to measures of hate, an attribute to which it should not be related.

6. Predictive Validity

   - The SAT is said to have high predictive validity because students' scores on the test are strongly correlated with their grade-point average after two years in college.
   - If children's attachment styles as measured in the Strange Situation test are correlated with their ability to establish and maintain long-term romantic relationships in young adulthood, you can say that the test has relatively strong predictive validity.

- Observations of aggressive behavior in young children would be said to have low predictive validity if they do not correlate strongly with the appearance of aggressiveness when those children become adults.
- If experiencing physical or sexual abuse in childhood is found to be only moderately correlated with various kinds of psychological disorders in adolescence, then the predictive validity of abuse experiences would be only moderate.
- A test of mental arithmetic ability would have high predictive validity if it were strongly correlated with a job candidate's ability to do mental arithmetic in a work situation. However, if smart cash registers make mental arithmetic unnecessary, the mental arithmetic test might be invalid for predicting the person's success on this job.

Reliability Versus Validity

- A good bathroom scale will provide a reliable and valid measure of your weight, but that same scale will be invalid (inaccurate) as a measure of your height. So, we cannot say that a test is inherently valid or invalid. We can only describe its validity for certain purposes. If the scale has not been properly set to zero, it will reliably provide you with the same inaccurate weight measurement every time you step on it on a given day. In this example, the scale will be reliable but not valid.
- An ultra-reliable Swiss watch will give you the correct time, every time, but if it is set for the wrong time zone, the time shown on the watch would be invalid for the place where you are located.
- You decide to give yourself a few extra minutes in bed in the morning, so you set your clock ahead by 10 min. Thus, when the alarm goes off at 7am each morning, it is really only 6:50am. In this case, your clock will reliably go off at 7am, even though it is not really 7am. Again, the clock is reliable, but not valid.
- A researcher notices that very anxious people tend to pull their hair more than less anxious people do, and claims that people's typical level of anxiety can be measured by counting the amount of hair on their heads. Assuming an accurate method is available for identifying the percentage of the skull covered by hair, that percentage would be a *reliable* measure of anxiety. It would remain fairly stable over short periods of time, and different observers using the same measurement tool would presumably agree on the results. But this highly reliable measure of hairiness would be an invalid measure of trait anxiety because the amount of hair on people's heads can be due to their age, gender, health habits, genetic proneness to baldness, and a host of factors entirely unrelated to anxiety.

Biological Aspects of Psychology: Functions and Dysfunctions

As we mentioned in the Preface, this chapter does not include descriptions of brain regions, anatomical or neuroanatomical structures, biological systems, or other neuroscience topics, nor does it include explanations of where brain regions are, what they do, or how they do it. Instead, it contains examples focused on what can happen when problems in these regions, structures, and systems create various kinds of cognitive, emotional, and behavioral disorders. We have chosen examples that we think will not only enhance your explanations of biological aspects of psychology, but also make those explanations more interesting to your students. They should also be helpful debunking myths about the brain, such as that we only use 10% of it.

Biological Bases of Behavior

Our first example is designed to illustrate both the integrated nature of the central and peripheral nervous systems and the complex chain of physical and biological processes that underlie even the simplest forms of behavior.

If your teacher asks you, at the count of three, to raise your right hand and then lower it, you will surely be able to do so. But how? In order for you to follow these simple instructions, sound waves from your teacher's vocal cords have to travel through the air and reach your ears. These sound waves will enter your outer ear, pass down your ear canal, and strike your eardrum (tympanic membrane) which will then begin to vibrate. These vibrations will cause similar vibrations in a series of three small bones (ossicles) in your middle ear. Their vibrations will create waves in the fluid that fills a coiled tube (cochlea) in your inner ear and the motion of that fluid will bend tiny stereocilia on top of hair cells inside the tube. Each of those hairs is connected to nerve cells that travel together (as the auditory nerve) to the brain and the stream of combined messages from all these cells will stimulate the areas of your brain that receive sound. The pattern of stimulation provides information (sensations) about the frequency (pitch) and intensity (loudness) of the incoming sound.

If you are to *understand* (perceive) the sound waves your teacher made, your brain has to compare them to information about the patterns of sound that are already stored in your long-term memory. If and when the brain finds matching patterns, you will be able to recognize the stream of sound waves as a stream of meaningful words, in this case, the sentences that make up your teacher's instructions. If the teacher had been speaking an unfamiliar language, you would have still heard (sensed) the sounds, but you would not have been able to recognize and understand (perceive) meaningful words.

But the story is not over. Now the action shifts to the frontal lobes of your cerebral cortex, where most of your higher cognitive processes occur, including thinking, planning, and decision-making. While holding the information about the teacher's instructions in your short-term memory, you will have to retrieve information from long-term memory about what your cultural background and other aspects of your social learning has taught you about what is appropriate and inappropriate behavior in a classroom situation (including norms about complying with instructions and engaging in other social behavior). On the basis of all this information, you will make a decision about what to do when your brain understands the sound of the word "three." Assuming your decision is to comply, when you hear "three" you will have to execute that decision by remembering where the right side of your body is, and then directing neurons in the left motor area of the cerebral cortex that control movement of the right arm to send movement messages down nerves in your right arm. Through their connections to your muscles, stimulation from these nerves will cause certain muscles to contract and others to relax, thus allowing a smooth arm-raising movement. Sensors that tell the brain about the position and movement of various body parts (proprioception and kinesthesia) will confirm that your arm is raised, so even if your eyes are closed, as long as your teacher's instructions are still in your memory, you will know it is time to execute instructions to reverse the contractions and relaxations so as to bring the arm back to its original position. Once that happens your proprioceptive system will tell you your arm is lowered. Finally, your memory of this movement sequence will be compared to your memory of the teacher's instructions, and when it matches you will be aware that you have behaved correctly.

The Central Nervous System

1. Examples of the complexity and activity level of the human brain:

   - With about 7000 synapses on each central nervous system (CNS) neuron, communication can take place across an estimated hundred trillion synapses every second. For comparison, consider that there are only about 10 billion stars in the entire Milky Way.

- As an illustration of the energy required for brain activity, point out that though the brain accounts for only 2 percent of body weight, it uses more than 20 percent of the body's oxygen.

- There is a website that provides 52 relatively little-known facts about the brain and its complexity.

- Another website is full of good examples of the brain's complexity, including a case study illustrating that the cerebellum has functions that go well beyond balance and fine motor control.

2. Examples of modularity and networks in the brain:

- A useful analogy: The brain is like the head of a company with a vast array of employees (modules), each with a specific skill, which can be organized and reorganized from one moment to the next into many different work teams to perform many different tasks. In this way, some of the same brain areas might participate in many different psychological tasks, but the exact combination of which areas do so, and when, may differ from one function to another.

- For example, doing a math problem might require you to use several abilities, such as being able to read or hear a math problem, recognizing numbers and symbols, remembering the rules of addition or multiplication, keeping many numbers in your head as you do calculations, and reporting your answer. If damage in your brain's language areas made it hard for you to talk, you might not be able to answer the question, "How much is 2 plus 2?", but that would not mean that there is anything wrong with your mathematical ability.

- Disconnection syndromes provide examples of what happens when different modules in brain networks, some of which may themselves be intact, are prevented from interacting as they normally would. A classic example is *alexia without agraphia*, the inability to read while still being able to write. The shaded area of the image below (looking down at the brain, with the frontal lobes at the top of the drawing and the occipital lobes at the bottom) shows the location of damage that could produce this kind of disconnection syndrome. You might want to draw your students' attention to the fact that there is damage to the left occipital lobe, causing loss of vision, but only for what appears on the right side of the visual field. The patient can still see things that appear in the left visual field. However, there is also damage to the corpus callosum, which connects the left and right hemispheres of the brain. The damaged area of the corpus callosum would have allowed visual information from the left side of the world to cross from the right hemisphere into the left hemisphere, but now this pathway is blocked. Because the language-producing regions of the left hemisphere are intact, the person can still talk and write normally but can see only what lies in the left visual field. That information goes to the right hemisphere, but because it cannot cross into the left hemisphere, where most language functions reside, people with this disconnection syndrome cannot read what they have written. In effect, the visual processing of the words is disconnected from the brain regions that are needed to extract the meaning of the words they see.

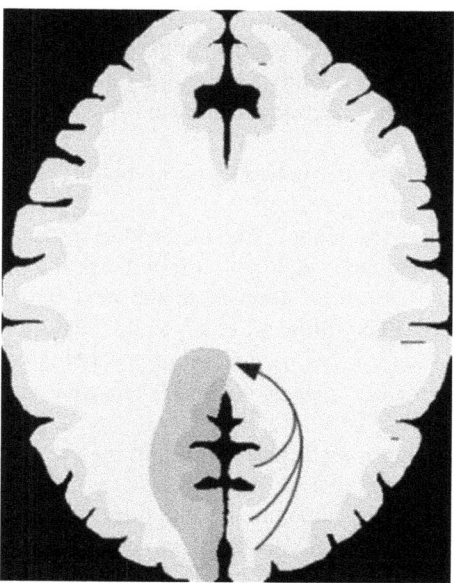

[Source: Bernstein, D.A. (2019). *Essentials of psychology* (7th ed.). Belmont, CA: Wadsworth Cengage Learning.]

- Another example of the modularity of brain systems is seen in the case of *acalculia,* a condition in which patients have difficulty performing simple mathematical operations (e.g., addition, subtraction), or even identifying which of two numbers is larger. Unlike dyscalculia, a developmental disorder affecting math abilities, acalculia is acquired, usually late in life as a result of brain damage from a stroke, trauma, or disease. The specifics of the disorder depend on the location of the damage, which supports the idea that different regions of the parietal cortex are involved in different aspects of numerical processing.

  For example, patients with lesions in the angular gyrus in the parietal lobe tend to show impairments in memorized mathematical facts, such as multiplication tables, but relatively unimpaired subtraction abilities. Patients with lesions in the intraparietal sulcus of the parietal lobe show deficits in subtraction but not in multiplication.

- Example of research methods to identify brain modules:
  It is possible to "shut off" a brain area using transcranial magnetic stimulation (TMS). In this procedure, a powerful magnet is held near a specified

area of a person's head, after which specific areas of the brain's cortex can either be temporarily stimulated or inactivated. In this way, a brain module can be temporarily removed from, or made to exert a greater role in, the networks in which it normally participates. By observing how a person behaves during TMS, experimental neuropsychologists can in effect create and analyze the impact of "reversible" lesions.
[Reference: Nevler, N. & Ash, E. L. (2015). TMS as a tool for examining cognitive processing. *Current Neurology and Neuroscience Reports*, *15*(8), 1–11.]
Note: Other examples of disconnection syndromes appear later in the chapter in the cases illustrating anterograde amnesias, Broca's aphasia, and Wernicke's aphasia.

3. Examples of neural plasticity:

   - Neural plasticity is at the heart of our ability to form new memories and learn new skills, as illustrated by the fact that more cells in the brain's motor cortex become involved in controlling hand movements in people who have learned to play a musical instrument.
     [Sources: Munte, T. F., Altenmuller, E., & Jancke, L. (2002). The musician's brain as a model of neuroplasticity. *Nature Reviews: Neuroscience, 3,* 473–478.
     Pascual-Leone, A. (2001). The brain that plays music and is changed by it. *Annals of the New York Academy of Science, 930,* 315–329.]
   - As non-musicians get better at making rhythmic finger movements, the amount of motor cortex devoted to this task increases.
     [Source: Munte, T. F., Altenmuller, E., & Jancke, L. (2002). The musician's brain as a model of neuroplasticity. *Nature Reviews: Neuroscience, 3,* 473–478.]
   - As opera singers train their voices, changes occur in brain areas that control vocalization.
     [Sources: Kleber, B., Veit, R., Birbaumer, N., Gruzelier, J., & Lotze, M. (2009). The brain of opera singers: Experience-dependent changes in functional activation. *Cerebral Cortex, 20*(5), 1144–1152.
     Kleber, B., Veit, R., Moll, C. V., Gaser, C., Birbaumer, N., & Lotze, M. (2016). Voxel-based morphometry in opera singers: Increased gray-matter volume in right somatosensory and auditory cortices. *NeuroImage, 133,* 477–483. https://doi.org/10.1016/j.neuroimage.2016.03.045]
   - MRI studies of individuals who were learning to juggle found an increase in the population of cortical neurons associated with processing visual information about moving objects.
     [Source: Draganski, B., Gaser, C., Busch, V., Schuierer, G., et al. (2004). Neuroplasticity: Changes in grey matter induced by training. *Nature, 427,* 311–312.]

- Merely imagining practicing movements causes changes in the motor cortex, as when athletes engage in exercises in which they visualize skilled performance-related actions, such as high-jumping.
  [Source: Olsson, C. J., Jonsson, B., Larsson, A., & Nyberg, L. (2008). Motor representations and practice affect brain systems underlying imagery: An FMRI study of internal imagery in novices and active high jumpers. *The Open Neuroimaging Journal, 2*, 5–13.]
- Mental practice has been applied in the form of "motor imagery training" to help people with cerebral palsy to improve their movement abilities.
  [Source: Cabral-Sequeira, A. S., Coelho, D. B., & Teixeira, L. A. (2016). Motor imagery training promotes motor learning in adolescents with cerebral palsy: Comparison between left and right hemiparesis. *Experimental Brain Research, 234*(6), 1515–1524. https://doi.org/10.1007/s00221-016-4554-3.]
- If for some reason a child's two eyes do not get a lot of early practice at focusing on the same objects at the same time, the brain begins to ignore sensory input from the "lazy eye," a condition called *amblyopia* that impairs the performance of fine motor skills and other tasks that require depth perception. (Other examples of problems related to critical or sensitive periods are presented in the chapter on development.) Until about the age of nine (depending on the severity of the problem), the condition may be improved by covering the dominant eye with a patch and giving the child intensive training of the "lazy" eye using video game apps such as "Captain LazyEye."
  [References: Astle, A.T., Webb, B.S., & McGraw, P.V. (2011). Can perceptual learning be used to treat amblyopia beyond the critical period of visual development? *Ophthalmic Physiological Optics, 31*, 564-73. https://doi.org/10.1111/j.1475-1313.2011.00873.x. PMID: 21981034; PMCID: PMC3428831.
  Webber, A.L., Wood, J.M., & Thompson, B. (2016) Fine motor skills of children with amblyopia improve following binocular treatment. *Investigative Ophthalmology & Vision Science, 57*, 4713-20. https://doi.org/10.1167/iovs.16-19797. PMID: 27607417.]
- Capitalizing on the fact that the human brain remains plastic to some degree throughout the life span, some companies are marketing "brain training" programs that are alleged to improve people's cognitive functioning. For example, see Lumosity and Brain HQ.

- Evaluative research has found that some of these programs have very limited ability to promote generalized improvement in cognitive skills. In fact, the Federal Trade Commission imposed a stiff fine on the Lumosity company for false advertising.
  [Sources: Simons, D. J., Boot, W. R., Charness, N., Gathercole, S. E., Chabris, C. F., Hambrick, D. Z., & Stine-Morrow, E. A. L. (2016). Do "brain-training" programs work? *Psychological Science in the Public Interest, 17*(3), 103–186. https://doi.org/10.1177/1529100616661983.
  Katz, B., Shah, P., & Meyer, D.E. (2018). How to play 20 questions with nature and lose: Reflections on 100 years of brain-training research. *Proceedings of the National Academy of Sciences U S A, 115*(40), 9897-9904. https://doi.org/10.1073/pnas.1617102114]
- Examples of research on other programs suggesting that they may have value for promoting more specific cognitive functions:
  Edwards, J.D., Xu, H., Clark, D.O., Guey, L.T., Ross, L.A., & Unverzagt, F. W. (2017). Speed of processing training results in lower risk of dementia. *Alzheimer's & Dementia: Translational Research & Clinical Interventions, 3*(4), 603-611. https://doi.org/10.1016/j.trci.2017.09.002
  Nouchi, R., Taki, Y., Takeuchi, H., et al. (2013). Brain training game boosts executive functions, working memory and processing speed in the young adults: A randomized controlled trial. *PLoS ONE, 8*(2), e55518. https://doi.org/10.1371/journal.pone.0055518
  U.S. Food & Drug Administration (2020). FDA permits marketing of first game-based digital therapeutic to improve attention function in children with ADHD. Published June 15, 2020.

4. Examples of localization of function in the brain

   - Early, incorrect, ideas about how localization of function was organized in the brain were embodied in phrenology.
   - A 1-min video shows a "psychograph" machine that was designed to measure the bumps and depressions on people's skulls, and was used to measure intelligence as well as personality traits. (For more on phrenology, see the personality and research methods chapters.)
   - An example of how case studies have promoted the scientific understanding of localization is provided by the 1861 case of Victor Leborgne, whose hospital nickname was "Tan" because after he had a stroke, that was the only word he could say. He later died and, at autopsy, neurologist Paul Broca found a small area of damage, in Tan's left frontal lobe, just in front of the primary motor cortex. After finding similar damage in seven other stroke patients with similar language problems, this area (Broca's area) was identified as related to the control of speech.

- You can see a photo of Tan's brain, with Broca's area circled here.

- A 90-s video summarizes the case of Tan and shows his brain.

- Another example of speech-related localization of function is provided by cases in which people with damage to Broca's area can produce words easily and correctly when they sing, but not when they speak. These cases suggest that the production of words that are set to music is handled by one part of the brain and spoken words by another.
  [Reference: Jeffries, K. J., Fritz, J. B., & Braun, A. R. (2003). Words in melody: An H(2)15O PET study of brain activation during singing and speaking. *Neuroreport, 14*, 749–754.]
- An example of applying research on localization of singing versus speaking is provided by speech therapists who are using "melodic intonation" therapy to increase fluency in Broca's aphasia patients by having them speak in a singsong manner.
  [Reference: Norton, A., Zipse, L., Marchina, S., & Schlaug, G. (2009). Melodic intonation therapy: Shared insights on how it is done and why it might help. *Annals of the New York Academy of Sciences, 1169*, 431–436.]
- The role of the left hemisphere in speech production is also illustrated by research in which sodium amytal is injected into the left internal carotid artery (which is the source for oxygenated blood to the left hemisphere). This Wada procedure—named for Juhn Atsushi Wada, the Canadian neurologist who first conducted it—temporarily puts one hemisphere "to sleep." When the left hemisphere is anesthetized, nearly all people temporarily lose their ability to speak.
  [Reference: Wada, J., & Rasmussen, T. (1960). Intracarotid injection of sodium amytal for the lateralization of cerebral speech dominance. *Journal of Neurosurgery, 17*, 266–282.]
- Another early case example of localization came from Italian ophthalmologists Antonio Quaglino and Giambattista Borelli, who, in 1867, published a paper describing a man who developed prosopagnosia, the inability to recognize familiar faces, after suffering damage to the right hemisphere of his brain (we offer more examples of this disorder later in this chapter.)
- A Far Side cartoon provides a humorous example of localization of motor function. It shows brain surgeons stimulating a patient's motor cortex and as the patient's leg kicks up in the air, one of them says "Whoa! That was a good one! Try it, Hobbs—just poke his brain right where my finger is." Here is the cartoon.

5. Examples of reflexive behavior triggered entirely within the spinal cord (which incidentally are relevant to the unconditioned response examples presented in the chapter on learning and to examples of early reflexes offered in the chapter on development):

- Your doctor taps your knee with a small rubber mallet and your foot automatically kicks upward.
- You accidentally touch something hot and your hand and arm instantly pull away.
- You see a ball coming fast, and straight toward your face, and you automatically duck out of the way.
- While you are sitting in a quiet library, a fire alarm suddenly sounds, causing you to startle.
- Near the beginning of the second movement of Haydn's Symphony #94, a sudden and unexpectedly loud chord occurs amid a soft and gentle flow of music. This chord caused massive startle reflexes in the first audiences to hear it. An audio clip for classroom use is available (the sudden loud chord comes at 47 s into the clip). Turn the sound way up if you want to create a startle reaction in your students.
- You are so deeply engrossed in whatever you are reading or writing that you do not see or hear someone approaching. When that person says "Hi," you practically jump out of your seat.
- You are so sound asleep that you did not hear your alarm, so your partner touches you on the shoulder and you wake up with a violent startle reaction.
- While sewing on a button, you accidentally stick your finger with a needle and automatically pull your finger away.
- You begin to salivate when food stimulates taste buds on your tongue.
- You sneeze when your nose is tickled or stimulated by pepper.

6. Examples of the consequences of spinal cord damage

   Paraplegia, a partial or total inability to feel or move the lower parts of the body, mainly the legs, exemplifies what can happen when disease or injury causes damage to nerves at or below the thoracic region of the spinal cord that normally transmit information back and forth between the brain and the somatic nervous system.
   - Charles Krauthammer was a famous example of this condition. While in his first year of medical school, he became paralyzed from the waist down after a diving accident caused damage to his spinal cord. After spending more than a year in a hospital, he completed medical school, became a psychiatrist, and participated in the creation of the third edition of the American Psychiatric Association's *Diagnostic and Statistical Manual of Mental Disorders*. He died in 2018. You can see his photo and read his obituary here.

- Franklin Delano Roosevelt, President of the United States from 1933 to 1945, was another famous example of paraplegia. His condition developed in 1921 as the result of polio, a once common but now virtually unknown viral disease that affects spinal nerves.
- A more sensational case of paraplegia occurred in 1978 when Larry Flynt, the founder of *Hustler* magazine sustained a spinal cord injury after being shot by a white supremacist who was upset about an interracial photo in the magazine. The story of his controversial career is portrayed in the Hollywood film *The People Versus Larry Flynt*.

Quadriplegia, also known as *tetraplegia*, is a partial or total inability to feel or move the arms, legs, and torso as the result of damage or disease that affects nerves at a higher (cervical) region of the spinal cord that normally transmits information back and forth between the brain and the somatic nervous system.
- World famous physicist Stephen Hawking provides an example of someone whose paralysis was caused by Amyotrophic Lateral Sclerosis (ALS; also known as Lou Gehrig's disease). It eventually left him almost completely paralyzed and able to communicate only through a speech generating device. Yet these devastating effects did not prevent him from making important scientific contributions as well as to educate the public about the universe right up until his death in 2018.
- After falling off a horse and suffering a spinal cord injury in 1995, Superman actor Christopher Reeve was told he would never again be able to move or feel his body. He refused to accept this gloomy prediction, and after years of devoted adherence to an exercise-oriented rehabilitation program, he regained some movement. By the time of his death in 2004, he was able to feel sensations from most of his body. Physicians and physical therapists hope to make such therapy programs even more effective in the future.
- Daryl Stingley was a wide receiver for the New England Patriots football team. His career was ended in 1978 at the age of 26 when a collision with another player caused a spinal cord injury that left him with quadriplegia. He died in 2007 from heart disease and pneumonia complicated by quadriplegia.

7. Example of the importance of myelin on the axons of neurons in the brain and spinal cord: When cells of the immune system cause inflammation that damages myelin, the result can be multiple sclerosis, or MS. Its symptoms can include double vision, blindness in one eye, muscle weakness and trouble with sensation or coordination, and can occur in isolated episodes or as sustained progressive worsening over time. In the relapsing remitting (RRMS) form, symptoms may disappear completely between episodes.

- This case example illustrates one pattern seen in MS: Ms. C., a 35-year-old woman, came to a neurology clinic for evaluation of long-term neurologic complaints, including a stumbling gait and a tendency to fall. Her visual acuity also seemed to change

The Central Nervous System

periodically during several years. Recently, after being under a lot of stress at work, she got the flu and her neurologic condition worsened such that she had significant tremors, could not hold objects in her hands, and was extremely exhausted. She also had several bad falls. Since that time, she had noticed joint pain, first just on the right side of her body, and later on the left. Then, she suddenly developed numbness on her entire right side. An MRI scan was performed at that time and revealed deterioration of myelin in both cerebral hemispheres. Other tests revealed abnormality in the optic nerves.

- A different pattern of MS symptoms appeared in a 27-year-old woman whose first indications of a problem appeared when she began to experience loss of vision in one eye accompanied by facial weakness, numbness and difficulty in speaking. An MRI revealed a lesion on her brainstem. Three months later, she started experiencing extreme fatigue and balance problems, possibly due to lower extremity weakness. The patient underwent a second MRI which revealed another lesion, this time in her right cerebral hemisphere. After being diagnosed with relapsing remitting multiple sclerosis, she began a course of physiotherapy to help control her fatigue, lower limb weakness, coordination, and to maintain general fitness.

- A 5-min video presents a number of different people describing the onset of their MS, its impact on their lives, and the role of the MS Society in supporting MS patients.

- Two 3-min videos available here and here show the stories and symptoms of adult males with MS. The second one shows a strategy for helping people without MS to appreciate what it feels like to have MS symptoms.

8. Examples of problems related to malfunctioning of glial cells:
Among their other functions, glial cells secrete chemicals to help repair damaged brain cells. An unfortunate byproduct of this response to brain damage is excessive inflammation, which can contribute to problems such as the chronic traumatic encephalopathy, or CTE, a brain disorder associated with repeated blows to the head (including in contact sports).

- One of the most publicized cases of CTE in a professional football player was that of former New England Patriot tight end Aaron Hernandez, who committed suicide in 2017. A post-mortem brain scan showed atrophy and damage, and prior to his death, he had shown symptoms associated with CTE, including depression, aggression, irritability, impulsivity, and anxiety, along with headaches and memory problems.
- Other NFL players who were found to have CTE after committing suicide include Junior Seau and Andre Waters.
- There are lists of the dozens of other former NFL athletes showing signs of CTE and there is a movie called *Concussion* that

describes the discovery of CTE and a doctor's efforts to raise awareness of it. You can see the trailer here.

- Stories about the consequences of CTE in extreme sports athletes are available here, as well as here.

- The story of a professional hockey player with CTE is available here.
- Malfunctions in glial cells also play a role in neuropathic pain—a condition in which the slightest contact with the skin is excruciating—by causing pain-sensing nerves to send their signals to the brain at a much higher than normal intensity.
- The ability of glial cells to over-excite neurons may also lead to seizure disorders such as epilepsy following head trauma.

9. Examples of symptoms that can occur when trauma or a stroke damages brain cells that are specialized to respond to certain kinds of input:

- A rare condition called Akinetopsia (motion blindness) occurs when trauma, stroke, or disease damages cells in the V5 area of visual cortex that are normally activated by the motion of objects. Patients with this disorder can see stationary objects clearly, but the object disappears as soon as it begins to move. It only reappears to the patient when it stops moving. To these patients, objects in the world seem to jump from one location to another. Here is a 3-min video that simulates what this looks like to a patient and presents other information about the condition.
- A case example of Akinetopsia describes a 70-year-old woman who was hospitalized following a stroke. She was alert, was able to identify figures, name objects, and also discriminate colors, but she was unable to discriminate moving objects from still objects. When walking in the hospital hallways, she often collided with other people because she was unable to see them moving toward her, and the result was falls and injuries. She eventually had to be placed in a nursing home specialized for visually handicapped and blind patients.
- A 4-min video presents a summary of the case of L.M., whose akinotopsia followed a stroke that damaged areas on both sides of the brain between the occipital and temporal lobes.

- Other akinotopsia cases, including classic ones, are available here.
- An even rarer condition called Astatikopsia creates problems opposite to Akinotopsia. Here, patients can see moving objects, but not stationary ones, so as a moving object comes to a stop, it disappears. In one case, a 61-year-old man told his neurologist that for more than a year he had a "loss of appreciation" of stationary objects, referring primarily to people, but being able to see them as soon as they moved. He cited specific examples such as when in a room filled with people, he would not be able to see a motionless person. He was nevertheless able to see fine detail, so he was able to perceive and accurately describe tiny insects if they were moving but not if they were stationary. His case is described in detail here.

10. Here are some examples of neuropsychological phenomena and neuropsychological disorders associated with damage to cells in particular lobes of the cerebral cortex (examples of more generalized neuropsychological syndromes are presented later):

Occipital lobe

- The most common problem caused by damage to the occipital lobe is blindness for information on one or both sides of the visual field. However, because some processing of visual information occurs in areas other than the occipital lobe, some people with occipital lobe damage show a phenomenon called *blindsight*, which allows them to respond to visual stimuli, but without being aware of seeing them. So, people with blindsight may duck when a flying object approaches their face but have no idea why they ducked. Also, if told that a ball has been placed on a table in front of them, they may be able to correctly name the color of the ball, but have no conscious experience of seeing it.
  [Sources: Cowey, A. (2010a). The blindsight saga. *Experimental Brain Research, 200*(1), 3–24.
  Cowey, A. (2010b). Visual system: how does blindsight arise? *Current Biology, 20*(17), R702–R704.]
- A 5-min video presents a short introduction to blindsight, shows experiments in which blindsight phenomena are artificially created in people with normal vision, and discusses the possibility that we have two separate visual systems.
- A 2-min video shows the apparent pathway for visual information processing that underlies blindsight.
- A 40-s video shows a patient who normally walks with a cane because he is blind across his entire visual field. In the video, researchers took away his cane and then asked him to walk down a corridor where they had placed obstacles. Though he claimed he could not see anything, blindsight allowed him to pass by the obstacles without bumping into them.

- A case study describes a 67-year-old man in Switzerland who had a stroke that left him blind throughout the visual field, but who denied any visual impairment (a form of anosognosia). He made up reports about what he was supposedly seeing, but all of them were incorrect except for faces. His case provides an example of blindsight for specific features of the visual world. [Source: Solcà, M., Guggisberg, A.G., Schnider, A. & Leemann, B. (2015). Facial blindsight. *Frontiers in Human Neuroscience, 29*, 1-6. https://doi.org/10.3389/fnhum.2015.00522]
(See the chapters on consciousness and sensation and perception for other examples of blindsight phenomena.)
- Occipital lobe damage can alter visual perception instead of blocking it. For example, in a condition called *palinopsia*, a person will continue to see an object for up to several minutes after the object has been taken away. Apparently, the damage caused brain regions involved in processing visual information to develop a kind of reverberating circuit that does not shut off when it should.
[Reference: Gersztenkorn, D. & Lee, A. G. (2015). Palinopsia revamped: a systematic review of the literature. *Survey of Ophthalmology, 60*(1), 1-35.]
- One case of palinopsia was apparently caused by a tumor in the occipital lobe. When the tumor was removed, the palinopsia disappeared.
[Reference: Khan, A. N., Sharma, R., Khalid, S., McKean, D., Armstrong, R., & Kennard, C. (2011). Palinopsia from a posteriorly placed glioma—an insight into its possible causes. *BMJ case reports*, bcr0820103273. https://doi.org/10.1136/bcr.08.2010.3273]

Parietal lobe

- Patients with damage to either the left or the right parietal lobe—but usually the right—often display a condition called *hemineglect* in which they ignore the side of the body and the side of space opposite the damaged hemisphere. For example, people with damage in the right parietal lobe might not eat from the left side of their plates, might not comb or brush the hair on the left side of their heads, or might not button their left shirtsleeve. They might ignore words on the left side of a page and not notice it when a person approaches from their left side.
[Reference: Langer, K. G., Piechowski-Jozwiak B., & Bogousslavsky J. (2019). Hemineglect and attentional dysfunction. *Frontiers in Neurology and Neuroscience, 44*, 89-99.]
[Additional examples of hemineglect are presented below in the section on neuropsychological syndromes involving perceptual disorders.]
- Another condition associated with parietal lobe damage or dysfunction—especially on the right side of the brain—is *simultanagnosia* (Chechlacz et al., 2012). Patients with this problem can see normally, but they have difficulty in seeing the "big picture" that appears when individual objects are grouped

together in meaningful ways. So, a patient who is shown this figure will only see a lot of "Ts," even though all those "Ts" make up a big letter "H."

```
T T T      T T T
T T T      T T T
T T T      T T T
T T T T T T T T
T T T T T T T T
T T T T T T T T
T T T      T T T
T T T      T T T
T T T      T T T
T T T      T T T
```

- Here is how one simultanagnosia patient responded when she looked at the figure above [Source: Shenker, J. I. & Roberts, M. H. (2016). Simultanagnosia: When all you can see are trees, the forest still rules. *Neurocase, 22*(3), 289–293.]
  EXAMINER: What do you see?
  PATIENT: I see T, T, T, T.... Do I keep going?
  EXAMINER: Anything else?
  PATIENT: T, T, T, T... lots of Ts.
  Examiner: Are there any other letters?
  PATIENT: No.
  EXAMINER: Is there an H?
  PATIENT: No, just Ts.
  EXAMINER: Is there a big letter?
  PATIENT: No, I don't see one.
  EXAMINER: Is there a big letter H?
  PATIENT: No.
  EXAMINER: Do the little letters together form the shape of a big letter H?
  PATIENT: I don't see how.
  EXAMINER: (Outlines the H with finger) Do you see how this is a big H?
  PATIENT: I don't see an H.

Temporal lobe

- If people suffer damage to areas in the temporal lobe that help to analyze visual information, they will still be able to see the objects, but might not be able to recognize what the objects are. As an example of this condition

(visual agnosia), a patient might look at an apple, but when asked to describe it, say "it's a rounded smooth spherical object with a thin protrusion at the top."
- Examples of how specific visual agnosia can be provided by cases in which the problem is restricted to particular dimensions of the visual world. So, some patients may lose the ability to recognize trees, dogs, and other living things, yet retain the ability to recognize cups, books, and other inanimate objects
[Reference: Wolk, D. A., Coslett, H. B., & Glosser, G. (2005). The role of sensory-motor information in object recognition: Evidence from category-specific visual agnosia. *Brain and Language, 94*(2), 131–146.]
- Other examples of the consequences of temporal lobe damage or dysfunction include problems with memory. So, if a tumor or infection or trauma or a stroke damages the medial temporal lobe and its links to other brain regions, people may develop a permanent amnesia syndrome and have difficulty in forming new memories. Similarly, if a seizure disorder or some other medical condition requires surgical removal of the hippocampus from both medial temporal lobes, patients may become unable to form new long-term memories. The most famous patient in this category was Henry Molaison (known as H.M.), whose case is described below in the section on amnestic disorders.
- Disruption of the functioning of the temporal lobes can also impair a person's ability to appropriately link emotional or motivational significance to events. Temporal lobe epilepsy (TLE), for example, may lead to what has been called the "TLE personality." One of these traits is a tendency to see mundane events as having great personal significance, and this can result in magical or sometimes paranoid thinking. Patients with TLE personality also display *hypergraphia*, a tendency to do a lot of writing and take a lot of notes, and they may also be slow to pick up on social cues. This last trait—along with their tendency to talk a lot—can make these people socially "sticky," meaning that it is difficult to gracefully end a conversation with them.
- A final example of damage or dysfunction in the temporal lobes is *palinacousis*, an auditory form of the palinopsia phenomenon mentioned earlier. In this rare condition, the patient continues to hear sounds long after the physical noise has disappeared. In one case, after having a stroke, a 71-year-old man began experiencing a troublesome new auditory phenomenon after hearing a dialogue on television. He stated that the dialogue rattled around in his head and repeated itself numerous times. These acoustic sensations continued after the television set was switched off and he could not stop them by covering his ears.
[Source: Park, S. H., & Kim, K. K. (2017). Palinacousis-auditory perseveration. *Journal of Epilepsy Research, 7*(1), 57–59.]
Two similar cases are available from this source:
Di Dio, A.S., Fields, M.C. and Rowan, A.J. (2007), Palinacousis—auditory

perseveration: Two cases and a review of the literature. *Epilepsia, 48*, 1801-1806.
- Students might also be interested in a milder form of this phenomenon, known as an "earworm," in which a song or melody persists in a person's mind. As described in this article, if the music is heard before bedtime, it can interfere with sleep.

Frontal lobe

- The case of "Tan" described above is an example of how damage to Broca's area in the left frontal lobe can create language problems, especially impairment in the ability to speak.
- Other cases illustrate that damage to other areas of either or both frontal lobes can disrupt executive functioning, including a person's ability to make judgments, plan, organize, and execute decisions, and engage in self-regulation. The most famous of these is the case of Phineas Gage, a Vermont railroad worker who, on September 13, 1848, suffered frontal lobe damage when an explosion sent a 3-foot, 7-inch, 1.25-inch diameter steel rod through his skull, piercing his frontal lobes as shown in the digitally remastered images available here. He survived with his speech, movements, and overall intelligence intact, but his personality changed. Previously responsible, judicious, and socially skilled, he became loud and profane, blurted out inappropriate comments, made poor decisions, and did not follow through with plans. One observer said, that "Gage was no longer Gage," but he seemed unaware of these changes. [Note: You might want to tell your students that Gage had more than just frontal lobe damage; he also had a brain infection and multiple seizures, making interpretation of the cause of his personality changes less clear.]
[References: DeRight, J. (2019). History of "frontal" syndromes and executive dysfunction. *Frontiers in Neurology and Neuroscience, 44*, 100-107.
Harlow, J. M. (1848). Passage of an iron rod through the head. *Boston Medical and Surgical Journal, 39*, 389–393.
- A 2-min video provides a recap of the basics of the Gage case.

- A 10-min video from Harvard's Warren Anatomical Museum focuses on Gage's life and death and the history of the display of Phineas Gage's skull. It also includes a discussion of phrenology and other skull casts on display at the museum.
- Another 8-min video hosted by Alan Alda provides details of the Gage case.

- A 12-min video offers a dramatic reenactment of Gage's accident and its results.
- Frontal lobe damage sometimes causes impairments in planning and organizing the various components of a cognitive task but does not impair the components themselves. In one case, even 8 years after surgery to remove tissue on both sides of his frontal lobes, a man could no longer hold down a job, do household chores, or even decide what to do next. Yet his performance on neuropsychological tests showed that he was of normal intelligence and thus had unimpaired mental capacity. He was accused of faking his disabilities, but his problems were real.
  [Reference: Eslinger, P. J., & Damasio, A. R. (1985). Severe disturbance of higher cognition after bilateral frontal lobe ablation: Patient EVR. *Neurology, 35*, 1731–1741.]
- Because areas in the prefrontal cortex allow us to understand sarcasm or irony, people with damage to these areas miss these aspects of spoken words. In one study, 25 people with prefrontal cortex damage listened to sarcastic stories such as this: "Joe came to work, and instead of beginning to work, he sat down to rest. His boss noticed his behavior and said, 'Joe, don't work too hard.'" A group of 17 people without brain damage immediately recognized that the boss was being sarcastic, but people with prefrontal brain damage did not. The deficits were greatest for patients with damage to the right prefrontal lobe.
  [Reference: Shamay-Tsoory, S. G., & Tomer, R. (2005). The neuroanatomical basis of understanding sarcasm and its relationship to social cognition. *Neuropsychology, 19*, 288–300.]
- Patients with frontal lobe damage may also exhibit *perseveration*, meaning that they say or think or do the same thing repeatedly because they are unable to plan what to say or do next. Some of them simply imitate the words others say (echolalia) or the actions they see others do (echopraxia). Their inability to plan leads some frontal lobe patients to display abulia, a reluctance to move, speak, or initiate interactions. They appear withdrawn and unmotivated; in extreme cases, they may display akinetic mutism: they literally never move or speak.
  [You might want to point out to your students that mild cases of abulia are virtually indistinguishable from those in which people with intact brains are simply unmotivated and uninterested in life, but that the latter cases are due to factors other than brain damage.]
  [Reference: Marin, R. S., & Wilkosz, P. A. (2005). Disorders of diminished motivation. *Journal of Head Trauma Rehabilitation, 20*, 377–388.]
- Frontal lobe malfunctions resulting in lack of inhibition of aggression have been proposed in criminal cases, including that of Joel Rifkin, a man who murdered 17 women in the New York City area between 1989 and 1993. In a video about this case called *The Mind of a Killer: Case Study of a*

Murderer, Rifkin is shown taking neuropsychological tests, including the Stroop test and finger-tapping impulse control tests as well as brain imaging studies. The video proposes that his killing spree resulted in part from a failure of the pre-frontal cortex to control the impulses generated by the limbic system. The video is expensive, but a free 7-min preview is available.
[Reference: *The Mind of a Killer: Case Study of a Murderer.* New York, N.Y.: Films Media Group, (2007), ©1999. ABC News Productions. Contents: Joel Rifkin's Murder Spree (7:07) – Joel Rifkin's Early Years (5:13) – Psychological Studies of Aggression (3:40) – Aggressive Impulses and Frontal Lobe Function (9:45) – Brain Abnormalities in Murderers (8:38) – Brain Scans Support Diminished Capacity Defense (4:22) – Links Between Dysfunctional Brains and Violence (4:52).]

11. Disorders related to split-brain patients illustrating hemispheric lateralization: [Note: Examples in this section, and the two that follow it, may help you to debunk the myth that people are either "left-brained" or "right-brained."]

- When a person's corpus callosum has been severed, the patient is said to have a "split brain." Research with these patients often involves having them sit in front of a screen that makes it impossible to see objects placed in their hands (see image below). They must depend entirely on touch information from the hands to identify the objects. They can do so if the object is placed in their right hand, because the touch information goes directly to the language-oriented left side of their brain. However, if the object is placed in their left hand, the touch information goes to the right side of the brain but—because of the severed corpus callosum—it cannot be transferred to the left side for verbal identification. One split-brain patient could use her left hand to correctly pick out a spoon from a group of other objects by its feel and shape, but when she was asked what she had just grasped, she replied, "A pencil." Her right hemisphere had recognized the object, but she could not describe it correctly because the left side of her brain did not see or feel it.
[References: Sperry, R. W. (1968). Hemisphere deconnection and unity in conscious awareness. *American Psychologist, 23,* 723–733.
Sperry, R. W. (1974). Lateral specialization in the surgically separated hemispheres. In F. O. Schmitt & F. G. Wordon (Eds.), *The neurosciences: Third study program* (pp. 5–19). Cambridge, MA: MIT Press.
Gazzaniga, M. S. (1967). The split brain in man. *Scientific American, 217* (2), 24-29.]

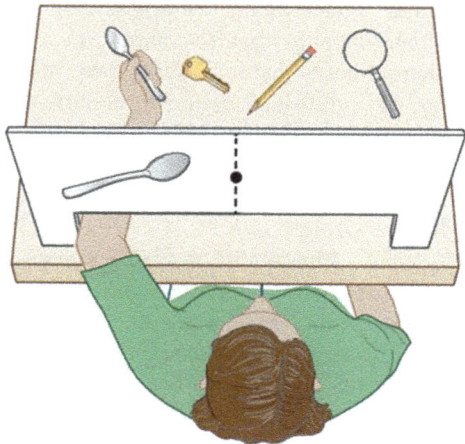

[Source: Bernstein, D.A., Teachman, B.A., Olatunji, B.O., & Lilienfeld, S.O. (2021). *Introduction to clinical psychology: Bridging science and practice* (9th ed.) Cambridge: Cambridge University Press.]

- A 10-min video from *Scientific American Frontiers* presents the case of "Joe," whose corpus collosum was surgically severed to control epileptic seizures. The surgery controlled the seizures, but left him with some interesting limitations and capabilities, including the ability to draw different objects with each hand at the same time.

12. Disorders associated with brain damage to the left cerebral hemisphere:

    - Broca's aphasia occurs as a result of damage from a stroke or trauma in left frontal lobe cortex, near motor areas that control facial muscles, and it makes it difficult for patients to speak or write correctly even though they still have fairly good understanding of spoken or written words. For example, in response to the question "What do you do with a cigarette, a person with Broca's aphasia replied, "Uh… uh… cigarette [pause] smoke it." His speech was meaningful but not fluent; it was halting and awkwardly phrased.
    - A 4-min video shows an interview with a man who developed Broca's aphasia following a stroke.

    - A 7-min video presents an interview with a 19-year-old woman who also developed Broca's aphasia following a stroke.

    - Examples of treatment for Broca's aphasia include the melodic intonation therapy (MIT) mentioned earlier, combined with noninvasive electrical stimulation of an area of the *right* hemisphere that is involved in the ability to sing. This stimulation appears to enhance the effects of MIT.

[Reference: Vines, B. W., Norton, A. C., & Schlaug, G. (2011). Non-invasive brain stimulation enhances the effects of melodic intonation therapy. *Frontiers in Psychology, 2* (article 230), 1–10.]
- Damage to *Wernicke's area*—a portion of association cortex in the left temporal lobe near the area of the sensory cortex that receives information from the ears—can create many symptoms. For example, this area (named for Carl Wernicke, the Polish neurologist who identified it in 1870) is involved in our ability to extract meaning from spoken or written language, so patients with *Wernicke's aphasia* are no longer able to understand what they read or what others say. To these patients, other people seem to be speaking gibberish, which makes them feel that the world has suddenly become a strange place where everyone else has a language problem.
[Reference: Goodglass, H., & Kaplan, E. (1982). *The assessment of aphasia and related disorders* (2nd ed.). Philadelphia: Lea & Febiger.]
- Although Wernicke's aphasia patients have no difficulty in speaking, what they say may make little or no sense. In response to the request "Tell me what you do with a cigarette," one patient with Wernicke's aphasia replied, "This is a segment of a pegment. Soap a cigarette." So, his speech came easily, quickly, and without effort, but also without meaning.
[Reference: Lapointe, L. (1990). *Aphasia and related neurogenic language disorders.* New York: Thieme Medical.]
- Wernicke's aphasia patients also make naming errors, called *semantic paraphasias*, in which for example, when trying to name a pen, they call it a book.
- In severe cases, Wernicke's aphasia patients may be impossible to understand. For example, this is what one patient said when asked to describe a picture of a woman and her children in the kitchen: "Over here is the top of the rest for the other rapid if am a many red sitters."
[You might want to point out to your students that the speech of some Wernicke's aphasia patients may sound so disorganized that it can seem like the "word salad" produced by some people with schizophrenia.]
- Unfortunately, people with Wernicke's aphasia often do not recognize their problems, and so may become puzzled, distressed, or angry when others fail to understand what they say. This anosagnosia (unawareness of disorder) can reduce these patients' motivation to participate in treatment.
- A 90-s video presents an interview with a man with Wernicke's aphasia.

- Unlike other forms of aphasia that appear suddenly as the result of a stroke or brain injury, *primary progressive aphasia* (PPA) is a neurological syndrome in which impairment of language capabilities comes on slowly and gets progressively worse. The patient may or may not have difficulty understanding speech, but eventually almost all patients become mute and unable to understand spoken or written language. PPA is considered a form of dementia because its origins lie in neurodegenerative diseases such as

Alzheimer's disease or frontotemporal degeneration that damage brain tissue in language areas. The specific early symptoms depend on exactly where that damage occurs. A 3-min video shows an example of PPA in a man who now struggles to speak.
- A 2-min video shows a woman with a different variant called logopenic PPA.
(Additional examples of the effects of neurodegenerative diseases are presented later in this chapter.)

13. Disorders associated with damage to the right cerebral hemisphere:

- The right hemisphere plays an important role in the accurate expression and perception of social communication, and damage to it can cause a variety of deficits, depending on where the damage occurs. For example, people with right-hemisphere damage often have difficulty understanding the overall point of a paragraph, the plot of a story, or the punch line of a joke.
- People with right hemisphere damage may also have difficulty understanding metaphors. For example, they might interpret the statement "I cried my eyes out" to mean the speaker's eyes actually fell out, or that "she's a princess" means the person is actually part of a royal family.
- Right hemisphere damage sometimes leads to an inability to understand subtle aspects of speech, such as indirect requests. So, when asked "Could you pass the salt?" the person may say "yes" rather than actually doing so.
- People with right hemisphere damage may display *expressive aprosodia*, meaning that their speech no longer contains the intonations, tones of voice and rhythms (prosody) that help express the emotions they are trying to convey. For example, they may speak in a robotic monotone, but may learn to finish sentences with "I am angry," "I am sad," or other tags that help the listener understand the intended emotional message.
- People with right hemisphere damage may also fail to take social situations into account when they speak. So, for example, if a person with an intact brain and typical social skills needed change for the copy machine and they noticed someone nearby engrossed in reading a book, the person would probably say something like "Excuse me, I am sorry to interrupt" before making a request for change. Someone with right-hemisphere damage might simply approach, ignore what the other person is doing, and say "Do you have change for a dollar?"
- Similarly, a person with right-hemisphere damage may engage in inappropriate social communication, such as by telling obscene stories or jokes at a wedding, a funeral, or in other inappropriate situations.
- Right hemisphere damage may also result in *receptive aprosodia*, in which the patient may not notice or understand the meaning of other people's hand gestures, emotional expressions, or other social cues. These deficits can create difficulties in social relationships. For example, when another person says "I'm trying to concentrate here," the patient may ignore this unspoken

request for silence and keep right on talking. The patient may also miss the social signals and body language—such as standing up and saying "OK, well, nice talking to you…"—that convey the other person's wish to end a conversation.
- People with receptive aprosodia also tend to miss the meaning of tone of voice. For example, if someone says, "Well, that was really smart" in a tone that meant just the opposite, a person with receptive aprosodia may hear only the words themselves, and being grateful, say "Thanks!"

Syndromes of Neuropsychological Disorder

1. Amnestic disorders

- In 1953, at the age of 27, Henry Molaison (known for decades only as H.M) had such severe epilepsy that surgeons removed parts of both his left and right temporal lobes, including parts of the hippocampus on both sides in the hope of stopping his uncontrollable, life-threatening seizures. The surgery did help control the seizures, but it left him with permanent anterograde amnesia (he died at the age of 82 in 2008). When H.M. met someone new, he was unable to recall the meeting moments later, so the person seemed to be a stranger no matter how many times they met again. H.M. could not even remember that time was passing, so he had few clues that he was getting older. He did realize, however, that he had a memory problem, and put it this way: "At this moment everything looks clear to me, but what happened just before? That's what worries me. It's like waking from a dream. I just don't remember."
[References: Milner, B. (1970). Memory and the medial temporal regions of the brain. In K. H. Pribram & D. B. Broadbent (Eds.), *Biology of memory*. New York: Academic Press.
Squire, L. R. (2009). The legacy of patient H. M. for neuroscience. *Neuron*, *61*(1), 6–9.]
- H.M. provides a striking example of how surgery, accident, or disease can create disconnections between brain modules that result in some abilities being lost while others are spared. His procedural memory remained intact, allowing him to perform everyday tasks as usual, and despite his amnesia, H.M. had good language function; he recognized objects; he thought and reasoned; he remained intelligent, pleasant, and sociable; and he carried on very normal-sounding conversations. He was even quite aware of his memory problem
- Musician and conductor Clive Wearing developed both anterograde and retrograde amnesia after having contracted herpesviral encephalitis in 1985. The following summary of his situation appears on Wikipedia:

"He spends every day "waking up" every 20 seconds, "restarting" his consciousness once the time span of his short-term memory elapses (about 30 seconds). During this time, he repeatedly questions why he has not seen a doctor, as he constantly believes he has only recently awoken from a comatose state. If engaged in discussion, Wearing is able to provide answers to questions, but cannot stay in the flow of conversation for longer than a few sentences. If asked about his current situation, he becomes very angry and upset, as he cannot obtain an explanation for his condition and thus feels interrogated. He remembers little of his life before 1985; he knows, for example, that he has children from an earlier marriage, but cannot remember their names. His love for his second wife, Deborah, whom he married the year prior to his illness, is undiminished. He greets her joyously every time they meet, either believing he has not seen her in years or that they have never met before, even though she may have just left the room momentarily. When he goes out dining with his wife, he can remember the name of the food (e.g. chicken); however he cannot link it with taste, as he forgets what food he is eating by the time it has reached his mouth."

- A 3-min video provides a brief description of the Wearing case, though it is incorrectly titled "The man with no short-term memory."

- A longer (48-min) video about his case is also available.

- The Wearing case is another example of the way in which various abilities can be disconnected. He has had no ability to form new memories since 1985, but his ability to play music is unaffected.

- An 8-min video presents a case similar to Wearing's, also due to hippocampal damage following a viral infection.

- A 3-min video of another similar case, this time involving damage resulting from an accident with a miniature fencing foil, is available.

- A 5-min video interview with "K.C." illustrates a rare case in which a motorcycle accident caused damage to the hippocampus and elsewhere that created anterograde amnesia as dense as H.M. and Clive Wearing, but also a form of retrograde amnesia that is confined to episodic memories. So, "K.C." has no memory of personal experiences before the accident (or of the accident itself) but retains memory of a lifetime of factual information (semantic memory).

Syndromes of Neuropsychological Disorder

- On July 25, 2011, Kay Delaney, a nursing home manager in Newton, England, fell at work and suffered a head injury that left her with retrograde amnesia so severe that she forgot virtually everything she had learned about everything and everyone she had known over the previous twenty years. Now in her 60s, she thinks she is still 34, and the last thing she can remember is putting her three children to bed in the early 1990s. A description of Kay's case can be found here.

- Case studies show that anterograde amnesia patients may still be able to form memories, though not conscious ones. H.M. and others with similar brain damage will show improved performance after repeated practice with a puzzle task even though they cannot remember the practice sessions. Some show differing patterns of eye movements when looking at previously seen versus never-seen pictures, or changes in heart rate or skin conduction in response to familiar versus unfamiliar stimuli.
  [References: Jacoby, L. L., & Kelley, C. M. (1987). Unconscious influences of memory for a prior event. *Personality and Social Psychology Bulletin, 13*, 314–336.
  Verfaellie, M., & Keane, M. M. (1997). The neural basis of aware and unaware forms of memory. *Seminars in Neurology, 17*, 153–161.]

- When strokes, tumors, vitamin deficiencies, excess alcohol use, or other factors damage the medial dorsal region of the thalamus or certain areas of prefrontal cortex, anterograde amnesia is often accompanied by *confabulation*, in which patients fill in memory gaps with reports that they believe to be true, but are not. A 90-s audio clip presents a patient with severe brain damage creating completely false statements.

2. Disorders of consciousness

    - The result of severe damage to the reticular activating system can be a temporary or permanent coma; in cases of less severe damage the patient may enter a persistent vegetative state (PVS) or a minimally conscious state (MCS). Patients in MCS appear unconscious but can still follow simple commands (e.g., touch your nose, look up), make verbal or gestural responses to yes or no questions (e.g., blink once for yes, twice for no), say a few words, smile or cry in response to happy or sad stimuli, reach for objects, and follow moving objects with their eyes.
    - A 4-min video presents the case of a brain-injured firefighter who had been in MCS and then, after ten years, suddenly woke up. Nevertheless, the story has a sad ending.
    - A 40-s video contains a news report on a little girl who was hit by a car. It provides an example of how brain-damaged patients previously in a coma can progress to MCS.

- Patients in a PVS are unable to do the things that MCS patients are capable of, but may open their eyes and appear to wake up in daytime and close their eyes and appear to sleep at night. A 5-min video shows examples of some PVS patients, and suggests that it might be possible to determine if they are conscious by identifying changes in brain activity (as measured by fMRI) in response to commands.
- A 90-s video shows the fMRI technique being used with a patient who is in a PVS.

- A 5-min video presents the case of a young man who entered a PVS that doctors thought would be permanent but from which he spontaneously emerged.
  [Note: you might want to explain to your students that, dramatic as it is, sudden or even gradual recovery from PVS or MCS is extremely rare.]
- Disruption in the functioning of both cerebral hemispheres as a result of alcohol or other drugs, the side-effects of medication or surgery, fever, seizures, chemical imbalances, hormonal disorders, and infections can lead to delirium, which can include periods of sleepiness, disorientation, and confusion alternating with periods of agitation, restlessness, hyper-alertness, hypersensitivity to stimulation, and even hallucinations.
- A 2-min video describes and illustrates typical behaviors seen in patients with delirium.

- A 6-min video presents more details about delirium and shows a number of patients who had, or were role-playing, the condition.

- Anosognosia, a lack of awareness of neurological or psychological disorder, can result from damage to the frontal or parietal lobes, usually on the right side, but as described earlier in relation to Wernicke's aphasia, also on the left side. The first part of a 4-min video summarizes this condition and its causes (e.g., stroke, tumor, Alzheimer's disease, Huntington's disease) as well as its appearance in association with schizophrenia and bipolar disorder. The video includes an interview with Russell Weston, a man with severe delusions who killed two police officers during an armed attack on the U.S. capitol building in 1998, but who has no awareness of being disordered. The latter part veers off into community treatment for mentally ill offenders.

Syndromes of Neuropsychological Disorder 61

- Here is an example to help students understand the anosognosia phenomenon: The brain is the organ that we use to figure out when something is wrong. If you have pain in your arm, sensory neurons tell the brain about it, but if the brain itself is hurt, it has nowhere to send its message, leaving a person unaware of a problem.
- As mentioned earlier, anosognosia can pose a serious obstacle to rehabilitation programs. For example, people in whom a right-hemisphere stroke left them with hemiplegia or hemiparesis, may refuse to acknowledge that there is weakness or paralysis in all or part of the left side of their body, and thus also refuse to engage in any efforts to solve a problem they "don't have."
- A 6-min video summary of anosognosia includes case descriptions of anosognosia for hemiparesis and blindness. The last part morphs into a commercial for Curiosity Stream, so you might want to stop the video at about 5:40.
- One example of the successful treatment of anosognosia is presented in the case of a patient who was unaware of the sudden and bizarre involuntary movements he had been making for several years, even if he looked at himself doing so in a mirror. However, when a neurologist made a video of the behavior and showed it to the patient, the patient immediately recognized the problem.
  [Reference: Shenker, J. I., Wylie, S. A., Fuchs, K., Manning, C. A., & Heilman, K. M. (2004). On-line anosognosia: Unawareness for chorea in real time but not on videotape delay. *Neurology, 63*(1), 159–160.]

3. Perceptual disorders

- As mentioned earlier, patients with damage to either the left or the right parietal lobe—but usually the right—often display a condition called hemineglect in which they ignore the side of the body and the side of space opposite the damaged hemisphere.
- Hemineglect can be so extreme that patients may perceive parts of their bodies as belonging to someone else. One such patient woke up in the middle of the night and tried to throw his leg out of bed because he thought that it belonged to an invading stranger.
  [Source: Sacks, O. (1990). A leg to stand on. New York, NY: Summit Books.]
- Here is an example of a drawing of a clock and a flower by a patient with right parietal lobe damage and left side hemineglect:

[Source: Bernstein, D.A. (2019). *Essentials of psychology* (7th ed.). Belmont, CA: Wadsworth Cengage Learning.]

- A 6-min video describes hemineglect and presents interviews with patients who have this condition.
- Neural pathways from the occipital lobe to the parietal lobe have been called the "where" system because it analyzes object location and where the objects are in relation to one another. Damage to this system can produce the disorder called simultanagnosia described earlier.
- Pathways from the occipital lobe to the temporal lobe have been called the "what" system because neuronal activity along this pathway helps us to identify what we see. Damage to this pathway can create *visual agnosia*, the inability to recognize seen objects. For example, a patient called "Max" could clearly see an apple resting on a table in front of him. He could describe it and even draw a picture of it, but could not say what it was.
- Though patients with visual agnosia cannot recognize objects by sight, they can do so by feel. For example, as mentioned in the research methods chapter, when neurologist Oliver Sacks showed a glove to his patient "Dr. P.," the patient could not say what it was. Instead, he said, "A continuous surface, infolded on itself. It appears to have … five outpouchings, if this is the word … a container of some sort." However, when Sacks allowed the patient to put on the glove, Dr. P. exclaimed, "My God, it's a glove!"

[Reference: Sacks, O. (1985). *The man who mistook his wife for a hat*. New York: Summit Books, p. 13.]

- Some visual agnosia patients cannot name anything they see, while others are impaired only when trying to name certain object categories. For example, there are patients whose visual agnosia is restricted to manufactured objects, such as cars, books, or glasses; they can still correctly recognize and name trees, dogs, or other living things. There are opposite cases, too, in which the patient can name on sight manufactured objects, but not living things. These cases exemplify the basis for suggestions that recognition of natural versus manufactured objects depend on neuronal processing in somewhat different brain areas.
[References: Riddoch, M. J., Humphreys, G. W., Akhtar, N. A., Allen, H., Bracewell, R. M., & Schofield, A. J. (2008). A tale of two agnosias: Distinctions between form and integrative agnosia. *Cognitive Neuropsychology, 25*(1), 56–92.
Thomas, R., & Forde, E. (2006). The role of local and global processing in the recognition of living and nonliving things. *Neuropsychologia, 44*(6), 982–986.]
- A 5-min video presents a case example of visual agnosia in an adult male. His description of the experience is very useful in helping students understand the subjective nature of this condition.
- Visual agnosias can be even more specific. For example, the man in the video just mentioned cannot name objects in the world but can easily identify faces. This is because there appears to be a brain network that is specialized for recognizing faces. As mentioned earlier, if that network is damaged, people may develop prosopagnosia, an inability to recognize faces, even very familiar ones; they cannot even recognize their own face in a photo or a mirror. This condition usually follows from damage in both temporal lobes, but it can sometimes occur following right-sided damage alone.
[References: Barton, J. J. (2011). Disorder of higher visual function. *Current Opinion in Neurology, 24*(1), 1–5.
Collins J. A., & Olson I. R. (2014). Beyond the FFA: The role of the ventral anterior temporal lobes in face processing. *Neuropsychologia, 61*, 65–79.
Gainotti, G. (2013). Is the right anterior temporal variant of prosopagnosia a form of "associative prosopagnosia" or a form of "multimodal person recognition disorder"? *Neuropsychology Review, 23*(2), 99–110.
Watson, R., Huis In't Veld. E. M., & de Gelder, B. (2016). The neural basis of individual face and object perception. *Frontiers in Human Neuroscience, 10*, 66.]
- A 4-min video presents another case of prosopagnosia, this time of a photographer and firefighter whose brain injury resulted in the inability to recognize faces, including her own. She describes the  sadness associated with this condition, which has essentially cut her off emotionally from her family. An interesting element of this video is that the patient could not recognize her mother by looking at a photo of her face, but instantly identified her once she could see the clothes her mother was wearing in the photo.

- As in the cases of blindsight patients being able to see without awareness and anterograde amnesia patients forming new, but unconscious memories, some prosopagnosia patients can recognize faces without being aware of it. For example, in looking an array of photographs, they may not be able to say if a face is familiar or not, but they show greater fMRI and EEG responses to familiar versus unfamiliar ones.
  [Reference: Simon, S. R., Khateb, A., Darque, A., Lazeyras, F., Mayer, E., & Pegna, A. J. (2011). When the brain remembers, but the patient doesn't: Converging fMRI and EEG evidence for covert recognition in a case of prosopagnosia. *Cortex, 47*(7), 825–838.]
- The fact that some people with intact brains may nevertheless have a hard time recognizing other people's faces illustrates that there can be an inherited condition known as developmental prosopagnosia.
  [Reference: Barton, J. J., & Corrow, S. L. (2016). The problem of being bad at faces. *Neuropsychologia, 89*, 119–124.]
- There is a 6-min video in which Oliver Sacks describes his own lifelong difficulty in recognizing faces (including his own), and also certain places.

- A quick guide to developmental prosopagnosia is available and there is also a 5-min video that includes an interview with a woman with this condition.

- An online test for "face blindness" is available.
- In a different kind of face-related perceptual disturbance, people come to believe that a familiar person has been replaced by an "imposter." This false belief is known as *Capgras syndrome* (named for the French psychiatrist who first reported it in 1923). The damage seen in Capgras syndrome tends to be in the temporal lobes, where brain areas that help recognize faces become disconnected from those that give us a sense of familiarity.
  [References: Ramachandran, V. S. (1998). Consciousness and body image: Lessons from phantom limbs, Capgras syndrome and pain asymbolia. *Philosophical Transactions of the Royal Society of London. Series B: Biological Sciences, 353*(1377), 1851-1859.
  Capgras, J., & Reboul-Lachaux, J. (1923). L'illusion des sosies' dans un delire systématisé chronique. *Bulletin de la Societe Clinique de Medecine Mentale, 2*, 616.]
- Capgras delusions are often permanent, but in at least one case, they were cured by anti-seizure medication.
  [Reference: Shenker, J. (2013). Reversible Capgras Syndrome due to temporal lobe dysfunction: S616. *Annals of Neurology, 74*, S–31.

- A 10-min video presents the case of a man who developed Capgras syndrome in relation to his parents following a car accident that damaged his brain. The video mentions an incorrect, but interesting, psychoanalytic explanation for the condition and then contrasts it with the biopsychological explanation. The case is particularly interesting because although the patient's delusion occurred while looking at his father, it disappeared when he spoke to him on the telephone. This phenomenon confirmed the involvement of damage to the patient's visual system.
- The *Fregoli delusion* is a related and rare disorder in which a person comes to believe that different people are in fact a single person who changes appearance or is in disguise. There is often a paranoid quality to this belief in that the patient claims they are being pursued or persecuted by the person they see as being in disguise. The disorder may be related to damage to the right frontal and left temporo-parietal areas of the brain.
- In cases of acquired achromatopsia, damage to the thalamus or the V4 area of the visual cortex leaves a person unable to see color even though the color-sensing cone cells in the person's retinas are normal. The thalamic damage is usually caused by a tumor; the cortical damage usually stems from physical trauma, hemorrhage or a tumor.
  [Reference: Heywood, C. A., Wilson, B., & Cowey, A. (1987). A case study of cortical colour "blindness" with relatively intact achromatic discrimination. *Journal of Neurology, Neurosurgery, and Psychiatry, 50*(1), 22–29. https://doi.org/10.1136/jnnp.50.1.22]
- A 4-min video provides an overview of inherited rather than acquired achromatopsia. It offers examples of what the world looks like to achromats and includes a scientific explanation of the cause of the disorder.
- Here are short summaries of 11 cases of individuals with congenital achromatopsia who have overcome the condition to lead successful lives, including musicians Ken Kase and John Kay, and skier Staci Mannella.
- Agnosias can appear in systems other than vision. For example, patients with somatosensory agnosia (also called tactile agnosia) can recognize objects by sight but have difficulty doing so by touch. So, for example, if they pick up and feel the shape and contours of a spoon without looking at it they will not be able to say what it is. If the brain damage causing this condition is on only one side of the brain, the left side, for example, the patient's agnosia would be evident only when trying to recognize objects by feeling them with the right hand; left-handed tactile recognition would be intact.
- Patients with auditory agnosia lose the ability to understand language, write from dictation, and repeat words, though they can recognize nonverbal sounds, such as those coming from a sewing machine or a car engine. In one case, a 65-year-old man was admitted to a neurosurgery department with a head injury that caused bleeding in the temporal lobe on the left side of his

brain. Afterward, he could speak fluently, he could read and understand written words, and he recognized nonverbal sounds, such as laughing, instrumental music, a baby crying, a telephone ringing, or a dog barking, but he did not follow oral commands and could not repeat or write words spoken to him. He said that the sound of people speaking was experienced as an unpleasant buzzing. After six months of cognitive rehabilitation treatment, his ability to understand verbal language was improved somewhat if the speaker spoke slowly and directly in front of the patient's eyes, but his comprehension of spoken language was restricted to individual words; he could still not understand sentences.
[Reference: Kim, J. M., Woo, S. B., Lee, Z., Heo, S. J., & Park, D. (2018). Verbal auditory agnosia in a patient with traumatic brain injury: A case report. *Medicine, 97*(11), e0136.]

- Patients with a rare disorder called dysmetropsia, also known as Todd's syndrome or Alice in Wonderland syndrome (AIWS), experience distortions of size perception several times a day. Objects, including parts of their own bodies, may appear smaller (micropsia) or larger (macropsia) than they actually are, or they may appear to be closer (pelopsia) or farther (teleopsia) away than they actually are. In patients who experience alterations of their body parts, the head and hands seem out of proportion, usually disproportionately large. There is sometimes also a loss of the sense of time, which may seem to pass abnormally slowly or quickly. Some patients experience strong hallucinations. The syndrome is seen in both adults and children, and though its symptoms may cause anxiety or panic, the disorder does not appear to be dangerous. Its cause(s) are uncertain, but the syndrome is often associated with migraine headaches, temporal lobe epilepsy, brain tumors, and encephalomyelitis. Treating this condition through anti-migraine drugs can be effective, but chronic cases that have been described as untreatable may simply disappear, especially in children.
[Reference: Weissenstein, A., Luchter, E., & Bittmann, M. A. (2014). Alice in Wonderland syndrome: A rare neurological manifestation with microscopy in a 6-year-old child. *Journal of Pediatric Neurosciences, 9*(3), 303–304.]
- The story of a child's AIWS told by her mother is available and includes information suggesting that, in this case at least, the syndrome may have a hereditary component.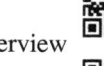
- A 2-min video showing a child with AIWS and a short interview with a doctor is available.
- Allochiria is a neurological disorder in which patients respond to stimuli presented to one side of their body as if the origin of those stimuli were on the opposite side. In somatosensory allochiria, a touch on the left arm will be reported as a touch on the right arm. If the auditory or visual senses are affected, images or sounds will be reported as coming from the side opposite to their actual source. This disorder is linked to lesions in the right parietal lobe and may occur in association with hemineglect.

- In a disorder called somatoparaphrenia, patients deny ownership of a limb or even a whole side of their body. If clearly shown that the limb is, in fact, part of their body, these patients create elaborate stories about whose limb it really is or how it became attached to their body. In extreme cases, these delusions lead the patient to care for the limb as if it were a separate being. The condition is associated mainly with extensive damage to the right side of the brain.
  [Reference: Vallar, G. & Ronchi, R. (2009). Somatoparaphrenia: A body delusion. A review of the neuropsychological literature. *Experimental Brain Research, 192*(3), 533-551. https://doi.org/10.1007/s00221-008-1562-y]
- In rare cases, brain damage can lead to alien hand syndrome (AHS), also called Dr. Strangelove syndrome, in which patients perceive one or more of their limbs acting independently, without conscious direction. In one case, a 77-year-old woman had been told to stop her anticoagulation medication temporarily in preparation for surgery. Two days later, she became terrified as she watched her left hand began stroking her face and hair, seemingly on its own. For 30 min, she could not control this movement, even through the efforts of her right hand. When control finally returned, she experienced numbness and weakness in her left upper arm. When her husband took her to the hospital, he noticed that she was dragging her left leg as she walked. CT and MRI scans revealed that she had had strokes in both parietal lobes, although this syndrome is more commonly associated with surgery on the corpus callosum, brain tumors, aneurysms, and neurodegenerative diseases.
  [Reference: Panikkath, R., Panikkath, D., Mojumder, D., & Nugent, K. (2014). The alien hand syndrome. *Baylor University Medical Center Proceedings, 27*(3), 219–220. https://doi.org/10.1080/08998280.2014.11929115]
- A case study presents the story of a 55-year-old woman who had been experiencing alien hand syndrome for nearly 30 years. It appeared following surgery that severed her corpus callosum in order to control severe epilepsy. Her symptoms include having one hand engage in activities (e.g., undressing) that she does not consciously direct and that she struggles to stop using her other hand.
- Here is a 30-s clip from the movie *Dr. Strangelove* in which Peter Sellers' alien hand tries to kill him, and from which the alien hand syndrome's alternate name comes.

4. Disorders of Movement

- *Praxis* is the ability to tell motor systems in the brain about the combinations of movements that are needed to perform a specific learned task. Brain damage, tumors, disease, or other causes can disrupt this ability, resulting in various forms of *apraxia*.
  One example is ideomotor apraxia, which involves difficulties in performing skilled movements. So, when brushing their teeth, patients with this condition will perform each step in the process in the proper order but have difficulty in

positioning their hands to hold the brush or in timing their brushing motions. These people may also use a finger or other body part as if it were a tool, perhaps brushing with their forefinger, or using their finger to stir sugar into a cup of coffee. They may also be unable to figure out how to use tools that they once used with ease.
[Reference: Wheaton, L. A., & Hallett, M. (2007). Ideomotor apraxia: A review. *Journal of the Neurological Sciences, 260*(1–2), 1–10.]

- There is a 2-min video showing the movement difficulties displayed by a woman with ideomotor apraxia.
- Patients with ideational apraxia can perform the individual movements needed to complete a task but do so in the wrong order. For example, a woman may be able to easily uncap a tube of toothpaste, wet her toothbrush, squeeze paste onto the brush, insert the brush into her mouth, and make the proper brushing movements, but will get the sequence wrong. She might put the brush in her mouth before putting paste on it, or she might squeeze the tube before unscrewing the cap.
- A 10-min video presents an interview with a 72-year-old woman with ideomotor apraxia during which she demonstrates varying degrees of difficulty with various kinds of motor tasks. The webpage where the video appears also contains a very detailed case history. Her condition first appeared following an inner ear infection but her doctors hypothesize that its actual cause is a neurodegenerative disease process in her right parietal lobe.
- A 6-min video presents examples of dyspraxia, a somewhat less severe form of apraxia, in this case with elements of both ideomotor and ideational apraxia. The video includes tips for helping people with this condition.
- This article contains reminders of 7 of the most memorable cases from the writings of Oliver Sacks.

5. Dementia (Major Neurocognitive Disorder)

- Often a precursor to dementia, mild cognitive impairment (MCI), also called mild neurocognitive disorder, appears as problems with memory, language, thinking, and judgment that are more severe than normal age-related changes. A 4-min video tells the story of a man with a family history of Alzheimer's disease (AD) whose physical and cognitive test results reveal that he already has MCI.
- A 3-min video from Emory University presents an overview of MCI, including causes that may be treatable and the fact that not all cases lead to Alzheimer's disease.

- A 7-min video presents the story of a 74-year-old woman who was diagnosed with MCI and of how she was living with it. More details about her and her case are presented on the same page where you will find the video. These details include the fact that five years after the diagnosis, she decided to end her life rather than live through the final stages of a condition that she felt sure was leading to Alzheimer's disease.
- An example of efforts to slow the progress of MCI is a program called Computerized Cognitive Training (CCT), which has been described as helpful or not helpful, depending on which reviews you read. Discussion of the program can provide an excellent opportunity for students to engage in critical thinking. Relevant references are listed below.
  Overviews of the controversy are available here and here
  [References: Harvey, P. D., McGurk, S. R., Mahncke, H., & Wykes, T. (2018). Controversies in computerized cognitive training. *Biological Psychiatry: Cognitive Neuroscience and Neuroimaging, 3*(11), 907-915.
  Hill, N.T., Mowszowski, L., Naismith, S.L., Chadwick, V.L., Valenzuela, M., & Lampit, A. (2017). Computerized cognitive training in older adults with mild cognitive impairment or dementia: A systematic review and meta-analysis. *American Journal of Psychiatry, 174* (4), 329-340. https://doi.org/10.1176/appi.ajp.2016.16030360]
- The case that led to identification of Alzheimer's disease, the most common cause of dementia, was that of Auguste Deter. After her death in 1906, neurologist Alois (or Aloysius) Alzheimer examined her brain and discovered dead and dying nerve cells that had become twisted and misshapen (neurofibrillary tangles) and abnormal debris outside of nerve cells (amyloid plaque).

- A photo as well as fascinating details of Auguste Deter's life and the progression of her symptoms are available.

- Here is a typical example of the symptoms of early-onset Alzheimer's disease, retrieved in edited form:
  "This 58-year-old woman was referred to our memory clinic with a 2-year history of repetitiveness, memory loss, and executive function loss. Magnetic resonance imaging revealed mild generalized cortical atrophy. Progressive cognitive decline was evident by the report of deficits in instrumental activities of daily living performance over the past 9 months. Word finding and literacy skills were noted to have deteriorated in the preceding 6 months according to her spouse. Examples of functional losses were being slower in processing and carrying out instructions, not knowing how to turn off the stove, and becoming unable to assist in boat docking which was the couple's pastime. She stopped driving a motor vehicle about 6 months

before her memory clinic consultation. She had no surgical history and no history of smoking, alcohol, or other drug misuse. Blood screening was normal. There was no first-degree family history of presenile dementia. Neurocognitive assessment at the first clinic visit revealed a Mini Mental State Examination (MMSE) score of 14/30; poor verbal fluency (patient was able to produce only 5 animal names and 1 F-word in 1 min) as well as poor visuospatial and executive skills. She had fluent speech without semantic deficits. Her neurological examination showed normal gait, muscle tone and power, mild ideomotor apraxia on performing commands for motor tasks with no suggestion of cerebellar dysfunction. Her speech was fluent with obvious word finding difficulties but with no phonemic or semantic paraphrasic errors. Her general physical examination was unremarkable without evidence of presenile cataracts. She had normal hearing. There was no evidence of depression or psychotic symptoms.

Over the next 4 years, she continued to decline in cognition and function such that admission to a care facility was required with associated total dependence for basic activities of daily living. She developed muscle rigidity, motor apraxias, worsening perceptual, and language skills. After 1 year in the care home, she was admitted to the acute care hospital in respiratory distress. CT brain imaging during that admission revealed marked generalized global cortical atrophy and marked hippocampal atrophy. She died of pneumonia at age 63; an autopsy confirmed the diagnosis of AD."

- Here is a case example of early- to middle-stage Alzheimer's disease, retrieved in edited form from www.alzheimers.org:
  A woman in her late 60s was referred for a neurological workup due to concern about dementia. Her family indicated that there has been gradual memory decline for the past four years. Now, the patient quickly forgets conversations, she misplaces items which results in her thinking that other people must have moved or taken the items, she occasionally forgets to go to doctor appointments, and she has gotten lost while driving her car in a familiar location. The patient's family also reported that the patient's memory for long-term information seems a bit fuzzy. For example, it was stated that the patient remembers vacations from the past, but when talking about them, she seems to mix up details from various vacations. The patient is not particularly concerned about her difficulties and she is not all that interested in treating her memory decline. Her family, however, is quite concerned.
- A 3-min video shows a case of a woman with early-onset Alzheimer's disease. Additional details are presented on the same page below the video.

- Here is a case example of late-stage Alzheimer's disease, retrieved in edited form from www.alzheimers.org:
  A male in his early 80s had previously been diagnosed with Alzheimer's dementia, and at the time of this evaluation, he was living at home with assistance from his family and paid caregivers. He is now unable to learn almost any new information, and long-term memories are also weak (sometimes forgetting who his wife and children are). He is sometimes hard to understand due to slurring of words, and he appears to see people who are not in the room. He needs help bathing, dressing, cutting his food, and using the toilet. Due to falls, he is usually transported to medical appointments in a wheelchair. During the evaluation, he was unable to state his age, the current month, the current year, or the city where he was located. He was read a list of 3 words but could not remember any of them after just 1 minute. His family noted that they are struggling to provide care to him, and they asked whether it would be appropriate to consider moving him to a residence with a memory care unit.
- A 3-min video shows the case of a woman with relatively early-onset Alzheimer's disease who is participating in a trial of a nutritional program for slowing the progress of the disorder. [Note: You might want to ask your students to think critically about the conclusions presented in the video, and what additional information they would want to see before accepting those conclusions.]
- Examples of famous people thought to have (or have had) Alzheimer's or related diseases include: Robin Williams, Gene Wilder, Pat Summit, Sandra Day O'Connor, Rosa Parks, Etta James, Glen Campbell, Norman Rockwell, Ronald Reagan, Perry Como, Charles Bronson, Charlton Heston, Rita Hayworth, Sugar Ray Robinson, Floyd Patterson, Aaron Copeland, Burgess Meredith, Peter Falk, James Stewart, Casey Kasem, Otto Preminger, Iris Murdoch, Margaret Rutherford, Fred Trump (Donald's father), Gordie Howe, James Doohan, and Estelle Getty. (You may have to explain who some of these celebrities are, or were.)
- In contrast to the progressive dementia caused by AD, vascular dementia can occur suddenly or over a relatively short period when a stroke, or a series of "mini-strokes" cause a loss of blood supply to parts of the brain that are involved in memory and other psychological functions. It is the second most common type of dementia after AD. An example of the difference between vascular dementia and dementia caused by AD is that while vascular dementia patients show memory loss, including forgetting of recent events, their hippocampus may be well preserved. So vascular dementia patients may still be able to form new memories.

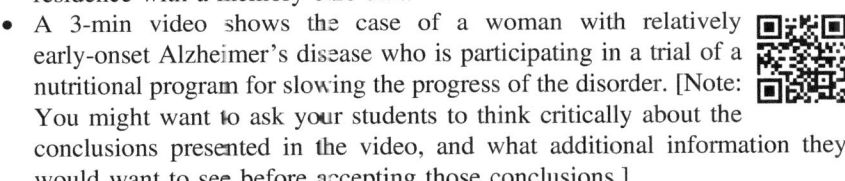

- Dementia can also occur as a symptom of Parkinson's disease, a neurogenerative disorder which at first damages or destroys neurons in motor areas of the brain, impairing speech, movement, and locomotion, but which later can create loss of memory and other cognitive functions. A 3-min video provides an emotional first-person account of what it is like to care for a person with Parkinson's dementia.
- A 4-min video presents a Parkinson's patient discussing her motor symptoms (without dementia), and how they have improved following deep brain stimulation surgery.
- Famous cases of Parkinson's disease include: Ozzy Osbourne, Alan Alda, Neil Diamond, Linda Ronstadt, Michael J. Fox, Muhammad Ali, Brian Grant, Janet Reno, Maurice White, Billy Connolly, Billy Graham, Charles Schulz, George H.W. Bush, Jessie Jackson, and Pope John Paul II.
- Some cases of dementia result from frontotemporal degeneration (FTD), a neurodegenerative disease that gradually kills nerve cells in the brain's temporal or frontal lobes, often on one side more than on the other.
- Examples of frontotemporal dementia symptoms include (a) the primary progressive aphasia mentioned earlier, (b) a variant in which there are dramatic changes in personality, behavior, judgment, empathy, and foresight, and (c) disturbances of motor function including amyotrophic lateral sclerosis (ALS), a motor neuron disorder also known as Lou Gehrig's disease.
- Famous cases of Lou Gehrig's disease (other than Lou Gehrig himself) include: Stephen Hawking, Dwight Clark, David Niven, Dennis Day, Jacob Javits, Huddie William Ledbetter ("Lead Belly"), Mao Zedong, and Sam Shepard.
- Dementia is also a symptom of the later stages of Huntington's disease, a rare neurodegenerative disorder which, like Parkinson's disease, first affects motor coordination, producing involuntary jerking or writhing movements (chorea), muscle rigidity or contractions (dystonia), slow or abnormal eye movements, impaired gait, posture and balance, and difficulty with speech or swallowing. Eventually, it leads to cognitive decline and dementia. Huntington's disease usually begins in middle age. It is caused by an inherited defect in a single gene and is incurable.
- The most famous case of Huntington's disease was that of folksinger Woody Guthrie.
- A 3-min video summarizes the anosognosia that sometimes accompanies various forms of dementia.

Assessment of Neuropsychological Disorders

1. Tests in the Halstead-Reitan Battery

Test name	Designed to measure
Categories test	Mental efficiency, ability to derive a rule from experience, and ability to form abstract concepts
Tactual performance test	Abilities such as motor speed, tactile and kinesthetic perception, and incidental memory
Seashore rhythm test	Nonverbal auditory perception, attention, and concentration
Speech-sounds perception test	Language processing, verbal auditory perception, attention, and concentration
Finger oscillation or finger tapping test	Motor speed
Trail-making test	Visual scanning, cognitive sequencing, and executive function
Dynamometer or strength of grip test	Right- versus left-side comparison of physical strength
Sensory-perceptual exam	Whether the patient can perceive sensory information separately and with standard variations in the location of the stimulation used
Tactile perception tests	Tactile perception
Aphasia screening test	Several aspects of language usage and recognition

- The first 27 slides of a slide show present a detailed description of each subtest (using slightly different names than those in the table above), along with photos of the equipment used.

2. Tests in the Luria-Nebraska Neuropsychological Battery consist of 269 test items covering the following 11 areas:

- Reading
- Writing
- Arithmetic
- Visual capacity
- Memory
- Expressive language (speaking)
- Receptive language (comprehension)
- Motor function
- Rhythm skills
- Tactile ability
- Intellectual (cognitive) abilities

   The results can be presented as scores on each of these areas, and in summary scores to indicate pathognomonic signs, as well as right hemisphere and left hemisphere functioning. The probability of brain damage is assessed by comparing an individual's score on each of the 11 areas listed above to those

typically seen in people of the patient's age and education level. For example, if test scores deviate significantly from these norms in five to seven areas, neurological impairment is seen as likely. Eight or more scores above the norm are seen as definite signs of neurological disorder.
- Slides 28-33 of a slide show describes the Luria-Nebraska test, though in less detail than for the Halstead-Reitan battery.

The Peripheral Nervous System

1. Examples of autonomic nervous system (ANS) functions and dysfunctions:

    - If your hands get cold and clammy when you are nervous, it is because the ANS has created perspiration and decreased the blood flow in your hands.
    - If you suddenly have to run to catch a bus, the ANS frees needed energy by stimulating the secretion of glucose-generating hormones and promoting blood flow to your muscles.
    - When you have eaten a meal, the ANS acts to increase your heart rate and constrict your peripheral blood vessels so as to maintain blood pressure and blood flow throughout the body, including the brain.
    - Disorders of the autonomic nervous system (autonomic neuropathy) occur when the nerves that control involuntary bodily functions are damaged. These disorders, a few of which are described below, can affect blood pressure, temperature control, digestion, bladder function, and sexual functioning.
    - People with orthostatic hypotension experience a sudden drop in blood pressure when they stand up, which leads to a decrease in blood supply to the brain and consequent feelings of dizziness, lightheadedness, or fainting. Orthostatic hypotension can cause complications, especially in older adults, such as fractures from falling as a result of fainting.
    - People with postprandial hypotension experience a sudden drop in blood pressure after a meal, resulting in dizziness, lightheadedness, or fainting for 15 to 90 min after eating. The condition results from the failure of the ANS to make enough of the adjustments described above in order to compensate when normal digestive processes cause blood to be diverted to the stomach and small intestine, leading to a significant drop in blood pressure. Postprandial hypotension is common in adults over the age of 60.
    - In a rare degenerative disorder called pure autonomic failure, patients experience not only orthostatic hypotension, but erectile dysfunction in men, a decreased ability to sweat, elevated blood pressure when lying down, and changes in gastrointestinal and urinary habits. It is seen mainly in middle-aged to older adults, and is slightly more common in men than women.

- In an autonomic disorder called afferent baroreflex failure, nerves that normally relay information to the brain about blood pressure fail to do so consistently, causing alternating periods of blood pressure that is either too high or too low. People with this condition experience dizziness and fainting as well as headaches, sweating, and skin flushing. The causes include hereditary defects in blood pressure-sensing nerves in the neck, damage to those nerves following surgery or radiation therapy, and stroke-related damage to areas of the brain where blood pressure information is normally received.
- Familial dysautonomia is a rare inherited condition that affects the development of both the autonomic and somatic nervous systems. Patients with this disorder not only have the unstable blood pressure associated with afferent baroreflex failure, but also experience reduced sensitivity to pain and temperature and an absence of tears when crying. Other common symptoms include difficulty swallowing, severe vomiting or gastroesophageal reflux, poor muscle tone, excessive sweating, overproduction of saliva and mucus, and blotchy reddening of the skin when excited or eating. They may also develop chronic breathing problems due to reflux of stomach acid or food and have vision problems due to progressive damage to the optic nerves. When under stress, these people with familial dysautonomia may experience dramatic high blood pressure and heart rate accompanied by vomiting or retching, a condition known as an autonomic crisis. [Source: Retrieved here]
- An overview of numerous other autonomic nervous system dysfunctions is available.

2. Examples of somatic nervous system functions and dysfunctions.

- Here is an example of normal somatic nervous system (SNS) functioning: As you lie on the beach you can feel the heat of the sun, enjoy the coolness of the can of soda in your hand, and smell the salty air, all because your SNS is taking this sensory information and sending it to the central nervous system for perceptual processing. The central nervous system evaluates the warmth and the smells that arrive, and also sends messages through motor neurons to muscles that allow you to turn over, sit up, or put on more sunscreen.
- Disorders of the somatic nervous system (somatic neuropathy) occur when trauma or disease affect the functioning of the nerve roots, ganglia, or sensory and motor nerves. These disorders, a few of which are listed below, can have a variety of negative consequences.
- Guillain–Barre syndrome is an inflammatory autoimmune condition caused when, as with multiple sclerosis in the central nervous system, the body attacks the myelin coating of its own peripheral nerves. The syndrome often occurs as a result of viral or bacterial infection, exposure to toxins, lymphoma, or the side effects of surgery or immunization.

- Myasthenia gravis is a disease of the places at which motor nerves transmit their impulses to muscles (the neuromuscular junction). It, too, is an autoimmune disease in which the body's immune system cells attack its own skeletal muscles.
- Trigeminal neuralgia, like other neuralgias, is a disorder of a cranial nerve, in this case, the fifth (trigeminal) nerve. Because this nerve is linked to the facial area, trigeminal neuralgia causes periods of intense, stabbing, electric shock-like pain in the lips, eyes, nose, scalp, forehead, upper jaw, and lower jaw. It is the most common of all neuralgias.
- In the case of the "disembodied lady," Oliver Sacks described "Christina," a healthy young woman who had lost the ability to feel the position of her own body. This case provides an example not only of how the somatic nervous system tells us about the location and movement of our body parts (proprioception and kinesthesia), but also plays an important role in our sense of self. Shortly after Christina checked into a hospital for minor surgery, she began to have difficulty holding onto objects, and then began to have trouble moving. When she got up from bed she flopped onto the floor like a rag doll. Christina seemed to have "lost" her body. She felt disembodied, like a ghost. Eventually, she could not walk or use her hands and arms. Then, on one occasion, she became annoyed because she thought that a visitor in her room was tapping her fingers on a tabletop, but it was actually Christina's own fingers that were doing the tapping. Like patients with the alien hand syndrome described earlier her body was acting on its own, doing things she did not know about. Sacks' neurological examinations and tests revealed that Christina had lost all sensory feedback about her joints and muscle tone and the position of her limbs. She had suffered a breakdown, or degeneration, of the sensory neurons that normally bring proprioceptive and kinesthetic information to her brain. In his case description, Sacks pointed out that our sense of our bodies is based partly on seeing the location of its various parts, but also partly on the feedback that the brain gets from the position of muscles and joints. Christina eventually regained some ability to move about. For example, if she looked intently at her arms and legs, she could coordinate their movement somewhat. She was able to leave the hospital and resume many normal activities, but Christina never recovered her sense of self. She still feels like a stranger in her own body. Sacks speculated that her condition might have been caused by an excess of vitamin B6, also known as pyridoxine, which is known to be capable of damaging sensory neurons.
[Source: Sacks, O. (1985). *The man who mistook his wife for a hat.* New York: Summit Books.]

Endocrine System Functions and Dysfunctions

1. The endocrine system is a collection of glands that regulates functions such as metabolism, growth and development, tissue function, sexual function, reproduction, sleep, and mood by releasing hormones into the blood where they affect target organs and tissue including, for example, the thyroid, the testes and ovaries, the pancreas, gallbladder, adrenals, mammary glands, uterus, stomach, kidneys, liver, intestines, and bones.

   - In the realm of reproduction, for example, when the sex hormone estrogen is secreted by a woman's ovaries, it activates her reproductive system. It causes the uterus to grow in preparation for nurturing an embryo; it enlarges the breasts to prepare them for nursing; it stimulates the brain to enhance interest in sexual activity; and it stimulates the pituitary gland to release another hormone that causes a mature egg to be released by the ovary for fertilization. Male sex organs, called the testes, secrete androgens, which are sex hormones such as testosterone. Androgens stimulate the maturation of sperm, increase a male's motivation for sexual activity, and increase his aggressiveness.
   - Another example can be seen in responses to stress. When the brain interprets a situation as threatening, the pituitary releases adrenocorticotropic hormone, which causes the adrenal glands to release the hormone cortisol into the bloodstream. These hormones, in turn, act on cells throughout the body, including the brain. One effect of cortisol is to activate the emotion-related limbic system, making it more likely that you will remember stressful or traumatic events. The combined effects of the adrenal hormones and the activation of the sympathetic system result in a set of responses called the fight-flight response, which prepares us for action in response to danger or other stressors. With these hormones at high levels, the heart beats faster, the liver releases glucose into the bloodstream, fuels are mobilized from fat stores, and we enter a state of high arousal. (See the chapter on health, stress, and coping for examples of other fight or flight responses.)

2. Examples of endocrine system disorders:

   - The most common endocrine system disorder is diabetes, a condition in which the body does not properly process sugar (glucose) because the pancreas fails to produce the insulin (or in Type 2 diabetes, not enough of the insulin) needed to do so. The result is excess sugar in the blood, which, in turn, can lead to increased thirst, frequent urination, extreme hunger, weight loss, fatigue, irritability, blurred vision, slow-healing sores, frequent infections of the gums, skin, and vagina. Long-term complications of diabetes include serious health problems such as cardiovascular disease, as well as damage to nerves, kidneys, eyes, ears, and feet. Diabetes is also a risk factor for Alzheimer's disease and depression.

- In hypothyroidism, the thyroid gland does not produce enough thyroid hormone to meet the body's needs, which can cause many of the body's functions to slow or shut down completely. Early-stage symptoms, such as fatigue or sensitivity to cold, are usually mild but over time can become more noticeable problems such as constipation, dry skin, weight gain, facial puffiness, hoarseness, muscle weakness, elevated cholesterol, tender, stiff, or aching muscles, pain, stiffness or swelling in the joints, heavier than normal or irregular menstrual periods, thinning hair, slowed heart rate, depression, impaired memory, and enlargement of the thyroid gland (goiter).

- Graves' disease is an immune system disorder that results in the overproduction of thyroid hormones (hyperthyroidism). Symptoms include anxiety and irritability, fine tremor of the hands or fingers, heat sensitivity, an increase in perspiration or warm, moist skin, weight loss (even though food intake remains normal), enlargement of the thyroid gland (goiter), changes in menstrual cycles, erectile dysfunction or reduced libido, frequent bowel movements, bulging eyes (Graves' ophthalmopathy), fatigue, thick, red skin usually on the shins or tops of the feet (Graves' dermopathy), rapid or irregular heartbeat (palpitations), and sleep disturbance.

- Images of patients with Graves' ophthalmopathy and Graves' dermopathy can be found here and here.

- Reduced levels of estrogen or testosterone secretion from the ovaries or testes, which tends to occur in late adulthood, can lead to osteoporosis, a condition in which bones become so weak and brittle that a fall or even mild stresses can cause a fracture—most often in the hip, wrist or back. Symptoms of the disorder appear gradually as back pain caused by a fractured or collapsed vertebra, loss of height, and a stooped posture.

- Images that illustrate the postural consequences of osteoporosis can be found here.

- Addison's disease, also called adrenal insufficiency, is a relatively rare disorder caused by the adrenal glands' insufficient production of the hormones cortisol and, often, aldosterone. The symptoms of this condition can appear gradually in the form of extreme fatigue, decreased appetite and weight loss, darkening of the skin, low blood pressure and fainting, salt craving, low blood sugar (hypoglycemia), nausea, diarrhea or vomiting, pain in the abdomen, muscles or joints, irritability, depression, loss of body hair, or (in women) sexual dysfunction. In some cases, though, symptoms of Addison's disease can appear suddenly due to acute adrenal failure (called an Addisonian crisis) that can be life-threatening. In such cases, the person may

experience severe weakness, confusion, pain in the lower back or legs, severe abdominal pain, vomiting and diarrhea, and reduced consciousness or delirium.
- In contrast to Addison's disease, overactivity in the adrenal glands can cause Cushing's syndrome, in which the glands produce too much cortisol (the disorder may also appear in patients who are taking too much corticosteroid medication). The symptoms of this disease include the appearance of a fatty hump between the shoulder blades, a rounding of the face, pink or purple stretch marks on the skin, increased susceptibility to bruising, slowed healing of infections, cuts and insect bites, high blood pressure, bone loss and, on occasion, type 2 diabetes.
- Gigantism is a serious condition that is nearly always caused by an adenoma, a tumor of the pituitary gland. Gigantism occurs in patients who had excessive growth hormone in childhood. The pituitary tumor cells secrete too much growth hormone, leading to many changes in the body, including an abnormally large amount of growth.
- Images of people with gigantism can be found here.

Sensation and Perception

It is not always immediately obvious to students how sensation and perception are relevant to psychology as they understand it, but we have found that providing examples of the failures of perception, such as those seen in visual illusions, can generate intense interest. We also find that students become engaged by a discussion of naïve realism and demonstrations that perception is a representation and not a direct copy of the external world. Providing examples of neurological disorders of sensation or perception can also help students appreciate the relevance of these basic processes and the differences between them (see also the chapter on the biological aspects of psychology).

Discussion of myths related to perception, such as the alleged influence of subliminal messaging in advertising, the non-existent "tongue map", and the supposed operation of ESP (extrasensory perception) provides another avenue for stoking students' interest.

Sensory Systems

Artistic Renditions of the Senses

1. Here are two examples of how artists have depicted the five senses. The first comes from the Lady and the Unicorn tapestries, housed in the Museum of the Middle Ages (Cluny) in Paris, France. High resolution images of all of the tapestries are available here at the museum website and on wikimedia here. As an example, below is an image of the tapestry that depicts "sight":

Source.
- An analysis of the meaning of the Lady and the Unicorn tapestries can be found here.
2. Another example of an artistic representation of the senses can be found in the paintings of Jan Bruegel the Elder entitled *Allegory of the Senses* that are part of the collection of the Prado Museum in Madrid, Spain. Images of these paintings can be found on the museum's website here and on Wikipedia here. As an example, here is an image of the painting that depicts "sight".

Source.

3. An artist's rendition of what infants can see in the first 6 months is shown in images in Fig. 22 of this review article on infant vision. [Reference: Teller, D.Y. (1997). First glances: The vision of infants. The Friedenwald lecture. *Investigative Ophthalmology and Visual Science*, *38*(11), 2183–2203.]

Human and Non-Human Visual Systems

1. Eagles have visual acuity at least 4 times that of humans. A nice graphic and description of what it would be like to experience eagle vision can be found here.
2. The compound eyes of insects provide an interesting contrast to the human eye and are described in an article and 13-min video that can be found here. Towards the end of the video is a rendition of what the world might look like to an insect.
3. A description of research examining whether dogs experience visual illusions in the same way that humans do can be seen here.
4. A recent "citizen-science" project revealed that cats, who like sitting in boxes, will sit in ones defined only by an illusory contour. An NPR story about this research can be found here.
[Reference: Smith, G. E., Chouinard, P. A., & Byosiere, S. E. (2021). If I fits I sits: A citizen science investigation into illusory contour susceptibility in domestic cats (Felis silvestris catus). *Applied Animal Behaviour Science*, *240*, 105,338.]
5. An NPR interview with Ivan Schwab in which he discusses the evolution of the eyes of many different animals can be found here.

Human and Non-Human Auditory Systems

1. Dogs can hear frequencies higher than those audible to humans (see the absolute threshold demonstration later in this chapter).
2. An example of elephants' use of sounds to recognize other elephants is discussed in a very brief interview here.

3. Examples of the sounds bats emit during echolocation can be heard here and a beautiful 2-min Smithsonian video of a bat flying and echolocating in slow motion can be seen here.

Human and Non-Human Olfactory Systems

1. The African elephant (among the most sensitive) has about five times as many olfactory receptor genes as humans as described here. [Reference: Niimura, Y. (2014). Olfactory receptor genes: Evolution. *eLS*. Available here: https://yosniimura.net/papers/Niimura_ELS_2014.pdf]
2. Dogs have more olfactory receptors than humans. This and other explanations for their better olfactory sensitivity are discussed here.

3. Dogs' sense of smell and why they are better than artificial machine olfaction, is described in this 11-min video. An update to this work can be found here.

4. The fact that moths also have high olfactory sensitivity, as has been demonstrated by using their antennae to create the "smellicopter", is described here.

5. The star-nosed mole has an unusual nose with unique properties, including the ability to smell under water. It is described near the end of this 3:13-min video and in this video.

6. Although commonly regarded as a less important sense, human olfaction has been underestimated. Humans can detect some odors better than other animals can, have relatively large olfactory bulbs (which seems to be important in olfactory ability) and the number of olfactory neurons does not vary as much across species as is the case with other physical features. Figures associated with these findings can be found in this article:
McGann, J. P. (2017). Poor human olfaction is a 19th-century myth. *Science*, *356*(6338), available here.

Human and Non-Human Gustatory (Taste) Systems

1. Examples of the differences in numbers of taste buds and in taste experience in across species are discussed here.

2. An example of high taste sensitivity is seen in channel catfish, which have taste buds all over their bodies. Photos of a catfish and a short description can be found here and a video can be seen here.

3. An example of the complexity of the sense of taste can be seen in the fact that it is quite common for people to believe that they have lost their "taste" sense when in fact they have actually lost smell function. Loss of smell results in reduced or lost "flavor" perception. It is relatively more difficult to damage the taste system.
[Source: Hawkes, C., & Doty, R. L. (2009). *The neurology of olfaction*. Cambridge University Press.]

4. An example of the interdependence of smell and taste is revealed in a 5:12-min segment on NPR. This clip explores both the concept of supertasters and the reason some people find cilantro to be "soapy" (it is due to olfactory receptor genes, not taste).

5. Another example of the interdependence of smell and taste may also be seen in the perceptual consequences of Covid-19. Although there is some evidence for taste loss due to Covid-19 infection, the scientific consensus appears to be that the loss is primarily an olfactory one. Self-reported taste loss is likely due to olfactory loss (see the Hawkes & Doty, 2009 reference listed above).

6. A short video of Rachel Ray and her audience testing to see if they are supertasters can be seen here.

7. This clip can also be found (at the bottom of) a website devoted to supertasters, found here.

   - A Scientific American Frontiers video on supertasters can be found here.

Human and Non-Human Tactile (Touch) Systems

1. The star-nosed mole's nose (see the olfaction section) is made up of 22 fleshy tentacles that have 100,000 nerve fibers (the human hand has about a fifth of that number).
2. There is evidence that tickling is pleasurable for rats. This is shown behaviorally here.

3. The neural underpinning of tickling (in a rat model) is explored here.

4. Touch Sensitivity

    - Examples of the power of touch include the ability to recognize many objects by touch alone (e.g., your coffee mug, a light switch, your cell phone) and is used for activities like buttoning your shirt and brushing your teeth. Though these are somewhat visually-guided actions, you can do them perfectly well with touch alone. For example, we know a man who carries a cloth bag full of flash drives, iPhone cables, ear buds, paper clips, international adapter plugs, and the like in his briefcase. He has no trouble finding the object he wants simply by reaching into the bag and "feeling around."
    - Likewise, newborn babies can recognize objects visually (e.g., pacifiers of various shapes) that they have only had experience with in their mouth. [Source: Kaye, K. L., & Bower, T. G. (1994). Learning and intermodal transfer of information in newborns. *Psychological Science, 5*(5), 286–288. https://doi.org/10.1111/j.1467-9280.1994.tb00627.x]
    - A somatosensory equivalent of "blindsight" known as "numbsense" is described in an article that can be found here.

    - Braille is an example of another important function that the touch system can serve. The case of Helen Keller provides a famous example of the value of the touch system. A short commemorative story and video about her can be found here.

5. Cross-modal sensory effects

    - An example of how we believe what we see rather than what we feel can be seen in the rubber hand illusion described in this 3:12-min video found here and in this 4:33-min video that describes some possible ways in which the illusion can be used in creating virtual reality and in the treatment of phantom limb pain.

- Another example of how vision overwhelms audition is seen in the McGurk effect, which can be experienced here and here.

- An example of the dominance of visual information over information from the other senses can be experienced in this 5-s video of a ball being thrown at the camera. We flinch even though there is no real threat of being hit!
  [Note: You might want to use this example in relation to the unconditioned responses described in the chapter on learning.]

6. Pain

- The experience of pain and our reactions to it provide examples of how touch warns us of danger.
- An example of the complexity of pain is seen in cases of phantom limb and phantom limb pain, described in this 9-min video that can be found here and described here.

7. Pain Control

- Examples related to gate-control theory include interfering with the signals that pain fibers normally send to the brain by rubbing the area around an injury, putting ice on the painful site, and using electrical stimulation or creams that produce temperature sensations. This may also help explain why scratching relieves itching.
- Secretion of endorphins can reduce the perception of pain that occurs during contact sports, childbirth and military combat by sending signals down the spinal cord to block incoming pain signals.
- Here is an example of research that applied gate control theory to chronic pain conditions such as neuropathy that are caused by damage or inflammation in the peripheral nervous system that sensitizes incoming pain pathways. Neuropathy patients in this study reported reductions in their pain after receiving "whole body vibration therapy," a technique in which they stand on a rapidly vibrating platform for three-minute sessions three times a week for a month. The researchers interpreted the results to suggest that the spinal pain gate was overwhelmed by the harmless non-painful vibration sensations, making it impossible for pain signals to enter.
  [Reference: Kessler, N. J., & Hong, J. (2013). Whole body vibration therapy for painful diabetic peripheral neuropathy: A pilot study. *Journal of Body Work and Movement Therapies, 17*(4), 518–522.]

- An example of using self-hypnosis to reduce pain during surgery is presented in the case of Bernadine Coady, which appears in the consciousness chapter.
- Other pain control examples include this one suggesting that swearing can increase pain tolerance.
  [Reference: Stephens, R., Atkins, J., & Kingston, A. (2009). Swearing as a response to pain. *Neuroreport, 20*(12), 1056–1060.]

- An example of using virtual reality to control pain is described here.

  As summarized by the developers, "SnowWorld shifts the patient's concentration away from their pain to an icy, virtual environment bathed in cool blues and whites, where their only task is to throw snowballs at an endlessly advancing group of penguins. It might seem silly, but the results speak for themselves: burn patients experienced 35 to 50 percent less pain when immersed in VR, about the same reduction as a moderate dose of opioid painkillers."

- Capsaicin has been used to ease pain, as described at the end of a Scientific American Frontiers video on supertasters, which can be found here.

Proprioceptive Systems

1. Kinesthesia

    - You can provide students with an example of a kinesthetic illusion by asking them to cross their pointer and middle fingers and stroke the inner pointer with a finger of the other hand. When someone else does the stroking, the students will confuse which finger is being touched. Other examples of this so-called Aristotle Illusion are described here.

2. Equilibrium/Vestibular system

    - Some amazing examples of humans' ability to maintain balance on cables stretched high above canyons can be seen here.

    - Even more incredible balancing in ballet dancing can be seen here. (Note: the narration is in Chinese).

    - Seasickness is an example of a problem that can arise due to overstimulation of the vestibular system. See a description and treatment here.

Disorders of Sensory Systems

1. You can find an example of technology that is being developed to cure blindness here.
2. An alternative to the standard eye chart that tests reading full sentences rather than single letters is described here. This test is used to determine the smallest print size required for reading in normal and "low" vision.
   [Source: Calabrèse, A., Owsley, C., McGwin, G. & Legge, G.E. (2016). Development of a reading accessibility index using the MNREAD acuity chart. *JAMA Ophthalmology, 134*(4), 398–405. http://archopht.jamanetwork.com/article.aspx?articleid=2487490]
3. Loss of the sense of smell is one of the earliest signs of neurodegenerative diseases such as Alzheimer's and Parkinson's.
   [Source: Doty, R. L. (2017). Olfactory dysfunction in neurodegenerative diseases: Is there a common pathological substrate? *The Lancet Neurology, 16*(6), 478–488.]
4. Smell loss has been found to be a significant marker of 5-year mortality, as described in this news story.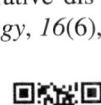
   [Reference: Adams. D. R., Kern, D. W., Wroblewski, K. E., McClintock, M. K., Dale, W., & Pinto, J. M. (2018). Olfactory dysfunction predicts subsequent dementia in older US adults. *Journal of the American Geriatrics Society, 56*(1), 140–144.]
5. Smell loss has been found to be a common early symptom of Covid-19. An excellent summary of this research can be found here.
6. Parosmia (particularly in the context of smell dysfunction as a consequence of Covid-19) is described at this website, where you will find a 4:17-min video about a person who has parosmia and another full webinar on the topic.
7. A case of phantosmia in which a woman had an odor "stuck" in her head is described here.
8. Specific anosmias (inability to smell a particular aroma) can have a genetic basis. For example, people who lack one particular olfactory receptor gene cannot smell the flowery component of cilantro (see the section above on interdependence of smell and taste).
9. For an example of a disorder in the kinesthetic system, see the case of "the disembodied woman" in the chapter on biological aspects of psychology.
10. Many other examples of sensory disorders can be found in the chapter on biological aspects of psychology, including *palinacousis*, an auditory perseveration syndrome in which sounds seem to continue even after they have objectively ceased.

Psychophysical Measurements

Detection/Absolute Thresholds

1. Here are examples of approximate human detection thresholds under more or less ideal circumstances where there are few interfering stimuli. Under less than ideal, but more typical, circumstances, detection thresholds are higher.

Sensory system	Detection threshold
Vision	A candle flame at 30 miles on a dark, clear night
Hearing	Tick of a watch under quiet conditions at 20 feet
Taste	1 teaspoon of sugar in 2 gallons of water
Smell	1 drop of perfume diffused into the entire volume of a 3-room apartment
Touch	The wing of a bee falling on your cheek from a distance of 1 cm

[Source: Galanter, E. (1962). Contemporary Psychophysics. In R. Brown, E. Galanter, E. H. Hess, & G. Mandler (Eds.), *New directions in psychology*. New York, NY: Holt, Rinehart & Winston.]

2. Here are some examples of psychophysical measurement of detection thresholds for vision:
   - Gabor patches—a sinusoidal grating in a gaussian vignette (pictured here)

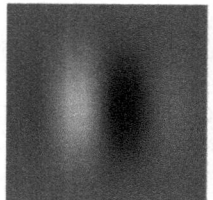 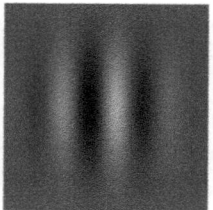 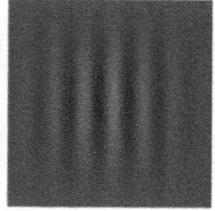 

   are often employed and presented on a computer screen. In this case, the detection threshold is defined as the amount of contrast (difference between light and dark bars in the Gabor patch) required for a person to just detect the presence of the stimulus.
   - There is a 2-min video at that describes how to test grating acuity in children.
   - Contrast sensitivity (inverse of threshold) can be measured with a Pelli Robson contrast sensitivity chart like this one:

Psychophysical Measurements

[Reference: Pelli, D. G., Robson, J. G., & Wilkins, A. J. (1988). The design of a new letter chart for measuring contrast sensitivity. *Clinical Vision Sciences*, 2(3), 137–199.]

- An example of a contrast sensitivity function (differential thresholds for different spatial frequencies) can be experienced here. You could involve students in a classroom activity that allows them to determine their own contrast sensitivity, using a chart such as this, found here.

- An example of using psychophysical methods to measure *changes* in perception (and cognition), including contrast sensitivity, task switching and motion perception, after playing action video games can be found here.

3. A practical example of a detection threshold in vision would be the size of the smallest tumor that a radiologist can detect. A related detection threshold would be the minimum *contrast* between the tumor and surrounding tissue needed for detection.
4. A more common example of an absolute threshold for vision would be the ability to detect a star in the night sky.
5. The ability to see more stars as dark adaptation occurs is an example of a factor that affects visual thresholds. Examples of other factors that affect visual thresholds (or the contrast sensitivity function) include light level, participant's age, attention, species, and certain visual disorders (e.g., glaucoma, cataracts, amblyopia and strabismus).
6. Psychophysical measurements using *olfaction* are enjoyable for students and relatively easy to demonstrate in the classroom. While it doesn't lead to a threshold, per se, odor discrimination is indeed a psychophysical/ behavioral method. An example of a way for students to test their ability to identify odors can be found here.

7. Here is a simple example of an olfactory detection threshold test (using the *method of limits*) that uses a swab of isopropyl alcohol (70% vol) and a ruler. The packet with the alcohol swab is torn open and, using the ruler, placed about 30 cm below the participant's nose. Each time the participant exhales, the swab is placed 1 cm closer to the nose. This is continued until the participant can detect the odor.
    [Reference: Davidson, T.M., & Murphy C. (1997). Rapid clinical evaluation of anosmia: The alcohol sniff test. *Arch Otolaryngol Head Neck Surg, 123*, 591–594.]
8. Determination of a two-point touch threshold can be particularly instructive if two areas of skin that have different sensitivity are measured (e.g., two sides of the forearm). As a class activity or an out-of-class assignment, you can ask students to take 2 toothpicks and choose two places on the body to test. They should measure how far apart the toothpicks must be at each skin location for them to tell that there are two points of contact.
    Reference: Mancini, F., Bauleo, A., Cole, J., Lui, F., Porro, C. A., Haggard, P., & Iannetti, G. D. (2014). Whole-body mapping of spatial acuity for pain and touch. *Annals of Neurology, 75*(6), 917–924.
9. Examples of two-point discrimination thresholds for pain and touch across the whole body are illustrated in figures in this paper.
    [Reference: Mancini, F., Bauleo, A., Cole, J., Lui, F., Porro, C. A., Haggard, P., & Iannetti, G. D. (2014). Whole-body mapping of spatial acuity for pain and touch. *Annals of Neurology, 75*(6), 917–924.]
10. An example of finding a detection threshold for *audition* would be to ask how loud a radio has to be for one to detect that it is on. Note, of course, that the detection threshold would change depending on circumstances. For example, one would have to turn up the volume in order to hear it when you have the air conditioner running or the windows open. Thus, the detection threshold is higher (and sensitivity is lower) under those conditions. A meme that the students might relate to can be found here.
11. The volume control on a radio can be used as another example of the *method of limits,* or an example of *hysteresis* by showing that the threshold is lower when you use *descending limits* compared to *ascending limits*. Further, you could use this as an example of a *top-down* effect on perception (see other examples below and in the chapter on thinking and cognitive abilities). If you start with a sound above threshold, listeners have expectations about what they should be hearing, which makes it easier to detect the stimulus. Finally, you can point out that if the person who is trying to hear the radio is the one adjusting the volume, that is like a *method of adjustment.*

Psychophysical Measurements 93

12. Absolute thresholds for different frequencies in hearing can be experienced here and here and here.

13. Here is an example of the effect of age on auditory detection thresholds: Hearing loss, particularly at high frequencies, increases with age, so if you are a more "senior" instructor, your students will be amused to discover that they can hear frequencies you cannot. This is the basis of the "mosquito ringtone" that most students, but not older teachers, can hear. Students may already be familiar with this phenomenon, but a short video demonstration can be found here.

Difference Thresholds/Just Noticeable Difference (JND)

1. How large does the change in a tumor's size have to be before it is noticed on repeated mammography screenings?
2. You taste your morning coffee and it is not as sweet as you would like it to be. How much more sugar do you need to add to notice a difference in sweetness?
3. You taste some mashed potatoes or scrambled eggs and decide you want them to be saltier. How much more salt do you need to add in order to notice a difference in saltiness?
4. How much sugar, salt, caffeine, citric acid or umami/monosodium glutamate (MSG) needs to be added to a glass of water until each taste (sweet, salty, bitter, sour or savory, respectively) can just barely be detected.
5. Are two lines the same vertical orientation?
   They are not—they differ by 1°). How different would their vertical orientation need to be for you to tell that they are different?
6. These two lines differ in thickness, but you probably cannot tell. Therefore the difference is *below* your difference threshold.
7. The thickness of these two lines differs enough that you can see the discrepancy; thus the difference is *above* your difference threshold.
8. You might find that changing the volume on your TV's remote control by one unit is not enough to notice a difference in sound intensity but changing it by 2 units is noticeable.

9. When you have your eyes examined and the optometrist asks you to choose which of two lenses creates a "clearer" image, you are helping the optometrist to determine a difference threshold.
10. Musicians have to discriminate between notes when they tune their instruments.
11. Can you tell the difference between the colors of two different skeins of yarn that come from different dye lots? The importance of dye lot numbers is demonstrated in two silent videos showing perceptible and imperceptible differences in yarns. You can find them here.
12. A change in temperature over the course of a day may be perceptible (thus, it is at least a just noticeable difference), but how different do two temperatures have to be for you to detect a difference? Note: The average change in world climate involves differences that are well below what is a JND for humans.
13. Examples of the application of Weber's Law:

    - A $1 off sale on an item that costs $1.99 will be much more noticeable than a $1 off sale on an item that costs $199. This illustrates the basic feature of Weber's law, namely that the size of a noticeable difference will be a constant fraction of the original amount.
    - The cost difference between $10 and $11 will be more noticeable than the difference between $100 and $101.
    - A difference in length between a 2-inch line and a 2 ½ inch line will be more noticeable than the difference between a 12-inch line and a 12 ½ inch line.
    - The difference in brightness between two dim lights will be more noticeable than the same difference in brightness between two bright lights.
    - The difference in loudness between two soft sounds will be more noticeable than the same difference in loudness between two loud sounds.
    - The amount of hair cut from the head of someone with short hair will be more noticeable than an equivalent amount of hair cut from the head of someone with long hair.
    - A 20-pound weight loss will be more noticeable on a 120-pound person than on a 220-pound person.
    - An example using random dot patterns shows that there is a noticeable difference between 10 and 20 dots but not between 110 and 120 dots. You can find an image for this example on this Wikipedia page.
    - If you are carrying a book and someone asks you to carry another book, you would notice the change in weight. But if you were carrying 10 books and you were asked to carry one more, you might not notice the difference.
    - What is the *just noticeable difference* you can detect in the weight of pennies on the palm of your hand? If there are 3 to start with, how many would have to be added to detect that there are more? You can ask students to try this, first starting with 3 pennies and later starting with, say, 20. They will see that more pennies will have to be added to 20 than to 3 in order to detect a difference. This exercise reflects both difference thresholds and Weber's Law.

Psychophysical Measurements

14. Being able to tell that two faces differ is another example of a difference threshold. You would more likely be able to distinguish between faces of your own race (see the other race effect in the chapter on memory).
15. Can you tell the difference between genuine Nike sneakers and counterfeit "knock offs"? If the difference is perceptible, then you have established a difference that is above threshold for that task. Here is a picture that can help distinguish between the sneakers. The many young men who devote considerable time to buying and selling sneakers are examples of people who are very sensitive to subtle differences between real and fake Nikes. Related examples include jewelers who can detect fake diamonds, and art experts who can detect fake paintings.

Signal Detection Theory (SDT)

1. Here is an example of using signal detection theory to analyze weather forecasting via radar images. Even with the latest Doppler radar systems, weather forecasters sometimes fail to warn of a tornado (a "miss") that local residents can clearly see. The forecasters' task is not easy, because their radar systems are so sensitive that they don't just detect a tornado's spinning funnel but also harmless patterns created by swirling dust and swarming insects (a "false alarm"). So a tornado's telltale radar "signature" will always appear against a potentially confusing background of visual "noise." Whether or not that signature will be picked out and reported depends both on the forecaster's sensitivity to the signal and on the response criterion being used. In establishing the criterion for sounding a warning, the forecaster must consider the consequences. If the response criterion is too low (also referred to as too "liberal"), and warnings are issued at the slightest hint of a tornado, there would surely be false alarms that would unnecessarily disrupt people's lives, activate costly emergency plans, and even lead people to ignore future warnings. But setting the criterion too high (also referred to as being too "conservative"), so that warnings occur only when the forecaster is certain of a tornado, could allow a dangerous storm to go unreported. Such a miss could cost many lives if it left a populated area with no warning of danger. In other words, there is a tradeoff. To minimize false alarms, the forecaster could set a very high response criterion, but doing so would also make misses more likely.

The figure below provides examples of how expectations or assumptions can change the response criterion and how those changes might affect the accuracy of a forecaster's decisions.

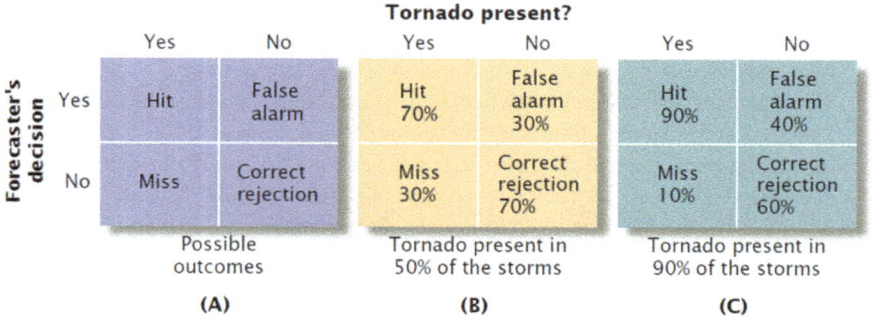

[Source: Bernstein, D. A., Penner, L.A., Clarke-Stewart, A., & Roy, E. J. (2012). *Psychology* (9th ed.) Belmont, California: Wadsworth Cengage Learning.]

If a forecaster knows it's a time of year when tornadoes occur in only about 50 percent of the storm systems seen on radar, a rather high response criterion would be appropriate. That is, it will take relatively strong evidence to trigger a tornado warning. The hypothetical data in section B of the figure above show that under these conditions, the forecaster correctly detected 70% of actual tornadoes but missed 30 percent of them. Also, 30% of the tornado reports were false alarms. Now suppose the forecaster learns that a different kind of storm system is on the way and that about 90 percent of such systems spawn tornadoes. This information is likely to increase the forecaster's expectation that a tornado signature will appear, thus lowering the response criterion. The forecaster will now require less evidence of a tornado before reporting one. Under these conditions, as shown in section C of the figure, the hit rate might rise from 70% to, say, 90%, but the false-alarm rate might also increase from 30 to 40%. A forecaster's hit rate and false-alarm rate will also be affected by the forecaster's sensitivity to tornado signals. Those with greater sensitivity to these signals will have high hit rates and low false-alarm rates. Forecasters with less sensitivity are still likely to have high hit rates, but their false-alarm rates will be higher, too.

2. An example of stimuli that nicely demonstrate the detection of a "signal" in the context of visual "noise" can be found in the Snowy Pictures Task, which includes random dot patterns with and without a "signal" in them. The pictures can be found in the appendix (p. 13 and 14) of the document found here.
[Reference: Whitson, J. A., & Galinsky, A. D. (2008). Lacking control increases illusory pattern perception. *Science, 322*(5898), 115–117.]

3. Imagine that you have a gas stove in your house. An important function of olfaction is to detect danger, such as a gas leak. In the context of SDT, one might need to decide whether or not the gas company needs to be called—i.e., is there a gas leak? As shown in the table below, when no leaking gas is present and you correctly recognize this, you will have made a *correct rejection*. You are likely unaware of even noticing the absence of a gas smell, and there are no negative consequences. However, if there is a gas leak and you detect it, this

would be a *hit*—the gas company should be called and you should get out of the house! Not detecting a gas leak would be a dangerous *miss*. If you *think* you smell gas when there is no leak, that would be a *false alarm*.

	Target Odor Present (odor + diluent) + H_2O	Target Odor Absent (diluent only) + H_2O
Respond "Yes"	✓ Hit	✗ False Alarm
Respond "No"	✗ Miss	✓ Correct Rejection

The consequences of a *miss* in this situation are potentially lethal, so one would not want to make such a mistake. The consequences of a *false alarm* might be a bill from the gas company to check out your stove. Deciding whether or not to call the gas company would depend on your *criterion*—you might have a very *liberal criterion* and call the gas company every time you have any concern that there might be a gas leak. Or you might have a very *conservative criterion* and only call the gas company when you were very confident that there was a leak.

4. Other examples of contexts in which SDT can be applied:

- Attempting to detect weapons of mass destruction from satellite images.
- Detecting tumors in x-rays. Clearly there is a tradeoff between not wanting to "miss" any tumors and having too many "false alarms", which would needlessly worry patients and cost a lot of money in additional testing.
- In the criminal justice system, we would rather let a guilty person go free than incarcerate an innocent person. In terms of signal detection theory, we are applying a *conservative* criterion such that we are more likely to commit a *miss* than make a *false alarm*. This example is worked through, along with a comparison to inferential statistics here.
- It is vital that *no* weapons pass airport security checkpoints. In terms of signal detection theory, security staff want a 100% *hit rate*. Thus, they apply a *liberal* criterion because they are more willing to accept a *false alarm* (e.g., inconveniencing a passenger) than to *miss* a weapon that could cause mass casualties.
- The applicability of SDT to Type I and Type II errors in standard inferential statistics can be illustrated with a table like this:

	Null Hypothesis is False	**Null Hypothesis is True**
Reject Null Hypothesis	✓ Correctly report an effect	✗ Incorrectly report an effect (Type I Error)
Fail to Reject Null Hypothesis	✗ Incorrectly report no effect (Type II Error)	✓ Correctly report no effect

L. Cameron (2020). Lecture notes.

- If you are waiting for an important phone call you might react to any sound coming from your phone as if it were a ring tone (a *false alarm*). Reacting to a phone sound only when it is a ring tone would be a *hit*. Failing to react to a ring tone would be a *miss* and not reacting to non-ring tone sounds from the phone call would be a *correct rejection*.
- When mobile phones were still new and owning one was a status symbol, all the businesspeople on commuter trains who had one would immediately reach for it if anyone's phone rang. For most people, this was a *false alarm*, but everyone set a low response criterion in order to avoid a *"miss"* and also to take the opportunity to show off their phones!
- A pregnancy test result that correctly indicates that a woman is pregnant is a "hit;" correctly indicating that she isn't pregnant is a "correct rejection." A positive result for a woman who is not pregnant is a "false alarm" and a negative result from a pregnant woman is a "miss." A funny and memorable illustration of the errors in this example is shown in this image in which a doctor tells an elderly man that he is pregnant (false alarm/a Type I error) and an obviously pregnant woman that she is not pregnant (miss/a Type II error).

Sensory Adaptation/Habituation

1. When you enter a movie theater there is usually a strong smell of popcorn. After a while, the smell seems to be gone. What changed is *your* ability to smell, not the smell itself. You have adapted to it.
2. You may forget that you are wearing glasses or a hat or a belt because your somatosensory system adapts to their presence. You also become adapted to the clothes you are wearing.

3. Prolonged exposure to a given color reduces sensitivity to that color and enhances sensitivity to the opposite color, as in any afterimage or aftereffect. One of the most powerful is shown here, and here and here.

4. An example of adaptation in temperature perception is found here.
5. If you put a lot of salt on your food you will adapt to it and your food won't taste as salty (you have reduced your sensitivity to salt).
6. After prolonged exposure to it, you will no longer notice the sound of a ticking clock or a humming fridge.
7. People who have been sleeping with a snoring partner for many years may no longer be disturbed by the noise.
8. After wearing distorting prisms (tilting, displacing or inverting), the visual system adapts and people can function relatively normally. The same can be done with "artificial ears" in which the interaural axis can be rotated so that the source of sounds is systematically shifted. People learn to correct for the rotation.
9. As you enter a darkened movie theater, it may seem so dark that you have trouble finding your way to a seat, but after a while dark adaptation will allow you to see much better. Later, when you step outside into daylight the environment will seem to be abnormally bright.
10. If you get up to go to the bathroom at night, your eyes will have dark adapted and you will likely be able to find your way without switching on the light.
11. A demonstration of the unusual droopy eyelid illusion, which occurs when only one eye is dark adapted can be found here.

12. A "positive aftereffect" can be experienced if one is dark adapted. A demonstration of this effect is described here.
13. Infants who see the same stimulus repeatedly will stop looking at it. (Examples of how habituation is used to study infants' sensory/perceptual abilities are presented in the chapter on development.)

14. If you live in the flight path for a major airport, you might become less sensitive to the sounds of take offs and landings.
15. People who live in big cities may stop noticing the noise of honking horns, sirens, and the like.
16. Indeed, for city-dwellers, silence may be disconcerting, as was illustrated in the movie *My Cousin Vinny*. The title character finds that his sleep is disturbed by the sound of an owl in the small town he is visiting, but he sleeps peacefully when he is thrown into a noisy jail (whose sounds are more familiar to him). You can see the relevant clip here.
17. Drug users may habituate to a drug they take frequently, increasing their tolerance and "need" for higher doses.

Perceptual Processes

Note: The title of this section might suggest that perceptual processes are separate from sensory ones, but it is our task as teachers to help students understand that the two overlap and that, as illustrated by the examples below, recognition and other aspects of perception are heavily influenced by top-down processes, including attention, memory, expectation, motivation, and emotion. Here is a potentially useful representation of the relationships among sensation, perception, and related processes:

Examples Contrasting Sensation and Perception

1. People with amusica or "tone deafness" provide examples of sensation accompanied by incomplete perception. These people can hear music but their perception of it is distorted such that they are not able to discriminate among pitches. A recent publication described here includes a series of behavioral and neurophysiological studies of amusica. The authors are quoted as saying "These findings are largely consistent with the hypothesis that amusics are relatively intact in early auditory processing, and are primarily impaired in later, conscious perceptual evaluation or categorization of pitch stimuli."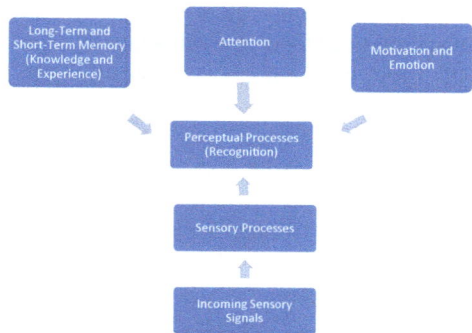
2. Disorders in sensory/perceptual processing, such as the agnosias described in the chapter on biological aspects of psychology, illustrate some of the distinctions between sensation and various aspects of perception. For example, someone with *apperceptive* visual agnosia might *sense* an object's contours—such as a dog lying on a rug—but be unable to recognize what it is.
Similarly, associative visual agnosias, such as prosopagnosia, or "face blindness" reveal that it is possible to *sense* an object and to *perceive* it as a face, but still be unable to *recognize* whose face it is.
3. Examples of stimuli used to differentiate between sensation and perception (or local and global processing) can be seen in the paintings of Giuseppe

Arcimboldo, which can be found here. Arcimboldo's paintings have  been used to explore visual processing in patients with agnosia (especially simultagnosia) and those with split brains, including cases in which the left-side processes faces and the right-side processes fruits (See the chapter on biological aspects of psychology for related videos).

4. Look at this image. If you cannot make sense of it, that is because your brain is receiving only raw visual *sensations* that can be organized in so many different ways that the brain's perceptual processes cannot recognize a meaningful object in the display. This is an example of primarily "bottom-up" processing.

Here is the same image with an object highlighted within. The highlighting gives your brain a way to organize what had been meaningless visual sensations into a meaningful perception, in this case a recognizable object. This is an example of "top-down" processing. Once your brain has created this perception, you will find it difficult or impossible to avoid experiencing it. (See other examples  later in this chapter.)

This same image, accompanied by two kinds of "help" to see the dog is available here.

5. A similar example is provided by the Coffer Illusion shown here and  here. In this case, you can easily *sense* a meaningful image but you may not initially *perceive* the circles within it.

6. Suppose that a friend is telling you about how she spent her weekend. You hear and understand every word until she suddenly begins speaking in French, a language you don't know. You will continue to hear the sounds your friend is making, but you will no longer have any idea what she is saying. Why? Because no matter what language she is speaking, the sound waves coming from your friend are just raw *sensations* that stimulate receptors in your ears and are converted into coded nerve signals that go to auditory areas of your brain. As long as these raw sensations came from English words, your brain could use its memory of the English language to translate the sensations into recognizable *perceptions* of what the sensations mean. When your friend began creating sounds that your brain could not recognize, you still experienced the sensations created by her voice, and you could still *perceive them as speech sounds* but you could no longer *recognize* what they mean.

Failures of Perception

Psychological scientists believe that human perception is more similar than different across individuals and that even when different people's experiences are not exactly the same at every moment, the *processes* of perception are the same for everyone. Offering some of the examples of visual illusions and auditory illusions listed below at the beginning of a course or a course section on perception can help students start to understand that perception is a *representation* of the environment, and not necessarily a *faithful* one. There can be failures of perception, meaning that we can't entirely trust our eyes. "Seeing is not believing".

1. That point is exemplified in this 2-min video of amazing cakes that look like other objects.
2. Magic tricks also demonstrate that seeing should not be believing as in the "vanish" in magic, amazing versions of which can be seen here.
3. Many students are attracted to the idea that each person has a *unique* perception of the world, yet they may be surprised and disturbed by demonstrations showing clear individual differences in perception. An example of an exception to the universality of perception can be seen in the case of the blue vs. gold dress phenomenon that took the Internet by storm in 2015. The fact that people find it hard to believe that other people see colors differently than they themselves do suggests that they do indeed presume that perceptual experiences are more or less universal.
   The individual differences involved in the dress phenomenon are demonstrated and discussed here.
4. The same type of illusion went viral in 2017. It involved sneakers that appeared pink and white to some people and teal and gray to others. An image and description of that illusion is described here.

5. This 1:25-min video helps people who see the shoes as gray and teal see them as pink and white.

6. This 1:27-min video helps people who see the shoes as pink and white to see them as gray and teal.

7. Other visual illusions also demonstrate that perception is a representation and that most people experience them in the same way. Several websites that present such illusions, including impossible and ambiguous figures, can be found here, here, here, and here.

8. As an example of illusions of motion, the waterfall illusion or motion aftereffect is powerful and robust, and its neural underpinnings are relatively well understood.
9. A demonstration of the same effect with spiral motion can be found here.

10. A more complex example of the same kind of motion can be found here. On that page you will find explanations of the phenomenon, further reading, and links to other demonstrations of the motion aftereffect. These motion illusions are also great examples of adaptation.

11. A blog with many humorous visual illusions can be found here. To keep up with some of the most recent illusions being developed, visit this site.

12. Examples of interesting impossible figures can be found here and here. (If you continue exploring this site, you will find many other amazing illusions and art, including some animated impossible figures).

13. Examples of ambiguous figures can be found here, and ambiguous (skull) illusions can be found here.

14. Fig. 1 in an article by Long and Toppino (2004), which can be found here, provides a summary of examples of the following impossible figures: the Necker cube, vase/faces, Maltese cross, wife/mother-in-law, duck/rabbit, Schroeder staircase, man/girl, rat/man, ambiguous triangles and overlapping squares.
 [Source: Long, G. M., & Toppino, T. C. (2004). Enduring interest in perceptual ambiguity: Alternating views of reversible figures. *Psychological bulletin*, *130*(5), 748–768.]

15. This video shows another way to disambiguate the old woman/young woman ambiguous figure.

16. The pin hole/shadow illusion is demonstrated in a compelling video found here.

17. Five amazing auditory illusions are described here, the first of which is the particularly powerful Barber Shop Illusion.

18. In an effect somewhat akin to the infamous blue/gold dress, the Yanny/Laurel effect demonstrates that the same sound can be perceived differently by different people. As with the dress, the responses are binary—heard either as one word (Yanny) or the other (Laurel), as shown here.

19. The compelling examples above should help you to demonstrate that perception provides a *representation* of the environment, but not an exact copy. In other words, the concept of naïve realism cannot be correct. Other evidence that perception is a representation include the facts that:

    - There are *limits of perception*. This is easily confirmed by the existence of microscopes, binoculars and telescopes to see things that are too small or too far away for human detection. (Some other examples of the limits of perception are provided in the section above on absolute/detection thresholds.)
    - Our *biology affects our perception*. As evidence, we know that other animals perceive the world differently than humans do. (See examples above of perception in dogs, eagle, bats).
    - *Perception is a function of both sensation and cognition*. (See examples of top-down influences on perception in this chapter and also in the chapter on thinking and cognitive abilities).

Perceptual Constancies

1. A number of examples of perceptual constancies can be found here (Note—there are also examples of Gestalt Laws of perceptual organization at this site, and examples of motion perception, but some of those links are broken.)
2. Shape, color, and size constancies are demonstrated in this image. The hot air balloons are perceived as being the same *shape* though they are seen from different angles. The red balloon is perceived as being a uniform red *color*, despite the differences in illumination.
Instead of perceiving these balloons has having various sizes, we interpret the scene as having depth with the "smaller" balloons interpreted as being further away.
3. An example of drawings of a chair and a footstool from multiple perspectives, demonstrating shape constancy can be found here.

4. Probably the most familiar example of failure of shape and size constancy can be seen in this image.
5. A firetruck looks red regardless of whether we see it outside illuminated by the sun, artificial light, a roaring fire or the flashing lights of an ambulance.
6. This image of a bowl of fruit under three levels of illumination demonstrates color constancy.

7. An excellent 13-min video that presents examples of color constancy and failures in color constancy (as in the dress and shoe illusions) can be found here.
8. Most people correctly interpret this picture as showing three people of normal size, despite the fact that the various spaces they take up on the viewers' retina are vastly different.

L. Cameron (2020).

9. Another example of failure of size constancy is the moon illusion, which is nicely illustrated and described here.

10. An interesting example and application of a failure of perceptual constancy is described and demonstrated in this blog post about judges of gymnasts on "rings".

Depth Perception

1. There are many monocular depth cues, as demonstrated in the photographs below (Source: L. Cameron, 2020). Each image can be used to demonstrate multiple depth cues, but there are particularly identifiable cues in each picture:

    - *Interposition and occlusion* are illustrated here. The trash can, sign, columns and lights all occlude parts of the scene, so they are perceived as being closer than the objects they occlude.

    - *Relative retinal size:* As mentioned above, the retinal image of each person in this picture is a different size, but they are perceived as being of about the same physical size at different distances from the viewer.

Depth Perception

- *Height in the visual field:* On the ground, objects that are more distant are usually higher than those that are nearby. Thus, the colorful tree on the left side of the road is perceived as more distant than the bushes on the left. Why don't the overhanging branches look the farthest away since they are actually highest in the visual field? Mainly because of linear perspective, as described in the next example.

- *Linear perspective:* These pictures show parallel lines that appear to converge, and objects that are closer to the point of convergence are perceived as more distant.

- *Texture gradient:* The "texture," or visual details, of objects becomes less distinct with increased distance, so as the cobblestones in this photo become less textured they are perceived as being further away.

- *Reduced Clarity:* This image shows that haze, blur, and blueness increase with distance, so hazy, blurry, and bluer objects in a scene are perceived as further away. This is why art students are taught to add a little blue to sections of a landscape that are to be perceived as very distant.

2. *Shading* is a particularly powerful depth cue, as can be seen in the so-called hollow face illusion demonstrated here. (See also the shape from shading examples in the section below on top-down influences on perception).
3. An illusion of a "floating trash bin" that arises from misinterpreting a dark blotch on the pavement as a shadow can be seen in here.
4. Many examples of depth cues are described in lecture notes on binocular vision from David Heeger (New York University), which can be found here.
5. A 10-min video lecture on how we perceive depth includes examples of depth cues mostly from photographs and can be found here.
6. Examples of the interdependence of size and distance can be seen in the classic Ames Room/Ames Window which is explored in this 17-min video. It is also demonstrated here and here.

7. Depth from motion is nicely demonstrated in "wiggle vision." Some examples are found here. Students may be able to provide other examples from memes/giphy with which they are familiar.

8. Many examples of outstanding two-dimensional street art that looks 3-dimensional are shown here.

9. Here is a picture of a shirt that gives the impression of depth using monocular depth cues.
10. Oculomotor cues to depth (Accommodation):

    - An image available here, demonstrates the change in shape of the lens to focus on an object at two distances.

    - The accommodation made by the human eye is different in detail, but similar in function to the lens of a camera, which can be moved forward or backward to bring the object of interest into focus.
    - You can point out to your students that poor focus leads to blurry images as occurs in myopia (nearsightedness), hyperopia (farsightedness) and presbyopia (farsightedness due to aging).
    - You can provide students with an example of accommodation by asking them to do the following: "Reach your two hands in front of you with the index fingers placed one in front of the other (though not completely overlapping) and at different distances from your face. While focusing on the index finger of your left hand, notice that the index finger of your right hand, is "out of focus". Now focus on the index finger of the right hand. That finger will now be in focus and the other will be out of focus. (The lenses of the eyes had to *accommodate* to bring each finger into focus.)

Oculomotor cues to depth: Convergence:

1. You can provide students with an example of convergence by asking them to follow a pen or a finger as it is moved toward and away from their nose.

2. An illustration of convergence (and divergence) can be seen here and a picture of a woman making a convergent eye movement can be seen here.

3. Retinal/binocular disparity is another very important cue to depth. There is a smaller difference, or disparity, between each eye's view of an object when the object is far away than when it is close by. The size of the disparity helps us estimate the object's distance. To provide your students with an easily understood example, ask them to hold a pen vertically about six inches in front of their nose, then close one eye and notice where the pen is in relation to the background. Now ask them to open that eye, close the other one, and notice how much

the image of the pen "shifted." (These are the two different views the eyes have of the pen). Now ask them to repeat this procedure while holding the pen at arm's length. They should notice that there is now less disparity or "shift," because there is less difference in the angles from which the two eyes see the pen.

4. The "Frankfurter" illusion, shown here, demonstrates "seeing double" and binocular rivalry or suppression. This illusion plays with depth cues.

5. The experience of depth that emerges from slightly different images presented to the two eyes (i.e., stereopsis from retinal disparity) can be seen in random dot stereograms. A simple demonstration of random dot stereograms and how they are created with some background about the developer, Bela Julesz, can be found here and here.

6. The development of autostereograms led to Magic Eye images, many examples of which can be found here.

Development of Depth Perception

Note: Some of the visual data examples provided here require an account on Databrary. See the Preface for details. The video examples described below can be found on Databrary by clicking the hyperlink for each source.

1. The "visual cliff" is an example of a method of testing depth perception in preverbal infants.

   - One video shows that babies learn from experience how to navigate cliffs, slopes and narrow bridges and that stopping at a cliff is not a sign of a fear of heights.
     [Source: Adolph, K. (2015). Science Friday: Babies on the brink. *Databrary*. Retrieved January 5, 2021 from http://doi.org/10.17910/b7.194.]

   - A video shows some of the ways in which researchers measure infants' ability to perceive depth.

   - Another video shows examples of various animals, with limited visual experience, being confronted with the visual cliff. It is based on the early work of Eleanor Gibson and Richard Walk.

[Source: Adolph, K. (2015). Excerpt volume: Gibson's "visual cliff". *Databrary*. Retrieved January 5, 2021 from http://doi.org/10.17910/B7.121
Reference: Gibson, E. J., & Walk, R. D. (1960). The "Visual Cliff." *Scientific American, 202*(4), 64–71.]

- An example of the specificity of learning is demonstrated in a video showing that 9-month-old babies confronted with the visual cliff don't try to cross from a seated position but do try when they are in a less-familiar crawling position. What determines whether they attempt to cross a crevice is their experience with moving in a particular way (e.g., crawling, walking, and the like). [Source: Adolph, K. (2014). Excerpt volume: Specificity of learning: Why infants fall over a veritable cliff. *Databrary*. Retrieved January 5, 2021 from http://doi.org/10.17910/B7KW28].

Perceiving Biological Motion

1. Examples of the point sources of light stimuli used to study biological motion can be found on Databrary. There is also this 2-min video with Mikhail Baryshnikov dancing and Michael Jordan playing basketball to demonstrate "bodies in motion".
   [Source: Bertenthal, B.I. (2014). Biological Motions. *Databrary*. Retrieved January 7, 2021 from http://doi.org/10.17910/B7W884
   Reference: Bertenthal, B.I. (1993). Perception of biomechanical motions by infants: Intrinsic image and knowledge-based constraints. In C. Granrud (Ed.), Carnegie symposium on cognition: visual perception and cognition in infancy (pp. 175–214). Hillsdale, NJ: Erlbaum.]
2. An example of biological motion, in this case a person walking in the presence and absence of visual noise, can be seen here.
3. Another example of a person walking can be seen here. Click on "BML Walker" and you will find that the attributes of the person, including sex and mood, can be manipulated. There are also links to participate in experiments, such as to guess the sex of the person whose biological motion is depicted by dots.
4. Examples of the optic flow pattern (the consequence of moving the body) in babies are documented here.
5. There are also examples of optic flow in Databrary.
   Source: Gilmore, R.O. (2014). An analysis of optic flow observed by infants during natural activities. *Databrary*. Retrieved January 6, 2021 from http://doi.org/10.17910/B7QP46.

Visual Search

1. Common examples of visual search tasks in daily life include looking for:

   - your keys on a crowded desk.
   - your car in a parking lot.
   - the jar of olives in your refrigerator.
   - your friend in a crowd.
   - your child on a playground.
   - your favorite brand of cereal on a supermarket shelf.
   - the spatula in a drawer of kitchen utensils and tools.
   - an app on your smartphone.
   - a book on your bookshelf.

2. Good examples of difficult visual search tasks include Where's Wally/Waldo pictures. There are two videos that include multiple Where's Waldo pictures. The first, which includes three different pictures and slowly zooms in on Waldo, can be found here. The second includes 6 pictures that are progressively more difficult and is available here.

3. Another example of a very challenging visual search task, in this case finding Sponge Bob among Minions, is illustrated here.

4. Efforts to spot the difference between two static images is another example of visual search. An interactive "spot the difference" game is available with artwork here. (New images are posted daily.)

5. Here are two other challenging visual search tasks. In this one you are searching for a phone and in this one you are searching for a cat.

6. An example of visual search in infants can be seen in this page on Databrary: Frank, M.C. (2014). Visual search and attention to faces during early infancy. *Databrary*. Retrieved January 5, 2021 from http://doi.org/10.17910/B75P47 [Reference: Frank, M. C., Amso, D., & Johnson, S. P. (2014). Visual search and attention to faces during early infancy. *Journal of Experimental Child Psychology, 118*, 13–26. https://doi.org/10.1016/j.jecp.2013.08.012]

Attention and Perception

1. Examples of selective attention include:

   - Focusing on your instructor during a lecture instead of the other students in the room.
   - Carrying on a conversation in a crowded room while ignoring conversations around you.
   - Concentrating on reading a book while someone nearby is watching TV.
   - Focusing on the movie you are watching and ignoring the sound of a snowblower outside.
   - Engaging with your cell phone—reading texts, dialing a phone number, reading a meme etc., while tuning out your instructor's lecture.
   - An example of the development of attention in babies can be found on this page on Databrary: Frank, M.C. (2014). Development of infants' attention to faces during the first year. *Databrary*. Retrieved January 5, 2021 from http://doi.org/10.17910/B7K01X.

   [Reference: Frank, M. C., Vul, E., & Johnson, S. P. (2009). Development of infants' attention to faces during the first year. Cognition, 110(2), 160–170.]

2. Examples of divided attention (also referred to as multi-tasking, but note that this is often really task-switching):

   - Checking your phone during class (don't do it).
   - Talking on the phone while driving (don't do that, either).
   - Texting while driving (really don't do it).
   - Texting while walking [see research by Hyman et al. (2009) in the chapter on research methods and statistics].
   - A humorous video with a serious and graphic conclusion about texting and driving from the South African government can be found here.
   - Playing a video game while talking on the phone.
   - Searching the Internet while having a conversation.
   - Cleaning your room while talking on the phone.
   - Feeding an infant while engaging in a conversation.
   - Taking care of multiple infants simultaneously.
   - Airline pilots, air traffic controllers, or nuclear power plant operators simultaneously monitoring multiple displays.
   - A receptionist who is scheduling an appointment while checking in a patient.
   - A waitress who is simultaneously delivering food and listening to customer requests in a busy restaurant.
   - A cashier at a deli who is bagging one customer's lunch while taking the telephone order of another.

- True story: One of the authors once saw a woman driving 70 miles an hour on I-94 outside of Chicago while eating Chinese food with chopsticks!

3. Examples of dissociating eye movements and attention

    - Basketball players can look at the person guarding them but attend to the ball or a teammate to whom they are going to pass the ball. There are plenty of examples of this in any professional basketball game, but this 32-s video shows a nice behind-the-back pass by LeBron James. It demonstrates the dissociation between looking and attending (he was clearly attending to the location of his teammate while looking elsewhere—shown very clearly in the final camera angle).
    - Another example occurs when you meet someone at, for example, a conference and have forgotten the person's name. Luckily people typically wear name badges at conferences, but it would be embarrassing to be caught reading the name badge of a person whose name you should know. Thus, you might find yourself looking at the person's face while you attend and try to read the name badge "out of the corner of your eye."
    - At a crowded party, you are looking at the boring person who has button-holed you, but you are really paying attention to another person nearby with whom you would like to have a conversation.

4. Here are some examples of the fact that *attention enhances perception*. They are a special case of the fact that knowledge affects perception (see also top-down processing later in this chapter and in the chapter on thinking and cognitive abilities):

    - In one early experiment examining the effect of attention on visual perception, researchers studied the visual areas in monkeys' brains and found that the activity of neurons in areas that process information about moving objects were more active when the monkeys were "paying attention" to the stimulus that it was processing.
    [Reference: Treue, S., & Maunsell, J. H. (1996). Attentional modulation of visual motion processing in cortical areas MT and MST. *Nature, 382*(6591), 539–541.]
    - The example above is better understood when the tricky concept of a receptive field is explained. (See also the section below on feature detectors.) Not long after the Treue and Maunsell (1996) study was published, researchers using psychophysical techniques demonstrated that when humans attend to particular locations in the visual field they require lower contrast (less difference between the light and dark-colored bars shown below) to detect the presence of one of these "Gabor" stimuli.

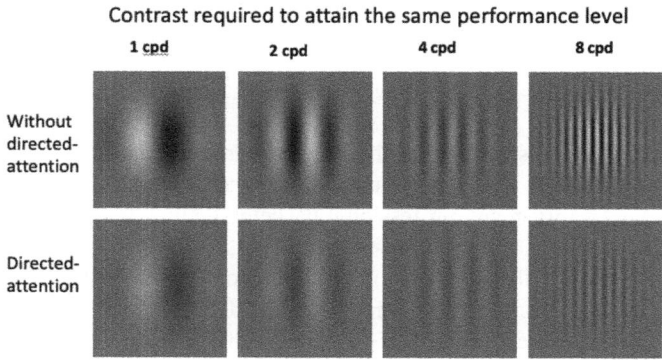

[Source: L. Cameron (2020), lecture notes].
[Reference: Carrasco, M., Penpeci-Talgar, C., & Eckstein, M. (2000). Spatial covert attention increases contrast sensitivity across the CSF: Support for signal enhancement. *Vision research*, *40*(10–12), 1203–1215. https://doi.org/10.1016/s0042-6989(00)00024-9].

5. Examples of failures of attention:

- "Flicker tasks," in which two photographs are alternated with a blank grey screen in between them can be used to induce change blindness. A classic example of two photos of an airplane with a big but hard-to-detect difference between them is shown in a 26-s video here.
- Another example, shown in a clever scene that is acted out in a 1:24-min "Whodunnit?" video, can be found here.
- Another example produced for a UK campaign to encourage drivers to watch for cyclists can be found in the 1:08-min video here.
- A more amateurish 2:17-min video in a high school classroom can be found here.
- Examples of the accidental "continuity errors" in movies can be found in the 2:17-min video clip found here.
- A series of video examples of inattentional blindness that go beyond the well-known "gorilla" video can be found here.

Attention and Perception

- An example of inattentional blindness can be seen in the magic trick demonstrated here and in this one.

- Pictures can also be changed slowly in a "gradual change" task and people often miss the change. Examples are seen in the 1:19-min video found here (from Dan Simons) and in the 54-s video shown here.

- There is an amusing example of failures of attention in a series of images from a Colgate commercial shown here and here.

- Descriptions of airplane crashes that were caused by failures of attention can be found
  here, here and here.
  [Note: there are many applications of cognitive psychology to aviation on the skybrary website.]

- Here is an example of the dangers of distracted driving, including when caused by the negative impact of "voice message apps" on perceptual-motor and cognitive tasks.

  Reference: Li, J., Dou, Y., Wu, J., Su, W., & Wu, C. (2021). Distracted driving caused by voice message apps: A series of experimental studies. *Transportation Research Part F: Traffic Psychology and Behaviour, 76,* 1–13.

Subliminal Perception and Subliminal Messaging

(See also examples of priming in the chapters on thinking and cognitive abilities and consciousness.)

1. Several examples of so-called "subliminal messages" are provided here, in the context of debunking myths about the supposed impact of subliminal messages.

2. Examples of advertisements that allegedly include subliminal messages can be found here and here.

3. A lesson plan for combatting myths about the alleged power of subliminal perception can be found here. It is part of a larger set of lesson plans for creating an introductory psychology course organized around debunking myths about human behavior and mental processes. Its homepage can be found here.

4. Some examples of research findings that suggest that subthreshold *olfactory* stimuli lead to behavior change (which could be considered a form of "subliminal perception") include:

   - Some odors added to the ventilation system of clothing stores in low concentration (thought to be below threshold), resulted in longer customer visits and had a positive effect on sales.

     [Reference: Teerling, A., Nixdorf, R. R., & Köster, E. P. (1992). The effect of ambient odours on shopping behavior. *Chemical Senses, 17,* 886.]

   - People exposed to a citrus-scented cleaning product demonstrated both increased mental access to the concept of cleaning and increased cleaning behavior.

     [Reference: Holland, R. W., Hendriks, M., & Aarts, H. (2005). Smells like clean spirit. *Psychological Science, 16*(9), 689–693. https://www.jstor.org/stable/40064295]

   - People rated neutral faces differently depending on the odor that was presented to them—more positively for pleasant odors and more negatively for unpleasant odors, but only if the odors were undetectable.

[Reference: Li, W., Moallem, I., Paller, K. A., & Gottfried, J. A. (2007). Subliminal smells can guide social preferences. *Psychological Science, 18*(12), 1044–1049. https://www.jstor.org/stable/40064701]

5. Another example of subliminal mental processing comes from blindsight, a condition in which patients with damage to the primary visual cortex might not be consciously aware of objects in their path, and yet navigate past them without bumping into them. Or they might duck when a ball is thrown at them, but without know why. (More examples are presented in the chapters on biological aspects of psychology and consciousness.)

Bottom-Up Perceptual Processes

1. Feature Detectors.

    - There is a 3:15-min video from Hubel and Wiesel that provides an example of a single (*simple*) cell in cat visual cortex that responds to an *oriented* bar of *light* in the cell's *receptive field*. It can be found here.

    - It might be helpful to first show this video to help students understand the method Hubel and Wiesel were using in the first video.

2. Other "basic" *features* that the visual system can detect include:

    - Spatial frequency (see image below)
    - Contrast (see image below)
    - Orientation
    - Phase (position with respect to a landmark)
    - Color
    - Motion

    Spatial Frequency gratings (Gabors); two contrast levels

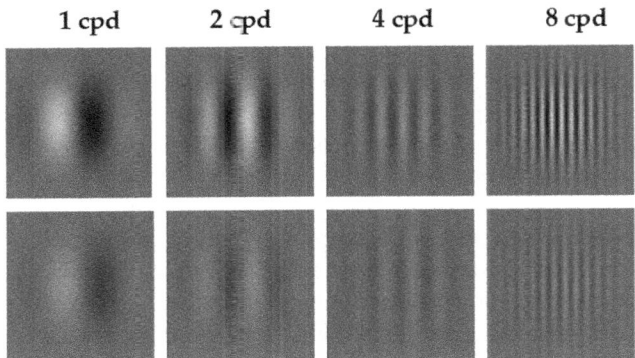

[Source: L. Cameron, lecture notes (2020)].

3. An example of how to conceptualize feature detectors can be found in the Pandemonium model, clearly demonstrated here.

4. There are also cells that respond to stimuli that are more complex than the basic features describe above, including things such as faces. A 38-sec video embedded in a news article shows activity in neurons that are selectively responsive to faces. It can be seen here.

5. Examples of specific regions of the brain subserving specific functions (i.e., localization of function) are provided in this 16:59-min Ted Talk by Nancy Kanwisher.
   (See also "localization of function" in the chapter on biological aspects of psychology).

Top-Down Influences on Perception

1. Illusory contours, such as the Kaniza Triangle shown here demonstrate perception without sensation (i.e., we see a shape that is not actually present, but that our *knowledge* of objects tells us should be there).
2. Here is another case of perception without sensation, as demonstrated by a mime's ability to lead us to perceive objects that do not exist but that our knowledge creates for us.
3. Two men are sitting at adjacent tables in a coffee shop when a woman walks by on her way to the counter. Both men can smell her perfume as she passes, but one of them finds himself holding back tears. Why should this be? The olfactory *sensations* that reached each man's brain were essentially the same, and they could both *perceive* them as perfume but one man's *experience* of the scent was very different. Based on long-term *memory*, his brain recognizes that this is the perfume worn for many years by his beloved wife before her untimely death.
4. An American tourist in Australia is having lunch when the waiter asks her if everything is ok with her meal. When she gives him a "thumbs up" to signify that all is well, he turns his back on her in disgust. Why should this be? The shape and movement *sensations* reaching the waiter's brain from her hand gesture were 100% accurate, but his *perception* of them was based on his *experience* of having been raised in a culture where the "thumbs up" gesture means the same as a middle finger gesture in the United States.
5. It is 2 a.m. when an armed robber enters a 24-h supermarket in an upscale community and fires a warning shot to get the store manager to open the safe. Several late-night shoppers are at the back of the store, but most of them had never before heard a live gunshot. As a result, when their brains received the

auditory *sensations* it created, they *perceive* the sound as a firecracker or a car backfiring. However, a shopper who had had experience in law enforcement, the military, or other environments involving gunfire would use that *experience* to correctly recognize the sensations as gunshots and call 911.

6. The fact that we do not experience a blind spot in our vision (even when one eye is closed) provides an example of the brain's ability to use knowledge and experience to "fill in" the visual information that is missing where the optic nerve leaves the eyeball.

7. *Shape from shading*, an example of which can be experienced here, illustrates that our *knowledge* about the typical source of light affects our perception; we know that light usually comes from above, so the darkness at the top of a disk is assumed to be a shadow and hence the disk is perceived as concave.

8. We use top-down processing to interpret ambiguous figures such as the image seen here as either a duck or a rabbit.

9. An example of how knowledge and expectation can permanently affect perception of ambiguous stimuli is provided by music clips that, when played backwards, make no sense unless one is told what to listen for. Several songs played backwards and forward can be found here.

10. When presented with the odor of parmesan cheese, people perceive it to be relatively more pleasant if they are told that it is cheese than if they are told that it is the smell of stinky socks.

11. An example of top-down processing can be seen in this humorous Candid Camera video in which people are shown abstract art and instructed to "see" the image in a particular way. The participants perceptions were clearly being influenced by the orienting descriptions provided by the Candid Camera staff.

12. Here is an example of how perceptions of facial expressions can be influenced by the context in which it is seen. Research participants perceived this man's expression as disgust when he was shown holding a dirty diaper (a), but that same expression was perceived as anger when it was digitally superimposed on a person in a fighting stance (b), and as fear when in defensive contexts (c and d).
[Reference: Aviezer H., Hassin, R.R., Ryan, J., Grady, C., Susskind, J., Anderson, A., & Bentin, S. (2008). Angry, disgusted, or afraid? Studies on the malleability of emotion perception. *Psychological Science, 19*, 724–732.]

13. Context can also shape expectations, which in turn influences perception. For example, we expect to see people, not gorillas, on city streets, so when a large gorilla escaped from Boston's Franklin Park zoo in 2003, a woman who saw him at a bus stop later said, "I thought it was a guy with a big black jacket and a snorkel on."
[Source: MacQuarrie, B., & Belkin, D. (2003, September 29). Franklin Park gorilla escapes, attacks 2. *Boston Globe.*]

14. Another example of top-down influences can be found in people's perception of a photograph of smoke billowing out of the World Trade Center on September 11th, 2001. Most people see nothing special in the smoke, but after a newspaper story claimed that the face of Satan appears in the smoke, people's expectations changed and they could then see it clearly. More information about the photographer, Mark Hamill, and his story can be found here.
15. Other examples of the influence of expectation on perception:

    - As you are driving along the street, looking for a particular store, you will be more likely to spot it on the block where you have been told it is than in an area where you did not expect to see it.
    - With deadly shooting incidents so much in the news, many people have become "set" to perceive ambiguous objects as weapons, especially in public places. In one such case, police in Olympia, Washington received a report of a man wearing a ski mask, carrying what appeared to be an assault rifle. A citywide manhunt ensued, and schools went into lockdown. The man had no idea what was going on until he noticed a helicopter tracking him. Police found that his "assault rifle" was actually an umbrella, and the "ski mask" just a black turtleneck and cap. Another misperceived umbrella in a sling caused a lockdown of four schools in Fredericton, New Brunswick, Canada after someone reported seeing a "gunman" near a high school. You can read about the case and see photos of the "gunman" here.
    - You have heard that a new employee in your office is prejudiced against members of your ethnic group. When you meet this person you are likely to perceive almost anything the person says as confirming that alleged prejudice. (See other examples of prior knowledge and self-fulfilling prophesies in the chapter on social psychology.)

16. An example of how our emotions can influence our perceptions is provided by research showing that people are more likely to see ambiguous objects as weapons if they are feeling angry or threatened.
    [Source: Baumann, J., & DeSteno, D. (2010). Emotion guided threat detection: Expecting guns where there are none. *Journal of Personality and Social Psychology*, *99*(4), 595–610. https://doi.org/10.1037/a0020665.]
17. Another example of the role of motivation: You are very hungry and looking for a restaurant in a strange town when you misperceive a sign for "Burger's Body Shop" as indicating a place to eat.
    [Source: Radel, R., & Clément-Guillotin, C. (2012). Evidence of motivational influences in early visual perception: Hunger modulates conscious access. *Psychological Science*, *23*(3), 232–234. https://doi.org/10.1177/0956797611427920.]
18. Motivation can also influence our perception of sporting events. You can probably remember a time when a referee incorrectly called a penalty on your

favorite sports team. You knew the call was wrong because you clearly saw the other team's player at fault. But if you had been cheering for that other team, you would have agreed with the referee's call.

Other examples of top-down influences on perception can be found in the chapter on thinking and cognitive abilities and in the chapter on memory (see in particular studies by Bartlett and Carmichael in the reproductive memory section).

Examples of Useful Classroom Demonstrations

1. Examples of demonstrations that illustrate many concepts in perception can be found here (courtesy of Anthony Barnhart, Carthage College). At this site you can find demonstrations for the following topics:

   - Color Constancy
   - Dark Adaptation & the Purkinje Shift
   - Ecological Psychology
   - Visual Feature/Conjunction Search
   - Hermann Grids
   - Mach Bands & Lateral Inhibition Demo
   - Mach Bands & Lateral Inhibition Workshop
   - Odor Detection
   - Odor Identification
   - Positive Afterimage
   - Signal Detection Theory
   - The Speech to Song Illusion
   - Stevens's Power Law
   - Taste Testing with Gymnema Sylvestre Tea

2. Other demonstrations relating to taste and smell are available on the Association for Chemoreception Sciences' website, here.

3. A series of, mostly low-tech, vision demonstrations can be found here.

Learning 4

Students may come to this material with an inaccurate conception of what learning is. They are likely to think that they are going to learn about how they learn in school. Thus, it is important to begin with an explanation and examples of associative learning. It may also be helpful to provide examples of how students can apply aspects of associative learning (e.g., using rewards) to improve their study habits and thus to perform better academically. The concepts in this chapter are readily observable in daily life. We hope that the examples provided will be a catalyst for generating your own additional examples of learning concepts, but remember that doing so can become very tricky, very quickly. Daily life does not provide many pure examples of the kinds of associative learning found in the laboratory, mainly because components of both classical and operant conditioning often operate in combination.

Classical Conditioning

1. The classic examples are Pavlov's experiments in which dogs came to salivate (CR) at the sound of a tone (CS) that had been paired with food. These experiments are described in most introductory psychology and psychology of learning textbooks. A 4-min video with original footage of Pavlov, narrated by Phil Zimbardo, can be found here.
2. The case of *Little Albert* provides an example of classical conditioning of fear. A 3-min video showing film of the learning trials can be seen here.

[Reference: Watson, J. B., & Rayner, R. (1920). Conditioned emotional reactions. *Journal of Experimental Psychology, 3*(1), 1–14.]

3. This 10-min video demonstrates human fear conditioning in a virtual environment.

[Reference: Huff, N. C., Zielinski, D. J., Fecteau, M. E., Brady, R., & LaBar, K. S. (2010). Human fear conditioning conducted in full immersion 3-dimensional virtual reality. *Journal of Visualized Experiments: JoVE,* (42) e1993. 10.3791/1993]

4. There were party hats at Liam's first birthday party. When his mother tried to put the party hat (neutral stimulus) on him, she (mistakenly) snapped him with the chin strap (US—snap of elastic). He cried (UR) and would never wear a party hat after that. Bringing a party hat (now a CS) near his face now makes him recoil and cry (CR).
5. When blowing up balloons (neutral stimulus) at Aidan's birthday party, one popped in his face (US) and startled him (UR). Now he is a bit afraid (CR) of blowing up balloons (CS).
6. Experienced moviegoers have learned that sudden scary events (US) that create startle reactions (UR) are usually preceded by foreboding music. As a result, the onset of such music alone has become a CS for tension and anxiety (CR).
7. For ten dry winter days in a row, Frank and his wife were startled (UR) by the static electric shocks (US) they got when they kissed while standing on their plush living room carpet. They now feel mildly anxious (CR) whenever they approach each other for a kiss (CS) in that room.
8. Students might remember that Harry, Hermoine, and Ron break into Gringott's bank in the final *Harry Potter* movie. They get past the fire-breathing dragon with the goblins because the goblins ring a bell (CS) that the dragon has been conditioned to associate with pain (US). As the goblins ring the bell the dragon recoils and howls (CR) as the group passes on into the vault.
9. One of the authors once lived in a house where the water temperature in the shower skyrocketed (US) if anyone opened a cold-water tap or flushed a toilet. Everyone in the family learned to jump out of the shower stream (CR) at the sound of the toilet flushing (CS).
10. That same author had a college roommate who liked to tease her by tickling the back of her neck (US). The roommate found it funny that the author would recoil and get goosebumps (UR). Eventually, the roommate would enter the room and simply cup her hand as though she was going to start tickling, and the sight of that cupped hand (CS) was enough to create goosebumps (CR).
11. A professor used a microphone while teaching a large class and had the unfortunate habit of occasionally walking in front of the amplifier's speaker, which resulted was a loud screeching sound (US). The first time this happened, the students were startled (UR), and over time, whenever the professor even approached the speaker, many of them had a startle reaction (CR).

12. Eli's grandma gives him a Tootsie Roll (US) every time she visits. His mouth waters when he puts the Tootsie Roll in his mouth (UR). Now when Eli sees his grandma (CS) arriving, his mouth begins to water (CR).
13. The first time Jamie had a glaucoma test—which involves a puff of air in his eye—the air puff (US) caused a reflexive blink response (UR). At every eye exam since, as soon as the glaucoma test instrument (CS) is put in front of him, Jamie starts blinking (CR).
14. After Lizzie had her wisdom teeth extracted and was experiencing pain and nausea, her mother fed her cold creamed corn (a food she loved). However, the corn became associated with pain and nausea. Lizzie was never able to eat creamed corn again and even thinking of cold corn (CS) made her nauseous (CR). Years later, when Lizzie's own daughter had her wisdom teeth extracted and was experiencing pain and nausea, Lizzie gave her painkillers crushed up in vanilla ice cream. Afterward, vanilla ice cream became a conditioned stimulus (CS) that make Lizzie's daughter nauseous (CR).
15. Another example of classically-conditioned food aversion is described at this website.
16. Yet another example of classically conditioned taste aversions is found in a study by Ilene Bernstein (1978), who gave one group of cancer patients Mapletoff ice cream an hour before they received nausea-provoking chemotherapy. A second group ate this same kind of ice cream on a day they did not receive chemotherapy; a third group got no ice cream. Five months later, the patients were asked to taste several ice cream flavors. Those who had never tasted Mapletoff and those who had not eaten it in association with chemotherapy chose it as their favorite. Those who had eaten Mapletoff before receiving chemotherapy found it distasteful.
[Reference: Bernstein, I. L. (1978). Learned taste aversions in children receiving chemotherapy. *Science, 200,* 1302–1303.]
17. Another chemotherapy-related example is the development of anticipatory nausea. In the years before effective anti-emetic medications became available, many cancer patients receiving chemotherapy treatments experienced nausea that was severe enough that, over time, the once neutral treatment room became a conditioned stimulus that provoked a conditioned nausea response (CR) even before the drugs were administered. A study describing this classically conditioned phenomenon is available here.
18. Honeybees reflexively extend their proboscis (UR) when their antennae are stimulated by sugar water (US). They can be classically conditioned to extend their proboscis (CR) in the presence of an odor (CS) if that odor is paired with sugar water. A 40-s video demonstrates this effect (you have to watch closely at about 11-s into the video). This conditioning technique has been used to train honeybees to detect

Covid-19 by smell, as is described here. (Other examples of classical conditioning in honeybees are available in this video that also discusses the effect of scent on emotion.)

19. Second order conditioning can occur in honeybees when a second odor is associated with the originally trained odor. Second-order (higher order) conditioning can also be seen in the classic experiments of Pavlov, where a second stimulus, say a light, is paired with a tone to ultimately produce salivation in the absence of the tone. An image of this process can be found here.

Simple Examples of Unconditioned Stimuli (US)

1. A splash/spray of water in the face
2. A sudden loud sound
3. A sudden bright light
4. Tickling
5. A pin-prick
6. Contact with a hot object
7. A poke in the ribs
8. An insect bite

Simple Examples of Unconditioned Responses (UR)

1. Reflexes, such as pulling a hand away from a hot stove
2. Closing your eyes or turning your head away from a spray of water
3. Putting your hands in front of face to avoid a rapidly approaching object
4. Startling at a loud noise such as a popped balloon
5. Squirming or curling when being tickled
6. Feeling nausea after eating or drinking too much
7. Crying out when you hit your finger with a hammer

Simple Examples of Conditioned Stimuli (CS)

1. A doctor's white coat after repeated painful medical procedures
2. The sight of a dog after one has been bitten by a dog
3. For a hungry person, the sound of a microwave bell that signals that dinner is ready
4. The smell of chocolate chip cookies after having become violently ill after once eating too many of them

5. A buzzing sound for someone who was recently stung by a wasp
6. The sound of a dental drill for someone who has recently had painful dental work
7. The sight of dark clouds and the sound of wind for someone whose home was once destroyed by a tornado
8. The sound of a motorcycle revving for someone who had been hit by one in the past

Simple Examples of Conditioned Responses (CR)

1. Closing your eyes and turning your head at the sound of a word that had been repeatedly followed by a spray of water in your face
2. Backing up and giggling when someone who has tickled you in the past approaches
3. Feeling nauseous when smelling chocolate chip cookies after being previously sickened from overeating them. (More examples of taste aversion are presented below.)
4. Experiencing anxiety at the sight of dark clouds after your home had once been destroyed by a tornado
5. Feeling anxious upon hearing the sound of dental drill
6. Feeling tense at the sight of someone holding a pin near a balloon after having seen that person pop balloons in the past
7. Feeling nausea at the sight of a place where one has previously received nausea-provoking chemotherapy
   [Note: In presenting examples of conditioned responses, it is a good idea to point out that they are evoked by a CS, not a US. Further, explain that although *conditioned* responses *resemble unconditioned* responses, they are usually not identical. For example, a CR may be less intense than a UR, as when an unconditioned startle reaction to the pain of an injection may become a conditioned anxiety response when re-entering the same medical office.]

Extinction in Classical Conditioning

1. In the classic Pavlov example above, if food no longer follows the tone, salivation upon hearing that tone ultimately stops.
2. After learning that certain music leads to scary events in movies, listening to the same music when nothing scary happens would reduce the fear response.
3. A classically conditioned fear of dentistry may extinguish over time if the fearful person finds a caring dentist who provides painless treatment and a soothing office environment.
4. A person who had developed a classically conditioned aversion to chocolate chip cookies after becoming ill after eating too many of them may eventually be able to eat them again because the conditioned response to their smell and taste may have extinguished.

5. A person's classically conditioned fear of cats, dogs, spiders, or other creatures may extinguish following treatment that provides controlled, gradual exposure to them as part of cognitive behavior therapy programs. (See below and in the chapter on treatment of psychological disorders for specific examples.)

Spontaneous Recovery

1. In the classic Pavlov example above, even after extinction of salivation (CR) to the sound of the tone (CS), that CR may temporarily recur if after some time passes the tone is presented again.
2. A nice graphical representation can be seen in Fig. 2 in this publication along with 4 general principles of spontaneous recovery. [Reference: Rescorla, R. A. (2004). Spontaneous recovery. *Learning & Memory, 11*(5), 501–509.]
3. A fear response may return spontaneously after treatment for post-traumatic stress disorder when a person is again confronted with the anxiety-producing stimulus.
4. A relapse, as in resuming smoking or drug use after therapy to quit smoking or drug use, could appear as spontaneous recovery when a person enters situations, such as a bar or a drug-using friend's apartment, where the association was formed. Here is a short video describing the many contextual cues that can lead to an urge to smoke.
5. Some smokers come to associate smoking with certain activities, such as drinking coffee. After quitting smoking, pouring a cup of coffee may result in an urge to smoke.
6. You are in a romantic relationship and then break up. When your "special song" comes on the radio you feel sad, but after hearing it many times, that feeling fades. Yet, after not having heard that song for years, you hear it again and to your surprise, that feeling of sadness returns.

Stimulus Discrimination

1. In the classic Pavlov example above, stimulus discrimination would be demonstrated if the dog does not salivate in response to a tone that is different from the original one.
2. After being in a car accident on a bridge last month, Giorgio gets nervous when he is approaching a bridge, but not in other driving situations.
3. In the example above in which Eli's grandma gives him a Tootsie Roll every time she visits, if Eli's mouth waters when he sees his grandmother but not his great aunt, he would be demonstrating stimulus discrimination.
4. James got sick after drinking too much vodka. Now the smell of vodka makes him slightly nauseous but the smell of rum does not.

Stimulus Generalization

1. In the classic Pavlov example above, stimulus generalization would occur if the dog salivates to tones that are similar, but not exactly the same as the original one.
2. After that accident on the bridge last month (described above), Giorgio gets nervous whenever and wherever he is driving.
3. In the example above in which Eli's grandma gives him a Tootsie Roll every time she visits, if Eli's mouth waters when he sees his grandmother and also when he sees his great aunt, he will have demonstrated stimulus generalization.
4. When Matt was two years old, his father accidentally sprayed insect repellent into his eyes during a camping trip. After that experience Matt would cry whenever someone would come near him with a spray can of insect repellent, and with any kind of spray can, including shaving cream.
5. If, after getting sick from drinking too much vodka, James developed a dislike for all hard liquor, James would be demonstrating stimulus generalization.

Applications of Classical Conditioning

Treatment of Anxiety: Systematic Desensitization

Two excellent examples of the use of systematic desensitization can be found here (Scientific American Frontiers, Season 6, Episode 5 demonstrates using virtual reality to reduce fear of height) and here (Season 9, Episode 5 addresses arachnophobia).

[*Note:* Many more examples of systematic desensitization are presented in the chapter on treatment of psychological disorders.]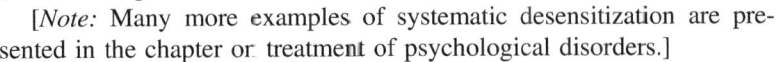

Treatment of Enuresis

1. Jenny wets the bed. Her parents place a pad under her sheets that sounds an alarm (US) that wakes Jenny up (UR) when the pad gets wet. Eventually Jenny won't need the alarm to wake up because the sensations of a full bladder (CS) will wake her up (CR).
2. This "bell and pad" system and its effectiveness are described in an article to be found here.
   [Reference: Gim, C.S., Lillystone, D., & Caldwell, P.H. (2009). Efficacy of the bell and pad alarm therapy for nocturnal enuresis. *Journal of Paediatric Child Health, 45,* 405–408].
3. An example of a commercially available bell and pad apparatus (in this case, called "Therapee") can be found here.

Predator Control and Animal Health

1. In the western United States, some ranchers lace a sheep carcass with enough lithium chloride to make wolves and coyotes nauseous. The predators associate nausea with the smell and taste of sheep and afterward stay away from the ranchers' flocks. Similar classical conditioning methods have helped ranchers to prevent grazing horses and cattle from eating poisonous plants.
[Reference: Pfister, J. A., Stegelmeier, B. L., Gardner, D. R., & James, L. F. (2003). Grazing of spotted locoweed (*Astragalus lentiginosus*) by cattle and horses in Arizona. *Journal of Animal Science, 81*, 2285–2293.]

2. A program supported by the government of India has greatly reduced human deaths from tiger attacks, as well as the need to kill marauding tigers. Stuffed dummies—connected by hidden wires to a shock generator—are placed in areas in which tigers have attacked people. When the animals approach they receive a shock (unconditioned stimulus), which they learn to associate with the human form. Humans thus become a conditioned stimulus for fear, and the tigers learn to avoid them (conditioned response). Shock collars used to keep dogs on the property of their owners work on the same principle.

Airport Security

An example of using classical conditioning principles to teach insects to detect explosive material is described in a study available here. The researchers showed that after the taste of sugar water was associated with the smell of a chemical used in certain explosives, wasps quickly  developed a conditioned response to the smell alone. When several of these trained insects were placed in a plastic tube and brought near the target chemical, they displayed an immediate attraction to it. Researchers hope that it may someday be possible to use these so-called Wasp Hounds and other similar devices to provide less elaborate and expensive methods for detecting explosives or drugs concealed in airline passengers' luggage.

[References: Rains, G. C., Utley, S. L., & Lewis, W. J. (2006). Behavioral monitoring of trained insects for chemical detection. *Biotechnology Progress, 22*, 2–8. https://doi.org/10.1021/bp050164p.

Tomberlin, J. K., Rains, G. C., & Sanford, M. R. (2008). Development of microplitis croceipes as a biological sensor. *Entomologia Experimentalis et Applicata, 128*(2), 249–257.

Olson, D., & Rains, G. (2014). Use of a parasitic wasp as a biosensor. *Biosensors, 4*(2), 150–160. https://doi.org/10.3390/bios4020150].

Operant Conditioning

1. Here are a few simple examples of learning through operant conditioning. More detailed examples are provided in the sections below.

   - You have learned that if you flip a light switch, a light goes on. If you flip a switch and no light goes on you are unlikely to continue flipping that switch. It may also lead to you try to figure out why a light doesn't come on (the light switch is disconnected or, more likely, a lightbulb has burned out).
   - You have learned that if you put your finger in an electrical outlet, you will get shocked.
   - You are complimented on your outfit by someone you would like to impress and thus are more likely to wear it again. If you are complimented by someone whose opinion you do not value, you may be less likely to wear that outfit again.
   - After you came home past curfew, your parents took away your driving privileges for two weeks. You never again miss a curfew.
   - You studied hard for an exam and earned an A. You are likely to study hard again for the next exam.
   - You notice that when you smile at people they are likely to smile back and thus you continue to smile at them.
   - You ask your dog to "give you a paw" and you give her a treat when she does. She'll be more likely to give you her paw next time you say "paw".
   - You post a story on social media and get lots of "likes". You are more likely to post stories again.
   - You are hungry and go to a vending machine for a snack. You put a dollar in the machine and it dispenses a candy bar. You are more likely to use that vending machine in the future.
   - You make a new dish for your family for dinner and everyone says it is delicious. You are more likely to make the dish again in the future.

2. This 4-min video shows a pigeon completing a word discrimination task for food reward in a Skinner Box and concludes with a short interview with B.F. Skinner.

The Law of Effect

1. A 2-min video dramatizing the law of effect, with footage of a cat escaping Thorndike's puzzle box can be found here.
   Note: This video could also be used as an example of insight (see the chapter on thinking and cognitive abilities).
   [Source: Thorndike E. (1988). Animal intelligence: An experimental study of the associative processes in animals. *The Psychological Review: Monograph Supplements*, 2(4):i-109. https://doi.org/10.1037/h0092987]

2. In this 2-min video, which demonstrates an owner teaching a dog to pick up a collar (using shaping), she pairs the sound of a clicker with food. The dog is likely to repeat the behavior because it has been rewarded ("produced a satisfying effect").
3. Being praised by your boss for showing up to work early makes it more likely that you will show up early again. By contrast, if you show up late and miss a critical meeting (perhaps the opportunity to work on a desirable project) or are scolded by your supervisor, you will be less likely to show up for work late again.
4. When young Max plays nicely with his friends at daycare, the daycare provider praises him. Max is more likely to play nicely with his friends in the future. When Max bites one of the other children, he is put into a timeout room. Max is less likely to bite another child again (we hope).
5. You worked hard on a presentation and you receive a lot of positive comments and requests for further information. You are more likely to work hard on your next presentation. By contrast, if you work hard on a presentation and receive negative feedback, you might be less likely to work hard on your next presentation.
   [Note: This scenario might also be used in relation to teaching about learned helplessness.]

Reinforcers

1. Examples of Primary Positive Reinforcers

   - Food
   - Water
   - Air

2. Examples of Secondary Positive Reinforcers

   - Praise
   - Attention
   - Trophies
   - Stars
   - Stickers
   - Money
   - Gift cards
   - Bonuses
   - Time off work or school
   - "Likes" on social media
   - Increase in followers/friends etc. on social media

3. Examples of Primary Negative Reinforcers (whose removal will strengthen behaviors that removed them):

- Electric shock
- Excessive heat
- Excessive noise
- Headache or muscle pain
- Pain of excessively spicy food
- Sunburn pain

4. Examples of Secondary Negative Reinforcers (whose removal will strengthen behaviors that removed them):

- Ridicule
- Lack of money
- Lack of respect from others
- Failure
- Being ignored by others
- Rejection by others
- Being at an undesired weight
- Anxiety
- Nagging by someone who wants you to complete a chore

Examples of Positive Reinforcement (Reward)

1. The "point system" in *Harry Potter* books is an example of reinforcement. For example, in *Harry Potter and the Sorcerer's Stone*, Dumbledore awards extra points to Gryffindor for the accomplishments of Hermione, Ron, Harry and Neville, seen here.

2. Other examples of positive reinforcement with house points, but also negative punishment with points taken away, can be found here.

3. Health authorities around the world set up positive reinforcement systems to encourage people to be vaccinated against the Covid-19 virus. Israel, for example, gave vaccinated people a *Green Pass* card that allowed them entry into certain businesses and events and decreased quarantine restrictions. The details are described in this article and at the website found here. In the US, positive reinforcers

offered to people who chose to be vaccinated included free beer, Krispy Kreme donuts, free rides on Uber and Lyft, tickets to the Great America theme park, and even a $1 million dollar lottery. Details are described here.

[Note: Potential problems associated with using positive reinforcement of vaccination—including the overjustification effect mentioned in the chapter on motivation and emotion—are described here.]

4. Some examples of cases in which maladaptive behavior is reinforced accidentally or unintentionally, and with unintended results:

- A child throws a fit in a grocery store and the parent gives her child a treat to stop the tantrum. The child's disruptive behavior will have been positively reinforced and the parent's reinforcing of that behavior will itself be made more likely in the future through negative reinforcement (when the disruptive behavior stops).
- Your dog is barking for food while you are eating dinner. You give him a morsel from your plate, and he stops barking. You will be encouraged (through negative reinforcement) to feed him from the table in the future and the dog will have been encouraged (through positive reinforcement) to come back to the table for more food.
- When Aidan was little, he liked to "cruise" around his crib, playing with toys and holding onto the sides. One day he threw his stuffed Curious George toy out of the crib. His mother didn't want him throwing things, so to give Aidan the idea that he had "hurt" the toy, she picked it up somewhat melodramatically said "Oh, poor Georgie! Poor Georgie!". When she put George back into the crib, Aidan immediately threw him out again. Obviously his mother's little dramatic turn served as a positive reinforcer of the precise behavior she wanted to discourage.
- Some people have a stronger tendency than others to experience anxiety and to engage in worrying about the future, such as whether they will pass a driving test, get a coveted job, be accepted into a club or academic program, or even get to the airport on time to catch their flight. The tendency to worry can develop into various kinds of anxiety disorders (see the chapter on psychological disorders). You might think that if anxious worrying is not followed by the bad consequences these people expect, they would stop worrying so much. That is not what happens, though, partly because good outcomes (passing the test, getting the job, joining the club, or catching the flight) serve as positive reinforcers for everything that preceded them, including worrying. We know of one case, for example, in which a man had been diagnosed with a potentially dangerous form of skin cancer but had to wait three weeks for the surgery that would tell him whether the tumor had spread or could be safely excised. As was his life-long custom, he imagined the worst possible outcome with all its attendant consequences (e.g.,

chemotherapy accompanied by nausea and hair loss, disfigurement, shortened life span, and the like). When at last the surgery was successful and no further treatment was necessary, he confided that he had been afraid to expect a good outcome because doing so would "jinx" him and lead to disastrous illness. The end result is that his tendency to worry about things large and small has once again been positively reinforced!
- A classic example of how superstitious behaviors can develop as a result of accidental reinforcement of those behaviors comes from B.F. Skinner's laboratory when he arranged for hungry pigeons to be reinforced with food on a fixed interval schedule (see below) regardless of how they behaved. This meant that the availability of food reinforced whatever each bird happened to be doing at the time it appeared. As a result, the birds learned to repeat the behavior that had apparently, but not really, caused food to appear. These "superstitious" behaviors differed from bird to bird, and including turning a certain number of times in one direction or another, bobbing the head, flapping the wings, and the like.
- The 1-min video available here shows a pigeon developing superstitious behavior patterns.
- The consequences of accidental reinforcement are provided by the endless examples of human superstitions, including those of professional athletes who engage in specific rituals prior to hitting a golf ball or shooting a free-throw that they insist help them to perform at their best because they are followed on a partial reinforcement schedule, at least, by success. Failure to execute these rituals can upset the athlete enough to disrupt performance (a punishing experience), and thus further solidify belief in the ritual's importance.
- Sports fans, too, develop superstitious behaviors. We know of one Pittsburgh Steelers football fan who insists that wearing exactly the same black and gold clothing and eating the same brand of lime-flavored chips while watching the team's games will ensure victory (he is wrong about that).
- Some college students always take tests wearing the "lucky" outfit they were wearing the last time they aced a test.

5. Cartoon examples:

- There is a Hi & Lois cartoon that shows a little girl laying happily between her parents in their bed and she is thinking to herself "This is great! I'll have to wake up crying in the middle of the night more often." Here, the parents have reinforced behavior that they probably didn't mean to reinforce. You can see the cartoon here.
- There is a cartoon showing a dog in a harness talking to another dog as Pavlov looks on. The first dog says "Watch what I can make Pavlov do. As soon as I drool, he'll smile and write in his little book." You can find the cartoon here.

- A cartoon at this site shows two rats in a cage. One says to the other "Boy, have I got this guy conditioned! Every time I press the bar down, he drops in a piece of food."
  [See also Table 4.1 below.].

Examples of Negative Reinforcement

1. We learn to push our TV's mute button through negative reinforcement; pressing it eliminates the sounds of a commercial or a commentator that we can't stand.
2. We learn to take pain relievers through negative reinforcement because after doing so, our pain disappears.
3. We learn to get out of unpleasant social situations through negative reinforcement, as when we end a boring date early after complaining of an imaginary headache.
4. A fear of spiders can be solidified through negative reinforcement if the fearful person escapes anxiety by changing the channel when a spider appears on a nature show.
5. We learn to fasten our seat belts through negative reinforcement because doing so stops that annoying reminder chime.
6. We learn to move to a different location when doing so eliminates annoying interference or static on our mobile phone.
   [See also Table 4.1 below.]

Examples of Punishment

1. Positive Punishment

   - Karen is an aggressive driver but she now stops for red lights because she received punishment in the form of an expensive traffic ticket for running a red light last week.
   - A child who discovers that pulling on the family cat's tail will result in being scratched by that cat will probably not do it again in the future.
   - Here and here are 30-s videos of office workers doing things whose consequences will make them unlikely to do in the future.

   - Numerous examples of positive punishment are contained in "Jackass" videos showing people doing stupid, dangerous things that result in pain or injury. You can find a compilation of such videos here. Videos like these allow the opportunity to help students understand that the negative consequences of a behavior does not define those consequences as punishment unless they result in a reduction of that behavior in the future. Many of the people in Jackass videos continue engaging in ill-advised activities.

2. Negative Punishment

- In Australia, child care support payments can be removed if parents did not get their children vaccinated, as described here.
- People who are convicted of driving while intoxicated may lose their driving privileges.
- People convicted of serious crimes can be sent to prison (freedom removed).
- A person who cheats on a partner may find that the partner ends the relationship.
- In a divorce settlement, a neglectful or abusive parent may lose child visitation rights
- A convicted felon may lose the right to vote while in prison.
- A passenger who disrupts a commercial airline flight may be banned for life from flying on that airline.
- A professional athlete who is found to have bet on the outcome of games may be banned from the sport for life.
- A misbehaving child might lose TV or computer privileges at home or be placed in a time-out room at school (time-out is designed to remove positive aspects of the environment).

3. Positive and Negative Punishment Combined
In *Harry Potter and the Order of the Phoenix* Dolores Umbridge punishes Harry Potter for saying that Voldemort has returned. Although it is true that Voldemort has returned, Umbridge has been sent by the Minister of Magic to ensure that Dumbledore and Harry do not try to seize the Minister of Magic's power by fabricating a lie. Here are the various forms of punishment used:

- Umbridge gives Harry detention (he has to come to her office at night), an example of negative punishment.
- Harry has to write lines "I must not tell lies.", an example of positive punishment.
- Harry has to use a "black quill" that makes his hand bleed with his hand-writing of the lines, an example of positive punishment
These forms of punishment are acted out in this 2:30-min scene.

In *Harry Potter and the Chamber of Secrets*, Ron and Harry take the Weasley's car and fly to Hogwarts after not being able to get onto the train at Track 9 ¾. The consequence of taking the car, and that it was spotted by muggles (non-magical people), was that Mr. Weasley is "facing an inquiry at work". Mrs. Weasley sends Ron a "howler" (a note brought by an owl that yells at the recipient, which is embarrassing—positive punishment). She threatens him with "If you put another toe out of line, we will bring you straight home" (negative punishment). You can see 1-min scene with the howler here.

Other *Harry* Potter examples:

- In *Harry Potter and the Prisoner of Azkaban*, Professor Snape gives Ron Weasley detention for talking back and Professor McGonagall takes away Neville's Hogsmeade visits for leaving passwords around and leading to Serious Black getting into a dormitory. This is an example of negative punishment.
- In *Harry Potter and the Half-Blood Prince*, Professor Snape gives Harry Potter detention for getting into a fight and seriously hurting Draco (negative punishment).
- Dobby the house elf punishes himself (bangs head on the dresser) for saying he hadn't met many decent wizards. This is an example of positive punishment. The 2-min scene where Dobby introduces himself and ultimately punishes himself can be seen here.

More examples of these concepts (along with descriptions) can also be found by scrolling through the slides on this website.

Table 4.1 Examples of positive and negative reinforcement and positive and negative punishment organized into four cells

	Add something	Remove something
Increase behavior	**Positive reinforcement** * Clapping and praising a small child for buttoning his shirt on his own * Giving a child money for high marks on a report card * Getting an "A +" for working hard in a class * Giving a gift card to a research participant * Throwing a ball for a dog after it retrieves the ball * Getting a bonus at work for a job well done * Giving a child an ice cream cone after good behavior on a shopping trip * Continuing to play with a puppy when it bites you * Giving a reward for returning a lost item (purse, bike, dog, etc.) * Getting a ribbon for participating in a race * Getting a prize for the best cake in a baking contest * Receiving frequent flyer miles for taking a flight	**Negative reinforcement** * Pain relief after taking a pain pill * End a boring date early after complaining of a (real or concocted) headache * Learning to fasten our seat belt because doing so stops that annoying reminder chime * Giving a tantruming child a treat to stop the tantrum (child gets positive reinforcement, parent gets negative reinforcement) * Bringing a crying baby into bed to stop the crying. (Negative reinforcement for parent; positive reinforcement for child) * Replacing the battery in a smoke alarm when it starts beeping * Cleaning your room so that your parents will stop nagging you about it * Crying "uncle" to stop someone who is twisting your arm * Paying a bill to stop unwanted "past-due" notices or phone reminders

(continued)

Operant Conditioning 141

Table 4.1 (continued)

	Add something	Remove something
	* Winning an Oscar for outstanding acting * Receiving a trophy for winning a soccer tournament	*Banging on the apartment wall to stop noisy neighbors from screaming at each other * Putting in earplugs to reduce the noise level on an airplane flight
Decrease behavior	**Positive punishment** * Swatting a dog with a newspaper for peeing on the floor * Spanking a child for running into the street * Shock delivered to a dog by a collar that senses when the dog is beyond the perimeter of the yard * Getting a speeding ticket for driving too fast * Scolding a teenager for sneaking out of the house at night * Corporal or capital punishment for committing a crime * Getting burned when touching a hot stove * Getting sick after eating spoiled food * Writing lines, such as "I must not lie" when caught in a lie * Getting a fine for overdue books at the library * Being charged a fee for paying a credit card bill late * Being injured due to overexertion during an extensive workout	**Negative punishment** * Taking away a child's dessert for throwing toys after being told to stop * Taking away a teenager's driving privileges for staying out past curfew * Sending a child to her room or putting her in time out for fighting with a sibling * Taking away the toy that children were fighting over * Being put in time out for being disruptive in class * Loss of recess time for acting out in class * Being sent to prison for committing a crime (due to loss of freedom, but also appears as positive punishment because of imposition of discomfort and danger) * Taking away a teenager's computer or phone for visiting inappropriate websites * Taking your child away from the park when he child behaves badly * Being made to stay after school for bad behavior

Schedules of Reinforcement

1. Examples of continuous reinforcement:

   - A vending machine dispenses items every time money is inserted.
   - An ATM provides cash every time a customer enters the correct PIN.
   - Water comes out of a fountain or faucet every time we push the button or open the tap.
   - A SCUBA system provides oxygen to a diver with every inhalation.
   - A locked door opens each time you insert and turn the correct key or type in the correct code.

- Emergency services personnel answer every time 911 is dialed.
- Early in training, you give your dog a treat every time it approximates the behavior you are trying to teach.
- You have a great meal every time you go to your favorite restaurant.
- You always have fun when you go to parties at your best friend's house.
- Your romantic partner is always loving and supportive, no matter what the situation.
- You throw a pizza party for your employees every time they meet the day's production quota.

2. Examples of Partial Reinforcement: Fixed-Interval

- A worker is paid once a week or once a month.
- A child gets an allowance once a week.
- You throw a pizza party for your employees every Friday afternoon.
- A retiree receives a social security check on the fourth Wednesday of each month.
- You take your family out for dinner twice a month.
- An author gets a royalty check twice a year.
- A new employee gets a two-week vacation once a year.
- Listeners are not eligible to win prizes from a radio call-in quizzes until 10 days have passed since the last time they won.
- A car dealer gives customers free car washes, but only once a month.

3. Examples of Partial Reinforcement: Variable Interval

- A university teacher gives bonus points for class attendance every five days, on average.
- A grade school teacher gives bonus points or stickers to children who are seated and on-task when a tone sounds at random intervals.
- Drivers are stopped by police on a random basis and given gift cards if they are wearing their seatbelts.
- Many online businesses run their loyalty programs through apps that keep track of what customers buy, and when. The app can be programed to give a discount or some other reward to the first person who orders something through the app during a certain time period. After that reward has been dispensed, another will not be given until a certain amount of time has passed, at which point the first person to make a purchase on the app gets a reward. The time delay can vary randomly from one minute to eight hours.
- A beachcomber finds something of value after spending unpredictably varying amounts of time wandering along the beach with a metal detector.

Operant Conditioning   143

- No matter what you do or do not do, your romantic partner becomes interested in sex only now and then, and you never know when the next time will be.
- You stay in touch by email with your favorite aunt who occasionally sends you a nice check.

4. Examples of Partial Reinforcement: Fixed Ratio

- A rat in a Skinner box is given a food reward after every five bar-presses.
- Factory employees are paid for every fifth item they assemble or produce or repair.
- A tech-support agent is allowed to take a 15-min break after completing, say, 10 customer calls.
- A car salesperson gets a bonus after every 10th sale.
- A newspaper delivery person is paid a fixed amount for every paper delivered.
- Credit card customers get one airline mile for every dollar they spend using their card.
- Coffee shop customers with loyalty cards get every 10th cup free.
- A wine store gives customers a $5.00 gift card every time they have spent a certain amount in the store.
- Some stores and credit cards give back a percentage of the amount their customers spend.
- Airlines give members of their frequent flyer programs free first-class upgrades or elevated membership perks for flying a certain number of miles.

5. Examples of Partial Reinforcement: Variable ratio

- A pigeon in a Skinner box will get food after a varying number of key-pecks, averaging perhaps, around 10.
- Casino slot machines pay out only after an unpredictable number of button-pushes.
- For most golfers, good shots come only now and then, and often when least expected.
- A real estate agent will get a sale only after an unpredictable number of house showings.
- A predator in the wild will make a kill only after a variable number of attempts at prey.
- A professional baseball player will get on base or hit a home run only after a varying number of times at bat. This is why batting averages of about 35% are considered quite high.
- The business apps mentioned in the variable interval section above can be programed to dispense rewards after a random number of purchases. This the customer never knows how many purchases will be required to get a reward.

- A person trying to catch fish will be successful only after a varying number of casts.
- People may play the lottery every day, but will be rewarded with a prize only now and then (if at all) and after an unpredictable number of ticket purchases.

Discriminative Stimuli

1. A pigeon learns that pressing the response key in a Skinner box will not bring a food reward unless a green light is on. The green light is a discriminative stimulus for the availability of food rewards, and if the pigeon's behavior is affected by the light, that behavior is said to be under stimulus control.
2. You have learned that when the Krispy Kreme sign is lit, the donuts are fresh.
3. You have learned that when the "open" sign at your favorite pizza place is not lit, you will not be able to order a pizza.
4. You have learned that when on a date, but not at work, giving a compliment about someone's appearance may be reinforced.
5. You have learned that parties, but not funerals, are places where you will be rewarded with laughs for telling jokes.
6. Bears searching for food in Yosemite National Park campgrounds tend to break into minivans; it appears that they have learned that minivans are more likely than other vehicles to contain the goodies they are after.
   [Reference: Breck, S. W., Lance, N., & Seher, V. (2009). Selective foraging for anthropogenic resources by black bears: Minivans in Yosemite National Park. *Journal of Mammology, 90*(5), 1041–1044.]
7. You have learned that when your boss is red-faced and complaining about slow progress around the office, it is not a good moment to ask for extra vacation time.
8. You have learned that the presence of ominous, dark clouds means that you should bring an umbrella with you when you leave home.

Shaping

1. A clear example of shaping can be found when teaching toddlers to eat with a spoon. You can't expect toddlers to have adult-like skills immediately, so you might start by using praise to reinforce them for behaviors that vaguely approximate the target behaviors, and then raise the reinforcement criterion such that the child must display a slightly more advanced behavior in order to get praise. So you might first give praise for holding a spoon, but later give praise only when the spoon is held in the proper orientation, and even later when it is used to bring food toward the mouth and so on.

[Note: The shaping process in this case is also reinforced by the food itself as the child finds ways to gradually more efficiently transport it from dish to mouth.]

2. Shaping is used to teach animals many kinds of tricks. Here is a 2-min video showing the use of a "clicker," praise, and food to provide primary and secondary reinforcement to teach a dog to pick up a collar. Notice that the behavior is reinforced with operant conditioning but the association of the clicker with food would have been learned through classical conditioning.
3. Descriptions and videos about shaping and dog training can be found on this website.
4. At the top of this webpage is a video that demonstrates how to teach a dog to spin by shaping the behavior. The rest of the webpage demonstrates successive steps (shaping) to teaching a dog to roll over.
5. Language learning, especially second-language learning, occurs partly through shaping. You are rewarded in Spanish 101 for knowing and being able to use some basic grammar, but those same skills would be insufficient for Spanish 201, where more advanced language skills will be required to gain the same level of reward.
6. Similarly, as you try out your developing language skills in an international setting, your pronunciation will improve as you receive positive reinforcement for ever-better performance and punishment (i.e., not being understood) for errors.
7. Shaping is also at the heart of improving skill at athletics, from golf and weight-lifting to football and swimming to bike-riding and skate-boarding, as adjustments in behavior are rewarded by better outcomes.

Extinction in Operant Conditioning

1. You go to the vending machine every afternoon for a snack. You insert your money and select your snack. Every day the machine delivers a snack. Today you went to the vending machine and inserted your money and the machine did not deliver your snack. You plan to stop using the vending machine. Because reinforcement is or should be continuous for a vending machine, failure to deliver your snack will result in almost immediate extinction of your behavior (putting money in the machine).
2. As a psychology student you earn extra credit for participating in experiments. If extra credit is no longer offered, you may stop signing up for experiments.
3. Every day for the last week you have been texting someone you would like to know better, but have received no replies. Eventually, through the process of extinction, you give up and stop texting.

4. A child's misbehavior in class may be (inadvertently) rewarded by the attention it gets from the teacher and/or other students. The behavior might extinguish if it no longer attracted attention, and especially if more appropriate behaviors were rewarded instead. The process of withdrawing attention by ignoring the behavior is an example of extinction.
5. A humorous take on the frustration that may accompany an extinction experience can be found in this cartoon. It shows a dog in a prison cell talking to a cellmate about what happened to get him imprisoned. He says: "Bells rings, I get a treat…bell rings, I get a treat. It went on that way for days. Then, out of the blue…bells rings, I get *nothing at all*!! Nada! I mean, can you seriously call my attack unprovoked?" The title of the cartoon is "The dark truth about Pavlov's dog."
6. And here is an example of a case in which extinction should have taken place but didn't. One of the authors had a cousin Howard who, when he passed away in 2013 owed his wife, Gladys, $42 million. How could this be? Because throughout their 50+ years of marriage, whenever she contradicted something he said about facts or dates or events from the past, he always said "Wanna bet?" At first, the bets were only for a dollar or so, but over the years, the stakes rose and often included a double or nothing challenge. Howard's problem was that Gladys's memory has always been virtually perfect and remained so until her death. She could tell you the names and birthdays of everyone in her extended family on both sides, not to mention when she and Howard had parties, went on vacations, etc., and who was with them and what happened at each event. The bottom line is that over all those years, Howard NEVER won a bet yet he never stopped betting with Gladys.
[Note: This example provides an opportunity to discuss how cognitive factors—in this case, unrealistic optimism—can overcome the extinguishing effects of continuous punishment.]

Learned Helplessness

1. The classic apparatus used to study learned helplessness can be seen here. In the image, a dog is jumping over a divider to get from a floor that is delivering shock to one that is not. Learned helplessness will occur after experiences in which the dog cannot avoid the shock and then doesn't try to escape it even when escape is possible.
2. An example of this same laboratory paradigm with humans can be found in this experiment. The researchers not only replicated the results of helplessness research with animals but showed that helplessness tends to develop more easily in people with an external locus of control (see the chapter on personality).
[Reference: Hiroto, D. S. (1974). Locus of control and learned helplessness. *Journal of Experimental Psychology, 102,* 187–193.]

3. A form of learned helplessness appears in some people who have been protesting and fighting for various kinds of social change, but after seeing nothing changing they may cease their activism.
4. Learned helplessness may appear in people who experience repeated failure in their efforts to lose weight, stop smoking, give up alcohol or other drugs, eventually leading them to stop trying to change.
5. Some people who experience domestic violence show signs of learned helplessness in that they may stay in an abusive relationship even when it might be possible to leave it.
6. Some students, especially those without well-developed study skills, may find that no matter how hard they try, they are unable to achieve grades that are high enough to stay on track for graduation or to avoid going on probation. Without guidance to improve study skills, some of these students will assume that there is nothing they can do to succeed academically and may eventually drop out.
7. Learned helplessness is developed in circus elephants from an early age so that they do not to try to escape. When they are young, they are tethered to ground stakes by ropes that are too strong to break. Once they learn that escape is impossible, they no longer try, even when tethered to much thinner ropes that they are strong enough to break. A description of learned helplessness in circus elephants with some images can be found here.
8. It might be valuable to contrast examples of learned helplessness with examples of programs designed to promote learned optimism, resilience in the face of stressors and other concepts associated with positive psychology (see the chapter on psychological disorders). Here are some relevant references:

- Bradshaw, B.G., Richardson, G.E., Kumpfer, K., Carlson, J., Starchfield, J., Overall, J., Brooks, A.M., & Kulkarni, K. (2007). Determining the efficacy of a resiliency training approach in adults with type 2 diabetes. *The Diabetes Educator, 33,* 650–659.
- Waite, P. J., & Richardson, G. E. (2004). Determining the efficacy of resiliency training in the work site. *Journal of Allied Health, 33,* 178–183.
- Schulman, P. (1999) Applying learned optimism to increase sales productivity. *Journal of Personal Selling & Sales Management, 19*(1), 31–37. https://doi.org/10.1080/08853134.1999.10754157.
- Chadwick, M. (2019). A Reflection on harnessing learned optimism, resilience and team growth behaviour in order to support student groups. *Student Success, 10,* 104–111. https://doi.org/10.5204/ssj.v10i3.1410.

Applications of Operant Conditioning

Token Economies

1. Examples of token economies are shown in this 2-min video of children with autism, directed at teachers and including a brief description of how to set up a token economy. A longer (6-min) video, directed at parents and including a demonstration of three types of "tokens" can be found here.

2. Here is an application of a token economy to help children on hemodialysis to maintain weight.
   [Source: Magrab, P. R., & Papadopoulou, Z. L. (1977). The effect of a token economy on dietary compliance for children on hemodialysis. *Journal of Applied Behavior Analysis*, *10*(4), 573–578. https://pubmed.ncbi.nlm.nih.gov/599104/]

3. Here is an example of the use of token economies with children with autism during the Covid-19 lockdown in Italy.

   [Source: Degli Espinosa, F., Metko, A., Raimondi, M., Impenna, M., & Scognamiglio, E. (2020). A model of support for families of children with autism living in the COVID-19 lockdown: Lessons from Italy. *Behavior Analysis in Practice*, 1. https://doi.org/10.1007/s40617-020-00438-7]

4. When Helen was about 3 months old her pediatrician asked her mother how she was sleeping. Her mother said that she was sleeping through the night, but that her 4-year-old son Liam was waking her up at night. The pediatrician recommended a token economy in which Liam would earn a sticker every night that he didn't wake up his mom. After 3 stickers he could earn a trip to the gym at the college where his mother worked (a coveted prize). After 10 stickers he could earn a trip to the Museum of Science and Industry in Chicago (which was a full-day affair, including a ride on a commuter railroad, an even bigger prize). Liam immediately stopped waking his mother up and earned both prizes.

5. An example of using a kind of token economy in the classroom is provided by a professor who wanted to promote class participation in a large section of introductory psychology. Students who participated in class received coinlike tokens that they could exchange for extra credit. He found that students responded faster to the professor's questions and offered many more comments and questions when this token economy was introduced. The frequency of student questions and comments dropped again when tokens were no longer given, but students continued their quick responses to the professor's questions. By that time, apparently, the professor's social reinforcement was enough to encourage this aspect of classroom participation.

[Reference: Boniecki, K. A. & Moore, S. (2003). Breaking the silence: Using a token economy to reinforce classroom participation. *Teaching of Psychology, 30,* 224–227. https://doi.org/10.1207/S15328023TOP3003_05]

6. A home-based token economy was set up for "David" who, when he was about 5 years old had a hard time accepting defeat. In playing family board games he would get angry, frustrated and would cry whenever he lost a game. His parents instituted a token economy to change his behavior. They started a sticker chart and every time he lost a game and did not have a fit, they would place a sticker on the chart. Once David had earned 30 stickers, he was able to buy his most coveted toy at the time (the Bionicle, Makuta). This system immediately changed his behavior and he learned to accept defeat graciously. In fact, he sometimes would purposely lose games for the opportunity to earn a sticker!

7. The preceding example provides a good opportunity to discuss with students the need to carefully engineer token economies and other therapeutic operant conditioning programs so as to avoid unintended consequences. One of the authors once worked as a consultant at a school for children with behavior problems, where classroom misbehavior was put on extinction through the use of a time out room. This contingency worked well overall, but one disruptive child would, upon being reintroduced to the classroom after a brief time out period, immediately repeat the actions that got him put in time-out in the first place. That is not supposed to happen, and indeed, an investigation revealed that an interior wall between the time out room and an adjacent storage room did not go all the way to the ceiling. By scaling that wall, the youngster in question discovered that all the M&Ms used to provide reinforcement as part of various training programs were kept in the storage room. Needless to say, from his perspective, the "time out" room was anything but!

[Other examples of using operant principles in treatment programs are provided in the chapter on treatment of psychological disorders.]

Promoting Health and "Green" Behavior

1. An example of using positive reinforcement in the form of fun to encourage people to use stairs rather than an escalator can be found in this video.

2. In a 13-week field study in The Netherlands, commuters could earn daily rewards—including money and continued access to a free smartphone—by driving to work either before or after peak traffic hours, by switching to another mode of transportation, or by working from home. Results showed that rush-hour driving decreased and driving at other times and travel by other modes increased.

[Reference: Ben-Elia, E., & Ettema, D. (2011). Changing commuters' behavior using rewards: A study of rush-hour avoidance. *Transportation Research Part F: Traffic Psychology and Behaviour, 14*(5), 354–368. https://doi.org/10.1016/j.trf.2011.04.003.]

3. Another study showed that children will increase their intake of vegetables when they are rewarded for doing so.

 [Reference: Cooke, L. J., Chambers, L. C., Añez, E. V., Croker, H. A., Boniface, D., Yeomans, M. R., & Wardle, J. (2011). Eating for pleasure or profit: The effect of incentives on children's enjoyment of vegetables. *Psychological Science, 22*(2), 190–196. https://doi.org/10.1177/0956797610394662.]

4. Cities and states that charge a deposit on certain beverage containers and refund the money when the container is recycled illustrate another use of positive reinforcement to promote "green behavior." This 90-s video describes such programs.

5. An example of using punishment to treat a life-threatening disorder can be found in a case study of a child who developed chronic ruminative disorder at the age of 5 months. By the time he was hospitalized, he had been vomiting everything he ate for four months. All treatments had failed and with the child in critical condition at only 12 pounds, two psychologists suggested using mild electric shock whenever monitoring equipment indicated that pre-vomiting muscular contractions (reverse peristalsis) were occurring. It took only a few shocks to reverse the vomiting pattern, and after 12 days, vomiting had stopped altogether. The child's weight had increased 26 percent, and he was physically and psychologically healthy when tested six months, one year, and two years later. (Note: A photo of the child before and after treatment is included in the case report to illustrate the dramatic change.)
 [Reference: Lang, P. J., & Melamed, B. G. (1969). Case report: Avoidance conditioning therapy of an infant with chronic ruminative vomiting. *Journal of Abnormal Psychology, 74*(1), 1–8. https://doi.org/10.1037/h0027077.]

6. A similar case study, with photos, is available here.

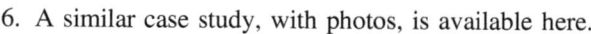

Observational Learning

1. The so-called Bobo doll studies are classic examples of observational learning. A 4-min video about the study, narrated by Albert Bandura, can be found here.
2. A list of examples of observational learning can be found here and here (including some cross-cultural examples and some illustrations).

3. On the subway in New York City one of your authors saw a child hitting his sister. After he had hit her several times, his mother turned, hit *him* and said, "Don't hit your sister!" [A question for your class: What aspect of the situation will be more influential? The punishment the boy received for hitting his sister, or the modeling of that same behavior by his mother?]
4. A similar scenario is presented in this cartoon that shows a mother smashing her kids' gaming console with a baseball bat while yelling "I have HAD it with you two and your violent video games!"
5. Some of the many things we can learn by observation include mechanical skills, social etiquette (e.g., table manners), situational anxiety, and attitudes (e.g., politics and religion), what foods are safe to eat, and objects and situations to fear.
6. A cartoon illustrates the fact that observational learning does not always take place. Some people seem unable to learn from other people's examples and have to learn things the hard way. The cartoon shows a group of kids looking at an outdoor basketball goal that has numerous hornets buzzing around a nest attached to the backboard. One of the kids says "Maybe we could play one quick game. They probably won't even know we're here."

Latent Learning

1. You may have learned the way to get to school or work even when you were a passenger in the car. So, although you didn't explicitly learn the directions, when you have to drive yourself you realize that you know the way.

   (Other examples appear in the chapter on cognition and cognitive abilities where we address cognitive maps, which we often develop more or less automatically.)

2. A list of examples of latent learning in both animals and humans can be found here.

3. A 10-min video describing the phenomenon of latent learning (and cognitive maps and observational learning) and the original experiment by Tolman & Honzik (1930) can be found here.
   [Source: Tolman, E. C., & Honzik, C. H. (1930). Introduction and removal of reward, and maze performance in rats. *University of California Publications in Psychology, 4*, 257–275.]

4. An example of latent learning in preverbal infants is described in this study.

 [Source: Campanella, J., & Rovee-Collier, C. (2005). Latent learning and deferred imitation at 3 months. *Infancy*, *7*(3), 243–262. https://psycnet.apa.org/record/2005-07635-002]

Non-associative Learning

Habituation

1. You no longer feel your eyeglasses, watch, belt, or shoes after having them on for some time.
2. After some time in a musty room, you no longer notice the musty smell.
3. After half an hour in a waiting room, you no longer notice the ticking of a large wall clock.
4. If that clock suddenly marks the hour with a loud chime, you will once again notice it through a process called dishabituation.
5. Examples of applying habituation and dishabituation to study cognitive development, including the development of object permanence (see the chapter on development) can be found in this 8:25-min video which includes some information at the beginning about the DVD "What Babies Can Do" (first minute). Nice data (plotted graphically) showing looking time decreasing with repeated exposure (habituation) and then the ability to discriminate between stimuli with looking time. The video points out the need for perception, eye movements and memory to do this task.

[Other examples of habituation and dishabituation are given in the chapter on sensation and perception.]

Sensitization

1. While breathlessly exploring a dark, spooky house, you might scream, run, or violently throw something in response to the unexpected creaking of a door.
2. After first taking drugs of abuse, users may become increasingly sensitive to them for a time (this is the opposite of drug tolerance) and this may help account for their strong wanting, or motivation, to repeat the experience.
3. People can become hypersensitive to certain otherwise harmless environmental substances such as pollen or cat dander, and the result is allergies.
4. After being badly frightened by a sudden loud noise (say, a car crash near the restaurant patio where you are having lunch), you may become hypersensitive to

much less intense sounds such as a car horn, for a while at least. In some cases of PTSD, this hypersensitivity can be long-lasting.
5. In water torture, drops of water repeatedly strike the same spot, such as the forehead, and over time the discomfort of the impact, which was zero at the beginning, increases dramatically.

Memory

5

Memory is an expansive topic that touches on many other areas of psychology. There are numerous classroom activities and short experimental protocols that are engaging and demonstrate important principles of memory. Moreover, students can readily apply many of the topics in this chapter, such as levels of processing, to enhance their study skills and habits.

Students are often intrigued both by people with exceptional memories, such as London taxi drivers, as well as by failures of memory, such as in false memory. Finally, there are several myths about memory than can be addressed, including: memory is like a videorecorder and eyewitness testimony is highly accurate and reliable.

Memory Storage

1. When asked to reflect on their memory, students often focus on the content of long-term memory storage. Of course, this is an important component of memory. Here are some pictorial examples of ways to conceptualize storage that could be used to compare and contrast to human memory storage.

   - A self-storage facility

   - Containers for dry goods

- Types of computer storage on the cloud

- Modular shelving/storage

- Computer memory example 1, example 2, and example 3

- A video example of a representation of long-term memory can be seen in the movie "Inside Out". A one-minute video clip exemplifying the characterization of LTM in that movie can be found here.

Examples of Sensory Memory (Sensory Registers)

1. Iconic (Visual) Memory also *Visual Persistence:*

    - Visual persistence creates a "sparkler's trail effect" as shown here and in a 40-s video here.

    - You might find that a short presentation of a photograph leaves a brief visual trace.

    - You're looking at your cell phone and its battery dies. You have a very brief memory of the screen before it went black.

Memory Storage

- You're looking at your computer screen just before the screensaver turns on. You have a brief memory of the screen before the screensaver appears.

- When magicians make a coin "vanish" by feigning its transfer from one hand to the other, they try to cause a quick reflection of light just before the coin goes out of view. They believe that, thanks to the persistence of vision, this increases the effectiveness of the illusory transfer of the coin. This 1-min video shows what this phenomenon looks like.

- Several everyday examples of iconic memory are available at this website.

- A 3:16-min demonstration of the classic Sperling (1960) experiment of iconic memory can be found here.

[Reference: Sperling, G. (1960). The information available in brief visual presentations. *Psychological Monographs: General and Applied, 74*(11), 1–29.]

- The thaumatrope (magic circle), which demonstrates visual persistence, is shown in a 15-s video here and directions for making a thaumatrope/pedemascope can be found here.

2. Echoic (Auditory) Memory

- You use echoic memory when you are processing spoken language. Interestingly, sometimes you have to ask speakers to repeat themselves because although you heard what they said (sensation), you didn't process it (perception). This seems to be particularly common when people are focused on their cell phones and hear something without fully processing it, which can lead to them saying, "Wait, what?" when they realize that they have missed some information that they think they might be interested in hearing. There is a brief period where the sound is still available in echoic memory.

- You are using your echoic memory as you listening to music, particularly if there is a pause in the music and you remember the last few notes before the pause.

- Other sounds that you can store in echoic memory include birds singing and the ocean lapping on the shore. You might play sounds like this and then stop them while the students attend to their echoic memory of the sounds.

3. Haptic (Touch) Memory

    - You are using touch memory when you run your finger over a textured surface, like a zipper, sheep skin, a dog/cat or your hair and remember what it feels like in the moment after you stop touching it.
    - Your memory of touching a hot stove persists over time after you have withdrawn your hand. The initial memory is sensory.
    - When you stop typing on a keyboard or on your phone, as you draw your hand away you may have a brief memory for the tactile sensation of typing.

Short-Term (Working) Memory

1. When you have a conversation with someone, you think about what they are saying and use that information to frame a response. You are using your working memory to do this.
2. Reading a phone number and repeating it over and over until you call the number uses STM or working memory. This was a particularly important use of working memory when rotary phones were common because of the delay imposed between dialing each number. This graphic of a woman using a rotary phone seems to highlight the challenge to working memory, which may be less obvious to today's students who are not familiar with rotary phones.
3. In "repeat after me" songs or during wedding or swearing-in ceremonies, you use your working memory to remember the phrase to be repeated.
4. Perhaps students will be more familiar with the challenge to working memory of remembering all the items that a restaurant server described as "Today's Specials". The challenge to the server of remembering all of the items in the daily specials is different, as it relies on long-term memory.
5. Recalling a debit or credit card number you just looked at while completing an online shopping order.
6. Remembering an authentication code presented on one webpage as you prepare to enter it into another.
7. You are planning a birthday party and you know that 10 children are coming. When you learn that Suzie and Isaiah cannot attend, you have to retrieve the original number of children expected, subtract 2 and substitute "8" as the

number of children coming. That new number will be held in working memory and may be placed in long-term memory.

8. While baking you try to add multiple ingredients in the appropriate quantities without looking back at the recipe. This is more taxing when using a new recipe than when using one that may have traces in long-term memory.
9. After looking at visual instructions, remembering the order of steps to fold/create a magazine box, a paper airplane or origami figure that you haven't made before.
10. While cooking, keeping track of which food is in which covered saucepan on the stove.
11. Attention is related to working and short-term memory. Servers at restaurants have to use attention to update their goal sets as they go through their workday, constantly updating orders and keeping track of tables and the status of their orders.
12. Other tasks that involve or require working memory:

- Reading
- Reasoning
- Solving problems
- Playing games
- Doing mental calculations (e.g., adding numbers, calculating a tip)
- Computer-language learning
- Following directions
- Telling a story
- Listening to a joke
- Ordering a meal
- Dialing a phone number
- Driving a car
- Imagining the route you're going to take to get to a destination
  Note: you might challenge your students to consider what cognitive tasks one can do *without* working memory. The number of items on that list will probably be quite small, as in zero.

13. Classic demonstrations/experiments of the capacity of working memory include:

- Memory span task: an example of a digit span test can be found here.

- The phonological similarity effect is observed in immediate serial recall tasks in which, for example, the letters *c, b, d, v* are recalled less accurately than *c, r, m, k,* and *cat, fad, pan, map* are recalled less accurately than *bar, kid, sun, toe*.

[Source: Chow, M., Macnamara, B. N., & Conway, A. R. (2016). Phonological similarity in working memory span tasks. *Memory & Cognition, 44* (6), 937–949.]

- A self-administered phonological similarity effect test can be found here.

- Classic empirical demonstrations of the capacity of short-term memory are described in these articles:
  Miller, G. (1956). The magical number seven, plus or minus two: Some limits on our capacity for processing information. *The Psychological Review, 63*, 81–97.
  Peterson, L. R., & Peterson, M. J. (1959). Short-term retention of individual verbal items. *Journal of Experimental Psychology, 58*(3), 193–198.

Long-Term Memory

1. Examples of classic quotes that summarize one of the prevailing questions in memory... Why do we remember some things and not others?... and a partial response, namely the importance of attention and depth of processing, include:

   - *Of some (experiences), no memory survives the instance of their passage. Of others, it is confined to a few moments, hours or days. Others, again, leave vestiges that are indestructible, and by means of which may be recalled as long as life endures. How can we explain these differences?* (James, 1890, p. 643)

   James, W. (1890). *Principles of psychology*. Holt.

   - *The time you spend thinking about material you are reading and relating it to previously stored material is about the most useful thing you can do in learning any new subject matter.* (Wickelgren, 1977, p. 346)

   Wickelgren, W. A. (1977). *Learning and memory*. Prentice Hall.

   - *Memory is assisted by anything that makes an impression on a powerful passion, inspiring fear, for example or wonder, shame or joy.* (*Bacon, 1620, 2000,* as cited by McGaugh, 2015, p. 15)

   McGaugh, J. L. (2015). Consolidating memories. *Annual Review of Psychology, 66*, 1–24

2. Types of long-term memory are shown in the figure and examples below:

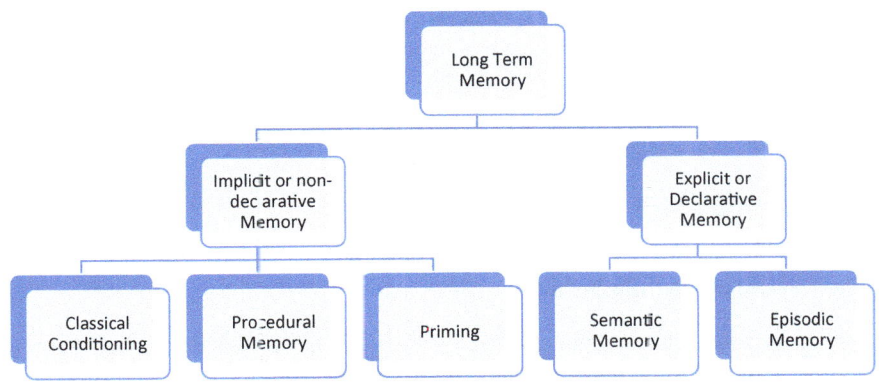

(Cameron, L. Lecture Notes)

3. Implicit (Non-Declarative) Memory

   - Classical Conditioning (see the chapter on learning)
   - Procedural Memory (e.g., how to ride a bicycle, play a musical instrument, swim, tie your shoes, make a cup of coffee, type on a keyboard, dance, do a cartwheel, tie a tie, drive a car, climb stairs, fold laundry, perform a mirror-tracing task). Another example is the case in which you can only recall an entry code or other number by using a key pad to actually punch it in.
   - Priming (see the chapter on thinking and cognitive abilities)

4. Explicit (Declarative) Memory: Semantic

   - Remembering that the freezing point is 32 degrees Fahrenheit, that a red light means stop, that Madison is the capital of Wisconsin, that Barack Obama won the 2008 presidential election, that the LA Lakers played the Miami heat in the 2020 NBA finals, that Michael Jordan played for the Chicago Bulls, that Emma Watson played Hermoine in the *Harry Potter* movies.
   - Remembering the meaning of the words *run, dog, pony* and *house*.

5. Explicit (Declarative) Memory: Episodic

   - Remembering the surprise birthday party you had for your best friend, your high school graduation, your first day at college, taking a quiz in your psychology class last week, watching the LA Lakers playing the Miami Heat in the 2020 NBA finals (in the bubble created due to the Covid-19 pandemic), a road trip you took with your family when you were in middle school, watching an episode of The Bachelorette with your friends last week.
   - Remembering where you were and with whom when participating as part of contact tracing during a pandemic.

[Source: Garry, M., Hope. L., Zajac, R., Verrall, A.J., & Robertson, J.M. (2021). Contact tracing: A memory task with consequences for public health. *Perspectives on Psychological Science, 16,* 175–187. doi:10.1177/1745691620978205].

Storing Long-Term Memories

1. Examples of how storing chunks of meaningful information can make it easier to remember that information:

   - It is easier to remember (262) 705–6588 as a phone number than to remember 2,627,056,588 as a string of numbers.
   - It is easier to remember the letters FBILOLMTVNBCBMW if you chunk them into the meaningful abbreviations FBI LOL MTV NBC BMW.
   - Here is an example of the fact that chunks can be quite complex. If you heard someone say, "The boy in the red shirt kicked his mother in the shin," you could probably repeat the sentence perfectly even though it contains twelve words and forty-three letters. You did it by organizing words rather than letters, in this case in three chunks: "The boy in the red shirt" was one chunk, "kicked his mother" was another, and "in the shin" was a third.
   - Experienced restaurant servers use chunking strategies to organize a lot of complex information about customers' orders into smaller chunks of information, allowing them to remember the details of numerous dinner orders without taking notes
   [Source: Bekinschtein, T. A., Cardozo, J., & Manes, F. F. (2008). Strategies of Buenos Aires waiters to enhance memory capacity in a real-life setting. *Behavioural Neurology, 20,* 65–70.]
   - Expert chess players can "chunk" items on a chess board if the pieces are arranged in a meaningful way, but not if they are random. This is described by chess master Viswanathan Anand here.
   (Another example can be found in the chapter on thinking and cognitive abilities.)
   [Source: Chase, W.G., & Simon, H.A. (1973). The Mind's Eye in Chess. In W.G. Chase (Ed.), *Visual Information Processing* (pp. 215-281) Academic Press. https://www.sciencedirect.com/science/article/pii/B9780121701505500111?via%3Dihub]

2. Examples of activities and drugs that can enhance memory storage (consolidation):

   - Repetition, as demonstrated by Ebbinghaus
   - Conditioning and reinforcement
   - Sleep

- Stimulants such as pentylenetetrazol, amphetamine, bemegride
- Stress hormones
- Caffeine
- Emotional arousal
[Source: McGaugh, J.L. (2015). Consolidating memories. *Annual Review of Psychology, 66,* 1-24.]

(Other examples are presented in the sections below on levels of processing and elaborative rehearsal).

Retrieval from Long-Term Memory

1. Examples of proactive interference

   - You learned Spanish in middle school and high school. When you start taking French in college, your knowledge of Spanish vocabulary interferes with your ability to learn French vocabulary and you keep calling a house "casa" rather than "maison". Or perhaps you use the indefinite article "una" from Spanish rather than the French "une".
   - Raneem El Welily, one of the best women squash players in the world has just retired. If she now tries to learn tennis and keeps forgetting that she gets a second serve, that would be an example of proactive interference; her prior knowledge of the rules of squash interfered with learning the rules of tennis.
   - For years, squash was scored such that only the server could score a point and games were played to 9 points. When the World Squash Federation first moved to a point-per-rally system with games played to 11 points, many people had trouble keeping track of the score. The old rule interfered with their ability to learn the new rule.
   - Yesterday when Professor Burling went to campus she parked in Lot A. Today she parked in Lot B. When she left school at the end of the day she started to walk towards Lot A, demonstrating proactive interference.
   - If you switch from an Android to an iPhone (or vice versa), knowledge of how to use the first device may interfere with your ability to use the new one.
   - If you switch from a Macintosh to a Windows computer (or vice versa), knowledge of how to use the first device may interfere with your ability to use the new one.
   - You learned the names of all of the players on your soccer team last season. This season you are having trouble remembering the names of your new teammates and you are confusing them with last season's team.
   - You have learned a dance routine until it was automatic. Now every time you try to learn a new routine the previous routine interferes.
   - If you have ever learned something incorrectly and then tried to correct it, you may have experienced proactive interference. Young children who take

music lessons once a week experience this. They learn an incorrect note, and at their lesson the next week, their teacher points out the mistake. However, it is very difficult to play the correct note because the old memory of the wrong note interferes with the new memory of the correct note.

2. Release from proactive interference

Note: this phenomenon was originally described in the context of short-term memory, but applications are often discussed in long-term-memory.

- Examples of word lists that demonstrate varying amounts of release from proactive interference based on semantic coding (from Wickens et al., 1976) are shown below. The critical question is whether memory is better on Trial 4, which it is when there is release from proactive interference.

Exp 1	Trial 1	Trial 2	Trial 3	Trial 4
Fruits	Banana	Pear	Lemon	Pineapple
	Peach	Grape	Plum	Lime
	Apple	Cherry	Apricot	Melon
Vegetables	Onion	Asparagus	Celery	
	Spinach	Potato	Radish	
	Carrot	Broccoli	Bean	
Flowers	Pansy	Violet	Honeysuckle	
	Lilac	Orchids	Clover	
	Daisies	Tulip	Poppy	
Meats	Salami	Ribs	Hamburger	
	Chops	Mutton	Veal	
	Roast	Sausage	Bacon	
Professions	Terms not provided			
Exp 2				
Non-alcoholic	Lemonade	Cider	Soda	Kool-aid
Beverages	Shake	Pop	Orangeade	Pepsi
	Cocoa	Juice	Cream	Tea
Alcoholic	Champagne	Bourbon	Gin	
Beverages	Brandy	Martini	Daiquiri	
	Vodka	Scotch	Rum	
Nonconsumable	Gasoline	Acid	Antifreeze	
Liquids	Ink	Kerosene	Perfume	
	Ammonia	Bleach	Mercury	
Meats	Salami	Ribs	Hamburger	
	Chops	Mutton	Veal	
	Roast	Sausage	Bacon	
Professions	Terms not provided			

[Source: Wickens, D. D., Dalezman, R. E., & Eggemeier, F. T. (1976). Multiple encoding of word attributes in memory. *Memory & Cognition, 4*(3), 307–310.]

3. Example of techniques or factors that induce release from proactive interference include:

- A context change between one set of items and the next (as in the word lists above)
- Directed forgetting of initial items
- Interpolated testing
   [Source: Bäuml, K. H. T., & Kliegl, O. (2013). The critical role of retrieval processes in release from proactive interference. *Journal of Memory and Language, 68*(1), 39-53.]
- Teaching a new skill at the end of a practice session can reduce proactive interference.
   [Source: Edwards, W. H. (2010). *Motor learning and control: From theory to practice*. Belmont, CA: Cengage Learning.]
- In one study, students were tested on information that was presented in a series of TV news stories. Memory generally declined for the series of stories, but not when the nature of the TV news stories changed on a critical trial. The change in the nature of the story resulted in a release from proactive interference.
   [Source: Gunter, B., Clifford, B. R., & Berry, C. (1980). Release from proactive interference with television news items: Evidence for encoding dimensions within televised news. *Journal of Experimental Psychology: Human Learning and Memory, 6*(2), 216–223. https://doi.org/10.1037/0278-7393.6.2.216]
- Changing the language in which information is presented.
   [Source: Goggin, J., & Wickens, D. D. (1971). Proactive interference and language change in short-term memory. *Journal of Verbal Learning and Verbal Behavior, 10*(4), 453-458.]
- Changing gender In one study, repeated presentation of female-typical occupations resulted in proactive interference but switching to male-typical occupations resulted in release of proactive interference in both college-aged and 6th grade participants. The gender stereotype was activated by presenting participants with tetrads of either "feminine" occupations (e.g., typist, school teacher, receptionist, babysitter, ballet dancer, singer, housekeeper, nurse, model, aerobics instructor, secretary, daycare worker, hair dresser, librarian, dressmaker, and decorator) or "masculine" occupational names (e.g., plumber, airline pilot, dentist, truck driver, firefighter, electrician, auto mechanic, surgeon, architect, coal miner, welder, police officer, industrial engineer, carpenter, brick layer, and janitor).
   [Source: Kee, D. W., Gregory-Domingue, A., Rice, K., & Tone, K. (2005). A release from proactive interference analysis of gender schema encoding for occupations in adults and children. *Learning and Individual Differences, 15*(3), 203-211.]

- Switching to recalling items on a grocery list after learning a set of numbers (e.g., phone numbers).
- A server trying to remember a table's food order without making notes could experience release from proactive interference if all of the food items came first and all the drink orders came second.

4. Examples of retroactive interference:

- You change your email address/password and later you can't remember your old email/password.
- A colleague gets married and you forget her maiden name now that you know her by her married name.
- After having learned French, you start learning Spanish and you forget the word for "house" in French because it is interfered with by the word "casa".
- You have learned the names of all of the players on your new soccer team. Now you are having trouble remembering the names of your teammates from last season.

5. The serial position effect provides examples of both proactive and retroactive interference.

- Here is an example of a typical serial position curve, showing primacy and recency effects and two forms of interference:

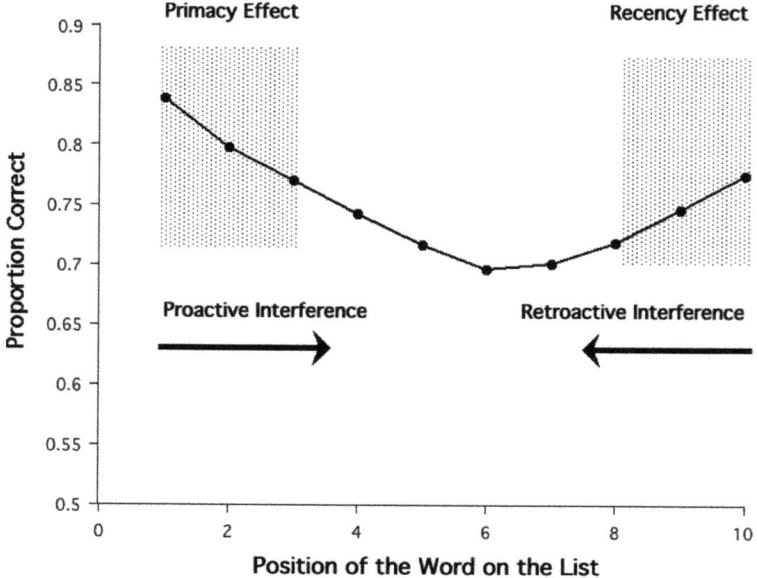

- The items at the beginning and end of a grocery list are likely to be remembered best.
- Information at the beginning and end of a speech will be remembered best.
- The information provided at the beginning and end of a television commercial are likely to be remembered best.
- Clicking on websites also demonstrates primacy and recency as people are more likely to click at the top and bottom of pages.
  [Source: Murphy, J. Hofacker, C., & Mizerski, R. (2006). Primacy and recency effects on clicking behavior. *Journal of Computer-Mediated Communication*, *11*(2), 522–535. https://doi.org/10.1111/j.1083-6101.2006.00025.x]
- Memory for information across a series of advertisements shows primacy and recency effects.
  [Source: Terry, W.S. (2005). Serial position effects in recall of television commercials. *Journal of General Psychology, 132*(2), 151-63. https://doi.org/10.3200/GENP.132.2.151-164.]
- An application of primacy and recency effects in human factors design can be found here.

Encoding and Levels of Processing

1. Examples of shallow encoding (visual or acoustic)

   - Focusing on visual features
   - Color-coding or re-writing notes
   - Making note cards (if just copying definitions without thinking about them)
   - Attending to the pronunciation of words

2. Examples of medium encoding (acoustic)

   - Learning material by song or rhyme
   - Learning concepts through nursery rhymes

3. Examples of deep encoding (semantic; see also release from proactive interference section above):

   - Elaborating on material
   - Putting ideas in your own words
   - Creating a mental image
   - Making connections to other information (e.g., concept maps)
   - Use method of loci—link concept to a place/route (see memory palace)
   - Studying by using examples

4. Another example of deep encoding is prospective memory, the ability to remind yourself to pay attention when you do tasks such as unplugging the iron, turning off the stove or locking the front door as you leave the house. This ability allows you to reassure yourself that these tasks were in fact completed. (More examples are presented later in this chapter.)
5. We know a mother of triplets who reported that her memory was taxed when the triplets were babies. It was a challenge for her to keep track of changing diapers, feeding and napping schedules. Paying close attention during the encoding of this information was critical to her ability to attend to the needs of all three babies. The same is true for day-care workers, which is part of the reason why they keep separate diaries of the activities of each child in the facility.
6. In one demonstration of the impact of shallow vs. deep processing (attributed to David Irwin and Janet Simmons), students listen to a series of silly sentences (e.g., "the lanky leprechaun wore lavender leotards"). Half the class is asked to rate how easy the sentences are to pronounce (shallow processing) and the other half is asked to rate how easy it was to generate a mental image of the sentences (deep processing). On a recall test (immediate or delayed), the students who create mental images significantly outperform those students who are focused on the surface-level characteristic of pronounceability. The full demonstration can be downloaded here [we cannot provide a QR code because this link downloads a Word file].
7. Here is a similar demonstration:
    At a moderate pace, read aloud the list of words below. Instruct half the class to count or estimate the number of vowels in each word and ask the other half to rate on a 1–5 scale how valuable each item would be to a person stranded on a desert island. The differing instructions can be given via distributed index cards, or differing presentation slides:
    Umbrella, gasoline, orchestra, yacht, hammer, diamond, university, macaroni, eyeglasses, garden, underwear, newspaper, alcohol, bouquet, microscope, camouflage, pollution, restaurant, insect, elephant, sulphur, lemonade, mosquito, bottle.
    After reading the list, displace from short-term memory the words in the latter part of the list by asking the students to spend about 30 s performing a distracting task, such as writing their name, address, phone number, academic major, home town, and favorite color. Then give them one minute to write down as many words from the list as they can recall (in any order). Retention scores from those who processed the words superficially (by counting or estimating vowels) will be much lower than those from students who processed the information more deeply by thinking about, and possibly visualizing, the usefulness of each item in a particular situation.
8. The table and graphic below provide examples of levels of processing described by Craik and Tulving (1975).

Level of processing	Typical encoding	Examples
Shallow	Visual/structural	Visual features—letter type; image color*;
Medium	Acoustic/phonemic	Sound features—rhyming; song; image shape*
Deep	Semantic	Word meaning; or image meaning*; Connect to previous knowledge; application

*Color, shape and meaning as examples of levels of processing are described here.

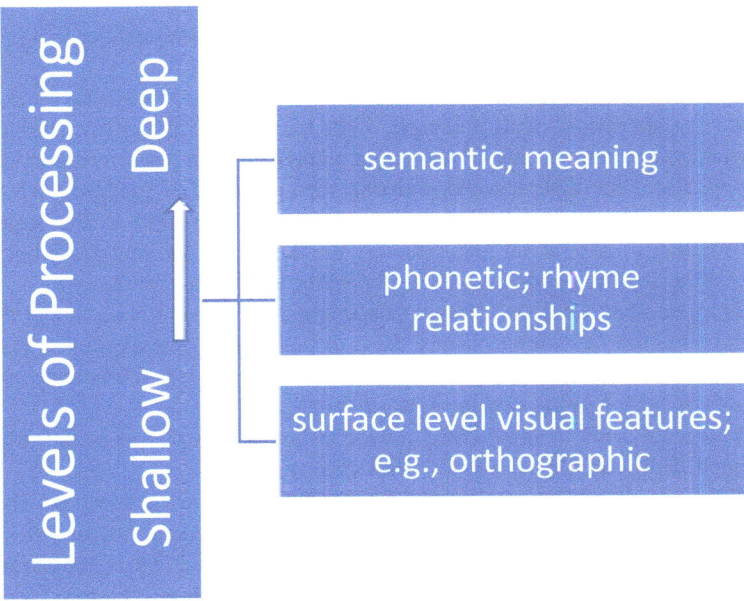

[Reference: Craik, F. I., & Tulving, E. (1975). Depth of processing and the retention of words in episodic memory. *Journal of Experimental Psychology: General, 104*(3), 268–294.]

Encoding Through Rehearsal

1. Examples of maintenance rehearsal (shallow encoding)

   - Reading a phone number and repeating it over and over until you call the number.
   - Repeatedly reciting your shopping list as you walk around a grocery store.

- You have been sent to the coffeeshop to buy coffee for each of your six coworkers. As you walk to the coffeeshop you continuously repeat the six coffee orders in your mind.

    (Note: Smart phones have largely obviated the need for this sort of rehearsal. Of course, paper and pencil also work to outsource this memory task!)

2. Examples of elaborative rehearsal (deep processing):

    - You have been sent to the coffeeshop to buy coffee for each of your six coworkers. As you walk to the coffeeshop you think about Kayla and how sweet she is and so you remember that she wants sugar in her latte. Then you think about Paul and how energetic he is and so you remember that he wants a double-espresso. And so on.
    - Sara is a world-class shopper. She has mental images of all the cities where she has shopped as well as images of the locations of all her favorite stores on each street in those cities. When Sara wants to remember information about a new store, she adds it to her existing mental image of the street where it is located. She thinks about the new store in relationship to the stores surrounding it. Sara is not just repeating the address of the new store but is also relating it to the addresses of all the other stores that she knows.
    - To remember a person's name, you might connect something about them or the situation in which you met them to their name. For example, when you met James you talked a lot about workout routines, so you associate him with a gym, which helps you to think of "Jim" for James.
    - You meet a man named Bill Crews and you notice that he is tall, like your uncle Bill who always wore a crew cut hairstyle.
    - Magician Doc Eason performs a remarkable magic trick where about 20 people pick cards from a deck. He cannot see the cards they choose, but he later correctly associates each card with each person. More remarkably, he also remembers the names of all the audience members. He does so by having memorized a standard set of jokes that he uses with specific names. When he makes the joke upon learning their name, he associates that joke with the person. To remember each name, he just needs to recall the joke he used with each person. You can see an example of him doing this here. Note the small quips and comments he makes when he learns names in order to engage in elaborative encoding. Doc discusses his strategies for learning names in this 7-min video.
    - Another example of elaborative rehearsal would be to consider whether information that you are learning or trying to remember (e.g., a word list) applies to you, such as: "Does the word *generous* apply to me?" This results in better memory for material, a phenomenon known as the self-reference effect.

An example of a self-reference effect test can be found here.

[Sources: Bentley, S. V., Greenaway, K. H., & Haslam, S. A. (2017). An online paradigm for exploring the self-reference effect. *PloS one, 12*(5), e0176611.
Rogers, T. B., Kuiper, N. A., & Kirker, W. S. (1977). Self-reference and the encoding of personal information. *Journal of Personality and Social Psychology, 35*(9), 677.]

- An internet post that describes examples of elaborative interrogation can be found here. The post begins with a description of elaborative interrogation and then (towards the end) provides three examples from different academic disciplines.

- An example of a way to train oneself to use elaborative rehearsal can be found at the San Francisco Exploratorium website.

- Creating a concept map is a way to make connections and deepen processing and learning on a given topic. An example of a concept map and instructions for creating them can be found here.

- The value of elaborative rehearsal techniques is exemplified in the story of Josh Foer, a science reporter and author of the book *Moonwalking with Einstein* who won the USA Memory Championships after only a year of practicing such techniques. He tells the story here in this 20-min TED talk. Ironically, he says he still sometimes can't recall where he left his car keys.

- A 5-min video of Joshua Foer describing a technique for memorizing the first 100 digits of pi can be found here.

- Examples of ways to train your memory can be found here. Don't forget to select the English language option on the website.

[Source: Maguire, E., Valentine, E., Wilding, J., & Kapur, N. (2003) Routes to remembering: The brains behind superior memory. *Nature Neuroscience, 6*, 90–95. https://doi.org/10.1038/nn988]

- A description of the Person Object Action system for elaborative rehearsal can be found here.

- A 14-min video that describes techniques for memorizing lists of numbers using several methods can be found here.

- This news article reports on a study that showed how people can improve their memory using a memory palace or mind palace (method of loci).

  [Source: Dresler, M., Shirer, W. R., Konrad, B. N., Müller, N. C., Wagner, I. C., Fernández, G., ... & Greicius, M. D. (2017). Mnemonic training reshapes brain networks to support superior memory. *Neuron, 93*(5), 1227–1235.]

- On this website you can find four TedTalks that address how to improve one's memory, including using a memory palace.

Mnemonic Devices

[Note: Mnemonic devices do not necessarily reflect elaborative rehearsal, nor do they guarantee deep processing.]

1. Categorical Clustering:

   - Remembering your shopping list by category—fruits and vegetables, meats, dairy, non-food items
   - You might remember a coffee order of your coworkers by type of drink—drip coffee, iced-coffees and teas
   - Categorize a list depending on their functions—you are going to Target and you remember that you have to buy three items from the grocery section, two from the pharmacy and two from men's wear.

2. Pegwords:

   - Felicia memorizes the school rules by forming interactive images between two words. For example, one is a gun—no weapons at school. Two is a shoe—proper attire at school. Three is a tree—outside play is to remain on the playground. (Source: Students can also test their knowledge of mnemonic devices at that website.)

   - Another example of the pegword system is described here.

3. Method of loci (see memory palace examples above).
4. Acronyms:

    - ROYGBIV for the colors of the rainbow
    - OCEAN for the Big Five personality traits
    - HOMES for the five Great Lakes

5. Acrostics

    - Every Good Boy Deserves Fudge/Does Fine (Treble clef)
    - Thirty days hath September...
    - Please Excuse My Dear Aunt Sally (order of mathematical operations)
    - My Very Excellent Mother Just Served Us Nine Pizzas (names of planets); or My Very Excellent Mom Just Served Us Noodles (no more Pluto)
    - When Jeff Left Home Jack Got Fat (Presidents on US bills)
    - On Old Olympus' Towering Tops, A French and German Viewed Some Hops (cranial nerves).

6. You can purchase a course on improving memory, including by using mnemonics, at this website. The website also includes a free podcast about improving memory.

Flashbulb Memories

1. Examples of major events that were encoded as flashbulb memories, usually because of the emotions evoked at the time:

    - The assassination of John F. Kennedy in 1963
    - The Challenger disaster in 1986
    - The death of Lady Diana in a Paris car accident in 1997
    - The terrorist attacks of September 11th, 2001
    - The fire at Notre Dame cathedral in Paris in 2019
    - Presidential elections of Barack Obama in 2008 and Donald Trump 2016
    - The royal weddings of Prince William and Kate Middleton in 2011 and Prince Harry and Meghan Markel in 2018

    [Sources:
    Brown, R., & Kulik, J. (1977). Flashbulb memories. *Cognition*, 5(1), 73–99.
    Neisser, U., & Harsh, N. (1992). Phantom flashbulbs: False recollections of hearing the news about Challenger. In E. Winograd & U. Neisser (Eds.), *Emory symposia in cognition, 4. Affect and accuracy in recall: Studies of "flashbulb" memories* (p. 9–31). Cambridge University Press. https://doi.org/10.1017/CBO9780511664069.003

Talarico, J. M., & Rubin, D. C. (2003). Confidence, not consistency, characterizes flashbulb memories. *Psychological Science, 14*(5), 455–461.
Hirst, W., Phelps, E. A., Meksin, R., Vaidya, C. J., Johnson, M. K., Mitchell, K. J., ... & Mather, M. (2015). A ten-year follow-up of a study of memory for the attack of September 11, 2001: Flashbulb memories and memories for flashbulb events. *Journal of Experimental Psychology: General, 144*(3), 604.]

2. If you ask them, your students will probably be able to provide examples of events that were encoded as flashbulb for them, personally.
3. An example of how emotion and memory are related is described in this 2-min video in which Elizabeth Phelps discusses memory and confidence in memory for the events of 9/11.

4. An example of how learning with retrieval practice can mitigate the effects of stress in a testing scenario is found in this 3-min video.

[Source: Smith, A. M., Floerke, V. A., & Thomas, A. K. (2016). Retrieval practice protects memory against acute stress. *Science, 354*(6315), 1046–1048.]
5. This video, from minute 12:30 to 21:15, shows how memory can be affected by emotion. It describes a series of experiments providing an example of how negative emotion can enhance memory and suppressing emotion with beta-blockers can impair it.
[Sources: Cahill, L., & McGaugh, J. L. (1995). A novel demonstration of enhanced memory associated with emotional arousal. *Consciousness and Cognition, 4*(4), 410–421.
Cahill, L., Prins, B., Weber, M., & McGaugh, J. L. (1994). β-Adrenergic activation and memory for emotional events. *Nature, 371*(6499), 702–704.]

Encoding Specificity Principle

1. In a classic study, participants read a target word (i.e., piano) in one of two contexts: The man *lifted* the piano or the man *tuned* the piano. Recall for the target word was better if the question matched the context (e.g., "something heavy" vs. "something that makes nice sounds.")
[Source: Barclay, J. R., Bransford, J. D., Franks, J. J., McCarrell, N. S., & Nitsch, K. (1974). Comprehension and semantic flexibility. *Journal of Verbal Learning and Verbal Behavior, 13*(4), 471–481.]
2. In another classic study, participants learned (and were tested) either on land or in the water. Memory was better when the learning and testing conditions matched, as shown in the graph below.

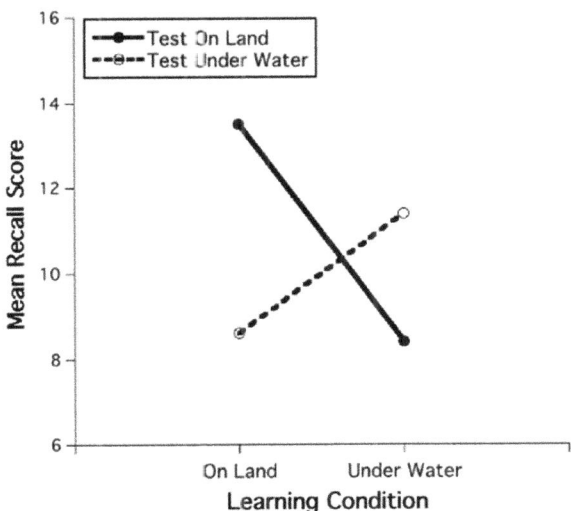

L. Cameron (2020), Lecture notes.

Note: this example provides an excellent opportunity to discuss the concept of a statistical interaction.
[Source: Godden, D. R., & Baddeley, A. D. (1975). Context-dependent memory in two natural environments: On land and underwater. *British Journal of Psychology, 66*(3), 325–331.]

Examples of People with Exceptional Memory

1. Taxi drivers in London, England provide an excellent example of people with extraordinary memory (for specific information), which is developed with practice. Given the complicated and extensive layout of streets in London and the large number of "places of interest", it takes aspiring taxi drivers two years to pass a test known as The Knowledge.
   Note: This example can also be used in the context of discussing brain plasticity as well as the role of the hippocampus in memory consolidation.
   [Sources:
   Maguire, E. A., Gadian, D. G., Johnsrude, I. S., Good, C. D., Ashburner, J., Frackowiak, R. S., & Frith, C. D. (2000). Navigation-related structural change in the hippocampi of taxi drivers. *Proceedings of the National Academy of Sciences, 97*(8), 4398–4403.

Maguire, E. A., Woollett, K., & Spiers, H. J. (2006). London taxi drivers and bus drivers: A structural MRI and neuropsychological analysis. *Hippocampus*, *16*(12), 1091–1101.]

2. A case of exceptional memory is shown in this 5-min video with Kim Peek, the inspiration for the 1988 movie *Rain Man*, starring Dustin Hoffman. Peek could apparently remember everything he had ever read and could nearly instantaneously compute a person's precise age when given a birth date.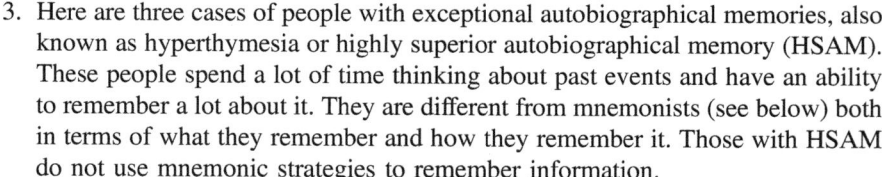
3. Here are three cases of people with exceptional autobiographical memories, also known as hyperthymesia or highly superior autobiographical memory (HSAM). These people spend a lot of time thinking about past events and have an ability to remember a lot about it. They are different from mnemonists (see below) both in terms of what they remember and how they remember it. Those with HSAM do not use mnemonic strategies to remember information.

    - Jill Price was the first reported case of HSAM. You can watch Diane Sawyer's interview with her here.
    [Source: McGaugh, J.L. & Leport, A. (2014). Remembrance of all things past. *Scientific American*, 40–45.]
    - You can find a news story from the BBC, including this 4-min video, about Bob Petrella, a man with HSAM here.

    - A 47-min documentary about HSAM, centered around the case of a British man named Aurelien, but also covering the cases of Jill Price and Bob Petrella can be found here.

4. Mnemonists

    - "*S*" (S.V. Shereshevsky) is one of the most famous cases of a mnemonist. He was studied extensively by neuropsychologist Alexander Luria. There is an interesting article that appeared in *The New Yorker* in 2017 about this case.
    [Reference: Luria, A.R. (1968). *The mind of a mnemonist: A little book about a vast memory*. (Ser. Discus books). New York: Basic Books.]
    - Rajan Mahadevan could recite from memory the first 31,811 digits of pi. You can see him reciting approximately the first 100 digits of pi at about 4 min into this 24-min video, which includes a discussion and demonstration of Rajan Mahadevan's memory.
    [Sources:
    Thompson, C. P., Cowan, T., Frieman, J., Mahadevan, R. S., Vogl, R. J., & Frieman, J. (1991). Rajan: A study of a memorist. *Journal of Memory and Language*, *30*(6), 702–724.
    Thompson, C. P., Cowan, T. M., & Frieman, J. (2013). *Memory search by a memorist*. New York: Psychology Press.

Biederman, I., Cooper, E. E., Fox, P. W., & Mahadevan, R. S. (1992). Unexceptional spatial memory in an exceptional memorist. *Journal of Experimental Psychology: Learning, Memory, and Cognition, 18*(3), 654–7.]
- Akira Haraguchi holds the unofficial record of reciting 100,000 digits of pi. You can see him recite the first 1000 digits in 1:42 min in a speeded recording found here.

- Cases of exceptional memory for music are described here.

5. People with eidetic (photographic) memory
[Note: This phenomenon seems to be extraordinarily rare in adults; it is more commonly seen in children.]

- A well-documented case of eidetic memory in a 23-year-old Harvard University teacher and artist is described by Stomeyer and Psotka (1970). This woman was able to recall the complete text of a poem in a familiar, but foreign, language. In one set of experiments she was able to conjure up an eidetic image and use it to see depth in a random dot stereogram.
[Source: Stromeyer, C. D., & Psotka, J. (1970). The detailed texture of eidetic images. *Nature, 225*(5230), 346-349. https://doi.org/10.1038/225346a0]
- A "Shass Pollak" is a Polish person who has memorized the complete Talmud. A description of the feat by some men is described by Stratton (1917).
[Source: Stratton, G. M. (1917). The mnemonic feat of the "Shass Pollak". *Psychological Review, 24*(3), 244. https://sci-hub.se/https://doi.org/10.1037/h0070091]
- Franco Magnani provides another example of eidetic memory. He was able to create amazingly accurate paintings of his hometown in Italy even though he had not seen it for more than 30 years.
[Source: Sacks, C. (1992, July 27). The landscape of his dreams. *The New Yorker.*]
- Stephen Wiltshire is a British artist who can draw incredibly accurate pictures of cityscapes that he has only seen briefly. You can read more about him here and watch a 3-min video of him creating a cityscape here.

6. It may be fun to talk with your students about fictional characters who have a so-called photographic memory. Some examples include:

   - Mike Ross on the TV series *Suits*
   - Lisbeth Salander from Stieg Larsson's *Millennium* series (e.g., The Girl with the Dragon Tatoo)
   - Diana Prince, aka Wonder Woman
   - Funes, a Jorge Luis Borges character who appears in the 1942 short story "Funes the Memorious". In this fictional work about a man plagued by the persistence of his memory after suffering a head injury, Borges writes: "To think is to forget a difference, to generalize, to abstract," and: "In the overly replete world of Funes there were nothing but details, almost contiguous details." Funes may or may not be an example of hyperthymesia, but he shares some features.
   - A short blog entry with three examples of fictional characters with eidetic memories can be found here.

Retrieval

Recall

1. Serial Recall (where order matters)

   - A phone number
   - A credit card number
   - A poem
   - Lyrics of a song
   - Steps to putting together a piece of IKEA furniture
   - Spelling a word

2. Free Recall (where order does not matter)

   - A shopping list
   - States and their capitals
   - Presidents of the United States
   - Events of your day
   - Answers to trivia questions
   - Important concepts learned in a class
   - An example of a short-term free recall test can be found here.

3. Cued Recall

   - Being given the first letter of a word or name to help you recall it
   - Being given a description or category of a word (e.g., "a kind of fruit") to help you recall it
   - Seeing response options on a multiple-choice test
   - Naming states (and capitols) when provided with a blank map of the United States; or naming the capitol when given the state or vice versa
   - One word can cue another, such as "lion" to recall tiger*
   - Sentence completion, such as: A _____ has stripes*
   - Considering one's internal state (e.g., mood) or "spatio-temporal context" when information was learned can serve as a cue for recall* (See also the section on state-dependent memory, below.)
   - Cued-recall was used in the famous Milgram experiment (i.e., participants had to remember a word pair, such as blue-ball, and then in the memory test were given "blue" and had to remember "ball").

[*Source: Higham P.A., & Guzel M.A. (2012) Cued recall. In: Seel N.M. (eds) *Encyclopedia of the sciences of learning*. Springer, Boston, MA. https://doi.org/10.1007/978-1-4419-1428-6_694].

Recognition

1. You might recognize a word that you learned in your Spanish class (although you've forgotten what it means).
2. You might recognize the face of your former Spanish teacher; you may or may not be able to recall the person's name.
3. If someone says, Is that Ms. Lopez? you might remember that that is the name of your former Spanish teacher.
4. You might recognize an object even if you have forgotten or don't know its name. Here is an object you probably know, but whose name you may have forgotten. And here is an image of the silver part of a pencil, which you certainly recognize, but the name of which (a ferrule) you may not be able to state.
5. Who played Jim Lovell in *Apollo 13*? You might know but be unable to *recall* the name. However, if someone asks: Was Jim Lovell played by Tom Hanks in *Apollo 13*? you might *recognize* that Tom Hanks is the name of that actor.
6. What is the capitol of British Columbia, Canada? If you can't recall it, this question might help: Is Victoria the capital of British Columbia? You might *recognize* that Victoria is the capital, even though you didn't know or perhaps were thinking that it is Vancouver.

7. Likewise, is Springfield the capital of Illinois? You might *recognize* that Springfield is the capital, even if you couldn't come up with the answer without prompting.
8. Examples of the application of retrieval in learning might be particularly appealing to students.

   - Retrieval practice is described in this video. and at this website and this one.

Prospective Memory

1. The Irving Berlin song *Remember* contains lyrics that will be unfamiliar to most of your students, but provide a nice example of prospective memory. One stanza goes like this:

   Remember the night, the night you said, "I love you,"
   Remember?
   Remember you vowed by all the stars above you,
   Remember?
   Remember we found a lonely spot,
   And after I learned to care a lot
   You promised that you'd forget me not,
   But you forgot to remember

2. As mentioned earlier, prospective memory is your "to do" list—what you want to remember to remember. A memorable graphic can be found here.
3. Some examples of prospective memory include remembering:

   - to take medicine.
   - to stop at the grocery store on the way home from work.
   - to call for a doctor's appointment.
   - to finish a presentation for class.
   - to grab your umbrella as you leave a restaurant even though it is no longer raining.
   - to keep an eye on the water that you have put on the stove to boil.
   - to take your lunch to school or work.

- to return a book to the library.
- to take out the trash when you get home from work.

4. A description and some examples of prospective memory can be found here, which includes a video describing the difference between younger and older adults on a prospective memory task—i.e., sending a postcard back to the researchers. (Spoiler alert: older adults perform better on the task.)

Context-Dependent Retrieval

1. Students might be interested to know that recall of learned material is enhanced when testing occurs in the same context (i.e., classroom) in which learning took place. For example, when students take an exam in their regular classroom, they can use items in the room such as the clock on the wall or the instructor's podium as cues to details from a lecture they heard in that room. Thus, students might not perform quite as well if they take exams in a location other than their classroom because that other location does not contain those contextual retrieval cues.
   [Reference: Smith, S. M., Glenberg, A., & Bjork, R. A. (1978). Environmental context and human memory. *Memory & Cognition, 6*(4), 342–353.]
2. Bilinguals may remember information better if it was presented and tested in the same language than in a different one.
   [Source: Marian, V., & Fausey, C. M. (2006). Language-dependent memory in bilingual learning. *Applied Cognitive Psychology, 20*(8), 1025–1047.]
3. You might remember material better if you learn and are tested in the presence of the same odor.
   [Source: Cann, A., & Ross, D. A. (1989). Olfactory stimuli as context cues in human memory. *The American Journal of Psychology, 102*, 91–102.]
4. You might remember words better when background music matches in learning and test conditions.
   [Source: Mead, K. M., & Ball, L. J. (2007). Music tonality and context-dependent recall: The influence of key change and mood mediation. *European Journal of Cognitive Psychology, 19*(1), 59–79.]
5. Another example of context-dependent retrieval tends to occur with age. By the time they are in their 60s, people often find themselves getting up from a chair, going into the kitchen or bedroom, or the study, or wherever, then stopping to look around, but having no idea why they went there! These people soon learn that the solution (which works every time) is to go back where they started, sit back down, and allow some retrieval cue in that environment to remind them what they meant to do. (This phenomenon is also called the context reinstatement effect.) They can then get up again, but this time use prospective memory efforts and/or maintenance rehearsal to keep the goal in STM.

State-Dependent Retrieval

1. You might remember information better if you are tested while under the influence of alcohol if you were under the influence of alcohol when you learned that material.
   [Source: Weissenborn, R., & Duka, T. (2000). State-dependent effects of alcohol on explicit memory: The role of semantic associations. *Psychopharmacology, 149*(1), 98–106. https://doi.org/10.1007/s002139900349].
2. This study showed that if people learn material under the influence of marijuana, they will remember it better if are tested on it while under the influence of marijuana. Remember to tell students that people's memories work best when they aren't using any drugs or alcohol during encoding or retrieval.
   [Source: Eich, J. E., Weingartner, H., Stillman, R. C., & Gillin, J. C. (1975). State-dependent accessibility of retrieval cues in the retention of a categorized list. *Journal of Verbal Learning and Verbal Behavior, 14*(4), 408–417.]
3. Lydia had several cups of coffee during the evening when was studying for the psychology quiz she would take the next morning. She overslept and didn't have time for coffee, and she did not do well on the quiz. Later, while drinking coffee with friends, she was amazed that she could now remember some of the material that had escaped her during the quiz.
4. Here are two cartoons that play on state-dependent retrieval:

   - A Callahan cartoon, found here shows a picture of one man saying to another man "I wonder if you'd mind giving me directions. I've never been sober in this part of town before."

   - A Ski Ninjas cartoon, found here, shows a character looking at notes on his phone and he's saying "I don't know what any of these notes mean, I was really drunk when I wrote them. Maybe I could use state-dependent memory: Get really drunk again, and remember what they mean." But he is in a coffee shop!

5. These studies showed that people's memory was better when in matching *mood states* (e.g., happy/sad) during encoding and retrieval of information.
   [Sources:
   Eich, E. (1995). Mood as a mediator of place dependent memory. *Journal of Experimental Psychology: General, 124*(3), 293–308. https://doi.org/10.1037/0096-3445.124.3.293
   Eich, E. (1995). Searching for mood dependent memory. *Psychological Science, 6*(2), 67–75.]

6. Another example of mood dependent retrieval is a study showing that people had better memory when they were in the same mood (neutral/anxious) during learning and testing.
   [Source: Robinson, S.J. & Rollings, L.J.L (2010). The effect of mood-context on visual recognition and recall memory. *The Journal of General Psychology, 138*, 66–79. DOI:10.1080/00221309.2010.534405].
7. Another study found that you might have a better memory if you're in the same *fear state* during learning and testing.
   [Source: Lang, A. J., Craske, M. G., Brown, M., & Ghaneian, A. (2001). Fear-related state dependent memory. *Cognition and Emotion, 15*(5), 695–703.]
8. A *New Yorker* cartoon found here plays on these findings. It shows a couple arguing, and one partner says to the other "I can't remember what we're arguing about, either. Let's keep yelling and maybe it will come back to us".

Memory Failure and Its Consequences

1. Here is an example of a disaster caused in part by forgetting:

   Several years ago, an air traffic controller at Los Angeles International Airport cleared an incoming flight to land on runway 24L. A couple of minutes later, the pilot of that flight radioed the control tower that he was on approach for runway 24L, but the controller did not reply because she was talking to another pilot. After finishing that conversation, the controller told a SkyWest commuter pilot to taxi onto runway 24L for takeoff, completely forgetting about the plane that was about to land on the same runway. The incoming jet hit the commuter plane, killing thirty-four people. The controller's forgetting was so complete that she thought the fireball from the crash was an exploding bomb. You can read more about the accident here.

2. Here is an example of less disastrous, but expensive and inconvenient, consequences of forgetting:
   In February 2002, prison warden James Smith lost his set of master keys to the Westville Correctional Facility. As a result, 2,559 inmates were kept under partial lockdown for eight days while the Indiana Department of Correction spent $53,000 to change locks in the affected areas. As it turned out, the warden had put the keys in his pocket when he went home, forgot he had done so, and reported the keys "missing" when they were not in their usual place in his office the next day.
   [Source: *Naples Daily News* (2002, March 9). Odds and ends.]

3. Because of failure to encode details, long-term memory for features of even very common objects (e.g., coins) may be poor. An interactive demonstration of this effect can be found at the San Francisco Exploratorium website.
[Reference: Nickerson, R. S., & Adams, M. J. (1979). Long-term memory for a common object. *Cognitive Psychology, 11*(3), 287–307.]

4. Likewise, although the Apple logo is very familiar to us, we might have trouble picking it out of a "line-up", as seen in this image.
[Reference: Blake, A. B., Nazarian, M., & Castel, A. D. (2015). The Apple of the mind's eye: Everyday attention, metamemory, and reconstructive memory for the Apple logo. *The Quarterly Journal of Experimental Psychology, 68*(5), 858–865.]

5. Examples of failures of encoding can also be demonstrated by people's inability to correctly answer questions such as these:

   - What is the color of the top stripe of the American flag?
   - How many sides are on a typical wooden pencil?
   - In what hand does the Statue of Liberty hold her torch?

   [Source: Albrecht, K. (1980). *Brain Power*. Englewood Cliffs, NJ Prentice Hall.]

6. The Princess Card Trick is a nice example of memory encoding failure, and it can be seen here. This trick is attributed to Henry Hardin and was first described in print by T. Nelson Downs.
[Source: Downs, T. N. (1909). *The art of magic*. The Downs-Edwards Company.]

7. A particularly unfortunate example of forgetting comes from this story of a computer programmer who could lose millions of dollars in Bitcoin because forgot his password.

8. One study, by contrast, provides an example of people demonstrating good visual memory for details. Researchers found that people could accurately select images in a forced-choice task in three conditions—when the original item was paired with a novel item, an exemplar of the original item, or an item in a different "state". You can see the results of the study in this figure. Numbers beside the image pairs indicate number of participants who selected the correct item.
[Source: Brady, T. F., Konkle, T., Alvarez, G. A., & Oliva, A. (2008). Visual long-term memory has a massive storage capacity for object details. *Proceedings of the National Academy of Sciences, 105*(38), 14,325–14,329.]

Eyewitness Testimony

1. A 4-min National Science Foundation video on eyewitness testimony and its limitations can be found here.

2. One of the most powerful examples of a failure of eyewitness testimony and ensuing events is found in the story of Jennifer Thompson and Ronald Cotton. In 1984, Jennifer was raped at knife point. Using prospective memory, she tried hard to pay attention to and encode the details of the rapist's appearance but later incorrectly identified Ronald Cotton as her rapist. Cotton was convicted and spent more than a decade in prison until DNA evidence exonerated him. After his release Thompson and Cotton became friends and, together, they advocate for reform in wrongful convictions and procedures for eyewitness identification. A summary of the case can be found here. They wrote a book together and a 3-min video preview can be seen here.
   [Reference: Thompson-Cannino, J., Cotton, R., & Torneo, E. (2009). *Picking Cotton: Our memoir of injustice and redemption*. Macmillan.]

3. A *60 Minutes* episode on this case and eyewitness testimony in general is covered in a two-part series:
   Part 1 (13:00 min)

   Part 2: (13:06 min)

4. The original telling of this story (before Ronald and Jennifer meet) is described in a 52-min Frontline video called *What Jennifer Saw*, which can be found here.

5. Jennifer Thompson's TedX Talk (18:01 min) can be found here.

6. Elizabeth Loftus' 17-min TedTalk on the reliability of memory with examples of cases where an eyewitness made an incorrect identification can be found here.

7. Federal guidelines (1999) to reduce miscarriage of justice based on eyewitness testimony can be found here.

8. Examples of other cases in which eyewitness testimony resulted in wrongful convictions can be found on the National Registry of Exonerations webpage.

9. More information can be found about eyewitness identification reform at the Innocence Project website. Ronald Cotton's case is described on that website. The direct link is here.

10. Students can experience a mock crime and learn about potential problems with eyewitness identification at this BBC website.

11. A New Yorker cartoon showing how <u>not</u> to design a lineup can be found here. It shows a lineup in which one person stands out not only in height but in obviously evil appearance.

12. The Other Race Effect can have an impact on the accuracy of eyewitness identification because it is sometimes difficult for people to distinguish between faces of people from other races, particularly if they have limited contact with members of those races. It apparently played a part in the Jennifer Thompson/Ronald Cotton case described above. A photo of Ronald Cotton, whom Jennifer misidentified, and Bobby Poole (the actual rapist) can be seen here.

13. An example of faces used in a study examining the Other Race Effect can be found in Fig. 1 of a paper found here.
[Source: Lucas, H. D., Chiao, J. Y., & Paller, K. A. (2011). Why some faces won't be remembered: Brain potentials illuminate successful versus unsuccessful encoding for same-race and other-race faces. *Frontiers in Human Neuroscience, 5*, 20.]

14. Some celebrities of color are mistakenly identified for other celebrities of the same race. For example, Lisa Ling who has been mistaken for Lucy Liu is described in this darkly humorous 2-min video clip. Pictures of Lisa Ling and Lucy Liu side-by-side for comparison can be found here.

Likewise, Samuel L. Jackson has been mistaken for Laurence Fishburne, as occurred in this live interview. Pictures of Samuel L. Jackson and Laurence Fishburne side-by-side for comparison can be found here.

False Memory

1. Confirming the truth or falsity of a memory can be challenging, especially in cases of allegedly recovered memories of childhood abuse, but there are plenty of cases in which even vivid memories are clearly false ones. For example, the first time one of the authors taught the concept of flashbulb memory, she asked students if they remembered where they were when they heard about the death of Lady Diana. One student said that he remembered his teacher announcing the news in school on a Tuesday morning, but as the accident happened in the early hours of a Sunday, that memory was false.
2. An example of people "remembering" an event that they could not possibly have seen is provided by the case of an El Al Boeing 747 that crashed into an apartment building in the outskirts of Amsterdam in 1992. There was no video of the crash, but ten months later more than half of people studied reported that they had seen video footage on television.
[Source: Crombag, H. F. M., Wagenaar, W. A., & van Koppen, P. J. (1996). Crashing memories and the problem of 'source monitoring'. *Applied Cognitive Psychology, 10*(2), 95–104.]
3. Here is an example of a false memory as described by a pioneer of cognitive psychology, Ulric Neisser: "I recall sitting in the living room of our house—we only lived in that house for one year, but I remember it well—listening to a baseball game on the radio. The game was interrupted by an announcement of the attack, and I rushed upstairs to tell my mother." Years later, after reading scientific research on flashbulb memories, Neisser realized that this memory had to be wrong. *Pearl Harbor was attacked on Dec. 7, and there is no baseball on the radio in December.* [emphasis added]" Source of quote.

4. Examples of *inducing* false memories can be seen in this video. From minute 21:22 to 30:22, Daniel Schacter manages to implant false memories in the memory of Alan Alda (the interviewer) using both word lists and photographs.

5. This 9-min lecture includes an engaging demonstration of false memory. You might want to ask your students to play along to experience false memory for themselves.

6. Examples of word lists that promote false memories (i.e., lists of words that are semantically related to the absent target word) can be found here.
   [Sources:
   Roediger, H. L., III, & McDermott, K. B. (1995). Creating false memories: Remembering words not presented in lists. *Journal of Experimental Psychology: Learning, Memory, & Cognition, 21*, 803–814].
   Pardilla-Delgado, E., & Payne, J. D. (2017). The Deese-Roediger-McDermott (DRM) task: A simple cognitive paradigm to investigate false memories in the laboratory. *Journal of Visualized Experiments, 119*, e54793.]

7. False memories can be promoted by semantic associates (as noted above) or phonological associates (created by adding, deleting or substituting one or more phonemes to the absent target word) or lists of a combination of semantic and phonological associates. Here is an example of such lists for the target word "DOG".

Semantic associates	Phonological associates
Hound	Log
Puppy	Dodge
Bite	Dug
Mutt	Hog
Pet	Bog
Beware	Doff
Bone	Daub
Tail	Cog
Cat	Dock
Animal	Dawn
Paw	Fog
Poodle	Dig
Flea	Doll
Bark	Frog
Lassie	Jog
Vet	Dot

[Source: Watson, J. M., Balota, D. A., & Roediger III, H. L. (2003). Creating false memories with hybrid lists of semantic and phonological associates: Over-additive false memories produced by converging associative networks. *Journal of Memory and Language, 49*(1), 95–118. https://doi.org/10.1016/S0749-596X(03)00019-6].

8. This website provides several examples of false memories, including one from Jean Piaget. Piaget's story is described at this Oxford Reference website and here.

9. This 2:30-min video of the classic Loftus and Palmer study that demonstrated that memory is affected by verbs used in a question can be found here.
[Reference: Loftus, E. F., & Palmer, J. C. (1974). Reconstruction of automobile destruction: An example of the interaction between language and memory. *Journal of Verbal Learning and Verbal Behavior, 13*(5), 585–589.]

10. Some examples of ways in which people might experience false memories in daily life:

- You might "remember" that your friend Kelsey suggested that you try a yoga class, when in fact it was your friend Ashley who made that suggestion.
- You might "remember" putting your keys on the key hook when you entered the house when in fact you put them in your pocket or purse.
- You "remember" telling your significant other to buy chocolate chips at the store, but in fact you only thought about doing so.
- You might "remember" that you have met someone before, but they just look familiar.

11. Examples of factors that affect false memory and susceptibility to suggestion are found in two studies of news events:

- One study found that "voters in a real-world political campaign are most susceptible to forming false memories for fake news that aligns with their beliefs, in particular if they have low cognitive ability."
[Source: Murphy, G., Loftus, E. F., Grady, R. H., Levine, L. J., & Greene, C. M. (2019). False memories for fake news during Ireland's abortion referendum. *Psychological Science, 30*(10), 1449-1459. https://doi.org/10.1177/0956797619864887]

- Another study found that "people who are more knowledgeable about Covid-19 or who score better on a test of analytical reasoning, are less prone to reporting false memories following exposure to fabricated stories. In contrast, people who simply believe themselves to be knowledgeable are more likely to report memories for true stories but are not protected against false memories. People who are very anxious about Covid-19, or who engage with a lot of related content, are also more likely to report a memory for true (but not false) stories."
  [Source: Greene, C. M., & Murphy, G. (2020). Individual differences in susceptibility to false memories for COVID-19 fake news. *Cognitive Research: Principles and Implications, 5*(1), 1–8. https://www.ncbi.nlm.nih.gov/pmc/articles/PMC7716111/]

Schemas

Other examples of schemas are presented in the chapter on development and examples of concepts are presented in the chapter on thinking and cognitive abilities.

1. An example of a neural network model of an adult's schema for "egg" might look something like the image you can find here.

2. In this classic riddle, a schema in memory (in this case, a gender stereotype) affects our ability to solve it: A man and his son are in a terrible accident and are rushed to the hospital in critical condition. A surgeon looks at the boy and exclaims "I can't operate on this child, he's my son!" How can this be?
   If our memory contains a schema in which surgeons are male, we would fail to consider that this one is a woman.

3. In a classic example of the role of memory schemas in processing information, the following passage makes little sense unless you know its context, which activates a schema (for doing laundry):

   The procedure is actually quite simple. First you arrange things into different groups... Of course, one pile may be sufficient depending on how much there is to do. If you have to go somewhere else due to lack of facilities that is the next step, otherwise you are pretty well set. It is important not to overdo any particular endeavor. That is, it is better to do too few things at once than too many. In the short run this may not seem important, but complications from doing too many can easily arise. A mistake can be expensive as well... At first the whole procedure will seem complicated. Soon, however, it will become just another facet of life. It is difficult to foresee any end to the necessity for this task in the immediate future, but then one never can tell. After the procedure is completed one arranges the materials into different groups again. Then they can be put into their appropriate places. Eventually they will be used once more and the whole cycle will have to be repeated. However, that is part of life.

[Source: Bransford, J D., & Johnson, M. K. (1972). Contextual prerequisites for understanding: Some investigations of comprehension and recall. *Journal of Verbal Learning and Verbal Behavior, 11*(6), 717–726.]

4. The role of schemas in what we remember is exemplified in Bartlett's "War of the Ghosts." It reveals that when we fail to remember details, we fill them in based on those schemas (constructive memory). A description of the story in the Oxford Reference can be found here.
[Sources: Bartlett, F.C. (1932). *Remembering: A study in experimental and social psychology*. Cambridge. Cambridge University Press.
Johnson, M. K., Bransford, J. D., & Solomon, S. K. (1973). Memory for tacit implications of sentences. *Journal of Experimental Psychology, 98*(1), 203–205. https://doi.org/10.1037/h0034290]

5. An example of the power of schemas to influence what we remember about others is provided by a study in which people were told that the woman they were going to see in a video was either a waitress or a librarian. When later asked to describe the woman, those who thought she was a waitress recalled that she had a beer with dinner and watched TV. Those who thought she was a librarian remembered that she was wearing glasses and liked classical music.
[Source: Cohen, C. E. (1981). Person categories and social perception: Testing some boundaries of the processing effects of prior knowledge. *Journal of Personality and Social Psychology, 40,* 441–452.]

6. An example of how *schema violation* can be especially memorable comes from a study in which participants looked at pictures of men and women and were told a brief story about each, including whether the pictured people had cheated on their romantic partners. Because many people have schemas suggesting that women are kinder and less self-centered than men, participants were better at remembering pictures of cheating women than of cheating men.
[Source: Kroneisen, M., & Bell, R. (2013). Sex, cheating, and disgust: Enhanced source memory for trait information that violates gender stereotypes. *Memory, 21*(2), 167–181.]

7. An example of how verbal labeling of an object can affect our memory comes from a classic study on schemas in memory. Participants were shown figures like those in the left-hand column in the figure below, along with labels designed to activate certain schemas. When later asked to draw these figures from memory, the participants' drawings tended to resemble the items mentioned by the experimenter.

Figure shown to participants	Label given	Figure drawn by participants	Label given	Figure drawn by participants
O—O	Eyeglasses	O͡O	Dumbbell	C—Ↄ
⧖	Hourglass	⧖	Table	⧖
⁊	Seven	7	Four	4
▷—	Gun	(gun shape)	Broom	(broom shape)

[Source: Carmichael, L., Hogan, H. P., & Walter, A. A. (1932). An experimental study of the effect of language on the reproduction of visually perceived form. *Journal of Experimental Psychology, 15*(1), 73.]

Biological Bases of Memory

Note: We now know that memory is processed in many areas of the brain, but some areas (e.g., the hippocampus) are particularly important for processes such as consolidation.

1. Here are a few examples of brain damage that resulted in memory loss, including anterograde amnesia and retrograde amnesia (additional examples are presented in the chapter on biological aspects of psychology):

   - A case of retrograde amnesia can be found here. It includes a brief video with the patient, Kay Delaney, a British woman who suffered loss of memory of everything from the 20 years prior to a fall in which she suffered a head injury.

   - A somewhat controversial example of retrograde amnesia is Trevor Rees, the former bodyguard of Dodi Al-Fayed, Lady Diana's boyfriend. After experiencing severe head-injuries, he reportedly could not recall events surrounding the car accident that killed Al-Fayed and Lady Diana.

   - An example of anterograde amnesia due to a benign tumor in the temporal and frontal lobes is described by Oliver Sacks in this 5-min video. The patient named Greg is described as "The Last Hippie".

2. Research showing that taxi drivers in London, England (described earlier in this chapter) have larger posterior hippocampi than control individuals, appears to be an example of the important role of the hippocampus in memory consolidation. [Source: Maguire, E. A., Gadian, D. G., Johnsrude, I. S., Good, C. D., Ashburner, J., Frackowiak, R. S., & Frith, C. D. (2000). Navigation-related structural change in the hippocampi of taxi drivers. *Proceedings of the National Academy of Sciences*, 97(8), 4398–4403.]

3. A graphical representation of synaptic connections underlying memory consolidation can be found here.

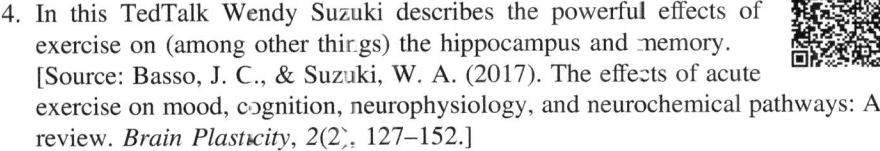

4. In this TedTalk Wendy Suzuki describes the powerful effects of exercise on (among other things) the hippocampus and memory. [Source: Basso, J. C., & Suzuki, W. A. (2017). The effects of acute exercise on mood, cognition, neurophysiology, and neurochemical pathways: A review. *Brain Plasticity*, 2(2), 127–152.]

Thinking and Cognitive Abilities 6

The topics covered in this chapter may be a challenge for students and may not immediately resonate with them. However, engaging them in puzzles and games that stimulate their thinking about problem solving and their own thinking can draw them in. As with memory, they may be impressed both by the powers and the weaknesses of human thinking. We start with examples of the functions of thinking and end with ways of measuring cognitive abilities.

Note that examples of other cognitive functions are covered elsewhere: memory is covered in its own chapter, language is covered in the chapter on development, and attention is covered in the chapter on sensation and perception.

The Functions of Thinking

The following two stories are examples of the overall value of thinking in human life and to introduce its role in problem solving, and decision making:

Dr. Joyce Wallace, a New York City physician, was having trouble figuring out what was the matter with a 43-year-old patient, "Laura McBride." Laura reported pain in her abdomen, aching muscles, irritability, occasional dizzy spells, and fatigue. The doctor's first hypothesis was iron-deficiency anemia, a condition in which there is not enough oxygen-carrying hemoglobin in the blood. There was some evidence to support this idea. A physical examination revealed that Laura's spleen was a bit enlarged, and blood tests showed low hemoglobin and high production of red blood cells, suggesting that her body was attempting to compensate for the loss of hemoglobin. However, other tests revealed normal iron levels. Perhaps she was losing blood through internal bleeding, but other tests ruled that out. Had Laura been vomiting blood? She said no. Blood in the urine? No. Abnormally heavy menstrual flow? No. As Dr. Wallace puzzled over the problem, Laura's condition worsened. She reported more intense pain, cramps, shortness of breath, and loss of energy. Her blood was becoming less and less capable of sustaining her, but if it was not being lost, what was happening to it? Finally, the doctor looked at a smear of Laura's blood on a microscope slide. What she saw indicated that a poison was destroying Laura's red blood cells. What could it be? Laura spent most of her time at home, and her teenage daughters, who lived with her, were perfectly healthy. Dr. Wallace asked herself, "What does Laura do that the girls do not?" She repairs and restores paintings. Paint. Lead! She might be suffering from lead poisoning! When the next blood test showed a lead level seven times higher than normal, Dr. Wallace had found the answer at last.

To solve this medical problem, Dr. Wallace relied on her ability to think and, more specifically, to weigh the evidence for and against various hypotheses to reach decisions about what tests to order and how to interpret their results.

[Source: Adapted from Bernstein, D.A. (2019). *Essentials of Psychology* (7th ed.). Belmont, CA: Wadsworth Cengage Learning. p. 238.]

"Failure is not an option!".

Excellent problem-solving and decision making are required at NASA and the space program. Examples of this were demonstrated throughout the nearly fatal Apollo 13 mission. This is depicted in the 1995 movie *Apollo 13*, starring Tom Hanks. Here is a description of a particularly memorable scene, which demonstrates an articulation of a problem and a commitment to solving it.  In this scene Gene Kranz assembles a group of scientists and engineers to deal with the problem of power to get the Apollo 13 spacecraft back to earth. He starts by saying "Are you telling me you can only give our guys 45 h? That brings them to about there…" as he draws an "X" on a blackboard, indicating that the ending place of the rocket would be in space, not on earth. "Gentlemen, that's not acceptable." Then one NASA engineer, John Aaron (played by Loren Dean) indicates that, in fact, even to get them to that point everything on the ship needs to be powered off to save energy for reentry. Kranz then indicates that they are going to need to figure out how to power back up a frozen computer and batteries. It has never been done before; never even simulated. Kranz says "Well, we're going to have to figure it out." He continues ".. find out how to squeeze every amp out of both of these goddamn machines." Back to the blackboard he points to the place in space where the ship was supposed to run out of power and says "I want this mark to be all the way back to earth with time to spare. We've never lost an American in space and we're sure as hell not going to lose one on my watch. Failure is not an option!" Later in the movie, there are scenes where John Aaron works with Ken Mattingly (played by Gary Sinese) to work through the power-up sequence that gets the astronauts the energy they need to fire up their computers for re-entry.

The Circle of Thought

1. A graphic example of the five main operations or functions of thought (describing, elaborating, deciding, planning, and guiding action) appears as *the circle of thought*.

The Functions of Thinking

Because the circle of thought begins as perceptual systems describe and elaborate sensory information from the world (including our own bodies), we offer here some examples of top-down perceptual processes that are particularly relevant to cognition (see also the chapter on sensation and perception). *Top-down influences on perception* include context, knowledge, expectation and motivation.

2. Here are some examples of context influencing perception:

- The Ebbinghaus (size) illusion shown here.

- The Müller-Lyer Illusion shown here.

- Simultaneous brightness contrast shown here.

- Context allows us to perceive the identical middle character in each of three words as either an "h" or an "a", so as to correctly see the display as a meaningful sentence ("The man ran") rather than as a nonsense string ("tae mhn rhn".)

THE MAN RAN.

- The partially occluded word is identical in the two sentences below, but context allows us to interpret them as "road" or "read" as is appropriate for the meaning of the sentence.

She walked down the road.

She liked to read.

- Another visual context example (the word "LOVE" is written with the "V" toppled over) can be seen in the image about half way down the page on this website.
- Reading poor handwriting or partially obscured text requires top-down processes that constrains what likely letters or words can be in a particular context. And some letters may look different in different contexts or different letters may look the same. Ask your students to say which obscured line of text below they find easier to read. Top-down processing should help them read the first line, but the words in the second line are not related, so context-based top-down processing cannot operate.

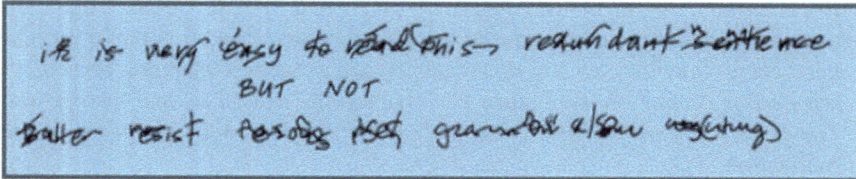

(*Note:* We believe that the top sentence reads: "It is very easy to read this redundant sentence" but we have no idea what the bottom sentence says!)
- The configural superiority effect is exemplified in the display below by the fact that people are faster at detecting a target (the counterclockwise tilted line) in context than when it is shown on its own.

Target, no context   **Target in context**

L. Cameron (2021), lecture notes
[Reference: Pomerantz, J. R., Sager, L. C., & Stoever, R. J. (1977). Perception of wholes and of their component parts: Some configural superiority effects. *Journal of Experimental Psychology: Human Perception and Performance, 3* (3), 422–435. https://doi.org/10.1037/0096-1523.3.3.422]
- Figure 1 in this manuscript shows two conditions in which (emergent) features provide context that result in a configural superiority effect and two conditions that do not.
[Reference: Wagemans, J., Feldman, J., Gepshtein, S., Kimchi, R., Pomerantz, J. R., Van der Helm, P. A., & Van Leeuwen, C. (2012). A century of Gestalt psychology in visual perception: II. Conceptual and theoretical foundations. *Psychological Bulletin, 138*(6), 1218–1252.]

- Top-down processing allows us to read the following paragraph:
  Aoccdrnig to a rscheearch at Cmabrigde Uinervtisy, it deosn't mttaer in waht oredr the ltieers in a wrod are, the olny iprmoetnt tihng is taht the frist and lsat ltteer be at the rghit pclae. The rset can be a toatl mses and you can sitll raed it wouthit porbeim. Tihs is bcuseae the huamn mnid deos not raed ervey lteter by istlef, but the wrod as a wlohe.
  Or in other words:
  According to a researcher (sic) at Cambridge University, it doesn't matter in what order the letters in a word are, the only important thing is that the first and last letter be at the right place. The rest can be a total mess and you can still read it without problem. This is because the human mind does not read every letter by itself but the word as a whole.
  [Note: This paragraph circulated on the internet a number of years ago and is known to have been a hoax (that is, there was no such research conducted at Cambridge University). While there is some truth to the claims about the way people read, a careful analysis of the claims and a reporting of what linguistics has to say about reading scrambled text can be found here.]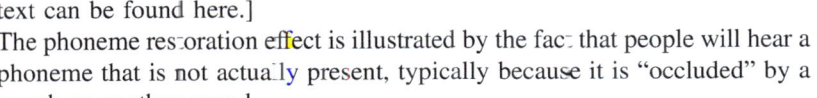
- The phoneme restoration effect is illustrated by the fact that people will hear a phoneme that is not actually present, typically because it is "occluded" by a cough or another sound.
  [Source: Warren. R. M. (1970). Perceptual restoration of missing speech sounds. *Science, 167*(3917), 392–393.]
- Here is a video of the Count from *Sesame Street* singing a song about how much he loves to *count*. The words "count" or "counting" are bleeped out of the soundtrack, and because most people know that bleeps are normally inserted to cover obscene words, many listeners will "hear" a profanity where the words "count" or "counting" should be. This knowledge-based top-down process can occur even in listeners who are familiar with *Sesame Street* characters and know what the missing word really is.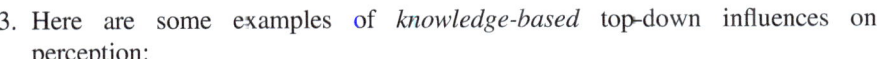

3. Here are some examples of *knowledge-based* top-down influences on perception:

   - *Native language comprehension.* You can easily understand a speech stream in your native language because your knowledge of that language allows you to partition the stream of sounds into meaningful words. If you listen to speech in an unfamiliar language, it can sound like a continuous stream of meaningless (and also accelerated) sounds because you do not have the top-down knowledge necessary to identify individual words.

- A classic example of how knowledge-based top-down processing can make it difficult to spot typos in written text is the sentence *"Paris in the the spring."* People often don't notice that the word "the" is repeated. It is especially easy to miss this error if the first "the" ends a line and the second one starts the next line, as in "Paris in the the spring."
- Another example of knowledge-based top-down processing occurs when you wake up in the middle of the night in your own dark bedroom and can safely navigate to the bathroom without turning on lights. In an unfamiliar house or hotel room, your lack of local knowledge can easily lead to a painful collision or fall unless you turn on a light.
- Knowledge-based top-down processes can also influence memory for objects, as exemplified in the experiment by Carmichael et al. (1932), described in the chapter on memory. It demonstrated that describing an ambiguous figure as, say, a crescent moon or the letter "C" influenced the drawings that participants created when later asked to reproduce figures they had seen.
- This video from the magicians Penn and Teller offers another example of knowledge- and expectancy-based top-down influences on perception, in this case taste perception. It shows that simple tap water will be judged to have noticeably different taste depending on what people are told about its origin and the labels on the bottles in which it is presented.
- In lexical decision tasks the observer has to judge whether an item(s) is (are) a word or not. When pairs of items are presented, people respond more quickly if the words are related (e.g., doctor-nurse) than when they are unrelated (e.g., doctor-bread) or if they are non-words (e.g., blar-plom). You can experience this effect here. The fact that people respond more quickly to the associated words is an example of prior knowledge affecting perception.
- Knowledge-based, top-down influences on planning, decision making, and guiding actions are exemplified during visual search tasks, such as when you are looking for your keys. You would start by looking on counter tops, in purses/pockets, and other places where experience says you might have left them (examples of other heuristics are presented below). You would not be likely to look in the refrigerator—unless that experience includes knowledge that your children enjoy playing tricks on you.
- Several forms of priming (repetition priming, lexical priming, conceptual priming, syntactic priming) provide additional examples of how prior experience can influence future perceptions, actions, and reactions:
  - Repetition Priming: Previous presentation of a word can increase the speed or accuracy of your reaction to the same word later.
  - Semantic Priming: Previous presentation of the color red can increase the speed or accuracy of your response to the word "apple" (as in a lexical decision task, see above).

- Conceptual priming: if you have been primed to think about *furniture*, you might more readily respond to the word "chair".
- Likewise, if you are having a conversation about gardening and someone mentions "squash", you would think of the vegetable. On the other hand, in a conversation about racquet sports, the mention of "squash" would more readily result in thinking about the sport of squash.
- In the classic old-woman/young-woman ambiguous figure, people either see the young or the old woman first. Priming with a less ambiguous figure can be used to influence whether an observer sees the old woman or the young woman first. This is demonstrated in this figure.
- After being primed with words such as "flowers" or "plants" you will be likely to unscramble the letters "efal" as "leaf" more readily than if you had been primed with words like "animal" or "building."
- An example of priming in magic can be seen in the use of a "force" to successfully execute a card trick. This example of priming not only demonstrates that people can be influenced to select the primed card but shows that they experience their selection as having been a free choice. [Source: Pailhès, A., & Kuhn, G. (2020). Influencing choices with conversational primes: How a magic trick unconsciously influences card choices. *Proceedings of the National Academy of Sciences*, *117*(30), 17675–17679. https://www.pnas.org/content/early/2020/07/09/2000682117]

4. Examples of the combined influence on perception of context, knowledge, expectation, and motivation can be seen in failures of human communication.

- Couples often misunderstand each other when one partner's interpretation of what the other partner says is influenced by experience-based knowledge of the other's habits, preferences, past actions, and biases. When this happens, each partner can end up feeling disrespected or accused or insulted—not so much by what the other said but by how the words were interpreted, and especially by assumptions about what the other person really meant.
- Consider also the communication that takes place between pilots and air-traffic controllers. These professionals use a special vocabulary and standardized phrases designed to increase the speed and efficiency of their communication, and as a result, these communications are usually short, with little of the built-in redundancy that in normal conversation allows people to understand a sentence even if some words are missing So, if a pilot eager to depart on time is waiting at the end of an active runway, hoping and expecting to receive the message "American 704 cleared for takeoff" when the actual message is "American 704 hold for takeoff," the results can be catastrophic. On March 27, 1977, just such a miscommunication apparently played a role in the worst accident in aviation history. Believing he had been cleared for departure, a KLM 747 pilot started his takeoff in slightly foggy conditions at an airport in Tenerife (Canary Islands). Moments before, a Pan

American 747 had landed on the same runway and had not yet turned off onto a taxiway. The resulting collision killed 583 people. Noise cancelling microphones, visual displays as well as auditory communication methods, and the use of slightly longer word strings have all been employed since this disaster to minimize or eliminate such top-down perceptual errors.

Mental Representations

Concepts

Bird

Features: has wings and feathers, can fly (typically), lays eggs.

Includes: robin, sparrow, crow, chicken, eagle, ostrich and penguin, etc.

Chair

Features: has legs, a back, can be sat on.

Includes: desk chair, recliner, kitchen chair, arm chair, rocking chair, etc.

Scissors

Features: has two blades, a connecting hinge and a pair of finger rings.

Includes: grooming scissors (for hair or nails), sewing scissors, kitchen scissors, medical scissors, gardening scissors (shears).

Formal concepts—e.g., shapes (square, equilateral triangle), numbers, order of operations, and formulas.

Natural/abstract concepts—e.g., home, game, honesty, justice, sandwich, and vegetable.

1. To help students experience the "fuzziness" of natural concepts, you can ask them to make a list of the features that define one of them. If you choose "vegetable," for example, students will soon discover that there are no rules or lists of features that apply to every vegetable. Tomatoes are not vegetables, but most people think they are. Rhubarb is a vegetable, but most people think it is not.
2. This "like a girl" video is a way to introduce the concept of *girl* that demonstrates the malleability of natural concepts and demonstrates how the concepts affect our thoughts and behaviors.

The ten most typical members or exemplars of three (superordinate) categories, selected by participants in a study by Rosch and Mervis (1975):

Furniture	Vehicle	Weapon
Chair	Car	Gun
Sofa	Truck	Knife
Table	Bus	Sword
Dresser	Motorcycle	Bomb
Desk	Train	Hand grenade
Bed	Trolley car	Spear
Bookcase	Bicycle	Cannon
Footstool	Airplane	Bow and arrow
Lamp	Boat	Club
Piano	Tractor	Tank

[Source: Rosch, E., & Mervis, C. B. (1975). Family resemblances: Studies in the internal structure of categories. *Cognitive Psychology, 7*(4), 573–605.]

Prototypes

1. A graphical example of the difference between exemplars and a prototype can be seen here.
2. Examples of prototypes of several concepts:

   - A prototypical piece of *furniture* is a chair.
   - A prototypical *weapon* is a gun.
   - A prototypical *motor vehicle* is a car or a truck.
   - A prototypical *bird* for a North American might be a robin or a wren.
   - A prototypical *hero* might be Superman or a fireman.
   - A prototypical *color* is red or blue.
   - A prototypical *animal* is a dog or a cat.
   [Source: Decyk, B.N. (1994). Using examples to teach concepts. In D.F. Halpern (ed.), *Changing college classrooms: New teaching and learning strategies for an increasingly complex world* (pp. 39–63). San Francisco: Jossey Bass.]

3. The prevalence of protoypes, in North American culture at least, is exemplified in the responses your students will give when you ask them to write down the name of a tool, a color, and a flower. About 60 to 80% of them will choose "hammer," "red," and "rose" because these are common prototypes of the concepts tool, color, and flower.
4. A simple example of how an amateur magician can use exemplars to "read minds" is seen in a trick that involves asking the audience to silently choose a number between 2 and 9, multiply that number by 9, and add up the two digits

of the resulting number (the total will always be 9), then subtract 5. The result of these operations will always be the number 4. Next the audience is asked to think of the letter of the alphabet that corresponds to "their" final number (this will always be D, because 1 = A, 2 = B, 3 = C, 4 = D). Finally, the audience is asked to write down the name of a country that begins with that letter (most people will think of Denmark), the name of an animal that begins with the last letter of that country (for most, that letter will be K, and most people will then think of kangaroo), and the name of a color that begins with the last letter of the animal they chose (for most, that letter will be O, and most people will think of orange). The magician then asks the audience to concentrate on the country, animal, and color they have "chosen" in order to transmit to the magician the information and can then either reveal a slide on which the words Denmark, kangaroo, and orange appear, or simply state that "There are no orange kangaroos in Denmark."

Cognitive maps

1. You can remember how to get from the front of your high school to your homeroom because you have a cognitive map of the school.
2. You can remember how to get from home to school or work or the grocery store because you have a cognitive map of your hometown.
3. A stranger to your town asks, "How do I get to the Coconut Point mall from here?" To answer the question, you use your cognitive map of the town to picture the roads and crossroads between your current location and the mall and generate a description of the best route. If, however, you know that construction has blocked a certain street, you would be able to use the same cognitive map to generate an alternate route that bypasses the obstacle.
4. This website and podcast starts with an example of how to direct a friend to your house using your cognitive map. The podcast also describes how to use cognitive maps in memory palaces (see the chapter on memory) and promotes a particular technique to improve memory (which we are not necessarily advocating for or promoting.)
5. Some studies have found that cognitive maps are created when playing video games, such as Minecraft. Playing such games can impact processing in the hippocampus. A news story describing one study can be found here.
[Sources: Clemenson, G. D., Henningfield, C. M., & Stark, C. E. (2019). Improving hippocampal memory through the experience of a rich Minecraft environment. *Frontiers in Behavioral Neuroscience, 13*, 57.
West, G. L., Konishi, K., Diarra, M., Benady-Chorney, J., Drisdelle, B. L., Dahmani, L., Sodums, D. J., Lepore, F., Jolicoeur, P., & Bohbot, V. D. (2018). Impact of video games on plasticity of the hippocampus. *Molecular Psychiatry, 23*(7), 1566–1574. https://doi.org/10.1038/mp.2017.155.]

6. As described in the chapter on memory, there is an effect on London taxi drivers' hippocampal volume as they develop the cognitive map necessary for them to pass "The Knowledge" test and receive their license.
7. The original description of a cognitive map in rats in Edward Tolman's (1948) paper can be found here. It is a readable (and funny) article which include images of experimental set-ups.
8. Cognitive maps are described along with two other strategies for spatial navigation in this short video.

Thinking and Reasoning

Examples of Formal/Logical/Deductive Reasoning

[*Note:* It may be helpful to explain that this form of reasoning is called deductive because it takes a general rule and applies it to *deduce* conclusions about specific cases.]

1. Astronomers estimate that the temperature at the core of the sun is about 27 million degrees Fahrenheit. Their estimate is based on *inferences* from other things that they know about the sun and about physical objects in general. Once they had telescopic observations that allowed them to calculate the energy coming from one small part of the sun, they could use knowledge of what solid geometry told them about the surface area of spheres to estimate the sun's total energy output. Further calculations told them how hot a body would have to be to generate that much energy. The formal, logical steps were of the "if–then" variety, namely if we know how much energy comes from one part of the sun's surface and if we know how big the whole surface is, then we can calculate the total energy output. In this example, the astronomers used algorithms, or mathematical formulas, that helped them reach a correct conclusion.
2. You conclude that *if* your friend José is two years older than you are, *then* his twin brother, Juan, will be two years older, too.

Examples of Informal/Inductive Reasoning

[*Note:* It may be helpful to explain that this form of reasoning is called inductive because its goal is to *induce* a general conclusion to appear on the basis of specific facts or examples.]

1. We use inductive reasoning whenever we are trying to assess the believability of a conclusion based on the evidence available to support it, such as:
   - Is a particular brain-training program effective for improving people's memory?

- Is the defendant in a murder case guilty beyond a reasonable doubt given the evidence and testimony presented by the prosecution?
- Which explanation of what caused an aircraft accident is most likely given the evidence available from the flight recorder, the cockpit voice recorder, eyewitness accounts, maintenance records, and weather data? (Every episode of Smithsonian Channel's show, *Air Disasters,* provides detailed illustrations of inductive reasoning processes.)
- In the case of "Laura McBride" described earlier, her doctor had to use evidence from the patient and from test results to determine the most likely cause of her illness.

Examples of Heuristics

1. You want to know if all swans are white. You have never seen a black one, but how many white swans would you have to see before concluding that all swans are white? If you were to use formal reasoning, you would have to look at every swan on the planet. A more practical approach is to base your conclusion on the number of observations that some mental rule of thumb, called a heuristic, leads you to believe is enough. In other words, you would take a mental shortcut to reach a conclusion, perception, prediction, or decision that is probably, but not necessarily, correct (there are black swans).
2. We use heuristics in many other situations, for example:

   - In making judgments about people, such as *stereotyping* based on limited information.
   - As mentioned earlier, if you have lost your keys, you don't use an algorithm (described above and below; in this case the algorithmic solution would be to do an exhaustive, sequential, non-directed search through your entire house). Instead, you use prior knowledge about where you are likely to have left the keys to direct or guide your search.
   - We use *scarcity* as a heuristic to judge the value of commodities. Scarcity is emphasized to increase sales by advertising limited time offers and—especially in TV and online shopping—displaying the ever-diminishing number of products still available.
   - If you are watching a tennis match and you want to guess who is going to win, you might use a recognition heuristic. That is, you might choose the player that is more familiar to you; the fact that you recognize that player may be related to how famous they are, which is a proxy for their ranking.
   - We follow Gestalt "laws" of perceptual organization even though they sometimes lead to incorrect perceptions (see the chapter on sensation and perception).

3. The Anchoring Effect/Anchoring Heuristic

- Here you can find a 90-s video in which Daniel Kahneman provides a classic example of anchoring in judging the average price of cars.
- In one early study on anchoring, participants observed a roulette wheel that was predetermined to stop on either the number 10 or the number 65. Afterwards they were asked to make a series of judgments such as the percentage of the United Nations that were African nations. First, they indicated if the number (10 or 65) was too high or too low and then they guessed the actual number (e.g., percent). In the UN example, participants whose wheel stopped on 10 guessed lower values (25% on average) than participants whose wheel stopped at 65 (45% on average)
[Source: Tversky, A., & Kahneman, D. (1974). Judgment under uncertainty: Heuristics and biases. *Science, 185*(4157), 1124–1131.]
- In another study, participants were asked either: "Did Gandhi die when he was older or younger than 9?" or "Did Gandhi die when he was older or younger than 140?" When people then estimated his age at death those who were asked the first question guessed a younger average death age (50) than those who were asked the second question (67). Incidentally, both groups underestimated of his actual age at death, which was 78.
[Source: Strack, F., & Mussweiler, T. (1997). Explaining the enigmatic anchoring effect: Mechanisms of selective accessibility. *Journal of Personality and Social Psychology, 73*(3), 437–446. https://doi.org/10.1037/0022-3514.73.3.437]
- Evaluating the degree to which a commodity is expensive or not depends upon an anchoring reference point. For example, in 2022 when gas prices in the United States spiked to an average of nearly $5.00 per gallon, it seemed very expensive because the gasoline had previously been priced closer to $3.00, which acted as an anchor.
- The anchoring heuristic operates in many bargaining situations. The asking price of a house, for example, can anchor the sellers' perception of its value. As a result, they may be reluctant to accept a lower price, even if their sales agent suggests that they should. The buyers' judgment of the house's value will also be anchored to some extent by the seller's asking price. Even if the buyers discover that the house needs some repairs, they are more likely to offer 90% of the price rather than, say, 50%.
- Anchoring heuristics can also affect probability estimates (e.g., likelihood of nuclear war or of being mugged in big cities). Suppose, for example, that Jean is getting ready to move from her small town to a big city for a new job. Her parents lived in that city 20 years ago in the same neighborhood where Jean wants to rent an apartment. Back then, the parents discovered that the area was plagued by crime, but Jean explains that in recent years it has seen many changes and improvements and now boasts one of the lowest crime

rates in the city. Jean's parents are glad to know that the crime is now less common there, but just cannot believe that the area is really all that safe.
- The length of a jail sentence could be seen as long or short depending on expectations (an anchor). There is some evidence that criminal sentences passed down by judges may be affected by recommendations from lawyers for the defense and the prosecution, which might serve as anchors.
- The anchoring heuristic presents a challenge for defense attorneys in U.S. criminal courts because the prosecution presents its evidence first. Once this evidence has created the impression that a defendant is guilty, some jurors mentally anchor to that impression and may not be swayed much by defense evidence to the contrary.
- The wait time at a restaurant can seem long or short depending upon your expectations, which act as an anchor. Your experience of waiting for 40 min will seem long if you have been told that the wait time will be 30 min, whereas it will seem short if you were told it was going to be an hour.
- Other examples of judgments affected by anchoring heuristics include:
    General knowledge (e.g., the freezing point of vodka, length of the Mississippi River, annual mean temperature in Germany)
    Legal judgments (e.g., punitive damage awards)
    Valuation and purchasing decisions (willingness to pay for a range of products)
    Forecasting (e.g., estimating an athlete's likely performance)
    Self-efficacy (e.g., estimating one's ability to solve a problem or do well at a task)
    [Source: Furnham, A., & Boo, H. C. (2011). A literature review of the anchoring effect. *The Journal of Socio-Economics*, *40*(1), 35–42. https://www.sciencedirect.com/science/article/pii/S1053535710001411]

4. The Availability Heuristic

- A graphical illustration from JamesClear.com of the root of the availability heuristic can be found here.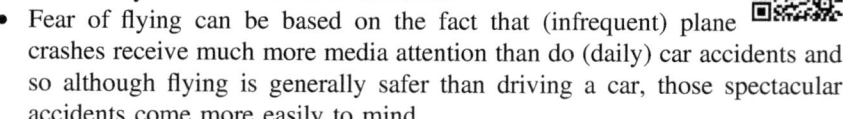
- Fear of flying can be based on the fact that (infrequent) plane crashes receive much more media attention than do (daily) car accidents and so although flying is generally safer than driving a car, those spectacular accidents come more easily to mind.
- We also tend to overestimate events such as shark attacks for the same reason that we overestimate the risk of flying.
- In the following riddle, the availability heuristic makes it difficult to come up with the solution: A father and son have a car accident and are both badly hurt. They are both taken to separate hospitals. When the boy is taken in for an operation, the surgeon says 'I cannot operate on this boy because he is my son'. How is this possible? Solution: the surgeon is a woman, but the availability heuristic (and gender role stereotyping) may have led you to assume the surgeon was a man.

- Concern over the Johnson and Johnson Covid-19 vaccine emerged in 2021 when a very small number of women (about 6 out of 6 million) developed blood clots and died after receiving it. These rare cases resulted in some vaccine hesitancy even though millions of people have had the vaccine with no serious side-effects. The "available" information focused on the small number of deaths.
- You may be hesitant to get a flu shot or other vaccination if you know someone who got sick after receiving one.
- Here are three other examples of the availability heuristic:
  People are likely to say that there are more English words that start with the letter "r" or "k" than those that have "r" or "k" as the third letter. This assertion is incorrect, but words that start with the letters "r" and "k" come to mind more readily.
  After hearing a list of names, including the names of celebrities, people are more likely to judge celebrities to be more numerous than they actually are. People's estimates of the probability of fires or car accidents increase after seeing a burned out house or an overturned car on the highway.
  [Source: Tversky, A., & Kahneman, D. (1974). Judgment under uncertainty: Heuristics and biases. *Science*, *185*(4157), 1124–1131.]
- The availability heuristic may partially explain why police officers are more likely to misclassify black people as guilty of a crime.
  [Source: Najdowski, C. J. (2011). Stereotype threat in criminal investigations: Why innocent Black suspects are at risk for confessing falsely. *Psychology, Public Policy, and Law, 17*(4), 562–591.]
- It is difficult for people to make sense of the science of climate change in the face of their personal experience with weather (and especially cold weather), which is the information that is most readily "available" to them. A description of how the availability heuristic leads to faulty judgments about the environment and climate change is available in a blog post found here.
  [Sources: Li, Y., Johnson, E. J., & Zaval, L. (2011). Local warming: Daily temperature change influences belief in global warming. *Psychological Science*, *22*(4), 454–459.
  Zaval, L., Keenan, E. A., Johnson, E. J., & Weber, E. U. (2014). How warm days increase belief in global warming. *Nature Climate Change*, *4*(2), 143–147.]
- Traumatic experience with hurricanes, tornadoes, and thunderstorms can change expectations and result in activation of the availability heuristic and creation of an "availability cascade".
- Media coverage of child abductions, violent crimes, and police shootings make those events more "available" and contribute to people's

overestimation of the true likelihood of such events. A small number of cases covered in the media creates images that are memorable. Moreover, the continuous coverage by the media of certain events, as well as the continued social media conversations about them, magnifies the threats.
- People are more likely to think they will win the lottery if they have just seen a news story about someone who won millions in a lottery.
- Because the dangers of the Covid-19 pandemic were so heavily reported, people may have been more likely to behave cautiously and abide by guidelines and restrictions even in situations that were unlikely to lead to infection. For example, it was not uncommon in 2020 to see people wearing masks while on Zoom calls or driving alone in their cars.
- The fact that people tend to hold the false belief that more people die from tornados than from asthma has been explained by the availability heuristic.
- This tendency is exemplified in a study in which people were asked to judge which of two means of death was more common. They frequently erred toward the cause of death that was more likely to be publicized. You can find the study here.

5. The Representativeness Heuristic

- In considering questions such as *What is the probability that object A belongs to class B?* people apply the representativeness heuristic. Here is a classic example:
A man is described as "meticulous, introverted, meek, solemn." What is the probability that this man is a farmer, a salesman, an airline pilot, a librarian or a physician? People tend to choose "librarian" based on stereotypes about the most representative characteristics of people in various jobs rather than on the base rate of those jobs in the population. When base rates are taken into account, the most appropriate judgment is "farmer" because farmers are more numerous in the population than any of the other jobs listed. The representativeness heuristic influences judgments even when people are told what the base rates are beforehand.
[Source: Tversky, A., & Kahneman, D. (1974). Judgment under uncertainty: Heuristics and biases. *Science, 185*(4157), 1124–1131.]
- Here is another example (also from Tversky & Kahneman, 1974) of a case where people use the representativeness heuristic (ignoring sample size) and come to the incorrect conclusion:
A certain town is served by two hospitals. In the larger hospital about 45 babies are born each day, and in the smaller hospital about 15 babies are born each day. As you know, about 50% of all babies are boys. The exact percentage of baby boys, however, varies from day to day. Sometimes it may be higher than 50%, sometimes lower. For a period of one year, each hospital recorded the days on which more than 60% of the babies born were boys.

Which hospital do you think recorded more such days?

(a) The larger hospital? (22% of students chose this answer)
(b) The smaller hospital? (22% of students chose this answer—the correct response)
(c) About the same (i.e., within 5% of each other)? (56% of students chose this answer)

- Gabrielle is tall, slender, extremely attractive, and lives in an expensive condo. If we were to judge that she is probably a fashion model because she resembles our stereotype of fashion models, we would be using the representativeness heuristic.
- A person's decision about whom to vote for in a presidential election can depend more on which candidate is more representative of the voter's conception of a president than on whether the voter agrees with the candidate's policies.
- A consumer may infer that a store (generic) brand is of a higher quality if its packaging resembles a national brand.
  [Source: Kardes, F. R., Posavac, S. S., & Cronley, M. L. (2004). Consumer inference: A review of processes, bases, and judgment contexts. *Journal of Consumer Psychology, 14*(3), 230–256.]
- Gamblers tend to prefer lottery tickets with random-looking number sequences "(e.g. 7, 16, 23. ...) over those with patterned sequences (e.g. 10, 20, 30, ...)" presumably because the random-looking numbers are more representative of what the gambler thinks of as a winner.
  [Source: Krawczyk, M. W., & Rachubik, J. (2019). The representativeness heuristic and the choice of lottery tickets: A field experiment. *Judgment and Decision Making. 14*(1), 51–57.]
- Investors may prefer to buy a stock that has had abnormally high recent returns (known as extrapolation bias) or may misattribute a company's positive characteristics (e.g., high quality goods) as an indicator of it being a good investment.
  [Source: Chen, G., Kim, K. A., Nofsinger, J. R., & Rui, O. M. (2007). Trading performance, disposition effect, overconfidence, representativeness bias, and experience of emerging market investors. *Journal of Behavioral Decision Making 20*, 425–451.]

[The three items immediately above were found at this website which lists numerous examples of the representativeness heuristic.]

Convergent, Divergent and Creative Thinking

1. Examples of convergent thinking include solving well-defined problems such as the Towers of Hanoi or perhaps when answering multiple choice questions. You use convergent thinking to answer the question: 5 + 5 = ?

2. Examples of divergent thinking (and creativity) appear when investigators try to identify the perpetrator of a crime or the cause of an accident, or when someone sits down to write a novel. You would use a form of divergent thinking called brainstorming to respond to questions and tasks like these:

   - How could/would you spend $1 million?
   - Write an essay after being given a single word as a prompt. (This task was used until recently as part of entrance screening at All Souls College at Oxford University).

3. The Alternative Uses Test is designed to measure divergent thinking. It asks people to generate as many uses as possible for common objects, such as a brick, a shoe or a paperclip. The test is described at this website.
   [Source: Guilford, J.P. (1967). *The nature of human intelligence.* New York: McGraw-Hill.]

4. Here is an example of responses to this alternative use question: "What can you use a newspaper for?" (Answers that relate to acquiring information or keeping up with current events would represent convergent thinking.) Divergent thinking responses included using newspaper to create a papier-mâché object, to light a fire, to pad a package, to cover oneself for warmth, to provide insulation from noise, to stuff shoes so that they keep their shape, to make a higher seat for a short child, to make a toy for a cat, to make an airplane, to wrap a box, to train a puppy, to humidify the air (by draping wet newspapers over a radiator), to make a ransom note (by cutting out letters from a newspaper), and to soak up water (by putting newspapers in wet shoes).

5. The Consequences Test contains items that require divergent thinking. The test includes items such as:

   - *Imagine all the things that might possibility happen if all national and local laws were suddenly abolished.*
   - *What would be the consequences if everyone suddenly lost the ability to read and write?*
   - *What would be the consequences if none of us needed food any more to live?*
   [Source: Guilford, J.P. (1959) Traits of creativity. In Anderson, H.H. (ed.), *Creativity and its cultivation.* (pp.142–161) Harper & Row.]

6. Divergent thinking is used in the game Scattergories. Players each generate their own set of words that meet constraints, such as *vegetables that start with the letter "C"*. The objective is to come up with unique responses (i.e., ones that no one else writes).

7. This 3:38-min video from the Harvard School of Continuing Education describes convergent and divergent thinking and gives examples of each.

8. When trying to solve the problem of a high accident rate at a particular intersection you (and perhaps your group) might first use divergent thinking to "brainstorm" all of the ways that one might try to decrease the likelihood of accidents occurring (e.g., decreasing speed limit, adding flashing lights around stop signs, adding temporary speed radar). You might say at this stage "There are no bad ideas." Once many ideas have been generated, you (and the group) can use convergent thinking to narrow down and select the best options, perhaps the "low hanging fruit" or those ideas that you expect will be maximally effective.
9. Here is an example of a problem that requires divergent thinking (and also breaking a mental set regarding the orientation of drawings):

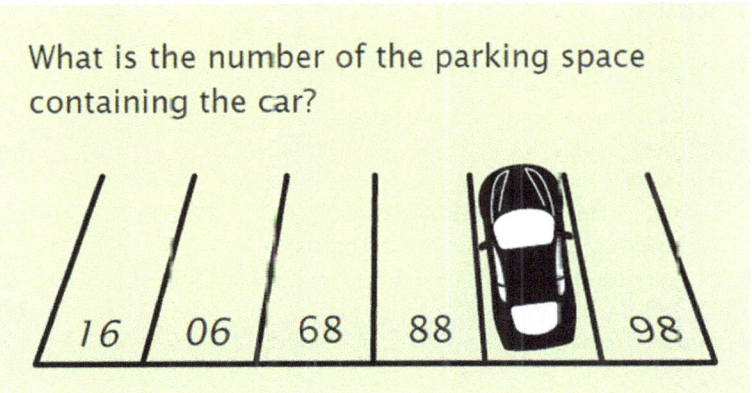

(If you turn the drawing upside down, it will immediately become obvious that the car is parked in space number 87.)
10. The Remote Associates Test of creativity can be found online here.
11. Examples of methods for improving creativity:

- This Veritasium video explains why boredom can be good for you and your creativity.
- It may surprise your students, but people are more creative when they make up sentences after being given a word or a picture that constrains their options. This effect is described by Catrinel Haught-Tromp here.
- Anecdotal support for the hypothesis that constraints facilitate creativity can be found in the pages of Dr. Seuss's bestselling children's book *Green Eggs and Ham*. As the story goes, Seuss's editor, Bennett Cerf, challenged him to write a book using only 50 words—including "Sam," "here," "there" and "anywhere." Previously, Seuss had penned *The Cat in the Hat* using only 255 words, so Cerf was upping the ante. More than up to the task, the limitation helped Seuss produce one of the most successful children's books of all time. Apparently, the 50-word limit imposed on Dr. Seuss served

to spark his creative genius. But how? Haught-Tromp explains that constraints work by "closing doors" and "narrowing the exploratory space. Fewer available options encourage a more focused, thorough search within the existing space, and facilitate mining and probing beyond the surface." By doing so, constraints increase the likelihood of finding novel associations—like "Sam I am"—and a more creative output.

[Source: Haught-Tromp, C. (2017). The Green Eggs and Ham hypothesis: How constraints facilitate creativity. *Psychology of Aesthetics, Creativity, and the Arts*, 11(1), 10–17. https://doi.org/10.1037/aca0000061]

Metacognition

1. Examples of metacognitive processes include

   - planning, monitoring and assessing thinking processes
   - self-questioning
   - reflection
   - assessing strengths and weaknesses (e.g., SWOT analysis—Strengths, Weaknesses, Opportunities, and Threats)
   - recognizing what helps you learn, remember, solve problems, and make decisions
   - thinking aloud

2. Metacognition includes

   - being aware that you have difficulty remembering names
   - monitoring your comprehension as you read
   - recognizing mistakes in your work
   - knowing that you know something but that you just can't recall it at the moment

3. This very short video describes the "metacognitive cycle".

4. A website devoted to metacognition for students, instructors and parents can be found here.

5. Application of metacognition to improve learning, particularly in college students, is described at about the 4-min mark in this video by Stephen Chew.

6. Exam wrappers, in which students reflect and respond to questions about their exam performance, are an example of using metacognition to improve learning.

7. This website about metacognition includes short videos with examples of students (one in elementary school and one in high school) using metacognitive strategies to complete math problems.
8. Here are some sample items from Schraw and Dennison's Metacognitive Awareness Inventory (MAI) that probe five aspects of metacognition (regulation of cognition):

   Information management strategies
   - I focus on the meaning and significance of new information
   - I create my own examples to make information more meaningful
   - I ask myself if what I'm reading is related to what I already know

   Debugging strategies
   - I stop and go back over new information that is not clear
   - I stop and reread when I get confused

   Planning
   - I think of several ways to solve a problem and choose the best one
   - I ask myself questions about the material before I begin.
   - I read instructions carefully before I begin a task

   Comprehension monitoring
   - I ask myself periodically if I am meeting my goals
   - I periodically review to help me understand important relationships

   Evaluation
   - I know how well I did once I finish a test.
   - I ask myself how well I accomplish my goals once I'm finished
   - I ask myself if I learned as much as I could have once I finish a task

   The full inventory is available here.

[Source: Schraw, G. & Dennison, R.S. (1994). Assessing metacognitive awareness. *Contemporary Educational Psychology, 19,* 460–475.]

Problem Solving

1. Examples of ill-defined problems

   - Solving a crime. See this website for an example of a game that involves solving a crime and has been used to study ill-defined problem-solving.
   [Source: Hołda, M., Głodek, A., Dankiewicz-Berger, M., Skrzypińska, D., & Szmigielska, B. (2020). Ill-defined problem solving does not benefit from daytime napping. *Frontiers in Psychology, 11,* 559.]

- Scenario: The population of your town is growing but you have limited water. What do you do to avoid a water crisis?
- Scenario: You're camping and you forgot the hammer you need to pound in the spikes for your tent. What do you do?
- What should you do for lunch, given that you have limited time?
- What meal should you prepare for a dinner party?
- What should you wear today if most of your clothes are in the laundry hamper? Or: what should you wear if you need to be able to wear something to work (i.e., something dressy) and you are going to ride a bicycle to work?
- How to complete a homework assignment given conflicting demands and time-constraints.
- Many ill-defined problems are encountered when conducting experiments, e.g., how to obtain a random sample of participants or how best to protect participants' data.
- Climate change is a very large-scale, complex, ill-defined problem.

[*Note:* These problems arise because there is an obstacle, often created by constraints, such as time or limited resources.]

2. Examples of well-defined problems

- A classic well-defined problem is the *Towers of Hanoi*, which can be played online here.
- The whole class of river-crossing problems provides another example of well-defined problems. (Note: the wording and set up of some of the versions below are dated and sexist). See this link for a variety of efforts to reword the problem; a description of the history of these problems can be found here.

Hobbits and Orcs
A nice graphic of this problem can be found here:
Three hobbits and three orcs arrive at a riverbank, and they all want to cross to the other side. There is a boat, but it can carry (at most) two creatures at a time. The constraint is that orcs can never outnumber hobbits on a river bank or they will eat them. Also, the boat has to be rowed by a creature—it cannot cross on its own. How can all six creatures cross the river without the hobbits being eaten by orcs?

Missionaries and cannibals
Three missionaries and three cannibals must cross a river using a boat which can carry at most two people, under the constraint that, for both banks, if there are missionaries present on the bank, they cannot be outnumbered by cannibals (if they were, the cannibals would eat the missionaries). The boat cannot cross the river by itself with no people on board.

Man and Wolf
A man has a wolf, a goat and a cabbage, and has to cross a river in a boat that can accommodate at most two of these possessions. He must not leave the wolf alone with the goat, or the goat alone with the cabbage, but it is ok to leave the wolf and cabbage together. How does he do it?

Friends and Sisters
Three friends, each with a sister, needed to cross a river. Each of them coveted the sister of another. At the river, they found only a small boat, in which only two of them could cross at a time. How did they cross the river without any of the women being harassed by the men?

Jealous Husbands
Three couples, husbands and their wives, are out walking and come to a river that they wish to cross. The only means available is a boat that could carry no more than two people. So evidently, they might be ferried across by twos, with one person returning the boat to pick up the next pair. However, there is a hitch. Being jealous, the husbands agreed that no wife can be left in the presence of another man unless her own husband is present. How can the crossing be achieved?

- Online versions of the river-crossing problem can be found here.

- A range of problems, including the river crossing problem, can be found here.

- Puzzles such as those shown here have constraints on how you can move the pieces

- The game of "hangman" can be played online here.

- Links to a variety of puzzles involving well-defined problems can be found here.

- Luchin's water jug problem is a classic example of a well-defined problem. (See the link under "mental set" below.)

- Here is a short (5:46-min) silent movie of Kohler's chimpanzees solving several well-defined problems.

3. Examples of insight problems

   - Many excellent examples of insight problems can be found in this publication.
     [Reference: Batchelder, W. H., & Alexander, G. E. (2012). Insight problem solving: A critical examination of the possibility of formal theory. *The Journal of Problem Solving*, 5(1), 6.]
   - The Number Reduction Task is an example of an insight problem. The task was used in one study that demonstrated that sleep improves insight. The task is described in the mental set section of this chapter. See also topics related to sleep in the chapter on consciousness.
     [Source: Wagner, U., Gais, S., Haider, H., Verleger, R., & Born, J. (2004). Sleep inspires insight. *Nature*, 427(6972), 352–355.]
   - This video shows a small group of students trying to solve a problem—how to lift 7 bricks with one hand. They fail to solve the problem that probably would be solved using insight. The students demonstrate functional fixedness (see below) and an inability to see the problem from a fresh perspective.
   - Here is an example of a word problem that requires an insight: "Water lilies double in area every 24 h. At the beginning of the summer, there is one water lily on a lake. It takes 30 days for the lake to become completely covered with water lilies. On what day is the lake half covered?" [The insight comes in recognizing that the lake would be half full the day before the final doubling (on day 30).]
     [Source: Davidson, J. E., & Sternberg, R. J. (Eds.). (2003). *The psychology of problem solving*. Cambridge University Press.]
   - Amory Danek has found that figuring out how magic tricks are done often happens through insight. Here is a description of the process and a video about it.

   - An example of a chimpanzee solving an insight problem can be seen in a two-minute video here.
   - An example of a pigeon solving Kohler's box and banana problem can be seen in a 1-min video here.
     [Reference: Epstein, R., Kirshnit, C, Lanza, R.P., & Rubin, L.C. (1984). 'Insight' in the pigeon: Antecedents and determinants of an intelligent performance, *Nature*, 308, 61–62.]

4. Examples of problem-solving processes: Algorithms.

   - Following each step in a recipe to bake a cake
   - Google, YouTube, and social media platforms use algorithms to "decide" what to recommend to you next, based on your previous "clicks".
   - An algorithm is used in the Number Reduction Task. (See details under "mental set" below.)

- A nice description of 3 basic (formal) algorithms used by programmers can be found here.

- A flowchart of Euclid's (formal) algorithm can be found here.

5. Examples of problem-solving processes: Using analogies

- Perhaps the most commonly used examples of analogies in the problem-solving and reasoning literature is Duncker's radiation problem and the so-called Fortress Story. These stories/problems can be found here along with a description of research that shows how difficult it can be for people to use the solution of one problem to find the solution of another.
  [References:
  Gick, M. L., & Holyoak, K. J. (1980). Analogical problem solving. *Cognitive Psychology*, 12(3), 306–355.
  Gick, M. L., & Holyoak, K. J. (1983). Schema induction and analogical transfer. *Cognitive Psychology*, 15(1), 1–38.]
- Examples of analogies can be seen in Miller's Analogy Tests, such as "Mason is to [stone] as Carpenter is to Wood. More sample problems can be found here.
- Analogies are used in teaching, such as, for example, when atomic structure is compared to the solar system. Likewise, a capacitor (two conducting materials separated by an insulator), is used as an analogy for the membrane of a neuron where the extracellular and intracellular fluids are the conductors, and the lipid membrane is the insulator.
- Examples of analogies in math problems are plentiful. If a child has solved a word problem that required addition, recognizing it as an analogy for another problem should help her solve the second problem.

6. Examples of problem-solving processes: Means-ends analysis (decomposition)

- If the problem you want to solve is to drive from New York to Boston in the minimum amount of time possible, then a means-ends analysis would involve keeping that ultimate goal in mind, but along the way considering any obstacles (traffic, weather conditions) and overcoming them as you try to minimize the time necessary to reach the goal.
- Another example would be writing a term paper. The ultimate goal of completing the paper would be kept in mind, but it would be broken up into subgoals (e.g., write an outline, gather information, write an opening paragraph, etc.), and obstacles to completing each subgoal would be overcome in sequence.

- Here is a blog post for a cognitive psychology course that describes using means-ends problem solving to complete the course by setting up and completing subgoals.
- Playing a game of chess requires a means-ends analysis. Your goal is to put your opponent into checkmate, but this cannot be done in one step. So, you create and complete subgoals, constantly revising them in response to your opponent's moves.
- The Towers of Hanoi, Hobbits and Orcs and many puzzles such as River Crossing (see the earlier section on well-defined problems) are examples of "search" problems that can be solved by using subgoals, and thus means-ends analysis.
- Another example: "I want to take my son to nursery school. What's the difference between what I have and what I want? One of distance. What changes distance? My automobile. My automobile won't work. What is needed to make it work? A new battery. What has new batteries? An auto repair shop. I want the repair shop to put in a new battery; but the shop doesn't know I need one. What is the difficulty? One of communication. What allows communication? A telephone... and so on." — [Source: Adapted from Newell, A., & Simon, H. A. (1972). *Human problem solving*. Englewood Cliffs, NJ: Prentice-Hall]
- An example of a crow solving a multiple part problem using subgoals is demonstrated here.

7. Examples of problem-solving processes: Working backwards

- One of the so-called "habits of highly effective people" is to "begin with the end in mind." In product development, designers start with the end product in mind and work backwards from there.
  [Source: Covey, S. R. (2013). *The 7 habits of highly effective people: Powerful lessons in personal change*. Simon and Schuster.]
- When solving time-management problems, working backwards can be very helpful. For example, if you know that you have a 4 pm flight, you also know that you have to be at the airport at 2 pm, which means that you need to leave your house at 1 pm (assuming you live a distance from the airport and will need to park etc.) You continue to work backwards to figure out what tasks (e.g. packing, closing up the house, taking the dog to the kennel, etc.) must be completed so that you are ready to leave your house at 1 pm.
- If you are planning to climb a mountain (e.g., Mount Everest), the best strategy is to envision the goal (being on top of the mountain) and figuring out what you would need at that point and then work backwards from there. So, you would figure out, first, what equipment and supplies are needed at the highest camp on the night before the attempt to reach the summit, then how many people are needed to stock that camp the day before, then how many people are needed to supply those who must stock the camp, and so on until a plan for the entire expedition is established. It is partly because of failure to

Problem Solving   221

  apply this strategy that climbers sometimes die on Everest.
  [Source: Adapted from Bernstein D.A. (2019). *Essentials of Psychology* (7th ed.). Belmont, CA: Wadsworth Cengage Learning. p. 248.]
  - Some math problems can be solved by working backwards. For example, in a subtraction problem you can work backwards by adding. Here is a word problem where that could work: *Sam's mom left a plate of cookies on the counter. Sam ate 2 of them, his dad ate 3 of them and they gave 12 to the neighbor. At the end of the day, only 4 cookies were left on the plate. How many cookies did she make altogether.*
  Source: This blogpost.
  - This classic problem from Sternberg and Davidson (2003) was described earlier in relation to insight, but it also lends itself to the working backwards strategy: "Water lilies double in area every twenty-four hours. At the beginning of the summer, there is one water lily on the lake. It takes sixty days for the lake to be completely covered with water lilies. On what day is the lake half covered?" The problem solver can use a solution method based on working backwards from the last day. Based on this method, the problem solver can ask what the lake would look like on the day before the last day and conclude that the lake is half covered on the fifty-ninth day.
  Here is the source.
  [Reference: Davidson, J. E., & Sternberg, R. J. (Eds.). (2003). *The psychology of problem solving*. Cambridge University Press.]

8. Examples of problem-solving processes: Using Experience
   A person who has dealt with a particular type of problem many times (an expert) will find it easier to solve such a problem the next time it is encountered than would someone who is facing the problem for the first time. Experts can bring to bear knowledge of all elements of the problem, can organize those elements in useful ways, can recall strategies that did and did not work in the past, and unlike the novice, can avoid letting irrelevant details distract attention from the "big picture" as they plan strategies. As a result, experts are usually better than novices at solving almost any problem in almost any realm, and solving it faster. This is why, at one time or another, most of us hire experts to build or repair our houses, handle our court cases, protect our property, invest our money, do our taxes, and help us address psychological problems.

   - Experts develop their knowledge through *deliberate practice*. Danish scientist and Nobel laureate Niels Bohr defined an expert as "A person that has made every possible mistake within his or her field." Malcolm Gladwell described expertise as a matter of practicing the correct way for a total of around 10,000 h.
   - Experts take advantage of chunking and other memory strategies to aid their problem-solving performance. That strategy is described in this blog post which includes a video of an expert recalling chess

board configurations and then describing how he remembered them. (See other examples of chunking in the memory chapter.)
- Experts have developed the ability to see similarities or analogies between current and past problems. Their experience makes experts better than beginners at identifying the common principles that underlie seemingly different problems.
- An experienced lawyer will grasp the implications of a new law far more quickly than a recent law school graduate.
- An experienced teacher will think of ways to promote students' interest in "boring" material that would never occur to a first-time teacher.
- An experienced business executive will realize that the same strategy that worked well to resolve a family problem at home can be adapted for use in dealing with conflicts among employees.
- A doctor who for years has specialized in open-heart surgery will be able to handle an unusual and potentially dangerous situation in the operating room with greater skill and aplomb than a general surgeon might.
- Expert radiologists show more effective patterns of eye movements when searching x-rays for tumors and other abnormalities.
  [Source: Kundel, H. L., & La Follette Jr, P. S. (1972). Visual search patterns and experience with radiological images. *Radiology, 103*(3), 523–528.]
- "Do it yourself" books, tutorials, videos, and blog posts designed to teach novices how to tile a floor or make money in the stock market or reach new heights in gaming, or even improve their classroom teaching skills are full of "pro tips" designed to help the reader avoid the "rookie" mistakes that the authors once made themselves.

Obstacles to Problem Solving

1. Mental Set

    - A classic mental set is induced in the Luchins' water jug problem demonstrated here.

    - The Number Reduction Task is another situation that can lead to a mental set. The task is nicely illustrated and described here.

    (See also the section on insight in this chapter and in problems related to sleep in the chapter on consciousness.)

    - Every time your wireless printer stops working, you reboot it and it reconnects to your network. Today, that solution didn't work because you failed to notice that your computer wasn't connected to the network.

- Here is the famous "nine-dot problem" (see also insight):

It challenges you to draw four straight lines that run through all nine dots without lifting your pen or pencil from the paper. Mental set leads most people to assume that the lines must be drawn within the frame of the dots or that they have to run through the centers of the dots. Here is a solution that breaks those mental sets:

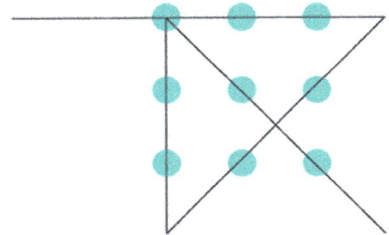

2. Functional Fixedness

- Examples of overcoming functional fixedness include:
  To solve the problem of joining two strings that are hanging from the ceiling, but too far apart to be reached by one person, this man tied a pair of pliers from the tool box to one string and started it swinging, like a pendulum, until he could reach it while holding the other string.

Using a tire as a swing or a football target
Using a wine bottle as a vase or candle holder
Using dental floss as thread
Using a book or a brick as a door stop
Using a towel as a curtain
Using a lacrosse stick to catch a bat in the attic
Using a fridge magnet tied to a chopstick to retrieve a metal object that fell into the kitchen sink drain

- Some of the most extraordinary examples of human problem-solving come from the story of the aborted Apollo 13 lunar mission, captured with the phrase "Houston, we have a problem." This story is brilliantly depicted in the 1995 movie *Apollo 13* starring Tom Hanks as Jim Lovell. The movie in its entirety can be used to demonstrate how people can come together to solve incredibly large problems, but here are two segments that provide particularly vivid examples of overcoming functional fixedness:

In the first scene, engineers and technicians at Mission Control debate the best way to try to get Apollo 13 back to earth using a "new flight plan." When debating which of various parts of the spacecraft could be used, Gene Kranz (played by Ed Harris) implores the scientists and engineers to be divergent thinkers, saying "I don't care what anything was designed to do. I care about what it can do."

In the second scene a group of men, including flight surgeons, at Mission Control approach Gene Kranz and say "Gene, we have a situation brewing with the carbon dioxide. We have a CO_2 filter problem in the LEM module. There are 5 filters on the LEM which are meant for 2 guys for a day and a half." They explain the dangers of too much CO_2—impaired thinking, brain asphyxia, blackouts… Kranz replies "What about the scrubbers on the command module?" The response: "They take square cartridges… and the ones on the LEM are round." Kranz says "Well, I suggest you gentleman figure out how to put a square peg in a round hole, rapidly." The next scene shows a group of scientists and engineers walking into a room and dumping onto a large table three boxes of objects that correspond to those that are on the spacecraft. The leader of the group says "OK people, listen up. The people upstairs have handed us this one and we have to come through. We have to find a way to put this [holds up one cartridge] into the hole for this [holds up another cartridge] using nothing but that [gesturing to all of the items on the table]". The response from the group is… "Let's get it organized." "Let's build a filter." "Let's get a pot of coffee going…" Later in the movie, Ken Mattingly (played by Gary Sinese) arrives at Mission Control with a group of guys carrying the unusual filter and instructions on how to build it on the spacecraft. The filter works, CO_2 levels drop, and there is a collective sigh of relief.

3. Confirmation Bias

   What the human being is best at doing is interpreting all new information so that their prior conclusions remain intact.—Warren Buffet

   No amount of experimentation can ever prove me right; a single experiment can prove me wrong.—Albert Einstein.

   - Obstacles to problem-solving frequently appear at the beginning of the process when people are trying to figure out what the problem is and what is causing it. It is in this diagnosis stage that people form and then test hypotheses about a problem. If they settle on the wrong hypothesis at the outset, they are in for a long and difficult experience. Here is a real life example described in the *London Daily Telegraph* in 1998: John Gatiss was in the kitchen of his rented house in Cheltenham, England, when he heard a faint "meowing" sound. Worried that a kitten had become trapped somewhere, he called for the fire brigade to rescue the animal. The sound seemed to be coming from the electric stove, so the rescuers dismantled it, disconnecting the power cord in the process. The sound stopped, but everyone assumed that wherever the kitten was, it was now too frightened to meow. The search was reluctantly abandoned and the stove was reconnected. Four days later, however, the meowing began again. This time, Gatiss and his landlord called the Royal Society for the Prevention of Cruelty to Animals (RSPCA), whose inspectors heard the kitten in distress and asked the fire brigade to come back. They spent the next three days searching for the cat. First, they dismantled parts of the kitchen walls and ripped up the floorboards. Next, they called in plumbing and drainage specialists, who used cables tipped with fiber-optic cameras to search remote cavities where a kitten might hide. Rescuers then brought in a disaster search team, which tried to find the kitten with acoustic and ultrasonic equipment normally used to locate victims trapped under earthquake debris. Not a sound was heard. Increasingly concerned about how much longer the kitten could survive, the fire brigade tried to coax it from hiding with the finest-quality fish, but to no avail. Suddenly, there was a burst of "purring" that, to everyone's surprise (and the landlord's dismay), was traced by the ultrasonic equipment to the clock in the electric stove! Later, the landlord commented that everyone assumed Gatiss's original hypothesis was correct—that the "meowing" came from a cat trapped in the kitchen. "I just let them carry on. If there is an animal in there, you have to do what it takes. The funniest thing was that it seemed to reply when we called out to it." (Adapted from Bernstein D.A. (2019). *Essentials of psychology* (7th ed.). Belmont, CA: Wadsworth Cengage Learning. p. 251).
   - This compelling video demonstrates confirmation bias with the "2–4–8" task.

- Typical responses to the Wason selection task demonstrate confirmation bias (and lack of attempts to falsify a claim). For a full description of the problem and the reasoning errors see this video.
- If a police officer on traffic patrol believes that young female drivers are more likely than other drivers to exceed the speed limit, the officer might be more likely to notice young female drivers speeding than to notice young male or older drivers doing the same.
- Some research suggests that during interrogations, some police officers are more likely to assume that, compared to white suspects, black suspects are guilty. Once they have made that assumption, confirmation bias may lead them to more aggressively seek and pay attention to evidence that supports their belief.
  [Source: Najdowski, C. J. (2011). Stereotype threat in criminal investigations: Why innocent Black suspects are at risk for confessing falsely. *Psychology, Public Policy, and Law, 17*(4), 562–591.]
- Someone who is afraid to travel by air is more likely than other people to pay attention to and remember every air accident, large or small, ever described on the news, and perhaps even to watch TV shows such as *Air Disasters*.
- If a student believes that her teacher is nicer to boys than to girls, she may be more likely to notice and remember instances in which the teacher was nice to boys.
- News stories about negative side-effects of the Covid-19 vaccines are likely to draw more attention from people who are reluctant to be vaccinated than from those who are confident in the value and safety of vaccinations. This example applies equally well to any vaccine, including the flu vaccine.
- A blog post that describes several examples of confirmation bias, can be found here.

- Research summarized here suggests that confirmation bias can lead some people to not only ignore facts that don't fit their views, but to create false memories of facts that do.

- In this study in the journal *Human Communication Research*, researchers asked people about their views on controversial topics, then showed them accurate statistics on those topics, including the decline in the number of Mexican immigrants to the United States from 12.8 million in 2007 to 11.7 million in 2014. Without being asked to memorize the statistics, the participants were later asked to write down the facts. When the facts didn't fit peoples' views, they tended to get the numbers wrong in the opposite direction. The lead author is quoted as saying that "We had instances where participants got the numbers exactly correct—11.7 and 12.8—but they would flip them around.... People can self-generate their own misinformation, it doesn't all come from external sources."

That same research summary highlights the role of confirmation bias in relation to everything from politics to religion to pandemics. It leads people to block out facts that contradict their views and attend selectively to facts and sources of information (such as particular news media), that support their views. The paper describes a recent brain-imaging study that found that the more confident people are in their views, the more likely their neural processing will change to decrease sensitivity to disconfirming information.
[Source: Coronel, J. C., Poulsen, S., & Sweitzer, M. D. (2020). Investigating the generation and spread of numerical misinformation: A combined eye movement monitoring and social transmission approach. *Human Communication Research*, 46(1), 25–54. https://doi.org/10.1093/hcr/hqz012]

- Confirmation bias can also increase people's tendency to not notice that supporting evidence for one's assumptions or conclusions is missing. As an example of this tendency, called ignoring negative evidence, suppose that when the electricity in your apartment goes out, you automatically assume that this is just another of the frequent power cuts that affect the whole building or the whole neighborhood. If that were true in this case, though, there should be no lights in the hallway or in other apartments that you can see from your window. If you don't bother to check for the *absence* of that evidence, the food in your refrigerator might go bad before you figure out that the problem is in the circuit breaker box in your apartment.
- In the "trapped kitten" case described above, when the "meowing" stopped for several days after the stove was unplugged and reconnected, rescuers assumed that the animal was frightened into silence. If there really were a kitten in the kitchen, it would probably not stay silent so long, but they ignored the possibility that their hypothesis was incorrect in the first place.
- On September 26, 1983, Lt. Col. Stanislav Petrov was in command of a secret facility that analyzed information from Russian early-warning satellites. Suddenly alarms went off as computers found evidence that five U.S. missiles were being launched toward Russia. Petrov hypothesized that a nuclear attack was under way. He was about to alert his superiors to launch a counterattack on the United States when it occurred to him that if this were a real nuclear attack, it would involve many more than five missiles. Fortunately for everyone, he realized that the "attack" was a false alarm.

4. Limitations of Expertise

- The same attributes that usually make experts better problem-solvers than novices can sometimes impair their problem-solving ability, especially if their experience leads them to see what they expect to see or if their well-learned and long-used strategies create mental sets that prevent them from seeing other, better alternatives. Because expertise can undermine as well as enlighten the problem-solving process, experts are often mocked, including in definitions attributed to Mark Twain and Will Rogers that an

expert is "an ordinary fellow from another town" and "a man fifty miles from home with a briefcase."
- Experts typically have a large store of knowledge about their area of expertise, but even confidently stated conclusions based on this knowledge can turn out to be spectacularly wrong. For example, Alfred Russel Wallace, the co-discoverer of evolution, stated that "[Phrenology] will prove to be the true science of the mind. Its practical uses in education, in self-disciplining, in reformatory treatment of criminals, and in the remedial treatment of the insane, will give it one of the highest places in the hierarchy of the sciences." [Source: Krauthammer, C. (1981, June). Science ex machina. *The New Republic*, 24.]
- The table below lists other examples of equally incorrect expert pronouncements. The first six come from *The experts speak: The definitive compendium of authoritative misinformation* [Cerf, C. & Navasky, V. (1998). New York: Villard Books.]

On the possibility of painless surgery through anesthesia: "'Knife' and 'pain' are two words in surgery that must forever be associated.... To this compulsory combination we shall have to adjust ourselves." (Dr. Alfred Velpeau, professor of surgery, Paris Faculty of Medicine, 1839)

On the hazards of cigarette smoking:
"If excessive smoking actually plays a role in the production of lung cancer, it seems to be a minor one." (Dr. W. C. Heuper, National Cancer Institute, 1954)

On the stock market (one week before the disastrous 1929 crash that wiped out over $50 billion in investments):
"Stocks have reached what looks like a permanently high plateau." (Irving Fisher, professor of economics, Yale University, 1929)

On the prospects of war with Japan (three years before the December 1941 Japanese attack on Pearl Harbor):
"A Japanese attack on Pearl Harbor is a strategic impossibility." (Maj. George F. Eliot, military science writer, 1938)

On the value of personal computers:
"There is no reason for any individual to have a computer in their home." (Ken Olson, president, Digital Equipment Corporation, 1977)

On the concept of the airplane:
"Heavier-than-air flying machines are impossible." (Lord Kelvin, mathematician, physicist, and president of the British Royal Society, 1895)

On the possibility of the rapid development of a Covid-19 vaccine:
On April 30, 2020, New York Times opinions editor Stuart A. Thompson argued against the U.S. government's claim that a Covid-19 vaccine could arrive within 12 to 18 months. He said "The grim truth behind this rosy

forecast is that a vaccine probably won't arrive any time soon. Clinical trials almost never succeed. We've never released a coronavirus vaccine for humans before..." He based his skepticism on interviews with biomedical experts, one of whom said that a vaccine likely wouldn't be approved until 2021 or 2022 at the earliest, and that "this is very optimistic and of relatively low probability." Thompson's article included a timeline suggesting that an approved vaccine would not be available until 2033. As it turned out, 12 months after the article appeared, vaccines from three manufacturers had been approved for emergency use and more than 200 million doses had been administered.

Decision Making

1. Examples of easy decisions (relatively trivial, low risk):

   - Do you want paper or plastic bags at the supermarket?
   - Do you want fries with that?
   - Coke or Pepsi?
   - Which movie to stream tonight?

2. Examples of risky decisions (where there are multiple attributes to consider and where outcomes are uncertain or not easy to predict):

   - Which college major should you choose?
   - Is it time to end this relationship?
   - Should I have a potentially dangerous surgical procedure?
   - Should we have a child?
   - Is it time to think about a nursing home for Dad?
   - Should I hire candidate A or candidate B as my new office manager?
   - Would I be better off renting an apartment or buying a house?
   - Should I buy the stock of a new company that could be the next Apple (or the next Enron), or of an established company whose share value and dividends have been stable for decades?

3. Examples of assigning utility and calculating expected value in multi-attribute decisions:

- In choosing a college major, a student must compare the value of an interesting, but not very marketable degree with the value of a less interesting but more lucrative degree.
- In choosing a college major, a student must estimate the employment value of each degree area four years from now, not just today.
- In deciding whether to play the lottery, a person must take into account the cost of the ticket(s), the potential value of having a winning ticket, and the probability of having a winning ticket.
- A Dilbert cartoon provides an example of why the laborious process of calculating expected value is not adopted by everyone.
- Another Dilbert cartoon illustrates that even carefully considered expected value analyses can lead to unsatisfactory decisions.

Biases and Flaws in Decision Making

1. Risk/loss aversion.

   - An excellent video illustrating the strength of risk/loss aversion on decision-making (Kahneman & Tversky) is available here.
   - Because of loss aversion, you might go to more trouble to collect a $100 debt than to win a $100 prize.

2. An example of bias in perceiving gains:

   - Suppose you could have a $10 gift certificate from a restaurant, but you would have to drive 10 miles to pick it up. Most people tend to behave as if the difference between $0 and $10 is greater than the difference between, say, $300 and $310. As a result, a person who won't drive across town after work to earn a $10 bonus on next week's paycheck might gladly make the same trip to pick up that $10 gift certificate.

3. Examples of misperceptions of outcome probabilities:

   - Several examples of the gambler's fallacy are described at this website.
   - An excellent summary of a number of examples of the gambler's fallacy are described here.

[Source: Chen, D. L., Moskowitz, T. J., & Shue, K. (2016). Decision making under the gambler's fallacy: Evidence from asylum judges, loan officers, and baseball umpires. *The Quarterly Journal of Economics*, *131*(3), 1181–1242.]
- Examples of bias in perceiving probability (overestimating the probability of rare events and underestimating the probability of frequent ones) include deciding to gamble and enter lotteries, to continue to smoke or vape or to engage in unprotected sex.

4. Examples of decision-making styles: Maximizers versus satisficers

- Maximizers will drive further to shop at a store that has more choices for each of the items that they need, whereas satisficers will choose a closer store with fewer options. (Interestingly, satisficers are more likely to be satisfied with their choices. "Satisficer" combines the words "satisfy" and "suffice")
- Maximizers are more likely to carefully consider all options on a multiple-choice test question and be more likely to change their answers, whereas satisficers are more likely to choose a response that sounds reasonable and not change it. In this case, the maximizer may be more likely to have selected the correct answer.
- A recent BBC article reviews maximizers and satisficers with some examples here.
  [Sources for the examples above:
  Schwartz, B., Ward, A., Monterosso, J., Lyubomirsky, S., White, K., & Lehman, D. R. (2002). Maximizing versus satisficing: Happiness is a matter of choice. *Journal of Personality and Social Psychology, 83*(5), 1178–1197. https://doi.org/10.1037//0022-3514.83.5.1178
  Dar-Nimrod, I., Rawn, C. D., Lehman, D. R., & Schwartz, B. (2009). The maximization paradox: The costs of seeking alternatives. *Personality and Individual Differences, 46*(5–6), 631–635.
  Iyengar, S. S., & Lepper, M. R. (2000). When choice is demotivating: Can one desire too much of a good thing? *Journal of Personality and Social Psychology, 79*(6), 995.]
- You can find a test called the Maximization Scale here. Items on this scale typically endorsed by maximizers include:
  When I watch TV, I channel surf, often scanning through the available options even while attempting to watch one program.
  When I am in the car listening to the radio, I often check other stations to see if something better is playing, even if I am relatively satisfied with what I'm listening to.
  I often find it difficult to shop for a gift for a friend.
  When shopping, I have a hard time finding clothing that I really love.
  I'm a big fan of lists that attempt to rank things (the best movies, the best singers, the best athletes, the best novels, etc.).

I find that writing is very difficult, even if it's just writing a letter to a friend, because it's so hard to word things just right. I often do several drafts of even simple things.

Whenever I'm faced with a choice, I try to imagine what all the other possibilities are, even ones that aren't present at the moment.

Cognitive Abilities

1. Examples of fluid intelligence:

   - Solving problems (such as the Tower of Hanoi and others described in the section above on problem-solving).
   - Completing tasks that use working memory, such as keeping track of the score in a tennis match, adding a column of figures, or multiplying two two-digit numbers.
   - Reasoning logically about facts, such as that if a suspect in a murder case was caught on a security camera miles away from the murder scene at the time a murder occurred, that person could not have personally committed the murder. But fluid intelligence would also allow you to recognize that the suspect might have ordered someone else to commit the murder.
   - Drawing logical conclusions, such as that if all As are B, and all Cs are B, it does not follow that all As are C. Specifically, if all gun owners are people, and if all criminals are people, it does not follow that all gun owners are criminals.
   - Solving puzzles, constructing strategies to deal with new problems, seeing patterns in statistical data, and engaging in speculative philosophical reasoning about, say, the consequences of particular social or political policies such as raising taxes or eliminating college tuition.
   - Completing analogies such as those mentioned above in relation to the Miller Analogy Test.
   - Assembling a complex jigsaw puzzle using a picture as a model for what the puzzle should look like at the end of the process.
   - Showing creativity (thinking outside the box) when solving problems.
   - Discarding irrelevant information or discredited hypotheses when conducting research.

2. Examples of crystalized intelligence:

    - Having a good vocabulary, perhaps in more than one language, knowing the multiplication tables, understanding written text.
    - Being able to recall personal memories from long ago (via long term memory).
    - Knowing facts about the world, including geographical locations, national capitols, significant dates in history, and other important and trivial information that allow one to perform at various jobs and to excel at Jeopardy!
    - Knowing the exact ingredients needed to prepare your favorite dishes.
    - Learning new words in your native language.
    - Memorizing new math formulae or facts.
    - Remembering the demographic statistics of a country you're reading about.
    - As an example of how fluid intelligence creates crystallized intelligence, consider a veteran police detective who has gained specific knowledge about how to "read" clues and people. This person may be able to examine the scene of a crime and notice clues that tell her when the crime took place. This specific knowledge (crystallized intelligence) gained from previous experience (previous applications of fluid intelligence) will increase her overall chances of solving the crime.

3. Examples of emotional intelligence:
    [*Note:* The concept of emotional intelligence is not universally accepted, but we include these examples so you can use them in your course if you wish.]

    - Traits seen as typical of emotional intelligence include:

        Being aware and responsive to other people's emotional state (i.e., being empathic).
        Regulating your own emotions.
        Being able to listen empathically to others.
        Being flexible with others.
        Being able to accept criticism and responsibility.
        Being able to move on after making a mistake.
        Being able to say no when you need to.
        Being able to share your feelings with others.
        Being able to solve problems in ways that work for everyone involved.
        Knowing why you do the things you do.
        Being nonjudgmental of others.
    - Your friend Lauren has been disciplined by your teacher and shares her feelings with you. You listen empathically, then objectively explain the possible reasons for the teacher's actions and advise Lauren on how to avoid similar situations in the future. If you can do this and not upset or offend Lauren, you will have used what some psychologists refer to as emotional intelligence.

- Here is an example of a police officer who uses emotional intelligence to do his job in a way that upsets and offends no one. At the time of this news story he had written over 25,000 traffic tickets without a single complaint.
- A case study of improving emotional intelligence is described here. This case is especially interesting because it involves someone who was a "people-pleaser," which may not be the kind of low emotional intelligence that typically comes to mind.
- Examples of several CEOs who are said to have high emotional intelligence are described here.
- Ronald Cotton (described in the eyewitness testimony section of the memory chapter) is an example of someone with high emotional intelligence. His ability to forgive Jennifer Thompson for incorrectly identifying him as her rapist showed, as Jennifer said, "grace and mercy" despite the fact that her testimony put him in prison for 11 years before he was exonerated by DNA evidence.
- This post describes several habits of emotionally-intelligent children with examples of behaviors for each habit.
- The movie *Inside Out* provides examples of what some psychologists consider to be emotional intelligence. You can find a synopsis here.
- Below are some examples of ways in which an employee was not demonstrating emotional intelligence. More details are available here.

  - Sue had recently completed several tasks behind schedule but didn't seem to realize the negative impact her behavior had on the projects of several colleagues.
  - Last week, Sue had allowed her frustration with another employee to escalate into an angry argument outside her cubicle, disrupting the work of employees in nearby cubicles.
  - During staff meetings, Sue has a habit of sharing her opinions, to the point of interrupting and even talking over quieter coworkers.
- An example of a fictional character who demonstrates very low emotional intelligence is Michael Scott, the boss on *The Office*.

Tests of Cognitive Abilities

[*Note:* See also examples of standardization in the chapter on research methods and statistics.]

1. Standardized Measures of Aptitude

    - SAT (originally known as the Scholastic Aptitude Test)
    - ACT (originally known as American College Testing)

- GRE (Graduate Record Examinations)
- MCAT (Medical College Admission Test)
- LSAT (Law School Admission Test).

2. Standardized Measures of Achievement

   - The Woodcock-Johnson Tests of Achievement IV.
   - The Wide Range Achievement Test (WRAT5)
   - The Kaufman Test of Educational Achievement (K-TEA-3)
   - The Wechsler Individual Achievement Test (WIAT-III).

3. Standardized Measures of Intellectual Functioning (Intelligence)

   - The Stanford-Binet Intelligence Scales (SB5)
   - Examples resembling items and tasks appearing on various verbal and nonverbal subscales:
     Vocabulary: Define words such as train, wrench, letter, error, and encourage.
     Memory for Sentences: Correctly recall sentences that were presented.
     Object Series/Matrices: Choose the correct order in which a series of pictures had been presented.
     Absurdities: Identify the mistakes or "silly" aspects of pictures in which, for example, a man is shown using the wrong end of a rake or a girl is shown putting a piece of clothing on incorrectly.
     Quantitative Reasoning Determine which numbers come next in a series of numbers such as the following: 32, 26, 20, 14, ____, ____.
     Verbal Relations: Indicate how three objects or words are alike but different from a fourth. For example, how are dog, cat, and horse alike but different from boy.
     Block Span: Separate blocks into rows coded with yellow and red stripes.
   - The Wechsler Adult Intelligence Scale (WAIS-IV)
   The table below shows examples of items similar to those on some verbal and nonverbal subtests of the WAIS-IV.

Subtest	Simulated items
Information	Where does lumber come from? What did Shakespeare do? What is the capital of France? What is the Malleus Malleficarum?
Comprehension	What should you do with a wallet found in the street? Why do imported cars cost more than domestic cars? What does "the squeaky wheel gets the grease" mean?

(continued)

(continued)

Subtest	Simulated items
Arithmetic	If you have four apples and give two away, how many do you have left?
	If four people can finish a job in six days, how many people would it take to do the job in two days?
Similarities	Identify what similar pairs, like hammer–screwdriver, portrait–short story, dog–flower, have in common
Digit Symbol/Coding	Copy designs that are associated with different numbers as quickly as possible
Digit span	Repeat in forward and reverse order two- to nine-digit numbers
Vocabulary	Define chair, dime, lunch, paragraph, valley, asylum, modal, cutaneous
Picture completion	Find missing objects in increasingly complex pictures
Block design	Arrange blocks to match increasingly complex standard patterns
Picture arrangement	Place increasing numbers of pictures in sequence to make increasingly complex stories
Symbol search	Visually scan and recognize a series of symbols

- The Wechsler Intelligence Scale for Children (WISC-V) and Wechsler Preschool and Primary Scale of Intelligence (WPPSI).

The drawing below illustrates items of the type included on the WISC-V:

Picture completion
What part is missing from this picture?

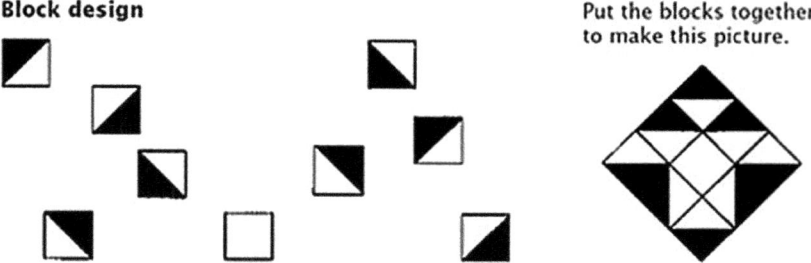

Block design

Put the blocks together to make this picture.

- Kaufman Assessment Battery for Children (K-ABC-II).
- The Raven's Progressive Matrices

- The Peabody Picture Vocabulary Test–Revised
- The Leiter International Performance Scale
- Naglieri Nonverbal Ability Test

4. Tests of Emotional Intelligence

- Mayer-Salovey-Caruso Emotional Intelligence Test (MSCEIT)
- Emotional and Social Competence Inventory (ESCI)
- The scales measured by this inventory, which can be found here, include:
  Emotional Self-Awareness: Recognizing one's emotions and their effects
  Emotional Self-Control: Keeping disruptive emotions and impulses in check
  Adaptability: Flexibility in handling change
  Achievement Orientation: Striving to improve or meet a standard of excellence
  Positive Outlook: Persistence in pursuing goals despite obstacles and setbacks
  Empathy: Sensing others' feelings and perspectives, and taking an active interest in their concerns
  Organizational Awareness Reading a group's emotional currents and power relationships
  Coach and Mentor: Sensing others' development needs and bolstering their abilities
  Inspirational Leadership: Inspiring and guiding individuals and groups
  Influence: Wielding effective tactics for persuasion
  Conflict Management: Negotiating and resolving disagreements
  Teamwork: Working with others toward shared goals. Creating group synergy in pursuing collective goals.

- You can find short emotional intelligence quizzes on this website.

Consciousness

As is the case when teaching about psychological disorders, the topics typically covered in a course or unit on consciousness usually generate intense student interest. Material on conscious and unconscious processes, sleep and dreaming, and hypnosis tend to generate nonstop questions and student requests for further reading. Be aware, though, that many students will also come to class with preconceived ideas about these topics, such as that it is dangerous to wake a sleepwalker, and that hypnosis can make people do things they would not otherwise do or help them remember forgotten events. We hope that the examples included in this chapter will satisfy your students' desire for more illustrations of various topics while also providing you with evidence that will help you debunk some of the common myths that surround those topics.

Studying Consciousness

1. The nature of consciousness

    A good introduction (for yourself and/or your students) to the nature of consciousness can be found in this 20-min TED talk video by Christoph Koch. An additional post by Koch is available here and a related article can be found here.

2. Introspection
   Wilhelm Wundt's goal was to study consciousness using introspection, which means "looking inward". A 7-min video provides examples of introspection as Wundt and Titchener used it.
3. The imprecision and other difficulties associated with introspection led John B. Watson and other behaviorists to argue that psychologists should ignore mental events and concern themselves only with observable behavior. However, although cognitive scientists now study consciousness using technologies such as brain scanning and other sophisticated methods mentioned in the chapters on biological aspects of psychology and on thinking and cognitive abilities, introspective methods are still being used. A prime example is the "think aloud protocols" in which research participants are recorded as they "speak" their thoughts while engaging in mental processes such as problem-solving or decision-making.
4. A 3:30 min video provides an example of using a think aloud protocol during a travel scheduling task.

Levels of Mental Processing

1. **Conscious**

   - You can correctly say what day it is, where you are, whether or not it is raining, and the like.
   - You are aware of feeling anxious and jittery while waiting to take an important test.
   - You are talking to a friend on the phone while at the beach and describing what you see.
   - You are reading a book and taking notes to remind yourself later of the book's main points.

2. **Preconscious**

   - You are playing trivia with some friends and trying to remember the name of the first American to walk on the moon. Suddenly, you blurt out "Neil Armstrong!" That name was stored in your memory at a preconscious level, but it was possible for you to bring it to the conscious level through the process of retrieval. [Note the link to material in the chapter on memory, particularly that retrievable information in LTM is essentially at the preconscious level]
   - Think about how your tongue feels against your teeth. Where were those sensations before you paid attention to them? Sensations coming from your

tongue were reaching your brain, but they were at the preconscious level, where you did not experience them even when your tongue is moving. However, you can easily become conscious of these sensations at any time, simply by paying attention to them. [Note link to sensation and perception]
- If you are wearing a belt, glasses, shoes, a watch, or a Fitbit, are they too tight, too loose, or just right? When you first put these accessories on today, you were probably conscious of how they felt, but–like sensations from your tongue–until you heard this question, the sensations coming from them were being processed at a preconscious level. That's because the sensations were unchanging, allowing you to get so used to them that they faded into the preconscious background. If one of these accessories suddenly loosens or bumps against something, you will immediately experience the resulting sensations at a conscious level.

[Note link to examples in the chapters on sensation and perception and on learning; the process of "getting used to" unchanging sensations is called habituation.]
- Ask the class what they had for dinner last night and point out that before the students heard the question, they were probably not thinking about that meal, but the memory of it was in their preconscious so they were probably able to bring it into conscious awareness.

3. **Nonconscious**

- Many ongoing biological processes such as regulation of blood pressure, heartrate, pulse, pupillary dilation, and muscle tone.
- Other examples of nonconscious, though not strictly mental, processes include regulation of body temperature and hormones such as insulin and cortisol, production of urine, and secretion of neurotransmitters and stomach acid.
- All the processes that maintain biological functions such as temperature at a more or less constant, or homeostatic, level for optimal functioning.
- It is possible to become indirectly aware of nonconscious processes and even to control them to some extent through laboratory-based biofeedback devices that connect to the body and provide a person with real-time information about biological processes such as pulse rate, blood pressure, muscle tension, and the like. You can get similar feedback through various smartphone apps, or you can approximate a laboratory biofeedback session by having a friend take your pulse at one-minute intervals while you sit quietly. First, establish a baseline pulse, then imagine a peaceful scene or think about lowering your pulse rate. Then ask your friend to softly say whether your pulse is higher or lower compared with the baseline. After four or five minutes of having this information "fed back" to you, you will probably be able to keep your pulse rate below the original baseline. Regardless of the biofeedback method used, the biological regulating processes themselves remain out of consciousness, so you still cannot experience them directly.

4. **Subconscious/unconscious** [Note: The examples in this section provide opportunities for you to point out that though this kind of mental processing does take place, it does not support mythical beliefs such as sleep learning and subliminal persuasion.]

- You and your best friend meet someone new at a party and you immediately dislike the person. You have no idea why you reacted that way, but after the party, your friend points out that the new person looks a little bit like someone who was always making fun of you in high school. In other words, that new person's appearance reminded you of a bully, but that information was at a subconscious level. Though you were not immediately aware of it, your friend's comment brought the information into consciousness, thus allowing you to better understand your negative reaction.
- A client in psychoanalysis is telling his therapist about his older sister, who is far more financially successful than he is. He mentions, too, how much he loves and admires her and how he worries about her safety because, as a real estate agent, she often has to show empty houses to strangers at night. He pauses, and then recalls a dream he had the night before in which he is walking behind his sister along a narrow and muddy mountain trail above a steep drop-off. When her foot suddenly slipped and it seemed she was about to fall, he abruptly woke up and a cold sweat. When the therapist asks what the dream might mean, the client says that it shows how much he loves his sister and wants her to be safe. The therapist would probably not immediately offer a different interpretation, but she wonders if the client might actually harbor strong but unconscious feelings of resentment, jealousy, and even hatred toward his sister and that, through internal defense mechanisms, these feelings are being translated into what he experiences consciously as love and concern.
[These first two examples can be used to contrast Freud's view of the *unconscious* as a level of mental activity where mainly unacceptable sexual, aggressive, and other impulses are hidden from awareness and the view held by modern cognitive scientists that the *subconscious* processes all kinds of information at a level that is normally out of awareness but that can nevertheless influence behavior, thoughts, judgments, and decisions.]
- Experimenters repeatedly played a recording of fifteen word-pairs in an operating room while medical patients had surgery under general anesthesia. After regaining consciousness, the patients were asked if they could recall hearing any word lists. None could do so, nor could they say if a recording had been playing at all. However, when the experimenters read one word from each word-pair and asked the patients to say the first word that came to mind, about 85 percent of the patients came up with the other member of the word pair at least some of the time.
[Reference: Kihlstrom, J. F., Schacter, D. L., Cork, R. C., Hurt, C. A., & Behr, S. E. (1990). Implicit and explicit memory following surgical anesthesia. *Psychological Science, 1*(5), 303–306.]

- Research participants watched a computer screen as an X was flashed in one of four locations. Their task was to indicate as quickly as possible where the X appeared. The place where the X appeared seemed to vary randomly, but it actually followed a set of complex rules (e.g., "If the X moves horizontally twice in succession, its next move will be vertical."). Over many trials, the participants' responses became progressively faster and more accurate. This suggests that they had learned the rules without knowing what they were, because when the experimenters began presenting the X in truly random locations, the participants' accuracy and speed deteriorated. However, even when offered $100 to correctly describe the rules that had guided the location sequence, participants were unable to do so, nor were they sure that any such rules existed.
[Reference: Lewicki, P. (1992). Nonconscious acquisition of information. *American Psychologist, 47,* 796–801.]
- In cases of blindness caused by damage only to the brain's primary visual cortex, pathways from the eyes are still connected to other brain areas that process visual information. Research suggests that these connections are responsible for a phenomenon called *blindsight*, in which there is a certain amount of visual information processing at a subconscious level, where a person is not aware of it. People who experience blindsight say they see nothing, but if forced to guess, they may still locate visual targets, identify the direction of moving images, reach in the correct direction for "unseen" objects, name the color of lights, and even discriminate happy from fearful faces. The same blindsight phenomenon has been created in visually normal volunteers using magnetic brain stimulation to temporarily disable the primary visual cortex. (See the chapter on biological aspects of psychology for more examples of blindsight phenomena.)
[References:
Allen, C. P., Sumner, P., & Chambers, C. D. (2014). The timing and neuroanatomy of conscious vision as revealed by TMS-induced blindsight. *Journal of Cognitive Neuroscience, 26,* 1507–1518.]
Azzopardi, P., & Hock, H. S. (2011). Illusory motion perception in blindsight. *Proceedings of the National Academy of Sciences of the United States of America, 108*(2), 876–881.
Cowey, A. (2010). The blindsight saga. *Experimental Brain Research, 200* (1), 3–24.]
- Priming studies show that people respond faster or more accurately to stimuli they have seen before, even if they do not consciously recall having seen those stimuli (see also examples in the chapters on sensation and perception and on thinking and cognitive abilities). For example, when people had to decide whether the figures shown here could exist in three-dimensional space, their choices were faster and more accurate for figures that —in a pre-experimental phase—had been flashed before their eyes at a subliminal speed, too fast for them to recognize consciously.

[Reference: Schacter, D. L., Cooper, L. A., Delaney, S. M., Peterson, M. A., & Tharan, M. (1991). Implicit memory for possible and impossible objects: Constraints on the construction of structural descriptions. *Journal of Experimental Psychology: Learning, Memory, and Cognition, 17,* 3–19.]

- Experimenters asked research participants to watch videos of television commercials while the ever-changing stock prices of fictional companies crawled across the bottom of the screen. Later, when the participants were asked to recall the stock prices of the various companies, they couldn't, so when asked which of these companies they liked best, they had to base their choices on their "gut reaction" to the company names. Those "gut reactions" were not random, though. Participants tended to prefer the companies whose stock prices had been rising over those whose stock had been falling. These results suggest that although your "lucky" choice of the fastest-moving supermarket checkout line might seem to have been based on a "gut feeling," if you had been to that store many times you might have gained useful information about the efficiency of various clerks that you did not know you had.
[Reference: Betch, T., Hoffman, K., Hoffrage, U., & Plessner, H. (2003). Intuition beyond recognition: When less familiar events are liked more. *Experimental Psychology, 50,* 49–54.]

- Research on implicit prejudice (implicit bias) suggests that people may hold negative stereotypes about minority groups but are not aware that they do so (see other examples in the chapter on social psychology). One example appeared in a study of physicians who said they were not biased against African Americans, yet were found to behave more negatively toward their African American patients.
[Reference: Penner, L. A., Dovidio, J. F. . . . Eggly, S. (2016) The effects of oncologist implicit racial bias in racially discordant oncology interactions. *Journal of Clinical Oncology, 34,* 2874–2878.]

- Other researchers have used the priming procedures described above to activate unconscious thoughts and feelings that can alter people's reactions to others without their awareness. In one study, white participants were exposed to subliminal presentations of pictures of black individuals. The participants were not consciously aware that they had seen these pictures, but when they interacted with a black man soon afterward, those who had been primed with the pictures acted more negatively toward him and saw him as more hostile than people who had not been primed.
[Reference: Chen, M., & Bargh, J. A. (1997). Nonconscious behavioral confirmation processes: The self-fulfilling consequences of automatic stereotype activation. *Journal of Experimental Social Psychology, 33,* 541–560.]

- Other studies suggest it is possible to prime unconscious negative stereotypes about other groups, too, including immigrants and people who are overweight.
[References:
Arendt, F., Marquart, F., & Matthes, J. (2015). Effects of right-wing populist political advertising on implicit and explicit stereotypes. *Journal of Media*

Psychology: Theories, Methods, and Applications, 27(4), 178–189. https://doi.org/10.1027/1864-1105/a000139.

Degner, J., & Wentura, D. (2010). Automatic prejudice in childhood and early adolescence. *Journal of Personality and Social Psychology, 98,* 356–374.]
- An example of efforts to measure implicit bias/prejudice in individuals takes the form of the Implicit Association Test (IAT), which uses a computer to record how quickly they come to associate pairs of words (such as "science" and "men," vs. "science" and "women") or to associate images with words (such as "good" with light-skinned vs. dark-skinned faces). If your students visit Project Implicit they can learn more about the test and use it to measure their own implicit attitudes about race, gender, sexuality, disability, age, and many other topics. Visiting Project Implicit Mental Health they can complete IATs tied to anxiety, depression, therapy, stigma of mental illness, suicide, and other mental health topics.

Biological Rhythms

1. Some biological rhythms are called *circadian* because they occur about once a day. The most common example is the sleep–wake cycle, but there are others. These include, for example, our ability to focus and sustain attention. For most people who sleep from 11 p.m. to 7 a.m., this ability tends to be at a low level in the morning (7–10 a.m.), to improve in the middle part of the day (10 a.m. to 2 p.m.), and then decrease later in the afternoon (2–4 p.m.), before improving again later in the afternoon and evening (4–10 p.m.), and finally decreasing continuously from 10 p.m. to 4 a.m., when it reaches its lowest level. It has been suggested that the time course of this aspect of cognitive performance should be taken into account when programming daily activities, such as school schedules, time allocated for studying, sports or work, as well as programming academic, medical, psychological, or neuropsychological tests.
[Reference: Valdez F. (2019). Circadian rhythms in attention. *The Yale Journal of Biology and Medicine, 92*(1), 81–92.]
2. Some graphics showing circadian rhythms can be found here.
3. An example of what happens when circadian rhythms are disrupted is the pattern of fatigue, sleepiness or sleeplessness, and impaired productivity experienced following international air travel—especially from west to east—(*jet lag*) or changing work shifts from night to day or vice versa. (See also the chapter on industrial/organizational psychology.)
4. Examples of individual differences in circadian rhythms can be seen in people with differing *chronotypes*; some have cycles of physiological and cognitive activation that prompt them to awaken early and be especially efficient in the morning ("larks") while others (called "owls") have rhythms that prompt them to sleep later (or want to sleep later) and to be especially efficient in the evening.

[If you take a classroom survey, most or all of your students should be able to classify themselves as one or the other.]
5. Some biological rhythms are shorter than a day, but longer than an hour. Examples of these *ultradian rhythms*, include patterns of rising and falling body temperature, urine production, bowel movements, physiological arousal (during wakefulness and sleep), hormone production, brain wave activity, and digestion.
6. Some biological rhythms are much shorter than one day, or even one minute. For example, when we are engaged in a task such as washing dishes or playing a video game, it feels as though our attention is focused continuously on the task and that we are in continuous control of our decisions and actions in performing each step. Yet cognitive neuroscientists have found that during such tasks our brains are actually going through repeated cognitive cycles consisting of sensation, conscious and unconscious perception, decision-making, and execution, each of which lasts a little less than half a second. This constant repetition of the cognitive cycle has led psychological scientists to suggest that what seems like our spotlight of attention is actually more like a strobe light of attention. So much as the stroboscopic phenomenon allows us to experience smooth movement in films and videos even though we are looking at a series of still images, our experience of continuous attention is a kind of illusion.
[References: Madl, T., Baars, B. J., & Franklin, S. (2011). The timing of the cognitive cycle. *PloS one*, 6(4), e14803.
VanRullen, R. (2018). Attention cycles. *Neuron, 99,* 632–634.]
7. An article describing cognitive cycles in non-technical language is available here.
8. Examples of *infradian rhythms*, which are biological rhythms that span more than a day, include the menstrual cycle in women, and, in other mammalian species, cycles of migration, mating, and hibernation.

Sleep Disorders

1. Narcolepsy

    - A 22-year-old woman came to the psychiatry department at a hospital in Korea because of her excessive daytime sleepiness and narcolepsy attacks. The daytime sleepiness began when she was around thirteen years old and had been getting worse. When she was in high school, she couldn't stay awake during her classes or exams. When she worked at a department store as a saleswoman after graduating from high school, she frequently dozed off standing up, and for this she was dismissed. She also got into a collision while driving due to a sudden sleep attack. Cataplexy developed as her daytime sleepiness got worse, and after the age of nineteen, it would occur almost every day. Cataplexy occurred when she laughed, got angry or exchanged

jokes. It even occurred when she was excited, surprised and embarrassed, and when she reminisced about happy moments. Her knees would suddenly buckle and her jaw sagged. She also complained of seeing ghosts or animals and hearing her name called when she was lying down at night. She experienced realistic and often scary dreams throughout the night; when she awoke, she was unable to move. There was no history of trauma to the head or any psychiatric illnesses. However, her father did suffer from constant sleepiness and fatigue, and also occasionally sudden muscle weakness of both knees when laughing. Both the father and the daughter were prescribed modafinil (a drug that promotes wakefulness) and venlafaxine (an antidepressant), and this resulted in reducing both their excessive daytime sleepiness and cataplexy, especially for the father. These cases exemplify familial narcolepsy, which is rare in comparison with the usual non-familial version.
[Adapted from Shin, Y.-K., Hong, S.-C., Cho, Y.-J., Jeong, J.-H., Han, J.-H., & Lee, S.-P. (2007). Case study of a narcoleptic patient with a family history of narcolepsy. *Psychiatry Investigations, 4,* 121–123.]

- Mr. A, an 18-year-old man, came to a psychiatry department in India complaining of excessive daytime sleepiness for the past 18 months, right after suffering high fever associated with an episode of typhoid and malaria. Despite sleeping well at night, he started sleeping for 5 to 6 h during the daytime. If not awakened, he would sleep for 19 to 20 h/day. He was unable to study, and this led to academic decline. After about three months, Mr. A. noticed that whenever he would laugh out loud or get angry, he would experience a sudden feeling of generalized body weakness, especially in the upper part of his body, along with drooping of his head and eyelids. In addition, he would have a sudden bending of his knees, leading to imbalance if he was standing. He would also have difficulty speaking and at times could not control his posture and would fall. These episodes would last for 8–10 s after which he would have complete recovery within 10–15 min without any deficits. He also reported visual images as he was falling asleep or waking up. He said he would see an unknown boy standing near him that others could not see. While experiencing these hallucinations, he would not be able to move his limbs or speak; such episodes of inability to move his limbs or speak would last for 5–10 min. Electroencephalogram and magnetic resonance imaging of the brain revealed no abnormalities. Over the following year, the symptoms continued to worsen. Different physicians, including neurologists and psychiatrists, diagnosed his condition as viral encephalitis, epilepsy, schizophrenia, and depression and he was treated with various combinations of modafinil (a drug that promotes wakefulness), antidepressants, antipsychotics, and anticonvulsants, all with no improvement. Finally, when a diagnosis of narcolepsy was considered, all previously prescribed medications were stopped, and he was started on methylphenidate, a stimulant medication used to treat attention deficit hyperactivity disorder. Within three weeks, all of his symptoms subsided and he remained symptom free for the two years during which his case was followed.

[Adapted from Gupta, A. K., Sahoo, S., & Grover, S. (2017). Narcolepsy in adolescence—A missed diagnosis: A case report. *Innovations in Clinical Neuroscience, 14*, 20–23.
See also Zhou, J., Zhang, X., & Dong, Z. (2014). Case report of narcolepsy in a six-year-old child initially misdiagnosed as atypical epilepsy. *Shanghai Archives of Psychiatry, 26*(4), 232–235.
See also Krishnamurthy, V.B., Nallamothu, V., & Singareddy, R. (2014). An interesting case of late age at onset of narcolepsy with cataplexy. *Journal of Clinical Sleep Medicine, 10,* 203–205. This case involves a relatively rare example in which narcolepsy appeared when the patient was in his 60s.]

- A 4-min video of a woman with narcolepsy and cataplexy is available here. It has a couple of sound interruptions, but is still usable.

- This 2-min video presents a woman with narcolepsy describing her condition and how it affects her life. There is also a short clip showing her falling asleep unexpectedly.

- Another excellent video, this one about 8-min long, presents a woman with an even more severe case of narcolepsy, describing her condition and how it affects every aspect of her life (includes many sample clips and efforts to combat the condition).

- This 6-min video shows the history and diagnostic process in a case of narcolepsy in a young woman.

- This 1-min video presents a brief story of a Spanish family whose 14 members all have narcolepsy.

- This 1-min video from Denmark describes narcolepsy and the accompanying text presents evidence of its being an autoimmune disease.

- This 5-min video shows a young woman fighting off her narcolepsy while trying to make a dance instruction video. Subtitles explain what is happening at each phase, which makes up for the poor audio.

2. Sleepwalking [*Note:* Examples in this section offer the opportunity to debunk the myth that it is dangerous to awaken a sleepwalker.]

- Case of Emma, 25, as described by Emma herself: I've been a sleepwalker my whole life. It used to drive my parents crazy, and to keep me safe as a kid my bedroom windows were always locked. I would often wander into my parents' room and stand at the end of their bed in silence—sometimes I'd mumble nonsense. I can only imagine how creepy that must have been. My mother remembers one night when I was about 12 and I threw a tantrum, telling her she never listened to me, even though I'd been talking complete rubbish up to that point.
- Case of Peter, 59: I've been sleepwalking for as long as I can remember and am constantly dragging my girlfriend out of bed as I'm convinced the front of the house is falling off. I once found myself on a window ledge chasing a thief who did not exist. As a child I thought I was the Man from UNCLE and fell face down on to the floor thinking I had been shot. I then calmly got up and went back to bed as if nothing had happened, according to my aunt. I've fallen out of bed on lots of occasions, including once in an apartment where the bed was eight feet above the floor. I constantly dream about tsunamis. I just live with it without taking any medication. Everyone who knows me seems to accept it. At the time I don't even know I am doing it, and if I wake up during sleepwalking I just get back into bed and fall asleep straight away. When I'm reminded of the incident sometimes it comes back to me and I relive it.
- Case of Eleanor, 28: The worst and most dangerous experience I had was when I was 21. I was home alone and I woke up at 3am in a bath full of lukewarm water with a razor in my hand. I had shaved the bottom half of my left leg. Luckily I hadn't cut myself. After a sleepwalk I never remember what I've dreamed about, but I think that night it was getting ready for a night out I had planned. I woke up and started panicking and hyperventilating—it was pretty scary.

  The last time I sleepwalked was at 22. I got up and went to sleep under the kitchen table. I never took any medication for it as it was very infrequent and usually I just wandered around my own bedroom. I used to freak out my first boyfriend when I sleepwalked: eyes open, talking incoherently and wandering about the house. He told me I looked like a demonic possessed doll. I didn't appreciate that, and we broke up a month or so later. On one occasion my ex-boyfriend also found me rummaging through the freezer—apparently, I was looking for chicken nuggets "because the man in the yellow sweater" really needed them and so did I. "Don't just stand there, help me find them," I exclaimed. The bizarre thing is, I am a vegetarian.
- Case of Zoe, 40: I first started sleepwalking when I was 11 or 12 years old. At university I would often get in the building elevator and go up and down a few times before returning to bed. I have also had more frightening night-terror experiences, where I am desperate to get out of my bedroom because I think the walls are covered in bugs. In my panic the only way out seemed to be the bedroom window. I woke up as I opened the window and the cold air hit me, just before I was about to jump out.

[Source of the previous 4 cases: Sleepwalkers' stories. *Guardian Weekly*. May 24, 2016. Retrieved here.]

- A Canadian man named Kenneth Parks began suffering insomnia in his 20s. On the night of May 23, 1987, he got out of bed, drove 14 miles to his in-laws' house, killed his mother- in-law and injured his father-in-law with a tire iron and a knife. After the incident, he drove himself to a police station and turned himself in. Up until this point, he had a good relationship with his in-laws, and his wife vouched for his lack of motive in the crime. He claimed he had been sleepwalking, and the following year, he was found not guilty of murder. You can read about the case here.

[The next 5 cases come from: Griffin, S. (2014). Ten terrifying tales of sleepwalking. *Health,* June 24th. Retrieved here.]

- James Currens has been a sleepwalker for a long time, but his most terrifying adventure occurred when he was 77. In 1998, Curren got up and sleepwalked out of his house, cane in hand, and right into a nearby pond. At this point, he woke up chest deep in water, but was unable to get out as he had become stuck in the mud. What made the incident really frightening was that he found himself surrounded by alligators. He used his cane to keep them at bay and began shouting for help. One of his neighbors heard him yelling and called the police. Using lights to scare off the alligators, the police managed to free Currens, who escaped with only small cuts from falling when entering the pond.
- A middle-aged woman in Australia reported sleepwalking episodes in which she would get out of bed, sleepwalk out of her house, and engage in sex with total strangers. This took place for several months, and neither she nor her partner realized it until the partner woke up one night and realized she wasn't there. After searching for her, he found her having sex with a stranger, completely asleep. Reports say that she has been successfully treated for the condition.
- A 55-year-old woman from Cheshire, England, engages in "sleep-eating". She has had to change her daytime diet and join a fitness club, because she can eat up to 2500 extra calories while asleep. She also cooks while she sleeps, using a gas oven, posing a danger should she leave the gas running unlit. She will sometimes eat inedible items, such as Vaseline, paint and washing powder. She put alarms on her doors in the hopes that they would wake her up, but to no avail. She is now in treatment.
- In 1887, Robert Ledru was one of France's finest detectives. Although living in Paris, he was working on a missing persons case in the coastal town of Le Havre when he was asked to investigate the death of a man found on the beach the night before. The man had been shot, and the only clues were the bullet, and the footprints left in the sand by the killer. Ledru examined the footprints and came to a horrible realization. The killer was missing the big

toe on his right foot. Ledru was missing this same toe, and had awoken that morning to find that his socks were wet. Furthermore, the bullet was the same type he used. He discovered that he had murdered another Parisian named Andre Monet while sleepwalking. The French police were reluctant to accept this theory, so they put him in a cell for overnight observation. The first night, he did sleepwalk, so the next night they left a gun loaded with blanks in his cell with him, and he shot at the guards in his sleep. It was ruled that Ledru could not be held responsible for his actions, but that he was still a threat, so he was exiled to a farm in the countryside, where he lived the last 50 years of his life with guards and nurses.

Here are a number of additional cases of sleepwalking homicides:

- This 4-min video describes several sleepwalking cases, one of which, like the case above, involves sleep-eating.

- This light-hearted 2-min video shows a woman sleepwalking while her son records it and later plays it back to her.

- This 1-min video shows a man entering his kitchen while asleep and pouring milk onto a countertop.

- There is a fascinating 4-min video about a man who claims to have no artistic talent while awake, but creates excellent artwork while asleep. [It offers an opportunity to ask students how they might design a study to test his waking artistic ability to confirm his claim.]

3. REM behavior disorder

- Case of James, 54: This patient was referred to a sleep disorder clinic because he broke his wrist diving out of bed while dreaming that he was about to be hit by a train. The previous month he hit his wife while dreaming a tiger was attacking him. According to his wife, James had been having similar experiences for a couple of years but could not always remember his dream content. James was very healthy and not on any medication. His physical examination findings were unremarkable, as was neuroimaging. His sleep study ruled out sleep disordered breathing but revealed REM sleep without atonia (i.e. muscle activity when the muscles should be at rest). James was

started on clonazepam (an antiseizure medication), which relieved his dream enactment behavior but caused daytime sleepiness, so he was switched to melatonin (a hormone associated with sleep onset) and within days felt a significant improvement.
[Source: Coeytaux, A., Wong, K., Grunstein, R., & Lewis, S.J.G. (2013). REM sleep behaviour disorder: More than just a parasomnia. *Rheumatology, 42*, 785–788.]

- A man in his late 60s with a 20-year history of REM behavior disorder came to a sleep treatment center reporting episodes of dream enactment behavior that were becoming progressively more violent, resulting in assault on his wife and self-injurious behaviors. Yelling occurred multiple times per night. Violent behaviors were reported every other night, such as punching through walls or striking furniture. The problem persisted despite treatment with standard medications (clonazepam and melatonin). Treatment with a central nervous system depressant drug (Xyrem) was followed by cessation of the disorder.
[Source: Liebenthal, J., Valerio, J., Ruoff, C., & Mahowald, M.A. (2016). Case of rapid eye movement sleep behavior disorder in Parkinson disease treated with sodium oxybate. *JAMA Neurology, 73*(1), 126–127. https://doi.org/10.1001/jamaneurol.2015.2904]

- The photo on the second page of this article shows a patient with chronic REM behavior disorder demonstrating the homemade restraint apparatus that he used every night for five years to prevent himself from leaving the bed and injuring himself during dream-enacting episodes.
[Source: Schenck, C.H. & Mahowald, M.W. (2002). REM sleep behavior disorder: Clinical, developmental, and neuroscience perspectives 16 years after its formal identification in SLEEP. *Sleep, 25*, 120–138.]

- There is a 4-min video about a man who was charged with domestic abuse and barred from contact with his wife because he beat her while asleep, presumably as a result of REM behavior.
- The story of Mike Birbiglia, who has made a career by talking and writing about his long history of sleepwalking can be found here.

4. Nightmares and night terror disorder

- Most common examples of nightmare content:

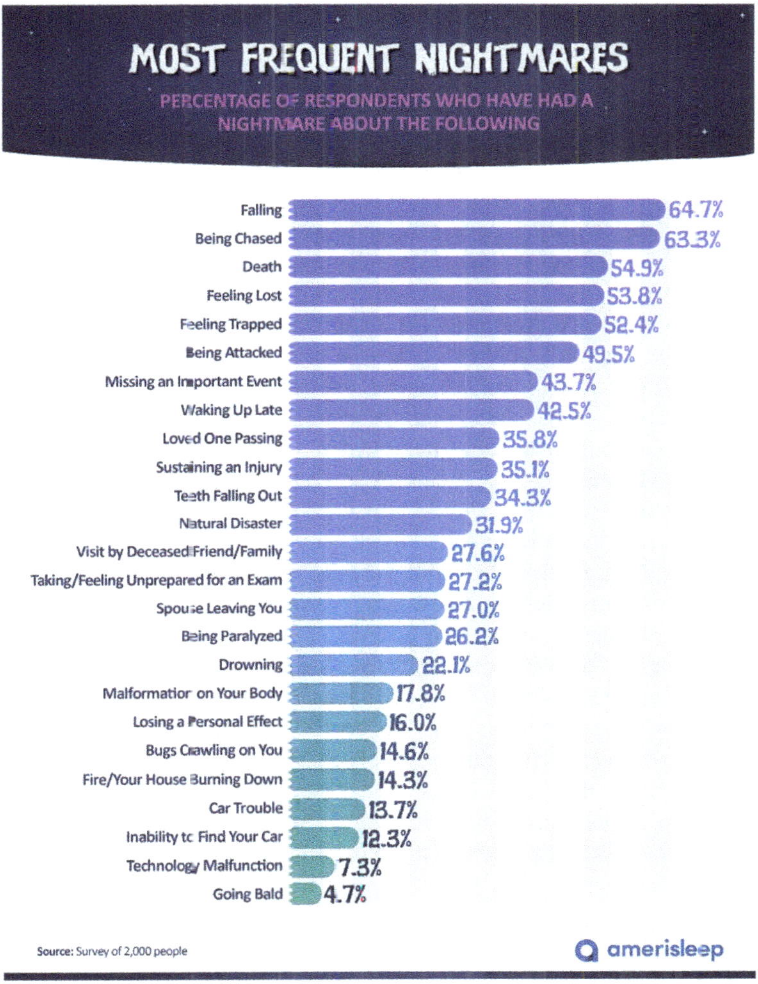

Sleep Disorders

MOST FREQUENT NIGHTMARES
PERCENTAGE OF RESPONDENTS WHO HAVE HAD A NIGHTMARE ABOUT THE FOLLOWING

Nightmare	Percentage
Falling	64.7%
Being Chased	63.3%
Death	54.9%
Feeling Lost	53.8%
Feeling Trapped	52.4%
Being Attacked	49.5%
Missing an Important Event	43.7%
Waking Up Late	42.5%
Loved One Passing	35.8%
Sustaining an Injury	35.1%
Teeth Falling Out	34.3%
Natural Disaster	31.9%
Visit by Deceased Friend/Family	27.6%
Taking/Feeling Unprepared for an Exam	27.2%
Spouse Leaving You	27.0%
Being Paralyzed	26.2%
Drowning	22.1%
Malformation on Your Body	17.8%
Losing a Personal Effect	16.0%
Bugs Crawling on You	14.6%
Fire/Your House Burning Down	14.3%
Car Trouble	13.7%
Inability to Find Your Car	12.3%
Technology Malfunction	7.3%
Going Bald	4.7%

Source: Survey of 2,000 people — amerisleep

[Source: Hyde, H. (2020). *What are the most common nightmares?* Retrieved here.]

- Here is a brief edited case example of sleep terror disorder (night terrors) in a young child in Brazil:
  We report a case of sleep terror in a 4-year-old boy, patient A. The parents observed that for the past month, after the patient went to bed, he woke up in the middle of the night. This behavior occurs once or twice a week. On these occasions, the child is found standing somewhere in the house, crying and seemingly disoriented with rapid breathing and profuse

sweating. When the parents attempt to comfort him or return him to his room, he becomes quite upset, striking out at them and screaming loudly. He continues to scream and fight for several minutes, followed by spontaneous cessation. Once the child is calmed, the parents can put him back in his bed, and he sleeps through the rest of the night without incident. In the morning, he wakes up in his usual happy mood and does not remember what occurred the previous evening. The parents are worried that he might be having seizures or developing a severe behavioral problem. Lab blood work-up is solicited, including an electroencephalogram (EEG). All returned normal results.

The recommended treatment for sleep terror disorder [for children] is to assure the parents that their child will probably grow out of this developmentally, but in this case we chose a selective serotonin reuptake inhibitor antidepressant—fluoxetine 20 mg per day, for 2 months, achieving good response after 6 weeks treatment.

[Source: Guzman, C.S. & Wang, Y.P. (2008). Sleep terror disorder: A case report. *Brazilian Journal of Psychiatry*, 30(2), 169. You can find the article here.]

- Here are excerpts from an adult Taiwanese example in which treatment of sleep terror disorder included drugs and procedures akin to cognitive behavior therapy:

A 58-year-old man in good health was seen in the sleep clinic because of frequent episodes of nighttime disturbances, which he described as "intense nightmares" for the past year. He described himself as a light sleeper in general with no sleep problems prior to the onset of these disturbances. He admits that in the past 5 years he has been in an almost constant state of increased anxiety and arousal related to severe health problems in his wife; he also noted that the onset of these disturbances coincided with a relapse in his wife's illness after a hiatus brought about by successful treatment. He experienced sudden awakening, always in the first 3–4 h of sleep. The prevalent feeling was that of agony and for some time after the event he felt "his heart pounding", shortness of breath, increased pressure in both ears, sweating, and tight muscles in his legs and arms. A few seconds later he had the feeling that something "terrible" had happened. He immediately thought of his wife, only to discover that she was awake and trying to comfort him, and then gradually all symptoms ceased. His wife reported that he woke her up with a scream, which the patient did not seem to remember. He pointed out that the occurrence of an episode largely depended on his emotional state. He noticed that the episodes became more frequent when he had heightened anxiety over the health of his wife. Furthermore, the patient stated that a specific nightmare preceded awakening. The patient was an avid reader of police novels and usually read in bed prior to sleep or in order to sleep. The ensuing nightmare always contained a similar set of events: the "criminal" of the novel pursued his wife; his facial characteristics were present to the extent that they were revealed in the novel or in some other cases absent if his identity had not yet come to light; the patient viewed the events from a close distance at a first-person angle and tried to intervene. When he realized that he could not stop the criminal he woke up in despair. In a few instances he managed to approach the scene and woke up while engaged in a physical struggle with his opponent. The setting of the scene was predominantly his house or a familiar street leading to it. The predominant theme here seemed to be his effort to help his wife and his frustration at his inability to do so or his agony even when he succeeded. Upon awakening, he also recalled visual events such as "insects crawling at the far end of the room" only to disappear when the bedroom light was turned on....

Although the episodes were initially associated with high levels of anxiety, it became apparent that the anticipation of an episode soon led to a self-reinforcing pattern characterized by catastrophizing, selective attention focused on the disturbances, and negative emotionality, all of which served in maintaining a state of heightened arousal, which in turn precipitated the disturbance by increasing arousal frequency. A secondary issue was that the patient associated his nightmares with the night terrors, creating an explanatory framework that accentuated the problem....

We decided to supplement a monthly course of 20 mg paroxetine nightly with a number of sleep-education sessions.... During the sleep-education sessions, information was provided about all aspects of sleep, current research was presented, and clarification was given to address misconceptions about the nature of and differences between nocturnal events such as nightmares and night terrors. This could help the patient understand the nature of the episodes, and their place in the continuum of sleep physiology, and also disassociate these episodes from REM events such as dreams. The aim was to minimize the daytime focus and anticipation, and hence the negative emotionality and arousal. This course of treatment was decided on because of the inquisitive personality and the high level of literacy of the patient. The patient also completed a sleep diary for 1 month after the seven 45-min sleep-education sessions.

The sleep of the patient improved slowly and incrementally over 1 month. Sleep onset latency was reduced from over 1 h to 20 min; his sleep efficiency was 0.86, which was relatively low but within the normal range. The [sleep disturbance] score decreased to 4.7, an elevated normal result, whereas the [anxiety test] score improved to 39, indicating mild anxiety. The patient and his wife reported that the attacks decreased slightly (from an average of 5/week to 4/week), but most noticeable was a decrease in the feelings of panic and terror after an attack. Furthermore, daytime anticipation and ruminations about the expected "attack" were reduced as the patient accepted the physiological nature of the nighttime events.

[Source: Mazarakis, T. (2014). A case of adult night terrors. *Tzu Chi Medical Journal, 26*(3),138–140. You can find the article here.]

- Here is an edited case example from Turkey in which treatment of adult sleep terror disorder using behavioral methods was ineffective and improvement came only after trying several different drug treatments:

  A 58-year-old...married female applied to the psychiatry outpatient services with complaints of nightmares, screaming in sleep, and not being able to wake up on time. The complaints started after a plate operation owing to hip fracture approximately two years ago. The patient received treatments of sertraline, quetiapine, alprozolam, and olanzapine for 6–7 months at unstable doses and duration without any improvement. Furthermore, her partner is obliged to wake up the patient because of her screaming in sleep and increased activity in bed. The patient's mind was busy with the nightmares during the day, but she could not precisely remember the content of her dream. As her sleep is affected at night, sleepiness and tiredness affects her functionality during the day. Following ... psychiatric evaluation, the psychotropic drugs were stopped by tapering the dose.... The patient was diagnosed with [night terrors] according to the Structured Clinical Interview (SCID-I) for the DSM Axis I disorders. Behavioral methods were selected as the first-step intervention, and the patient was required to maintain a sleep diary and was educated about sleep hygiene. During the follow-up, it was noticed that the patient could not write her sleep diary as she could not remember the associated nightmares.... She noted her experiences at night according to the statements of her partner, including that her face flushed, her breathing changed, and that there were sudden moves such as crashing and hitting her arms and hands. Because desired treatment results could not be achieved by only behavioral methods and the complaints of the patient continued in the follow-up, 75-mg/day clomipramine and 1-mg/day lorazepam were added to the treatment.... Complaints about falling asleep and inability to sustain sleep decreased; however, the medication was stopped because of no improvements in the symptoms of nightmare, night screaming, hyperactivity in sleep and tiredness in the morning, and an oral drop of 1-mg/day clonazepam was administered thereafter. Nightmares reduced by the third day, and the quality of sleep increased. Further, night screaming, acts of violent behavior in sleep, and extreme mental occupations reduced. This treatment was continued for one month more at the same dose, and the patient and her partner consistently reported that the symptoms were completely abolished. The administration of oral clonazepam drop (1 mg/day) has been continued for 8 months and was ended by tapering the dose by 0.2 mg (two drops) per week in a month. Neither an exacerbation of night terror attacks nor a sign of abstinence was observed during six months of follow-up after discontinuation.

  [Source: Sodan Turan, H., Gündüz, N., Polat, A., & Tural, Ü.

(2015). Treatment approach to sleep terror: Two case reports. *Noro Psikiyatri Arsivi*, *52*(2), 204–206. The article can be found here.]

5. Sleep apnea

- Case of Mark, 49: During a visit to Mark's physician for a routine cholesterol check, Mark's wife tells the doctor that Mark wakes up throughout the night, sometimes very abruptly, with choking sounds. She says that sometimes it also appears as if he is holding his breath for short amounts of time or even not breathing. When she wakes him, he is usually startled. When the doctor asks if Mark snores, she says that Mark has snored very loudly for as long as she can remember. The doctor questions Mark as to how he feels in the morning when he wakes up. Mark responds that he usually still feels tired and catches up on sleep by taking naps. The doctor refers Mark to a sleep specialist to determine the cause of his symptoms. The specialist performs a physical examination and takes Mark's medical history, including sleep and daily functioning habits for him and his family, and checks Mark's tonsils, uvula, and soft palate for enlarged tissues. Following the examination, the specialist suspects sleep apnea and orders an overnight polysomnogram (PSG) at the sleep center in a nearby hospital.

  While Mark sleeps, the PSG records his brain activity, eye movement, muscle activity, breathing and heart rate, airflow through his lungs, and oxygen percentage in his blood. He is monitored by staff at the sleep center while he sleeps. Mark's PSG report shows 24 awakenings in a recording period of 6.63 h, resulting in 1.1 h awake and 5.5 h asleep. He has a sleep onset latency of 5.5 min. His overall sleep efficiency is 84%. Throughout the recording period, he is in Stage 1 sleep for 116.5 min, Stage 2 for 203 min, and REM for 10.5 min. Mark showed obstructive apneas 226 times with the longest event reaching 41.7 s. He had 446 hypopneas with the longest being 37.9 s. Throughout the study, Mark's sleeping position was on his back.

  Based on this assessment, Mark's physician diagnoses him with obstructive sleep apnea (OSA), the most common type. The doctor explains that the disorder has been causing Mark to stop breathing for many seconds at a time while he sleeps. He says that this happens multiple times per hour because a sufficient quantity of air is not able to flow into Mark's lungs as he sleeps. The throat briefly collapses, causing the pause in breathing. In Mark's case, because he is overweight, the enlarged tissue in his throat restricts the throat area from being open enough to allow adequate air to flow to his lungs. This causes the amount of oxygen in his blood to drop. Patients move out of deep and into light sleep several times throughout the night, resulting in poor sleep quality. The doctor explains that this is why Mark usually still feels tired in the morning when he gets out of bed and fatigued during the day.

  The doctor tells Mark that there are currently no medications to treat the disorder, but there are other therapeutic methods that can be utilized to help him. The goal for Mark is to restore his regular nighttime breathing and decrease his snoring and daytime fatigue. Mark's doctor warns that if left untreated, his sleep apnea can increase the chance of having high blood pressure and even a heart attack or stroke. Since diabetes also runs in his family, it is also important to know that his sleep apnea could increase the risk for developing it. Other problems that could arise are work-related or driving accidents due to his daytime sleepiness.

His physician recommends that he try to lose some weight, and prescribes the most common treatment for sleep apnea, a continuous positive airway pressure (CPAP) machine. Mark is also advised to avoid alcohol, smoking, and medications that may make him drowsy (all things that make it harder for his throat to stay open while he sleeps) and to sleep on his side instead of his back to help keep his throat open.

In a follow-up phone call one month after beginning CPAP treatment, Mark's wife reports that he has more energy than before treatment and usually sleeps through the night.

[Source: Adapted from A case of sleep apnea. (2008). *Case Manager Studies*, January 2. Retrieved here.]

- Case of W.R., 84: This patient was referred to a sleep specialist by her physician following her complaints of daytime fatigue. She was diagnosed with obstructive sleep apnea. Her initial diagnostic sleep study indicated about 37 respiratory disturbances per hour, all occurring while she slept on her back. The longest event that occurred was a 47-s period of obstructive apnea with a decrease in oxygen saturation to 84%. She was treated using a CPAP system. Her medical history also included obstructive sleep apnea, hypothyroidism, hyperlipidemia, essential hypertension, coronary artery disease, congestive heart failure, gastroesophageal reflux disease, renal insufficiency, and gout. W.P is a widow of normal weight who lives alone. She is a nonsmoker and does not use alcohol or recreational drugs. She follows a low-cholesterol, 2-g sodium diet and restricts caffeine intake to one or two cups of coffee daily. She has a sedentary lifestyle with no regular exercise. Physical exam showed a decrease in the anterior–posterior diameter of her posterior oropharynx space with a recessed mandible. The CPAP consolidated sleep and resolved most of the snoring and apneic episodes. At her second visit to the sleep lab she reported that her new CPAP face mask fit better than her previous one and when seen for a follow-up appointment she reported a decrease in daytime sleepiness. Yet another new mask and increased humidification in the CPAP system resulted in her ability to use it for more than 6 h per night.

[Source: Adapted from Berry, D. (2008). Case study: Obstructive sleep apnea. *Medsurg Nursing, 17,* 11–16. https://www.proquest.com/openview/39b0f5f0 122720572e19fab24ae11858/1?cbl=30764&pq-origsite=gscholar]

- Case of Mr. A., 55, illustrating an alternative treatment approach. This patient sought chiropractic manipulative care for chronic low back pain in January of 2004. During the history-taking process, he also complained of suffering from obstructive sleep apnea (OSA) for the past 11 years. In 1998, he underwent surgery for the correction of a deviated nasal septum and to clear nasal obstruction by removing the adenoids and uvula. Despite surgery, OSA persisted and the patient was reliant on a CPAP device from 1993 to 2003. The patient rarely experienced 6 h of uninterrupted sleep; and even with the CPAP machine, he suffered from wakefulness and restlessness throughout the night. Consequently, the patient never felt fully rested in the morning and suffered from afternoon lethargy.

As OSA is known to be associated with chronic inflammation and obesity, the option of lifestyle management was presented. The patient made the commitment to pursue a state of wellness with nutrition and exercise, referred to here as anti-inflammatory lifestyle changes. The most tangible goal was weight loss, and the operational and mental goal was to promote an anti-inflammatory state with each meal and snack. The patient was encouraged to avoid the consumption of refined sugar, refined grains, and whole grains in favor of more nutrient-dense foods including vegetables, fruits, lean meats, fish, skinless chicken, omega-3 eggs, and nuts. If a starchy carbohydrate was desired, the recommendation was to consume a modest portion of sweet or other potatoes. The use of spices was encouraged to replace table salt. Ginger, turmeric, and garlic were recommended as well as others that appealed to the patient, as they have an anti-inflammatory effect. The patient adhered to several of these dietary changes; the consumption of junk food snacks and soft drinks was reduced to an occasional occurrence. The patient also made a conscious effort to "slow down when eating" and was mindful of feelings of fullness, so as not to overeat. Alcohol consumption was significantly reduced from 4 to 5 drinks several nights per week to 1 glass of red wine 3 to 4 nights per week. In August of 2005, the patient began taking several supplements that are thought to assist in the process of inflammation reduction including a multivitamin, magnesium (400 mg/d), fish oil (1.2 g of omega-3 fatty acids per day), coenzyme Q10 (100 mg/d), and an anti-inflammatory botanical (1.5 g of turmeric, ginger, and bioflavonoids).

Because the patient was initially sedentary, he was encouraged to exercise to facilitate weight loss and to increase feelings of well-being. He began to walk on a daily basis and gradually increased the intensity and distance. For approximately 1 year, from March 2005 to 2006, he engaged in weight training at a local gym. Since that time, he decided to substitute moderately heavy yard work for weight training and included core stabilization exercises. He currently jogs 4–5 days per week for approximately 60 min. In April and July of 2010, he completed 5-km races.

The status of OSA symptoms in this patient was assessed periodically when the patient sought manipulative care for his low back pain. Blood pressure, use of blood pressure medications, and body weight were also monitored. These assessments revealed a dramatic change in sleep habits after initiating lifestyle changes. Before lifestyle modifications, the patient reported that he rarely experienced 6 h of uninterrupted sleep, even while using the CPAP machine; and this was associated with long bouts of wakefulness throughout the night. By March of 2004, after 3 months of lifestyle modification, the patient no longer needed to use the CPAP device. Furthermore, since that time, the patient has reported 6–8 h of continuous sleep and feeling well rested upon waking; and according to the patient's spouse, there were no more snoring or apnea episodes during the night.

Numerous health and quality of life improvements also occurred during this nearly 7-year process. Most notable was the significant reduction in blood pressure from 140/90 mm Hg with antihypertensive medication to 120/80 mm Hg without medication. Despite a personal and family history of hypertension, the patient stated that this was the first time since the age of 25 years that his family physician considered reducing the dosage of his hypertension medication, which commenced approximately 2 years after lifestyle modifications began. At the time of this writing, the patient was no longer taking antihypertensives and maintained a blood pressure of 120/80 mm Hg. For the majority of the patient's adult life, he weighed between 210–260 lb. His weight before initiating lifestyle changes in January of 2004 was 225 lb. As of September 2010, he weighed 175 lb. The patient also reported several subjective improvements in quality of life, including increased sexual desire and pleasure despite a steady decline before lifestyle changes, increased energy and stamina during activities of daily living and exercise, increased positive mental attitude and body image, increased optimism, decreased frustration and decreased mood swings, better mental capabilities and clarity, improved quality of life and ability to pursue activities such as hiking, backpacking, and general increased feeling of well-being.

[Source: Adapted from Gala, T. R., & Seaman, D. R. (2011). Lifestyle modifications and the resolution of obstructive sleep apnea syndrome: A case report. *Journal of Chiropractic Medicine*, *10*(2), 118–125. You can find the article here.]

Sleep Deprivation

1. Laboratory case example: The aim of this study was to evaluate the effects of 72-h sleep deprivation on normal daily activities (work, family, and sports), and to investigate whether sleep can be chronically reduced without dangerous consequences. The participant in this study was an adult male (age 41). During the 72 h data were collected every 6 h, and compared to a pre-deprivation baseline on oxidative stress (D-Rom and Bap test), psychological responses (Profile of Mood States test and a measure of global stress), metabolic expenditure using a metabolic holter monitor, EEG records, and cortisol, and catecholamines level. During the 72-h sleep deprivation, no psychophysiological stress was recorded. The participant remained within the threshold of well-being. The only peak was recorded during the 66th h, but it was within the wellness threshold.

[Source: Adapted from Coco, M., Buscemi, A., Guarnera, M., La Paglia, R., Perciavalle, V., & Di Corrado, D. (2019). Sleep deprivation and physiological responses. A case report. *Journal of Functional Morphology and Kinesiology*, 4, 17.]

2. A famous case study of the effects of longer-term sleep deprivation comes from a 1959 "Wakeathon" during which New York City disc jockey Peter Tripp did not sleep for 201 h (8.4 days) to raise money for the March of Dimes charity and to break the current world record. He spent most of this time in a glass booth in Times Square, and the rest in a hotel room across the street being monitored by scientists. After three days, Tripp began laughing hysterically at nothing at all. He also became upset, confused and paranoid. He hallucinated—at first, simple patterns like cobwebs on people's faces, or insects which were really specks of paint on the table. But soon, the hallucinations became more intense, like waking dreams. He famously saw mice and kittens scurrying around the room. By the end of his sleepless stunt, Tripp was behaving in an apparently psychotic manner. He rummaged through drawers searching for non-existent money. He accused a technician of trying to harm him. He then claimed he was not Peter Tripp but an impostor. Nothing made sense to him.

On reaching his 200-h target, Tripp was made to stay awake for one final hour while doctors did more tests. They left the EEG sensors in place as he finally closed his bloodshot eyes and entered a deep 13-h slumber.  Unfortunately, there appeared to be permanent consequences to the event. Tripp's family noticed a difference in his personality; he was moody and depressed. He fought with his boss, and was fired from his  high profile job. He went on to have four divorces.

[Source: Adapted from an account in the New York Times by Rebecca Turner, *How Long Can You Survive Without Sleep?*, retrieved here.]

3. An example of a paper-and-pencil test of sleepiness is provided by the Epworth Sleepiness Scale. You can find it here.

Dreams and Dreaming

[Note: Dreams are familiar enough to students that they can all come up  with their own examples, so this section is meant to provide examples of less familiar dream-related phenomena and research methods for studying them.]

1. A basic introduction to sleep lab technology and dreaming is provided by this 13-min video filmed by Alan Alda in the laboratory of Dr. Robert Stickgold.
2. Researchers are experimenting with a wearable electronic device designed to incubate dream content while a person is falling asleep. The idea is eventually to allow controlled experiments on dreams and their effects

[Source: Horowitz, A.H., Cunningham, T.J., Maes, P., & Stickgold, R. (2020). Dormio: A targeted dream incubation device. *Consciousness and Cognition, 83*, 102,938.]

3. Researchers are experimenting with the use of virtual reality experiences to induce dreams of flying. Here is an edited version of the abstract of their report: Despite a high prevalence and broad interest in flying dreams, these exceptional experiences remain infrequent. Our study aimed to (1) induce flying dreams using a custom-built virtual reality (VR) flying task, (2) examine their phenomenological correlates and (3) investigate their relations to participant state and trait factors.... VR-flying successfully increased the reporting of flying dreams during the laboratory nap and on the following morning compared to both baseline frequencies and a control cohort. Flying dreams were also changed qualitatively, exhibiting higher levels of lucid-control and emotional intensity, after VR exposure. Factors such as prior dream-flying experiences and level of VR sensory immersion modulated flying dream induction. Findings are consistent with a new vection-based explanation of dream-flying and may facilitate development of dream flight-induction technologies.
[Source: Picard-Deland, C., Pastor, M., Solomonova, E., Paquette, T., & Nielsen, T. (2020). Flying dreams stimulated by an immersive virtual reality task. *Consciousness and Cognition, 83*, 102,958.]

4. Another example of current trends in dream research is called "dream engineering," in which researchers are interested in using virtual reality technology to direct dreaming and manipulate sleep, presumably for the benefit of humankind, but with obvious ethical implications.
[Source: Carr, M., Haar, A., Amores, J., Lopes, P., Bernal, G., Vega, T., Rosello, O., Jain, A., & Maes, P. (2020). Dream engineering: Simulating worlds through sensory stimulation. *Consciousness and Cognition, 83*, 102,955.]

5. The following edited abstract provides an example of dream researchers' efforts to teach people to engage in lucid dreaming:
Lucid dreaming offers many opportunities to study consciousness processes. However, ... frequent lucid dreamers are rare. Several studies demonstrated that a combination of a wake-up-back-to-bed (WBTB) sleep protocol and a mnemonic technique (MILD) showed promising results for increasing lucid dreaming. (MILD is a memory technique designed to create and carry out the intention to remember that one is dreaming.) To further investigate the effectiveness of this combined approach, we conducted a sleep laboratory experiment with four conditions. The general experimental procedure was the following: Participants were awakened after 6 h of sleep from a subsequent REM period and kept awake for 30 or 60 min, during which they were asked to practice MILD or a control task (e.g., reading). Then they returned to bed for a morning sleep period. In the first condition eleven students, who attended a seminar on sleep and dreams, spent one night in a sleep laboratory. To control for possible increased motivation caused by the seminar attendance, 15 participants in the second condition did not attend the seminar. In the third condition, 14 students

were tested with a shorter awakening period (30 min). In the fourth condition, 11 students slept for two non-consecutive nights in a sleep laboratory. Instead of MILD, on one night they read a book (fiction, unrelated to dreams), while in the other night they played a Nintendo Wii video game. In the first three conditions, six (54%), eight (53%), and five participants (36%) reported lucid dreams during the morning sleep period, whereas three, (27%), four (27%), and two participants (14%) produced the eye movement signals that they had been taught to give to indicate lucid dreaming. In the reading condition, one (9%) participant reported lucid dreams, but no eye movement signals. No lucid dreams were observed in the Wii condition. The findings of the present study show that by using a combination of WBTB and MILD, lucid dreams can be effectively induced in people who are not selected for their lucid dream abilities.
[Source: Erlacher, D., & Stumbrys, T. (2020). Wake up, work on dreams, back to bed and lucid dream: A sleep laboratory study. *Frontiers in Psychology, 11*, 1383.]

6. A simplified version of the same methodology achieved similar results.
[Source: Appel, K., Füllhase, S., Kern, S., Kleinschmidt, A., Laukemper, A., Lüth, K., Steinmetz, L., & Vogelsang, L. (2020). Inducing signal-verified lucid dreams in 40% of untrained novice lucid dreamers within two nights in a sleep laboratory setting. *Consciousness and Cognition, 83*, 102, 960.]

7. Examples of other lucid dreaming training techniques are described in a literature review that suggests only some of them show promise.
[Source: Stumbrys, T., Erlacher, D., Schädlich, M., & Schredl, M. (2012). Induction of lucid dreams: A systematic review of evidence. *Consciousness and Cognition, 21*(3), 1456–1475.]

8. An example of how scientific research on induction of lucid dreaming is finding its way into pop psychology is found in the course offered by Chris Hammond, "chief lucidity officer" at the World of Lucid Dreaming.

9. Utterly unscientific examples of the alleged meaning of every conceivable kind of dream content can be found here.

Hypnotic Phenomena and Applications

[*Note:* Examples in this section provide the opportunity to point out that hypnotic phenomena are influenced by many psychological and social factors including demand characteristics, but also to debunk the myth that people can be hypnotized against their will or made to do things, including commit crimes, that they would not do without being hypnotized.]

1. Hypnotherapists and stage hypnotists use hypnosis in an attempt to create effects such as:

   - forgetting or remembering of events or information
   - preventing or relieving pain
   - creating rigidity (cataplexy) of muscles, including eye muscles
   - dissociation (mentally removing oneself from a situation)
   - visualization of future events (including mental practice of some activity)
   - hallucination of non-existent stimuli or events (such as temperature changes or sounds)
   - compliance with post-hypnotic suggestions (such as to do or not to do certain things)
   - visualization of past events (including supposed age-regression)
   - experiencing time as slowing down or speeding up.

2. Age regression. The figure below shows the signatures of two adults before hypnotically induced age regression (top of each pair) and while age regressed (bottom of each pair).

   The lower signature in each pair looks less mature, but you can challenge your students to investigate if such changes are necessarily due to hypnosis by asking a friend to sign a blank sheet of paper, first as usual, and then as if he or she were five years old. Ask your students to consider, if the two signatures look significantly different, what this says about the cause of certain age-regression effects.

   Steve

   Steven

   Sue

   Sue

   [Source: E. R. Hilgard (1965). *Hypnotic susceptibility*. New York: Harcourt, Brace, Jovanovich.]

3. Pain control. Bernadine Coady of Wimblington, England, has a condition that makes general anesthesia dangerous for her. In April 1999, she faced a foot operation that would have been extremely painful without anesthesia. She arranged for a hypnotherapist to help her through the procedure, but when he failed to show up, she was forced to rely on self-hypnosis as her only anesthetic.

She said she imagined the pain as "waves lashing against a sea wall ... [and] going away, like the tide." Coady's report that the operation was painless is believable because, in December 2000, she had the same operation on her other foot, again using only self-hypnosis for pain control.
[Source: Morris, L. (2000, December 5). Hold the anaesthetic: I'll hypnotise myself instead. *Daily Mail*, p. 25.]

4. Similar cases in which patients use only hypnosis while undergoing lumpectomies for breast cancer can be found here.
5. Retrieving memory. Here is an abbreviated version of a hypnotherapist's description of the case of a woman who had lost a $15,000 diamond wedding ring:

Needless to say, when she and her husband arrived at my office she was upset and said she was willing to try anything to recover it. I explained that there was no assurance that a hypnosis session would be successful in helping her to find her ring, since there might be other variables involved, such as theft. I also explained that while I could not promise that she would find her ring, I assured her that her subconscious mind had a record of her last contact with the object and hypnosis could be useful in bringing that memory forward. I asked her to give me every available detail about the morning she lost the ring. Since it had happened on the previous Sunday, many of the details were still fresh in her mind. I had her recall what she was wearing, where she was, details about her movements, what the weather was like. She was able to give me many details, but the only memory of the ring was when she left home to buy breakfast for her family at a fast food restaurant. She said her last memory of her ring was when she was driving her vehicle, she looked at her hand on the steering wheel and admired the ring. She told me that after she realized the ring was missing, she began a frantic search. She and her husband had lifted the carpet, looked under every bit of furniture, gone through every bit of garbage, even followed the dog around thinking he may have swallowed it. They also searched every inch of their vehicle. I asked if it was possible that the ring may have fallen from her finger, or if someone else might have taken the ring after she put it someplace in her home. "No" was the answer to both questions.
I began the hypnosis session, slowly guiding the client through the events of that Sunday morning, questioning her about her every move. At one point, when I asked "What happened next?", she said she took her baby into the bathroom for a bath. "Then what? Take your time." I continued. She said, "I took the baby from the bathroom to the bedroom, laid her on the bed, there were no sheets on the bed because I was washing them." "What happened then? Did you take off your ring then?" I repeated, "Did you take off your ring when you laid the baby on the mattress?" "Yes!", she replied. "What happened then?", I asked. "I dressed the baby, then I got the bed sheets out of the clothes dryer and made the bed." I ended the session, bringing Natalie to a full waking state. I looked at the client and her husband and said, "You guys have been sleeping on your ring since Sunday! The ring is between your top bed sheet and the mattress!" They could not get out of my office fast enough! They returned home to find the ring

exactly where I said it was. The client called me immediately, she couldn't believe it!

Source: Adapted from Hypnotic World Case Histories and Studies, retrieved here. (Note that this case allows you to ask students to consider the possibility that the same line of questioning might have led to the same conclusion, but without hypnosis. It can also lead to discussion of hypnosis-related myths, such as claims that hypnosis can help eyewitnesses remember forgotten details about a crime or a criminal, and that it can help clients recover repressed memories, including memories of childhood abuse.)

6. Anxiety management. Here is a revised version of a hypnotherapist's case description:

The client made an appointment for driving test nerves. Her next exam was due in less than a week so I suggested that we arrange her session for the afternoon of the day before her exam. She told me that she had already taken her test 11 times and failed, not because she was not a competent driver, but because she panicked each time at the slightest mistake. After her first couple of failures she began to have panic attacks several days prior to her next test. She couldn't sleep the night before and was even physically sick on several occasions. She had already 300 h of driving experience and knew all the examiners, and they all told her that they were sorry they had to fail her for hitting curbs and other mistakes, but that they simply couldn't pass her. I think I was her last hope and I really believed that she was going to pass this time. Maybe it would have happened without hypnosis, but she had already decided that she was going to panic yet once more. She told me that she'd been hypnotized on stage once and was a good subject. I used my favorite induction, which rarely fails, taking her down a beautiful stairway and through the door of time—the door to tomorrow —the day of her driving exam. We went through an imaginary journey of her test where she felt so confident and competent—she was given several anchors to reinforce this confidence and projected to the end of her test to enjoy the experience of knowing that she had now earned her license to freedom. When the session was over I asked the client how she felt. She reported that she *knew* she was going to pass this time. I really wanted to wish her luck but didn't because I thought that might seem as though it was leaving things to chance so I simply asked her to phone me after the exam and let me know how it went. She said - "I'll phone you to let you know that I've passed". At exactly one o'clock the following day the phone rang. It was my client—she said—"I've passed—thank you so much".

[Source: Adapted from Hypnotic World Case Histories and Studies, retrieved here.]

7. Any part of this 20-min video showing a stage hypnotist doing hypnotic inductions on a public beach provides both a good example of hypnotic techniques and an opportunity to ask your students to consider alternative hypotheses—such as demand characteristics—that might account for the subjects' behavior.
8. There is a 14-min version showing the same hypnotist doing inductions on a college campus.
9. A 6-min video of a stage hypnotist doing a mass induction at a college show is available here.

Motivation and Emotion

Motivation and emotion are topics of great interest to students. They can be linked and applied to virtually all aspects of life, from weight control and sexuality to job performance and happiness. The links and applications are so numerous that many examples that could have been included in this chapter are listed instead in other chapters, as noted below. Because motivational and emotional concepts are so much a part of everyday life, we have found that while it is always helpful to have an arsenal of examples of those concepts, students are often able to come up with good examples of their own, including some of those presented here.

Sources of Motivation

The general drive to survive is one of the most basic sources of motivation. An example of how that drive can motivate extraordinary behavior is the case of Aron Rawson who, in April of 2003 was climbing alone in Utah's Bluejohn Canyon when he slipped and fell, dislodging an 800-pound boulder that fell on his arm. Unable to move the boulder or summon help, he remained trapped for five days and after running out of food and water, he used a pocket knife to amputate his arm to save his life. Here is a short clip of Rawson describing his decision-making process. A description of the movie (*127 Hours*) about his story can be found here.

Specific Sources of Motivation

1. Physiological

   - Need for food
   - Need for water

- Need for temperature regulation
- Need for sleep
- Hormones such as testosterone or estrogen can alter interest in sex

2. Emotional

- Fear leads a person to try to avoid being around dogs, heights, social situations, or air travel.
- Anger leads a person to physically or verbally attack someone who caused the anger.
- Jealously leads a person to try to control a romantic partner's social life.
- Love leads parents to endanger their own lives to protect their child.
- Compassion leads people to volunteer their time at food banks, homeless shelters, hospitals, and nursing homes.
- Envy leads a person to launch a nasty campaign on social media against a more successful co-worker
- Hatred leads a person to commit violent acts, including murder, against a reviled supervisor.
- Patriotic feelings lead military service members to risk their lives to fight for their country.
- Here are just three cases in which anger, hatred, envy, and jealously combined to motivate crimes of passion:

> When Leonard Rojas saw his wife leaving his brother's bedroom one morning in Alvarado TX, he confronted her about the possibly imagined adultery before shooting her at point blank range between the eyes and murdering his brother. He bought a bus ticket for Atlanta before confessing his murder to a security guard.

> Sahel Kazemi was in the undesirable position of being a famous football player's secret girlfriend when, in 2009, after being dumped by retired quarterback Steve McNair, she reportedly snapped and shot McNair twice in the body and twice in the head before committing suicide.

> In 2007, astronaut Lisa Nowak's fury at a love rival caused her to try to kidnap Colleen Shipman, an engineer who was involved with her boyfriend, William Oefelein. She drove from Houston, Texas, to Orlando, Florida, where she accosted Shipman in the parking lot of the airport and pepper sprayed her, trying to get her into the car. Shipman managed to alert a security guard and Nowak was subdued without causing any further harm.

> You can read about 27 crimes of passion here.

3. Cognitive

- Perceiving the world as a place full of caring people can lead children to want to explore that world, to be nice to others, and to expect others to be nice to them. [You might want to point out to your students that some children's television shows (e.g., Sesame Street, Mister Rogers, Dora the Explorer, Arthur, Curious George) reinforce this idea about the world.]
- Perceiving the world to be a dangerous place full of threatening people can lead people to distrust everything and everybody, causing them to push others away, and make themselves miserable in the process. [You might want to point out to your students that some children's television shows focus on conflict, threat, aggression and violence (e.g., Teenage Mutant Ninja Turtles, Frozen, Power Rangers) reinforce this idea about the world.]
- Believing that you have a great voice might lead you to enter a singing contest with high hopes of winning, even though—as seen in the early stages of many such contests—that belief may be obviously wrong.
- Believing in their ability to succeed at difficult tasks can lead people to persist at such tasks, even in the face of temporary failure.
- Believing that they are incapable of overcoming obstacles in life can lead people to give up at the first obstacle they encounter and to come to depend on others to solve their problems for them. (See also examples of learned helplessness in the chapter on learning.)
- Believing that you have control over the events and circumstances of your life leads you to develop and follow a detailed study plan in order to pass a difficult course, or to adopt a healthy lifestyle to prevent illness.
- Believing that the events and circumstances of your life are controlled mainly by luck or chance leads you not to bother studying very hard and simply hope that the exams in that difficult course will not be all that hard. Or you might not bother to eat healthy foods or exercise because you assume that getting a serious illness is all a matter of bad luck.

4. Social/environmental

- The encouragement of family members, their hopes for your success in getting a college degree, along with a desire not to disappoint them, may lead you to work much harder in school than you otherwise might have done.
- Your cultural background is such that you more or less automatically consider what your family will think about how you behave, what career choice you make, and whether, when, and whom you marry.
- The fact that all your closest friends have tattoos and body piercings leads you to get some of both, even though these things don't really appeal to you and you worry about whether you will regret doing so.

- The story of 20-year-old Donte Franklin who walked 8 miles each way to and from a part-time job, largely because of the influence of his recently deceased mother's teachings about responsibility is available here. He was quoted as saying that he walked "just to make my family proud."

Theories of Motivation

1. Instinct theory: Fixed- or modal-action patterns

- Spiders spin characteristic webs, birds build characteristic nests, animals of all kinds engage in stereotyped courting and mating behavior, including for example, when male stickleback fish instantly attack at the sight of a red spot on the belly of a male rival.
- Geese roll objects that aren't eggs into their nests, as can be seen in this 1-min video.
- Reflexes such as breathing, eye blink, rooting, sucking, swallowing, stepping, Babinski, grasping and Moro (see also the chapter on biological aspects of psychology, development, and learning)
- Yawn contagion between species is shown in this 1:30-min video and in this 2-min video.

- Innate facial expressions such as genuine smiles and disgust (see more examples in the section on facial expressions of emotion later in this chapter)
- Crying in a newborn infant

2. Instinct theory: Complex human behavior

[Note: The examples listed here can stimulate class discussions and/or serve as topics for papers about the strengths and weaknesses of evolutionary psychology, especially the theory that some of the complex social behaviors seen in humans today evolved over the centuries because they were adaptive for survival. The individuals in each generation who displayed these behaviors, the theory goes, were the ones who lived long enough to pass their genes on to the next generation. You might also want to point out alternative explanations for these behaviors, including cultural traditions, social learning, and gender differences in economic and political power.]

- People help others, even at the risk of their own lives, and do so especially for those to whom they are most closely related genetically. An example of this phenomenon appears to have occurred during the 1973 Summerland resort fire on the Isle of Man, UK.

[References: Sime, J. D. (1983). Affiliative behaviour during escape to building exits. *Journal of Environmental Psychology*, *3*(1), 21–41.

Sime, J. D. (1985). Movement toward the familiar: Person and place affiliation in a fire entrapment setting. *Environment and Behavior*, *17*(6), 697–724.]

- Aggression may serve to take needed resources away from others, to successfully defend oneself against potentially fatal attacks by others (and discouraging them from further attacks), intimidating those who would compete for one's sexual partner, reducing the chances that one's partner will be unfaithful, negotiating status and power hierarchies, deterring rivals from future aggression, and deterring mates from being unfaithful, among other examples.
- Today's mating choices may be influenced by the consequences of the choices made by our evolutionary ancestors, as seen in the fact that both men and women express a strong preference for a dependable, emotionally stable, and intelligent long-term partner who can help create a good environment for having and raising children.
- The fact that most males want to engage in sex sooner than most females do is said to reflect the efforts of males' evolutionary ancestors to maximize their genetic impact on the next generation.
- Males tend to prefer mating with females who appear most capable of successfully bearing children, as indicated by youth, good health, and a low waist-to-hip ratio.
- Females are more careful about mating choices than males are because they can produce relatively few children in their lifetimes, are thus more psychologically invested in them, and want to be sure they find a mate who can and will help to provide for them. Evidence supporting this tendency comes from a study showing that women are slower than men are to fall in love and say "I love you."

[Reference: Harrison, M. A., & Shortall, J. C. (2011). Women and men in love: Who really feels it and says it first? *The Journal of Social Psychology*, *151*(6), 727–736.]

Arousal Theory

Activities that *increase arousal* include:

- participating in novel activities, such as taking up a new hobby or learning a new language
- engaging in risky behaviors such as smoking, drinking alcohol, skydiving, white water rafting, bungee jumping, rock climbing
- watching sports competition or car races
- socializing
- being in a crowd

- being in a noisy environment
- watching an action movie or a comedy
- engaging in activities that satisfy curiosity, such as exploring a new place.

Activities that *decrease arousal* include:

- going for a slow, quiet walk
- taking a nap
- taking a bath
- reading for relaxation
- getting a massage
- being in a quiet environment
- being alone or with a small number of compatible people
- doing yoga
- meditating
- practicing progressive relaxation training (see chapter on treatment of psychological disorders).

Arousal and performance: Performance is generally thought to be best when there is an optimal level of arousal. There are, however, individual differences and the optimal level of arousal depends upon the complexity of the task. The optimal level of arousal tends to be lower for difficult, complex tasks and higher for easy, simple ones. For example:

- When first learning to drive or when driving in heavy traffic or in bad weather, performance will likely be better if the driver turns off the radio, asks passengers not to talk, and avoids other distractions that will add to cognitive load. (See also the section on attention and multi-tasking in the chapter on sensation and perception.)
- When studying for an exam, students should limit the amount of noise and distraction in their environment by turning off their phone and email. (Students are often quite interested in offering their perspectives on this bit of advice!)
- When engaged in a simple, mundane task like knitting, one of your authors finds that her performance is better and she persists at it longer if she also watches TV, listens to music or talks to her daughter.
- People whose jobs require them to do repetitive tasks such as packing boxes, stuffing envelopes, or working on an assembly line, typically perform better if they also listen to music or talk radio.
- When driving long-distances on a wide, straight road with little traffic, conversation, music or talk radio can help keep arousal high enough to avoid "highway hypnosis" and increase safety. (Note: Due to habituation, the high-risk nature of driving at high speed does not, in and of itself, always keep arousal high. Also, consider your daily commute and how you may complete it without incident and then have trouble remembering details of the trip because your

attention was not fully engaged in the task of driving. See also chapters on learning and memory.)
- Examples of consequences of arousal being too low include lethargy, poor or lackluster athletic or academic performance, and falling sleeping while operating machinery.
- Examples of consequences of arousal being too high include "blanking" on an exam or "choking" in an athletic competition.

Maslow's Hierarchy of Needs

1. Here is an example of the standard pyramidal representation of Maslow's hierarchy:

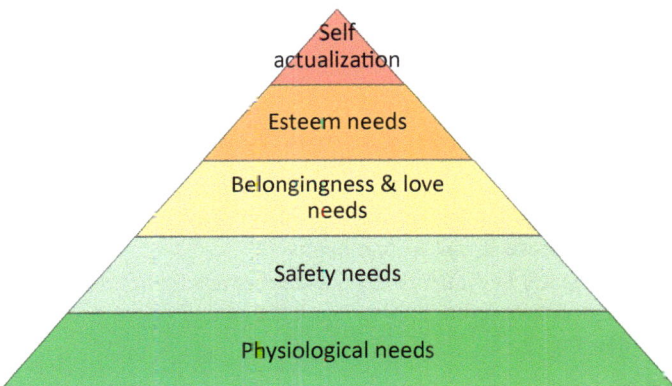

[Note: You might consider discussing with your students the criticism that this conceptualization of needs may not be universal, for example, that the hierarchy may differ somewhat between people in collectivist vs. individualist cultures.]

2. Here is an alternative to the pyramid shown above. It may better reflect the interaction/overlap among needs described by Maslow. This figure demonstrates the *dynamic* interaction among these needs over time. Notice that the need for self-actualization grows as the intensity of other needs decreases. *The pyramid above was color-coded to match this image.*

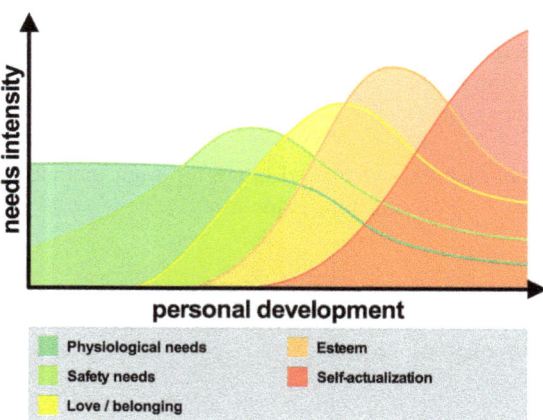

[Source: Philipp Guttmann, CC BY-SA 4.0 <https://creativecommons.org/licenses/by-sa/4.0>, via Wikimedia Commons].

3. The image above and some of the following examples of working towards self-actualization can be found here.

   - Developing strong relationships with others
   - Being a good parent, such as finding meaning in raising community-minded children
   - Pursuing interests for the intrinsic pleasure they provide, such as painting landscapes because it makes one happy
   - Developing skills and talents (e.g., creative, academic, athletic), such as an amateur dancer who continues to take classes and improve, but never makes money dancing

4. Examples of people who are/were self-actualized—including famous people identified by Maslow (such as Albert Einstein, George Washington, and Harriet Tubman)—are described here.

5. In this *Scientific American* article the authors identify the following unedited list of 10 "scientifically supported" characteristics of self-actualization, with examples of Self-Actualization Scale items endorsed by actualized people:

   - *Continued Freshness of Appreciation* (Sample item: "I can appreciate again and again, freshly and naively, the basic goods of life, with awe, pleasure, wonder, and even ecstasy, however stale these experiences may have become to others.")
   - *Acceptance* (Sample item: "I accept all of my quirks and desires without shame or apology.")

- *Authenticity* (Sample item: "I can maintain my dignity and integrity even in environments and situations that are undignified.")
- *Equanimity* (Sample item: "I tend to take life's inevitable ups and downs with grace, acceptance, and equanimity.")
- *Purpose* (Sample item: "I feel a great responsibility and duty to accomplish a particular mission in life.')
- *Efficient Perception of Reality* (Sample item: "I am always trying to get at the real truth about people and nature.")
- *Humanitarianism* (Sample item: "I have a genuine desire to help the human race.")
- *Peak Experiences* (Sample item: "I often have experiences in which I feel new horizons and possibilities opening up for myself and others.")
- *Good Moral Intuition* (Sample item: "I can tell 'deep down' right away when I've done something wrong.")
- *Creative Spirit* (Sample item: "I have a generally creative spirit that touches everything I do.")

The full Self-Actualization Scale can be completed at no cost here.

6. Examples of esteem needs include:

- To be accepted (by oneself and others)
- To be respected (by oneself and others)
- To be valued (by oneself and others)
- To have a sense of mastery in life (e.g., demonstrating proficiency in a second language athletics, or job responsibilities)
- To be independent and free (particularly strong in individualist cultures)
- To have recognition, fame, prestige

7. Examples of ways to fulfill belongingness and love needs include being part of

- clubs
- social groups (including family)
- teams
- gangs
- communities (e.g., religious)
- a group of co-workers

8. Examples of safety needs

- To feel physically safe in your home and community
- To experience emotional safety, such as feeling free to be open and honest with an intimate partner without fear of punishment
- To be financially secure
- To be healthy and experience happiness (subjective well-being)

9. Examples of physiological needs
   - To have breathable, oxygenated air
   - To regulate bodily processes such as temperature (homeostasis) via clothing appropriate for the environment
   - For health
   - To have food and water
   - To sleep

Intrinsic Motivation

1. Children are intrinsically motivated to play. Many examples of this can be found on Databrary. For example:

   - Adolph, K. (2014). *Children's social and motor play on a playground.* Databrary. Retrieved December 23, 2020 from https://doi.org/10.17910/B77P4V.
   - Adolph, K., Tamis-LeMonda, C., Gilmore, R.O. & Soska, K. (2016). PLAY Project: NICHD Workshop (2016–12-16). *Databrary.* Retrieved December 23, 2020 from https://doi.org/10.17910/B7.254.
   - Frank, M.C. (2016). *Sample play session video. Databrary.* Retrieved December 23, 2020 from https://doi.org/10.17910/B7.235.

2. Based on Daniel Pink's book *Drive*, this 1:49-min video suggests that intrinsic motivation is enhanced by autonomy, mastery and purpose. The video includes images of a classroom and of people paragliding, steering a boat, flying a kite, kicking a soccer ball on a beach, hiking to the top of a mountain—all examples of activities that people are likely to be intrinsically motivated to do (see also the section below on links between motivation and emotion that lists examples of how the experience of pleasure can motivate people to engage in a variety of behaviors).
3. Daniel Pink's engaging 18:23-min Ted talk provides examples of ways in which intrinsic motivation results in better outcomes than incentivized motivation.
4. Pink's work is based on self-determination theory, proposed by Richard Ryan and Edward Deci. A website about this theory with links to examples of applications of self-determination theory can be found here.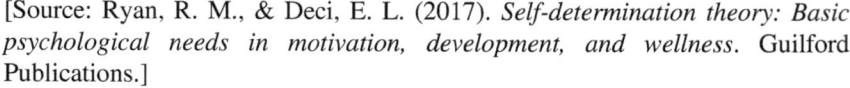
   [Source: Ryan, R. M., & Deci, E. L. (2017). *Self-determination theory: Basic psychological needs in motivation, development, and wellness.* Guilford Publications.]

5. A 5:46-min video about intrinsic motivation with the renowned motivational psychologist Edward Deci can be seen here.

6. An example of an applying an understanding of motivation to the challenges of keeping New Year's resolutions can be seen in this 3:05-min video with Ed Deci.
7. This website suggests some ways to increase intrinsic motivation in the workplace, including:

   - allowing employees 10% of their time to work on a project of their choosing,
   - giving employees more control and decreasing managerial control,
   - assigning "Goldilocks Tasks," which challenge people without overwhelming them, and
   - encouraging collaboration.

Extrinsic Motivation

1. Examples of external stimuli or incentives that create extrinsic motivation (see also reinforcers/rewards in the chapter on learning), include:

   - Money
   - Gift cards
   - Letter grades, credit or extra-credit, such as for participating in psychology experiments. [Note: you could discuss the ethical consideration of having the incentive be commensurate with the task.]
   - Trophies and ribbons (e.g., in athletic competitions)
   - Stars
   - Stickers
   - Pay raise or seasonal bonus
   - Time off (e.g., vacation)
   - Attention or praise
   - Awards
   - Recognition
   - "Likes" on social media posts

- Number of followers/friends on social media sites
- Food—giving employees or students a pizza party or other treats such as donuts or candy. As a corporate example, see Pizza Hut's "BookIt" program in which students are rewarded with pizza for reading.
- Extra recess
- Loyalty cards that offer incentives for consumers to purchase more goods and services
- Merit badges (e.g., Girl and Boy Scouts)
- Virtual badges (e.g., in online games)
- "Hidden" extrinsic rewards. For example, helping others, such as by assisting co-workers, volunteering your time at food banks, homeless shelters, hospitals, and nursing homes may bring intrinsic satisfaction, but may also be motivated, in part at least, by extrinsic rewards, such as looking better on job performance reviews or college applications.

2. Since students are likely to be familiar with badges on their games and apps, it might be interesting to discuss those as incentives. Badges are discussed in these two blog posts:

- The first one describes three examples of apps that meet the needs for autonomy, relatedness and competence, as described by the self-determination theory mentioned above.
[Source: Ryan, R. M., & Deci, E. L. (2017). *Self-determination theory: Basic psychological needs in motivation, development, and wellness*. Guilford Publications.]
- The second one, which provides an example of badges that work for scientists and explains the motivating factors, can be found here.

3. A list of examples of innovative incentives that can be used in school settings can be found here.

4. Other sets of examples of rewards in the context of schools can be found here and here.

5. There are many sites on the Internet with examples of using incentives in the workplace. You can find one of them here.

6. There are also a lot of websites that offer suggestions for how to maintain motivation in the workplace. For example:

   - On this website there is a 1:17-min video that provides examples of intrinsic and extrinsic motivation.

   - A spoof of incentives and extrinsic motivation is exemplified in this episode of the television series, *The Office*.

7. Here are some examples of survey items from a Work Preference Inventory that is used to assess intrinsic and extrinsic motivation in students and working adults:

   Intrinsic

   - I enjoy tackling problems that are completely new to me.
   - I want my work to provide me with opportunities for increasing my knowledge and skills.
   - What matters most to me is enjoying what I do.
   - I am more comfortable when I can set my own goals.

   Extrinsic

   - I am strongly motivated by the grade/money I can earn.
   - I want other people to find out how good I really can be at my work.
   - To me, success means doing better than other people
   - I prefer having someone set clear goals for me in my work.
   [Source: Amabile, T.M., Hill, K., Hennessey, B., & Tighe, E. (1994). The Work Preference Inventory: Assessing intrinsic and extrinsic motivational orientations. *Journal of Personality and Social Psychology, 66*(5), 950–67.]

8. Examples of extrinsic motivation undermining intrinsic motivation

   - The effect of extrinsic motivators undermining intrinsic motivation (sometimes referred to as the "overjustification" effect) was demonstrated in college students by Edward Deci (1971) and in preschool children by Lepper, Greene & Nesbitt (1973). The basic paradigm was to explore the motivation to participate in a task (e.g., completing a block puzzle or drawing with markers), then to introduce an extrinsic reward (i.e., money or "Good Player Award", respectively) for doing so, and then to observe the motivation to participate in the same task later. In these studies, participants given an extrinsic reward were less likely to engage with the task than control participants.

[Sources: Deci, E. L. (1971). Effects of externally mediated rewards on intrinsic motivation. *Journal of Personality and Social Psychology, 18*(1), 105–115.

Lepper, M. R., Greene, D., & Nisbett, R. E. (1973). Undermining children's intrinsic interest with extrinsic reward: A test of the "overjustification" hypothesis. *Journal of Personality and Social Psychology, 28*(1), 129–137.]

- Requiring class attendance or participation (i.e., giving a grade for attendance or participation) could overjustify attendance and/or participation, decreasing students' intrinsic motivation to attend, and to learn.
- Many professors are already intrinsically motivated to attend workshops on teaching. Introducing an incentive (gift card or certificate) for attending could overjustify participation in the workshop and undermine their motivation to do so.
- This post offers examples of how incentives like badges can "overjustify" behavior. In one example, an app called Untappd gives badges for drinking specific beers. But the author of the blog post points out that people are already motivated to drink beer. The post goes on to describe a Starbucks app that the blog poster describes as getting it "right". Starbucks uses a fixed-ratio schedule to reward members for their purchases (see also the chapter on learning).
- An example of how workplace incentives can go wrong can be found here.
- Offering a payment to receive a (Covid-19) vaccine could decrease motivation to get the vaccine by inadvertently signaling that vaccination is undesirable. (See also the chapter on learning.)

Achievement Motivation

1. Elliot and McGregor (2001) described a framework for achievement motivation known as the 2 (master/performance) × 2 (approach success vs. avoid failure) Achievement Goal Framework. Example items from their questionnaire include:

    1. I want to learn as much as possible in this class (mastery approach).
    2. It is important for me to do better than other students (performance approach).
    3. I worry that I may not learn all that I possibly could in this course (mastery avoidance)
    4. I just want to avoid doing poorly in this class (performance avoidance).

An example of this framework in the context of athletics is provided in this table:

	Mastery	Performance
Approach success	I really want to play better tennis and master the game	I really want to win the conference tournament
Avoid failure	I would not want to be an unskilled tennis player	I do not want to perform poorly in the conference tournament

[Source: Elliot, A. J., & McGregor, H. A. (2001). A 2 × 2 achievement goal framework. *Journal of Personality and Social Psychology, 80*(3), 501.]

2. Here is a simple example of achievement motivation: You are a reporter for a large daily newspaper. You have specific story assignments with deadlines that must be met. Each time you turn in an article, you feel energized. When your editor gives constructive criticism, you know it will help you do better with your next assignment. Your byline in the next day's newspaper is your reward. However, when offered a different subject matter to cover, say a sports story, you reject the opportunity because you don't feel you can do your best or might miss a deadline. If you can't do the task, you would rather not do it at all.

Eating Behavior

1. Examples of factors that affect the food we eat are described in this video.

2. Examples of how stress can affect eating habits is described here.

3. Examples of what constitutes a healthy diet (with accompanying graphics) in different countries can be found here.

4. Examples of diet consumptions across the globe can be found here.

Obesity

1. A 7-min video from the Centers for Disease Control on the obesity epidemic in the US can be found here.

2. A Body Mass Index calculator can be found here.

3. Here is a case study of an extremely obese 2-year-old boy (Access requires a subscription, however.). A video that prepares students for a discussion of this case study can be found here.

[Source: Wabitsch, M., Funcke, J. B., Lennerz, B., Kuhnle-Krahl, U., Lahr, G., Debatin, K. M., ... & Fischer-Posovszky, P. (2015). Biologically inactive leptin and early-onset extreme obesity. *New England Journal of Medicine, 372*(1), 48–54. https://www.nejm.org/doi/full/10.1056/NEJMoa1406653]

4. This video shows people reflecting on what it felt like to carry 10-pound sandbags to simulate weight gain.

5. Hypothalamic obesity is a disorder that results from damage to or a lesion in the hypothalamus. It is described here.

6. An example of two factors that can result in overeating in mice can be found here.

7. A potential hormonal (Lipocalin-2 (LCN2)) treatment for those with obesity has been described here.

[Source: Petropoulou, P-I., et al. (2020). Lipocalin-2 is an anorexigenic signal in primates. *eLife*. https://doi.org/10.7554/eLife.58949.]

8. An example of a male with anorexia nervosa is described in this news story.

(Other examples of eating disorders can be found in the chapter on psychological disorders.)

9. The Eating Attitudes Test™ may be of interest to students, particularly in discussing eating disorders. It can be found here.

Sexual Behavior

1. Examples of factors that affect sexual behavior:

   - Physiology (estrogen, testosterone, and other hormones)
   - Evolutionary forces (see the discussion of evolutionary psychology above)
   - Learning (e.g., sociocultural norms about what is and is not acceptable sexual behavior)
   - Physical environment (e.g., rufous-winged sparrows are desert birds that show no interest in sex during the dry season, but within ten minutes of the first rainfall, they vigorously court and copulate)
   - The photo below provides an example of the far less vital role of physical environments in controlling sexual behavior in humans, who have been known to have sex virtually anywhere, including on top of a bridge:

   - Social environment (more potentially desirable partners are likely to be available at bars, parties, and "swingers" clubs than in remote desert outposts or prisons)
   - Goals. One survey of college-age men and women have identified 237 stated reasons surrounding their efforts to have sex. The reasons included some that were obvious (e.g., "I wanted to experience physical pleasure"), some that were spiritual (e.g., "I wanted to get closer to God"), some that were altruistic (e.g., "I wanted the person to feel good about himself/herself"), and some that

were vengeful (e.g., "I wanted to get back at my partner for having cheated on me"). A factor analysis of the data yielded four main factors (physical, goal attainment, emotional, and insecurity) and 13 subfactors. The physical subfactors included stress reduction, pleasure, physical desirability, and experience seeking. The goal attainment subfactors included resources, social status, revenge, and utilitarian. The emotional subfactors included love and commitment and expression. The insecurity subfactors included self-esteem boost, duty/pressure, and mate guarding.
- [Reference: Meston, C. M., & Buss, D. M. (2007). Why humans have sex. *Archives of Sexual Behavior, 36,* 477–507.]

Surveys About Sexual Behavior

[Note: These also provide examples of how some psychologists study sexuality.]

1. Sample questions from the National Health and Social Life Survey are available here.

2. A survey of people's sexual knowledge is available here.

3. An LGBTData.com survey of the so-called "sexual personality" is available here.

4. A sex quiz for partners is available here.

Links Between Motivation and Emotion

1. Motivation can create or intensify emotional arousal, as when a "hangry" person (hungry + angry) starts shouting at a restaurant server because the person's dinner order has been delayed, or as in the case of this (2:14-min) video from a Red Lobster restaurant, because of the waiting time for a table.
2. In Oklahoma City, a "hangry" woman shot three McDonalds employees when she was told that the dining room was closed. You can find the story here.

3. Another example of hunger-related anger comes from a study that found lower levels of glucose in the blood (indicating greater hunger) associated with higher amounts of aggression between intimate partners. From the abstract: "We measured glucose levels in 107 married couples over 21 days. To measure aggressive impulses, participants stuck 0–51 pins into a voodoo doll that represented their spouse each night depending how angry they were with their spouse. To measure aggression, participants blasted their spouse with loud noise through headphones. Participants who had lower glucose levels stuck more pins into the voodoo doll and blasted their spouse with louder and longer noise blasts."

[Source: Bushman, B.J., DeWall, C.N., Pond, R.S., & Hanus, M.D. (2014). Glucose and intimate partner violence. *Proceedings of the National Academy of Sciences, 111* (17) 6254–6257. https://doi.org/10.1073/pnas.1400619111.]

4. The motivation-emotion link can be seen in the emotional consequences of motivational conflict, as when, for example, someone is considering two job offers. One offers a high salary but requires long hours and moving to an unpleasant climate, while the other boasts advancement opportunities, fringe benefits, and a better climate, but doesn't pay as much and involves an unpredictably changing work schedule. People faced with such decisions tend to experience worry, anxiety, irritability, and other negative emotions, and even after the decision is made, may feel regret or remorse driven by concerns that the decision might not have been the right one.

5. Other examples of motivational conflict situations that can arouse emotions such as irritability, worry, anxiety, or depression range from the relatively trivial to the momentous, including decisions about

- fixing versus selling a beloved old car
- choosing investments options that will yield the best return
- whether to get married
- whether to quit a good job to start one's own business
- whether to have or adopt a child
- divorcing
- retiring
- revealing a previously hidden sexual orientation
- having unpleasant, but potentially life-saving, medical tests
- having risky surgery (or authorizing it for a relative)
- putting an aging parent in a nursing home
- removing a terminally ill loved one from life support

6. Emotions can create, intensify or weaken motivation, as when:

   - love leads a person to donate a kidney to a relative or agree to a vacation at a hated location for the sake of a child or partner who adores that place
   - anger prompts a person to confront a fellow motorist or passenger (road rage or air rage)
   - jealousy leads a jilted lover to murder a former partner (and perhaps the partner's new lover)
   - sadness and anger at the loss of a murdered child may lead a parent to try to kill the killer or perhaps to become active in efforts to prevent future crimes against children. For a more specific example of the latter, see the story of John Walsh, founder of *America's Most Wanted*, found here
   - depression causes a person to consider or commit suicide
   - happiness prompts people to be friendlier or more generous than usual
   - fear prompts a person with acrophobia to avoid roller coasters, glass elevators, rooftop restaurants, or perhaps even movies about mountain-climbing
   - social anxiety leads a person to avoid parties, dances, clubs, and dating opportunities
   - depression causes a person to lose interest in work or family

7. The experience of pleasure can motivate people to engage in a variety of behaviors that they have learned, or expect, will be pleasurable, such as:

   - reading
   - writing
   - travel
   - seeking sexual contact
   - athletics
   - collecting things such as stamps, beer cans, golf balls, or fridge magnets
   - auto racing
   - bicycling
   - skydiving
   - volunteering
   - cooking
   - cleaning
   - target shooting
   - beachcombing
   - exploring caves

The Nature of Emotion

1. Examples of positive emotions can be found here and include:

    - joy
    - gratitude
    - serenity
    - interest (curiosity or fascination)
    - hope
    - pride
    - amusement
    - inspiration
    - awe
    - elevation (as when seeing someone engaging in an act of kindness)
    - altruism (the feeling you get from helping others)
    - satisfaction
    - relief
    - affection
    - cheerfulness
    - surprise (when something good happens)
    - confidence
    - admiration
    - enthusiasm
    - eagerness
    - euphoria
    - contentment
    - enjoyment
    - optimism
    - love
    - happiness (subjective well-being). An example of the relationship between money and happiness can be found in an international survey study found here that suggests happiness increases with income, but only up to the point of "income satiation," after which life satisfaction may decline.

2. Examples of negative emotions:

    - fear
    - anxiety
    - panic
    - anger
    - worry
    - disgust
    - sadness

- melancholy
- annoyance
- frustration
- rage
- guilt
- apathy
- despair
- grief
- jealousy
- loneliness
- shame
- embarassment
- boredom
- regret
- remorse
- contempt
- envy
- confusion

3. Examples of mixed emotions:

- feeling happiness, sadness, and anxiety as you watch your child leave for the first day of kindergarten
- feeling relief, sadness, and guilt after surviving a natural disaster in which others were killed or injured
- feeling regret, anxiety, worry, and excitement about new beginnings after having finally gotten out of a bad marriage or long-term relationship
- feeling pride and satisfaction about your financial success, but also sadness and some guilt at knowing that others are suffering in poverty
- feeling happiness and pride, but also some envy and anger when your sibling wins an athletic competition in which you were only mediocre
- feeling happy but also irritated while working in a job that pays well but requires you to be nice to people you don't like
- feeling anxious and worried about an upcoming surgical procedure, but also happy to have the problem addressed and confident that you will healthier in the long run
- feeling sadness at the loss of a sick elderly relative, but also grateful for having known the person and happy that the person is no longer suffering
- feeling love as well as sadness and anger toward a teenage child whose involvement in drugs has led to addiction

4. Examples of emotions that depend on perception of events:

   - An exam score of 75% may make you happy if your best previous score had been 50%, but it may cause deep distress you if you had never before scored below 90%.
   - The photo here shows two people experiencing either elation or disappointment in response to the same event, depending on whether they perceive the outcome of a wrestling match as making them the winner or the loser.
   - We know a woman whom we'll call "Gina" (not her real name) who met her new boyfriend's parents for the first time during a weekend visit to the parents' home in Florida. On the afternoon of their arrival, while having drinks in the parents' living room, the boyfriend and his father got into a heated disagreement about politics during which the father shouted angry insults at his son. Gina had no experience with this level of hostility in her own family background, and quickly became so anxious and fearful at the father's behavior that she silently skulked into the guest room. About half an hour later, Gina's boyfriend came in to let her know that it was nearly time to leave for the restaurant where his dad had made a dinner reservation. Astonished, she said "You mean that your father is still taking us all out to dinner?" Her boyfriend said, "Sure, Dad yells a lot when he gets annoyed, but it passes and everyone in our family is used to it." A pleasant family dinner followed. In short, the father's behavior created little or no emotional arousal in his son (or in his wife), while frightening the daylights out of the woman who would soon become his daughter-in-law. Over the next several years, she, too, found herself emotionally unperturbed when her father-in-law got angry.

Facial Expressions of Emotion

1. Examples of the seven most basic, more-or-less universal, facial expressions of emotion (joy, surprise, anger, contempt, sadness, disgust, and fear are available as Fig. 1 here.

2. A similar set of emotional facial expressions is available at Paul Ekman's website here.

3. An example of the role of culture in perceiving emotions is found in the "results" panel of Fig. 1 in a study comparing the emotion labels that people gave to various facial expressions. The top row in the figure shows expressions that western Caucasians saw as happy, surprised, fearful, disgusted, angry, and sad; the bottom row shows

expressions that East Asians saw as conveying those same emotions. (The letters next to each image represent the initials of the observers.)

[Source: Jack, R. E., Caldara, R., & Schyns, P. G. (2012). Internal representations reveal cultural diversity in expectations of facial expressions of emotion. *Journal of Experimental Psychology: General, 141*(1), 19.]

4. In Fig. 1 of this article, you can find a row of photos illustrating basic emotional expressions, as well as additional rows illustrating compound emotional expressions (i.e., conveying a mixture of emotions).

   [Source: Du, S., Tao, Y., & Martinez, A. M. (2014). Compound facial expressions of emotion. *Proceedings of the National Academy of Sciences, 111* (15), E1454–E1462.]

5. For a real-life illustration of compound emotional expressions, you might want to show your students this image at and ask them to guess what is going on and what combination of emotions these people are feeling. (The photo shows April Canter and her 9-year-old daughter, Megan, of Wilkes County, Ga., waving goodbye to their husband and father, a member of a Georgia Army National Guard Field Artillery Battalion that was leaving for training before possibly fighting in Iraq. Their emotions probably included sadness, anxiety, worry, dread, uncertainty, and hope.)

6. Facial expressions can serve a *social referencing* function, as when, for example, an inexperienced chess player might reach out to move the queen, but then catch sight of a spectator's pained expression, and get the message that this would be a bad move.

7. Another example of the social referencing function of facial expressions can be seen in the world of poker, where experts are always searching for "tells," including facial expressions or facial movements that they have learned are correlated with a particular player's having a good hand, or perhaps with bluffing. Interpreting these "tells" provide cues about whether to bet against that player, and how much.

8. Yet another example of facial expressions as social advice comes from a study of infants' decision about whether to crawl over a moderately deep "visual cliff." (See the chapter on sensation and perception.) When mothers standing at the opposite side of the "cliff" apparatus made a fearful face, no infant crossed the glass floor, but when they made a joyful face, most infants crossed.

   [Source: Sorce, J. F., Emde, R. N., Campos, J. J., & Klinnert, M. D. (1985). Maternal emotional signaling: Its effect on the visual cliff behavior of 1-year-olds. *Developmental Psychology, 21*(1), 195–200. https://doi.org/10.1037/0012-1649.21.1.195.]

9. An example of how environmental context can alter perception of facial expressions is provided by a study in which research participants interpreted a

particular expression as disgust when it appeared on the face of a person who was holding a dirty diaper, but that same expression was seen as anger when it was digitally superimposed on a person in a fighting stance.

[Source: Aviezer H., Hassin, R.R., Ryan, J., Grady, C., Susskind, J., Anderson, A., & Bentin, S. (2008). Angry, disgusted, or afraid? Studies on the malleability of emotion perception. *Psychological Science, 19*, 724–732. https://www.jstor.org/stable/40064981.]

10. An example of how a tilt of the head can influence the perception of emotion can be found in this study. A downward tilt of the head results in a lowering of the eyebrows and increasing the "v" shape they take in an angry face. This study showed that the downward tilt of the head intensified the perception of anger, but not other emotions.

[Source: Witkower, Z., & Tracy, J. L. (2020). How and why head position changes the perception of facial expressions of emotion. *Emotion.* Advance online publication. https://doi.org/10.1037/emo0000846.]

The Biology of Emotion

1. An example of how biological factors influence the expression of emotion is provided by the case of a man who has damage to the pyramidal motor system in the right hemisphere, which includes the motor cortex and which controls voluntary movements. As a result, he cannot create a convincing voluntary smile because he cannot move the left side of his face at will. However, a smile that expresses genuine pleasure or happiness is involuntary, and that kind of smile, like the other facial movements associated with emotions, is governed by the extrapyramidal motor system, which depends on areas beneath the cortex. As a result, he can smile normally when he feels happy. In contrast, a person with damage to the extrapyramidal system can pose convincing facial expressions at will, but they may remain straight-faced even when feeling genuine joy or profound sadness. You can see photos of these two types of smiles in the reference below.

[Reference: Hopf, H. C., Muller, F. W., & Hopf, N. J. (1992). Localization of emotional and volitional facial paresis. *Neurology, 42*(10), 1918–1923.]

2. This 7-min video shows a case example of the emotion-expressing consequences of left-hemisphere damage to the pyramidal motor system.

[*Note:* You need only show about the first three minutes of this video in order to illustrate this aspect of biological control over facial expression, but the rest of the video is interesting as well.]

3. Lie detectors are not infallible, but people who *believe* they are infallible may be more likely than non-believers to confess to their crimes. In one small town police station which had no polygraph, a kitchen colander was placed on a burglary suspect's head and attached by wires to a copy machine on which there was a sheet of paper that said "He's lying!" When he denied committing the burglary, an officer pressed the "copy button," and when the "He's lying!" paper emerged, the suspect confessed.

[Source: Shepherd, C., Kohut, J. J., & Sweet, R. (1989). *News of the weird*. New York: New American Library.]

4. Much less humorous examples of the intimidating impact of polygraph testing come from cases in Chicago in which the mere prospect of taking a lie detector test caused some suspects to give false confessions. In one such case, after being repeatedly questioned about the murder of his elderly neighbor, Donny McGee was told by a detective to "face the truth" and take a polygraph. McGee was taken to the polygraph room but was never given the test. Instead, according to the polygraph examiner's testimony, as soon as he entered the room, McGee began confessing. McGee denied doing so and when the case went to trial, a jury found him not guilty in 90 min. DNA evidence would later confirm his innocence. News stories detailing cases like this, and alleged polygraph test abuses in Chicago, are available here and here.

5. Here is a 6-min video of a former police detective and expert polygraph administrator showing how to fool a polygraph and questioning their value and accuracy in criminal cases. His work has resulted in his being charged with witness tampering.

6. Examples of what polygraph advocates say are the advantages of these devices are described in an article listing cases in which polygraphs showed suspects to be innocent but, because the tests were deemed unreliable, suspects were wrongly convicted and imprisoned, only later to be exonerated by DNA evidence. Google "Polygraphs and 215 Wrongful Conviction Exonerations" to gain free access to the article as a pdf.

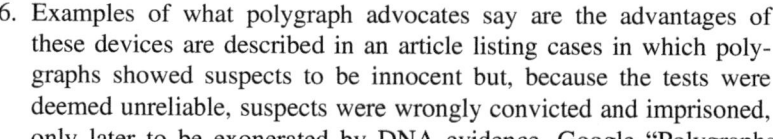

[*Note:* For more on the biology of emotion, see the chapters on biological aspects of psychology and health, stress, and coping.

Development 9

This chapter focuses on concepts in child development, including language and language development. We start with topics related to critical/sensitive periods and the important developmental question: To what extent are human behavior and mental processes due to nature and nurture? We end with some examples of moral reasoning. Examples of methods of testing children are found in the chapter on research methods and statistics.

Examples of some of the topics in this chapter come from a rich source of video data available here. Although Databrary is a repository that is open for all kinds of psychological content, most of the videos deposited so far focus on human development. Once you set up a Databrary account (see the preface for details), you will be able to gain access to the videos listed on this compendium's Databrary page, found here.

Critical/Sensitive Periods

1. You can find a very short video describing the need of infants to experience clear visual input in order to develop normal acuity here.

2. This short post describes the effect on vision of rearing kittens in deprived visual environments.
3. Here is a study showing temporary blindness induced in kittens reared in darkness for 10 days during a critical period of visual development.

© Springer Nature Switzerland AG 2022
E. L. Cameron and D. A. Bernstein, *Illustrating Concepts and Phenomena in Psychology*, Springer Texts in Education,
https://doi.org/10.1007/978-3-030-85650-2_9

[Source: Mitchell, D. E., Crowder, N. A., Holman, K., Smithen, M., & Duffy, K. R. (2015). Ten days of darkness causes temporary blindness during an early critical period in felines. *Proceedings of the Royal Society* B282:20142756. http://dx.doi.org/10.1098/rspb.20142756.]

4. Binocular vision/depth perception: Monocular deprivation results in reduced visual acuity as well as issues in depth perception and healthy development depends upon self-produced movement.

[Source: Held, R. and Hein A. (1963). Movement-produced stimulation in the development of visually guided behavior. *Journal of Comparative and Physiological Psychology*, 56(5): 872–876.]

5. Hearing: Lack of early input due to deafness results in inability to acquire functions such as language (see below), and input within the critical period (for example by fitting young children with cochlear implants) mitigates against this.

See this article.

6. Vestibular system: Appropriate input early in life underlies typical motor development. (See also examples of imprinting later in this chapter.)
7. Examples of psychological processes that develop *best* before particular moments in development and thus display weak critical periods, include:

- Phoneme tuning (organizing sound into meaning)
- Grammar processing
- Articulation control (speech production)
- Musical training
- Auditory processing
- Sports training

See the "strong vs. weak critical periods" section of this wikipedia page.

8. This 10-min Ted Talk by Patricia Kuhl describes critical periods in aspects of language acquisition. Some of the details from this Ted Talk are described in one of the many learning modules on Dr. Kuhl's website.
9. A classic case example of a critical period for language development is the "wild boy of Aveyron". He was a French child who, in the late 1700s, was apparently lost or abandoned by his parents at an early age and had grown up with animals. At about eleven years of age, he was captured by hunters and sent to Paris. What scientists observed was a dirty, frightened creature who trotted like a wild animal and spent most of his time silently rocking. Although the scientists attempted to rehabilitate the boy for more than

ten years, he was never able to live unguarded among other people, and he never learned to speak.

François Truffaut's 1970 film *L'Enfant Sauvage* (*The Wild Child*)—which dramatizes the story of the "wild boy" and the efforts of Jean Itard, the Parisian doctor who, circa 1800, tried to educate him—can be found on Amazon Prime and here. A 5-minute excerpt can be found here and the story is also summarized here.

10. There are similar and more recent cases of children who have been rescued after spending their early years isolated from human contact and the sound of adult language. Even after years of therapy and language training, these individuals are not able to combine ideas into sentences:

- A 1-h documentary film called *Genie: Secret of the Wild Child* (1997) tells the story of a case of extreme neglect. It includes discussion of relevant scientific questions about nature/nurture and critical periods, particularly with respect to language development, but focuses more on Genie's abuse and the distressing way in which she went through the social welfare system in the years just after she was discovered. The film is available here.
- A more specific discussion of critical periods occurs at about 7:00 min into this 12-min 2003 video about Genie.
[Source Rymer, R. (1993). *Genie: A scientific tragedy.* New York: HarperCollins.]
- An archive of information about the "wild boy," Genie, and other cases of feral or wild children is available here.

Imprinting

1. A 14-min 1975 National Geographic video about Konrad Lorenz and his work can be found here. It begins with a comment about nature and nurture, and at around the 3-min mark, shows standard imprinting of goslings on their parents. It then shows the more complicated process of goslings imprinting on humans, namely Lorenz's students.

(Note: this video includes some dated language.)

2. Another 2-min unnarrated video showing Konrad Lorenz and geese imprinting can be found at.

3. Here is a 90-s clip from PBS showing chicks imprinting on a man.

4. Here is a 3-min Animal Planet video showing ducklings imprinted on a cat.

Newborn Reflexes

1. A 2-min video demonstrating breathing, eye blink, rooting, sucking, swallowing, stepping, Babinski, grasping and Moro reflexes is available here.

2. A 1-min OPENPediatrics video about how to assess the Moro, palmar grasp and rooting reflexes is available here.

3. A 4-min video showing rooting, sucking, stepping, Babinkski, grasping, and Moro reflexes (along with examples of older babies who no longer show these reflexes) is available here.

4. A 3-min video of Berry Brazelton demonstrating how babies self-sooth and making the case for what babies can do is available here.

[Source: Als, H. Tronick, E. Lester, B.M. Brazelton, T.B. (1977). The Brazelton neonatal behavioral assessment scale (BNBAS). *Journal of Abnormal Child Psychology.* 5(3), 215–229. https://doi.org/10.1007/bf009136 93.]

5. Here is a 3-min video describing the APGAR test.

6. Here is a 6-min 1964 video showing Dr. Apgar teaching a nursing student how to score a newborn on the Apgar.

7. A historical summary, the correlation between low Apgar score and outcomes, a photograph of Dr. Apgar with a baby, and helpful tables are available in this article.

[Reference: Ehrenstein V. (2009). Association of Apgar scores with death and neurologic disability. *Clinical Epidemiology, 1,* 45–53.]

Maturation

1. Examples of maturation from late childhood through adolescence that will resonate with students can be seen in the characters of Hermione Granger, Harry Potter, and Ron Weasley across 7 years at Hogwarts School of Witchcraft and Wizardry. A graphical representation can be found here.
2. The four Brown Sisters photographed by Nicholas Nixon over 40 years are shown in 3-min videos here and here.

Teratogens

1. Examples of teratogens in general can be found here and here.

2. Thalidomide is a drug that was commonly given to pregnant women in the late 1950s and early 1960s to prevent morning sickness. It resulted in a variety of deformities in the women's babies. Information about this drug, and a 4-min video showing examples of the "Thalidomide babies" affected by it can be found here.
3. The biography of Brian Gault, a "Thalidomide baby" who was born without arms, appears in this book: B. Gault and H. Rogers, *Look, No Hands! The Inspiring Story of Brian Gault*, 2000. Hodder Christian Books. Brian's story is also presented here.
4. General information about fetal alcohol spectrum disorders (FASD) can be found at the CDC website, which includes some videos and podcasts. You will also find Brenna's illustrated story about a child living with FASD.

5. Here are YouTube videos of children and adults living with FASD.

6. Examples of the health effects of smoking during pregnancy can be found here and are described in this 2-min video.

7. Here is Amanda B's story of smoking during pregnancy and its effect on her baby, including videos.
8. If students ask about the claim that vaccines are teratogens that lead to autism spectrum disorder, here is a summary of the evidence debunking that claim.

Cognitive Development

1. Concepts from Piaget:

   - A quick tour (6:17 min) through *Piagetian stages* can be found here.

   - A longer (18:33 min) description is found in this video.

   - Renee Baillargeon describes *object permanence* and her studies of babies' understanding of impossible events, using the preferential-looking technique in a 3-min video in which she challenges the age at which object permanence appears.
     [Source: Baillargeon, R. (1987). Object permanence in 3½- and 4½-month-old infants. *Developmental Psychology. 23 (5), 655–664.* https://doi.org/10.1037/0012-1649.23.5.655.]
   - An example of peek-a-boo—a game that requires object permanence—is presented in this 1-min video.

- Examples of the A not B error are demonstrated in this (1:26-min) video.

- A 2-min video from the University of Minnesota and the Science Museum of Minnesota demonstrates assessment of egocentrism using Piaget's Mountain task. It is available here.

- A 7-min video showing one child who lacks conservation and one who has it is available here.

2. Some examples of Piagetian schemes/schemas/schemata are listed below, but additional examples are found under the heading of "Concepts" in the chapter on thinking and cognitive abilities.

- *Object schemas* include those for things such as animals (dog, cat); vehicles (car, truck) and furniture (chair, table). A 1-min video with examples of vehicle schemas is available here.
- Dana's schema for *books* is that they are a bound stack of paper with stories or other information written on each page. When her fifth-grade teacher suggests that each student read a book on the computer, Dana is confused until she sees that the same information can be presented on a computer screen. Dana has now revised her schema for books to include those presented through electronic media.
- *Person schemas* include those for sex/gender, occupation, race, and age. So you may expect your doctor to appear at an appointment wearing a white coat and acting formally and, perhaps, hurriedly. You may be (pleasantly) surprised if your doctor appears without a white coat and does not rush through addressing your concerns.
- *Event scripts*: what typically happens at a birthday party or a restaurant, on a plane trip or in a college classroom. As a college student, you have a script of how events should transpire in the classroom: students enter the classroom, sit in seats facing the professor, and take out their notebooks or electronic devices. The professor lectures while students take notes, until the bell rings and they all leave.
- *Social schemas/scripts*: how to behave at a birthday party, when you go to a restaurant (including differences between sit-down vs. fast-food establishments), on a plane trip, or in a college classroom.
- Examples of accurate *assimilation* include (a) seeing a German shepherd for the first time and categorizing it as a dog because you know your greyhound is a dog; (b) seeing a Prius and categorizing it as a car because you have a Toyota Corolla that you know is a car.

- Examples of inaccurate assimilation include seeing a pony and categorizing it as a dog or seeing a truck and calling it a car.
- Examples of accurate *accommodation* include (a) realizing that a cat is not the same as a dog, firming up the concept of dog, and creating a new one for cat; (b) realizing that a truck is not a car, firming up the concept of car and creating a new one for truck; (c) seeing a cheetah and realizing that it is a (big) cat.
- Example of an inaccurate accommodation: Coming to the conclusion that a small pickup truck is a car.
- *Equilibrium* and *disequilibrium* are described in a 1-min animated video in which students go from disequilibrium to equilibrium, but note that it does not describe how to get from one to the other. It is available here.
- Graphical representations of a scheme, assimilation, and accommodation can be found here and here.

- A schematic of Piagetian processes can be found here.

- Here is an application of Piagetian concepts through video games.

3. Concepts from Vygotsky:

- A quick tour of Vygotsky's major concepts, with an example, can be found in this 3-min video.

- A graphic illustrating Zones of Proximal Development (ZPD) is available here.

- Here is a graphic illustrating Zones of Proximal Development and scaffolding.
- Here are a number of examples of scaffolding for development at a range of ages and skill levels:

Cognitive Development

Skill to be acquired	Skill level	Scaffolding
Understanding language	Preverbal	Adult uses infant-directed speech. See section on "language development" in this 4-min video [QR code]
Using baby signs	Preverbal	Adult teaches baby signs to help child communicate before the baby can articulate (many) spoken words. See section on language development below.
Telling a story	Emergent literacy (i.e., cannot yet read words)	Provide child with wordless picture book that a child can narrate. An example of such a book is described in this 3-min video [QR code] The book provides a scaffold and the teacher can employ scaffolding by asking for details. An example of a 2nd grader narrating *Frog, Where are You?* can be found in a 4-min video here [QR code]
Complete a puzzle	Novice	Shaffer (1996) gives the example of a young girl who is given her first jigsaw puzzle. Alone, she performs poorly in attempting to solve the puzzle. The father then sits with her and describes or demonstrates some basic strategies, such as finding all the corner/edge pieces, and provides a couple of pieces for the child to put together herself and offers encouragement when she does so. Shaffer, R. (1996). *Social development*. Oxford: Blackwell. Source [QR code]
Writing a lab report	Novice (e.g., middle-school child)	A blog post at: [QR code] includes a link to a "scaffolded science lab report" [QR code] (Google doc in Read Only format)
Understanding the research process	Novice researcher/teacher	Use a research diary as a way of learning about the research process for:

(continued)

(continued)

Skill to be acquired	Skill level	Scaffolding
		A student: Gertstl-Pepin, C. & Patrizio, K. (2009). Learning from Dumbledore's Pensieve: A metaphor as an aid in teaching reflexivity in qualitative research. *Qualitative Research, 9*, 299–308. A teacher: Engin, M. (2011). Research diary: A tool for scaffolding. *International Journal of Qualitative Methods*, 296–306. https://doi.org/10.1177/160940691101000308
Learning to swim	Non-swimmer	A (1:36-min) video scaffolding learning to swim is available here 

- A number of other examples of the application of Vygotsky's concepts (ZPD) are provided here.
- Here are several examples of published articles that demonstrate the application of Vygotsky's concepts.
[Source: Sameroff, A. (2010). A unified theory of development: A dialectic integration of nature and nurture. *Child Development, 81*(1), 6-22.]

Delayed Gratification

1. Here is a 3-min video showing several children taking The Marshmallow Test.
2. Further examples of delayed gratification (including the dangers of instant gratification) in adults can be seen in two TedxTalks. A 13-min talk that includes a description of the Marshmallow Test can be found here. A 15-min talk that could be useful for college students to consider the power of grit, deliberate practice, and a growth mindset is available here.

Language

1. When defining language it can be helpful to contextualize it as one type of human communication, as demonstrated in this table:

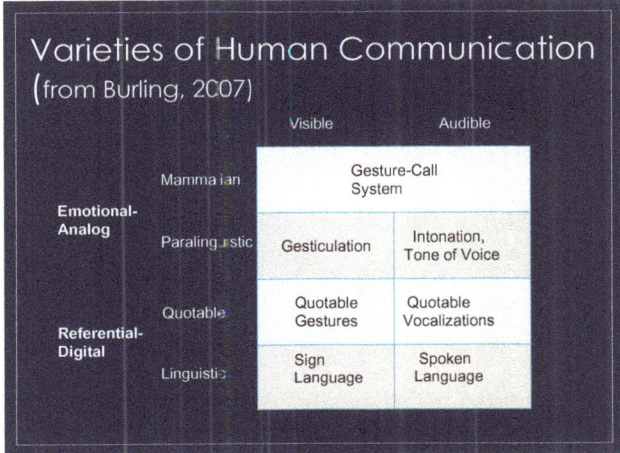

which is also available here.

[Source: Burling, R. (2007). *The talking ape: How language evolved* (Vol. 5). Oxford University Press on Demand.]

2. Examples of features distinguishing language from communication include that language:

    - is semantic/communicative
    - is creative/generative/productive
    - is regularly structured at multiple levels
    - is made up of arbitrary symbols
    - has flexibility of symbols
    - allows us to name all concepts, objects etc.
    - allows us to talk about things other than the here and now (i.e., displacement)

3. A 6-min video clip of Steven Pinker describing the essence of language is available here.

4. Here is a useful graphic for illustrating levels of linguistic structure:

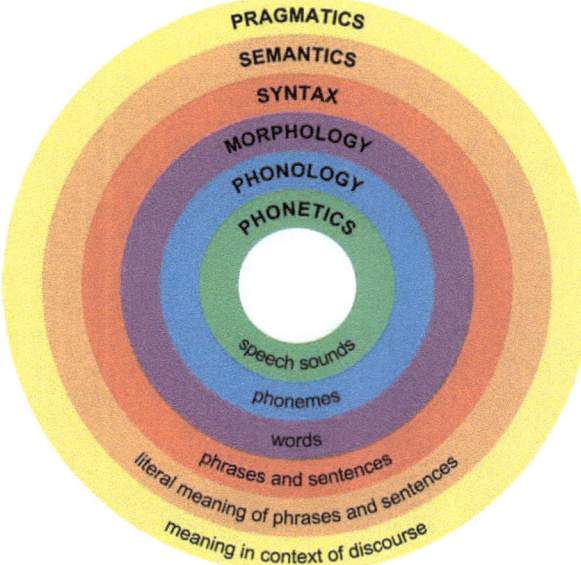

[From Wikimedia commons: Thomas, James J. & Cook, Kristin A., ed. (2005) Illuminating the Path: The Research and Development Agenda for Visual Analytics, National Visualization and Analytics Center, p. 110.]

5. Phonemes in English

- The 44 phonemes in English are identified and articulated in this delightful 5-min video.

- Here is a chart of the complete list of English phonemes, which comes from this website.

- This website lists all of the English phonemes, with examples.

Language   307

6. Morphemes in English

   - Here is a useful chart with examples of types of morphemes:

	Lexical morphemes	Grammatical morphemes
Free morphemes	Content e.g., cat, dog, bus	Function e.g., to, of, the
Bound morphemes	Derivational (prefix or suffix) e.g., re-, -er, -ize	Inflectional (suffix) e.g., -s - 's, -ed, -ing, -er, -est

[Note on examples in this chart:

-er signifies doer, as in teacher (derivational) or comparative, as in wider (inflectional)

-s signifies plural, as in cats and dogs, but not bus

-ed signifies past tense, as in walked, not bed]

[Source: Schmid, H.J. (2015), Morphology. In: N. Braber, L. Cummings, & L. Morrish (Eds.), *Exploring language and linguistics*. Cambridge: Cambridge University Press (pp. 77–110). This publication is available here.

   - Examples of words composed of multiple morphemes include:
     UN-BREAK-ABLE
     DIS-APPOINT-MENT
     DOG-HOUSE
     But not:
     CATASTROPHE
     MADAGASCAR
   - Examples of phonemes that are also morphemes:
     -s, as in cat-s
     a-, as in a-political
   - Children's knowledge of morphological rules using, for example, "Wugs" (Jean Berko-Gleason) are described here.

   - You can find a graphical illustration of the original wugs here.

7. The importance of word order (i.e., syntax) can be demonstrated with these examples of ambiguous sentences:

   - We ate salsa and chips lying in the hammock.
   - She gave the dog a bone that was well-behaved.

- I recommend Susan with no qualifications.
- Free Kamala Harris sticker.
- I saw a man with a telescope.
- We need more intelligent leaders.

8. Examples of sentences that demonstrate that syntax and semantics are separate:

    - Colorless green ideas sleep furiously. (Source: Noam Chomsky)
    - Giant 30-foot purple gerbils are attacking Boston. Note: The source of this example is a 6-min video on the innateness of language.

Animal Communication

1. A 10-min video from the *Scientific American Frontiers* series with Alan Alda (Season 9) showing examples of animal communication (Hamlet the pig, Rocky the sea lion, Washoe the chimpanzee and Alex the parrot) is available here.

2. This 7:42-min video reviews examples of ape language.

3. Here is a 5:11-min video clip from a full documentary: *Animals Like Us–Animal Language*.

4. There is a 4–part series on Kanzi, starting with this one.

5. A short segment on Kanzi can be seen in this Oprah show video. The relevant information is in the first 3 min.

6. Videos about Washoe can be found here, but note that it may take some time to load. The first half (28 min) appears to have been removed from YouTube, but the second half (31 min) is still available here.

7. There is a full-length (90-min) documentary on Nim Chimpsky, but it is focused on much more than language and presents a compassionate story of Nim's life.

8. Here is an 11-min video about Koko the gorilla.

9. Here is an 8-min video describing the dance of the honeybees.

10. A series of video examples of gestures of great apes can be found here.

Language Development/Acquisition

Infant-Directed Speech ("Motherese")

1. A sample of infant-directed speech can be heard in this (3:46) video in which infant 'Paul' orients to hear "motherese".

   [Source: Fernald, A. (1985). Four-month-old infants prefer to listen to motherese. *Infant Behavior and Development*, 8(2), 181–195.]

2. One hundred hours of mothers speaking to preverbal infants can be found here.

   [Source: Brent, M. R. & Siskind, J. M. (2001). The role of exposure to isolated words in early vocabulary development. *Cognition*, 81(2), 31–44.]

3. The main page of the *Child Language Data Exchange System Talk Bank* lists relevant YouTube videos covering topics from comprehension versus production in a bilingual child to overextensions. Note that these are uncurated examples of child language and conversation with parents. They include side issues that could provide interesting opportunities for teachable moments.

4. Here is a list of other videos related to language.

5. Here are some examples of funny things kids say that demonstrate important linguistic concepts.

Cooing

1. Short samples of child language at 3, 6, 9, 12, 18, 24 and 36 months, starting with cooing, can be found here.

2. Here is a 32-second video of a cooing baby.

Babbling

1. Here is a 23-s video of babbling.

2. Cute videos from 2011 show *Talking Twin Babies* carrying on a "conversation" in babble. They are available here and here.
3. At about minute 33:30 in this 1-h *Scientific American Frontiers* video (Season 2, Episode 3) there is a segment called "Babbling Babies", which describes research on babies babbling in sign language.

One-Word Stage (Holographic Speech)

Samples of speech in the one-word stage, and their possible meaning include:

- "Give" meaning "Give me the ball".
- "Mine" meaning "That doll is mine".
- "More" meaning "I want more milk".
- Here is a 30-s video clip of a baby laughing and saying "thank-you".
- Here is a 3:34 min narration of a "Day in the Life" of a child who uses "baby signs," which is primarily used to communicate in the one-word stage.

- A 12-s clip of a child using baby sign for "all done" is found here.

- A 20-s clip of a child using baby signs for "more", "milk" and "all done" is found here. Note videographer's reinforcement

Telegraphic/2-Word Speech

1. A mother reports that one of her son's first two-word combinations was "Mama in!" He was in his crib and wanted her to join him. She tells her students that she was so excited that he had just uttered a two-word combination that she, of course, jumped into the crib with him! (This is also an example of ways in which we reinforce children for speaking, and not for grammar.)
2. At 18-months, the same woman's daughter starting using two-word combinations, such as: "my baby", "big boy" and "Mama up."
3. For a summary of the full "grammar of the two-word stage," see Table 4 in Brown and Frazer (1964). Examples include: A block, Daddy book, Mummy go, See that, That bird, Two men.
   [Source: Brown, R. & Fraser, C. (1964). The acquisition of syntax. In U. Bellugi & R. Brown (Eds.), *The acquisition of language* (pp. 43–79). The University of Chicago Press.]
4. A complete corpus of Brown's original data from Adam, Eve, and Sarah can be found here.

Examples of Over-Regularization Errors

Goed for went	Waked for woke	Builded for built
Becomed for became	Blowed for blew	Leaved for left
Beated for beat	Bringed for brought	Lended for lent
Losed for lost	Runned for ran	Sticked for stuck
Quitted for quit	Shutted for shut	Swinged for swung
Rided for rode	Singed for sang	Telled for told

Social Development

Attachment

1. A 5-min black and white video of the original Ainsworth Strange Situation study with the securely attached infant "Eva" is available here.
2. A more recent 3-min color video of the Ainsworth Strange Situation, which involves a bit more distress on the part of the securely attached infant "Lisa" is available here.
3. Another 7-min video of the Ainsworth Strange Situation with commentary from psychologists and an example of insecure-avoidant attachment is available here.
4. A 7-min video shows secure and ambivalent attachment in the Strange Situation, along with commentary and discussion of the long-term consequences of attachment.
5. A 10-min black and white video showing Harry Harlow's studies with rhesus monkeys is available here.
6. Attachment/love is the topic of the first episode of the Netflix series *Babies* (2020; 48 min). It explores the topic of bonding and includes footage of the *still face* procedure and describes studies on the role of oxytocin and amygdala function on bonding.
7. Here is a learning module on attachment from Dr. Patricia Kuhl's lab.
8. Examples of three attachment styles can be seen in the trio of main characters in Harry Potter. Here is a description based on the article "Attachment styles at Hogwarts: From Infancy to Adulthood" by Wind Goodfriend in *The Psychology of Harry Potter: An Unauthorized Examination of the Boy Who Lived* (2006), available at this website. A pdf is available here.
9. Dr. Goodfriend discusses the three attachment styles of Harry, Ron and Hermione here.

Child-Rearing and Parenting Styles

(*Note:* This section provides examples of the permissive, authoritarian and authoritative parenting styles described by Diana Baumrind, as well as types that have been described more recently, including indifferent-uninvolved, free-range, and helicopter.)
[Source: Baumrind, D. (1966). Effects of authoritative parental control on child behavior. *Child Development*, 837–907.]

Summarizing Parenting Styles

1. This Psychology Today article includes movie clips demonstrating authoritative, authoritarian, permissive and rejecting-neglecting parenting. Respectively, the clips can be found here, here, here, and here.

2. Other examples of parenting styles depicted in movies are described in this BBC article.
3. Examples of responses typical of each parenting style when a child has not been doing her homework and brings home a poor report card:

   - Authoritarian: Child is grounded, no TV, loses phone privileges, etc. until grades improve.
   - Authoritative: Parent shows concern for child and asks what's going on. Access to phone and TV are limited until after homework is done and parent checks it. Parent checks to see if this helps the child stay on task.
   - Permissive: Parent assumes the problem has to do with the teacher and doesn't recognize what the child has done wrong.
   - Indifferent/uninvolved: Parent comments that this isn't good, but does nothing more.

4. Examples of responses typical of each parenting style when a child forgets to feed the family dog (his chore).

- Authoritarian: Parent yells at child to feed the dog.
- Authoritative: Parent explains that the dog suffers if she isn't fed and works with the child to figure out a way to remember.
- Permissive: Parent feeds the dog.
- Indifferent/uninvolved: Parent says and does nothing.

5. Examples of general statements made by parents who are typical of each parenting style:

- Authoritarian:
  "I usually insist that my children do what I think is right, even if they do not agree with me."
  "I expect my children to do what I ask immediately, without asking any questions."
  "My children should know what I expect from them and should conform to my expectations simply out of respect for authority."
- Authoritative:
  "Once a family policy about something has been established, I discuss the reasoning behind the policy with my children."
  "I let my children know what I expect but I am open to discussion if they feel this is unreasonable."
  "If I make a decision that hurts my children then I am willing to discuss it and admit if I have made a mistake."
- Permissive:
  "I think that children should have their own way as often as a parent does in a well-run home."
  "I feel that my children should make up their own mind and then do what they want to do, even if I don't agree."
  "I think parents should avoid giving children specific expectations and guidelines for their behavior."
  Quotations are from this source, at the bottom of the webpage.

Examples of Authoritative Parenting (High Support/High Demand)

1. The parents in *The Cosby Show*. An example of their parenting style is found here.
2. Atticus Finch as played by Gregory Peck in the movie version of *To Kill a Mockingbird*.
3. Mary Poppins
4. Maria, the governess/baroness, in the *Sound of Music*

Examples of Authoritarian Parenting (Low Support/High Demand)

1. Neil's father in *Dead Poet's Society,* shown here.

2. Queen in the movie *Brave* shown here.

3. Captain Von Trapp in the *Sound of Music*, as can be seen in this clip.
4. The wicked stepmother in *Cinderella*.
5. Red Forman in *That 70's Show*.

Examples of Indulgent or Permissive Parenting (High Support/Low Demand)

1. Amy Poeler as a "cool mom" in *Mean Girls* is shown here.

2. A clip from in *Big Daddy* with Adam Sandler can be found here.

3. In *Charlie and the Chocolate Factory,* Veruca Salt is a child indulged by her father. This is demonstrated at the start of this clip.

Examples of Indifferent-Uninvolved Parenting (Low Support/Low Demand)

1. Al and Peg Bundy in the TV series *Married with Children.*
2. Harry and Zinnia Wormwood, the parents of Matilda in the 1996 movie of the same name.

Examples of Free-Range Parenting

1. "Free-range" parents might let their young child:
   - take public transportation alone.
   - ride a bike to school alone.
   - go to the park alone.

2. The relaxed, Dutch approach to raising children is described in a 17-min lecture and an article.

Examples of Helicopter Parenting/Overparenting

1. Wynona Ryder's character in *Stranger Things* is described as being a helicopter mother.
2. The father in *Finding Nemo* has been described as a helicopter parent as demonstrated in this "first day of school" clip.
3. The parents who participated in the college admissions scandal by breaking the law to get their children admitted into prestigious universities. A summary of their cases is available here and there is also a 100-min docudramatic film about them on Netflix.

Miscellaneous Examples Related to Parenting and Child-Rearing

1. Here are photos of Skinner's "air crib" or "baby box".

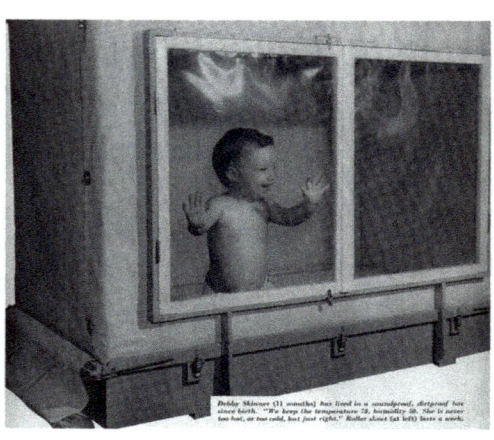 

2. Here is a description of the history of the air crib. A 2-min video shows Skinner's (other) daughter talking about the "baby tender."

3. An article describes the Finnish approach to child-rearing, which includes having the State provide expectant mothers with a "baby box" filled with sheets, baby clothes, and toys. When emptied, the box can be used as a crib for the newborn.

The Maternity package from 1947

4. Examples of differences in child-rearing practices, such as the amount of time mothers carry or are in contact with their infants, can be found at this website.
5. The results of parenting practices can be strongly affected by temperament, the child's individual style and frequency of expressing needs and emotions. It appears at birth and is constitutional, biological, and genetically based.

   - A summary of the three main types of temperament (easy, difficult, and slow-to-warm up) is available here.

   - A 5-min video showing various temperaments is available here.

Moral Development

Kohlberg's Stages of Moral Development

1. Here is a tabular overview of Kohlberg's stages, as exemplified in people's responses to the "Heinz dilemma."

Stage	What Is Right?	Should Heinz Steal the Drug?
Preconventional		
1.	Obeying and avoiding punishment from an authority	"Heinz should not steal the drug because he will be jailed."
2.	Making a fair exchange, a good deal	"Heinz should steal the drug because his wife will repay him later."
Conventional		
3.	Pleasing others and getting their approval	"Heinz should steal the drug because he loves his wife and because she and the rest of the family will approve."
4.	Doing your duty, following rules and social order	"Heinz should steal the drug for his wife because he has a duty to care for her," or "Heinz should not steal the drug because stealing is illegal."
Postconventional		
5.	Respecting rules and laws but recognizing that they may have limits	"Heinz should steal the drug because life is more important than property."
6.	Following universal ethical principles such as justice, reciprocity, equality, and respect for human life and rights	"Heinz should steal the drug because of the principle of preserving and respecting life."

2. The Heinz dilemma is more realistic than your students might think. For example, in 1994, a man was arrested for robbing a bank after being turned down for a loan to pay for his wife's cancer treatments. Here, you can read the story.
3. There is a website that describes the Heinz dilemma and includes a video that allows students to test their own stage of moral development.

4. The classic Trolley car moral dilemma and a variant are shown here.

5. Here are examples of everyday moral conflict situations.

6. Here is another series of moral dilemma scenarios, examples, and ethical dilemma questions.

Health, Stress, and Coping   10

Stress and its effects on physical and psychological health are, like psychological disorders and hypnosis, near the top of most students' list of high-interest topics, largely because they are so obviously relevant to the students' day to day lives. Indeed, teaching about stress and health is typically made easier because the examples you already have, and those you will find in this chapter, are likely to be matched by examples coming from your students themselves. The trick is to be sure that student-generated examples are good ones, and to immediately reconceptualize those that are not. Some students tend to think that their reaction to everyday stressors, such as going through final exams, is an example of posttraumatic stress disorder or that a supervisor who becomes angry from time to time is necessarily a case of burnout.

[*Note:* For an excellent overview of stress processes and consequences, consider assigning (or viewing for yourself) the one-hour video called *Stress, Portrait of a Killer* here.]

Stressors

1. Physical stressors

    - Staying up all night to study for a test
    - Running a marathon or participating in some other athletic competition
    - Having a cold, the flu, or Covid-19
    - Living through a heat wave without air conditioning
    - Being caught outside in a blizzard without warm clothing
    - Being lost in a desert without food or water

- Working a job that requires lifting heavy objects
- Running to catch a bus
- Being injured in an accident
- Undergoing surgery
- Drinking an excessive amount of alcohol
- Unpleasant side-effects of medication
- Partying all night
- Air travel across many time zones
- Chronic pain from a disease or injury
- Living or working in a noisy environment
- Harmful radiation
- Air pollution
- Sunburn
- Living or working in an overcrowded environment
- Physical or sexual assault

For more examples, see items from classic instruments such as:

- The SRRS [Holmes, T. H., & Rahe, R. H. (1967). The Social Readjustment Rating Scale. *Journal of Psychosomatic Research, 11*, 213–218.] You can find an online version of the scale here. A related scale that contains items especially relevant to college-age individuals is available here.

  [Reference: Renner, M. J., & Mackin, R. S. (1998). A life stress instrument for classroom use. *Teaching of Psychology, 25*(1), 46–48. https://doi.org/10.1207/s15328023top2501_15].
- Cohen, S., Kamarck, T., & Mermelstein, R. (1983). A global measure of perceived stress. *Journal of Health and Social Behavior, 24*, 385–396.
- The Daily Hassles Scale [DeLongis, A., Folkman, S., & Lazarus, R. S. (1988). The impact of daily stress on health and mood: Psychological and social resources as mediators. *Journal of Personality and Social Psychology, 54*, 486–495.]
- The Daily Hassles Scale-Revised [Holm, J. E., & Holroyd, K. A. (1992). The Daily Hassles Scale (Revised): Does it measure stress or symptoms? *Behavioral Assessment, 14*(3–4), 465–482. You can find a list of scale items here.]

2. Psychological/emotional stressors (can overlap with physical stressors)

    - Military combat
    - Natural disasters

- Living under threat of crime, terrorism, or pandemic infection
- Accidents
- Divorcing
- Relocating to a new residence
- Having a serious illness
- Caring for a sick or disabled relative
- Being unemployed or threatened with unemployment
- Being the target of racial, gender, or other kinds of discrimination
- Enduring extended periods of heavy academic or occupational workloads
- Long commutes in heavy traffic
- Continuing conflicts or bullying at work, at school, at home, or with extended family
- Difficulty finding affordable child care
- Car trouble
- Getting married
- Having a baby
- Working with technology that doesn't work.

Stress Responses

1. Physical stress responses (fight or flight; general adaptation syndrome)

- Rapid breathing
- Increased heartbeat
- Increased blood pressure
- Sweating
- Tremor
- Shivering
- Release of catecholamines (e.g., adrenaline, noradrenaline)
- Release of corticosteroids (e.g. cortisol)
- Release of endorphins
- Damage to cardiovascular system (heart, blood vessels)
- Suppression of the immune system
- Increased vulnerability to colds and flu
- Low energy
- Headaches
- Upset stomach
- Diarrhea, constipation, nausea
- Aches, pains, and tense muscles
- Increased vulnerability to "diseases of adaption" such as heart disease, stroke, hypertension, arthritis, and perhaps some forms of cancer.

- Worsening conditions such as diabetes, asthma, and skin disorders
- An early case example: On March 19, 1878, at a seminar at the *Académie de Médecine* in Paris, the famous French scientist Louis Pasteur showed his distinguished audience three chickens. One bird had been raised normally and was healthy. A second bird had been intentionally infected with bacteria but given no other treatment; it was also healthy. The third chicken that Pasteur presented was dead. It had been infected with the same bacteria as the second bird, but it had also been physically stressed by being exposed to cold temperatures; as a result, the bacteria had killed it.
  [Source: Kelley, K. W. (1985). Immunological consequences of changing environmental stimuli. In G. P. Moberg (Ed.), *Animal stress*. American Physiological Society.]

2. Psychological/emotional stress responses

   - Anxiety (possibly becoming an anxiety disorder)
   - Depression (possibly becoming a depressive disorder)
   - Impaired concentration
   - Confusion
   - Difficulty in making decisions, or making impulsive decisions
   - Reduced or exaggerated alertness
   - Forgetfulness
   - Impaired problem-solving ability (e.g., mental sets; functional fixedness—see chapter on thinking and cognitive abilities)
   - Nightmares
   - Suicidal thoughts
   - Angry outbursts
   - Irritability
   - Emotional numbness
   - Loss of enjoyment of life
   - Hopelessness
   - Agitation
   - Suspiciousness or mistrust
   - Tenseness
   - Ruminative thinking (intrusive thoughts)
   - Catastrophizing thoughts

3. Behavioral stress responses

   - Verbal aggression
   - Physical aggression (including domestic violence)
   - Abuse of alcohol
   - Use/abuse of illegal drugs
   - Increased smoking

- Increased caffeine consumption (e.g., coffee, energy drinks)
- Disengagement from social relationships
- Impaired occupational or academic performance
- Suicide attempts
- Infidelity
- Insomnia or hypersomnia
- Impaired sexual interest or performance
- Loss of appetite or overeating
- Accident proneness
- Tremulous voice
- Increased startle reactions
- Failure to exercise
- Quitting school or a job

Stress Response Mediators

1. Predictability

    - An early study looked at the effects of stressor predictability on physical stress reactions, particularly the formation of stomach ulcers. One group of rats received no shocks. Two other groups received tail shocks on a random schedule, either with or without first hearing a warning tone. All of the rats in the no-warning (unpredictable shock) group developed ulcers, while only about two-thirds of the warning (predictable shock) group did so. About 25 percent of the no-shock group developed ulcers. The animals in the unpredictable shock group also showed the most additional physical stress responses in the form of corticosteroid secretions and weight loss.
    [Source: Weiss, J. M. (1970). Somatic effects of predictable and unpredictable shock. *Psychosomatic Medicine, 32*(4), 397–408. https://doi.org/10.1097/00006842-197007000-00008]
    - Marine biologists in Portugal observed the physiological and physical responses of European sea bass to predictable and unpredictable stressors. They first taught the fish to associate the sight of a black-and-yellow-striped card with a stressor, namely a mesh net like the ones used to catch fish in aquaculture operations. The fish in the predictable group always saw the card a minute before the net swept through the fish tank, and so it served as a signal of the impending stressor. The fish subjected to unpredictable stress had no such warning: the card was displayed randomly, before or after the net appeared.
    During experimental trials, the researchers recorded changes in cortisol, a stress hormone, in response to predictable vs. unpredictable stressors. They also looked at the fishes' behavior, and measured activity in specific regions of their brains. The fish coped better with predictable stressors. In the

unpredictable stressor group, they found stronger stress responses, including higher cortisol levels and more changes in activity in two areas of the fishes' brains that are most similar to the amygdala and hippocampus in human brains. Fish in the unpredictable stress group also made more attempts to escape compared to fish that experienced predictable stress or no stressful events.
[Source: Cerqueira, M., Millot, S., Felix, A., Silva, T., Oliveira, G. A., Oliveira, C. C., ... & Oliveira, R. (2020). Cognitive appraisal in fish: stressor predictability modulates the physiological and neurobehavioural stress response in sea bass. *Proceedings of the Royal Society B, 287*(1923), 20192922.]

- People whose spouses died suddenly tend to display more immediate disbelief, anxiety, and depression than those who have had weeks or months to prepare for the loss.
[Sources: Schulz, R., Beach, S. R., Lind, B., Martire, L. M., Zdaniuk, B., Hirsch, C., et al. (2001). Involvement in caregiving and adjustment to death of a spouse: Findings from the caregiver health effects study. *Journal of the American Medical Association, 285*, 3123–3129.
Swarte, N. B., van der Lee, M. L., van der Bom, J. G., van den Bout, J., & Heintz, A. P. M. (2003). Effects of euthanasia on the bereaved family and friends: A cross sectional study. *British Medical Journal, 327*, 189.]

- A researcher exposed college students to an experimental priming manipulation that emphasized either the unpredictable aspects of college, the predictable aspects of college, or neutral features of the college environment. The students then completed a thought-listing task regarding their thoughts about college while blood pressure and pulse data were collected every two minutes. Students who had been exposed to the predictable manipulation appeared to be less stressed in that their thought lists included more references to the future and to their personal goals than those in the unpredictable or neutral conditions. They also had lower blood pressure and pulse pressure reactivity during the task.
[Source: Pham, L. B., Taylor, S. E., & Seeman, T. E. (2001). Effects of environmental predictability and personal mastery on self-regulatory and physiological processes. *Personality and Social Psychology Bulletin, 27*(5), 611–620.]

- A study of people with panic disorder, generalized anxiety disorder, or no disorder found that those with panic disorder showed stronger stress responses to unpredictable shocks than to predictable ones. On the other hand, people with generalized anxiety disorder showed stronger stress responses to predictable shocks.
[Source: Grillon, C., O'Connell, K., Lieberman, L., Alvarez, G., Geraci, M., Pine, D.S., & Ernst, M. (2017). Distinct responses to predictable and unpredictable threat in anxiety pathologies: Effect of panic attack. *Biological Psychiatry: Cognitive Neuroscience and Neuroimaging, 2*, 575-581.]

- The study above is consistent with other research showing that for some people, predictable stressors (those that occur every day, such as a daily commute or a noisy neighbor) can create cumulative stress responses that are as severe as unpredictable ones.
  [Source: Abbott. B. B., Schoen, L. S., & Badia, P. (1984). Predictable and unpredictable shock: Behavioral measures of aversion and physiological measures of stress. *Psychological Bulletin, 96*, 45–71.]

2. Sense of control

- In one study, "the authors exposed 10 healthy human volunteers to the stress of loud (100 dB) noise under controllable and uncontrollable conditions on two separate days. Subjects reported higher self-ratings of helplessness, lack of control, tension, stress. unhappiness, anxiety, and depression; had greater hypothalamic–pituitary–adrenal axis function as measured by elevations in plasma adrenocorticotropic hormone; and had higher levels of sympathetic nervous system and electrodermal activity after the uncontrollable stress condition than after exposure to controllable stress. Thus, lack of control over even a mildly aversive stimulus can produce alterations in mood as well as neuroendocrine and autonomic nervous system changes in healthy subjects."
  [Source: Breier, A., Albus, M., Pickar, D., Zahn, T.F., Wolkowitz, O.M., & Paul S.M. (1987) Controllable and uncontrollable stress in humans: Alterations in mood and neuroendocrine and psychophysiological function. *American Journal of Psychiatry, 144*, 1419–1425.]
- In another study. participants with panic disorder inhaled a mixture of oxygen and carbon dioxide that typically causes a panic attack. Half the participants were led to believe (falsely) that they could control the concentration of the mixture. Compared with those who believed that they had no control, significantly fewer of the "in-control" participants experienced full-blown panic attacks during the session, and their panic symptoms were fewer and less severe.
  [Source: Sanderson, W. C., Rapee, R. M., & Barlow, D. H. (1989). The influence of an illusion of control on panic attacks induced via inhalation of 5.5% carbon dioxide-enriched air. *Archives of General Psychiatry, 46*, 157–162.]

3. Cognitive appraisal of stressors

- In one of the first laboratory demonstrations of the impact of cognitive appraisal on stress reactions, three groups of students watched a film showing bloody industrial accidents. Before the film began, the "intellectualizers" were told to remain mentally detached from the gruesome scenes, the "deniers" were instructed to think of the scenes as unreal, and the "unprepared" were told nothing. Results showed that the intensity of physiological arousal during the film, as measured by sweat gland activity, depended on how the

viewers were instructed to think about the film. The unprepared students were more upset than either of the other two groups.
[Source: Lazarus, R. S., Opton, E. M., Nomikos, M. S., & Rankin, M. O. (1965). The principle of short-circuiting of threat: Further evidence. *Journal of Personality, 33*, 622–635.]

4. Social support

   - The impact of social support was exemplified in a study that "examined the relationship of naturally occurring social support from the spouse with the preoperative anxiety and postoperative recovery of 56 male coronary-bypass patients. Patients were divided into groups based on whether the overall quality of their marital relationship was perceived to be relatively good or bad at the time of surgery and on whether they received relatively high or low spouse support in the hospital (defined in terms of frequency of visits). A fifth group (n = 16), consisting of unmarried patients, enabled additional comparisons. The results indicated that, although groups were essentially equivalent in preoperative physical status, married patients who received higher hospital support took less pain medication and recovered more quickly than their low-support counterparts. In contrast, perceived quality of the marital relationship was a relatively insignificant factor. Speed of recovery for unmarried patients was generally slower than for married, high-support patients and faster than for married, low-support patients."
   [Source: Kulik, J.A. & Mahler, H.I. (1989). Social support and recovery from surgery. *Health Psychology, 8*, 221–38.]
   - Another study addressed the role of perceived social support and hugging as helping to protect against the tendency of a stressor to suppress the immune system. The researchers described the study as follows: "Using a sample of 404 healthy adults, we examined the roles of perceived social support and received hugs in buffering against interpersonal stress-induced susceptibility to infectious disease. Perceived support was assessed by questionnaire, and daily interpersonal conflict and receipt of hugs were assessed by telephone interviews on 14 consecutive evenings. Subsequently, participants were exposed to a virus that causes a common cold and were monitored in quarantine to assess infection and illness signs. Perceived support protected against the rise in infection risk associated with increasing frequency of conflict. A similar stress-buffering effect emerged for hugging, which explained 32% of the attenuating effect of support. Among infected participants, greater perceived support and more-frequent hugs each predicted less-severe illness signs. These data suggest that hugging may effectively convey social support."
   [Source: Cohen, S., Janicki-Deverts, D., Turner, R. B., & Doyle, W. J. (2015). Does hugging provide stress-buffering social support? A study of susceptibility to upper respiratory infection and illness. *Psychological Science, 26*(2), 135–147.]

- Similar results have been reported in this article.
  [Reference: Thomas, P.A. & Kim, S. (2021). Lost touch? Implications of physical touch for physical health, *The Journals of Gerontology: Series B*, 76, e111–e115 https://doi.org/10.1093/geronb/gbaa134]

5. Personality

   - Stress-hardy traits include optimism, resilience, hopefulness, high subjective well-being (happiness), and curiosity.
   - One study measured both hope and curiosity in a large group of volunteers, and, with their permission, tracked their health status as indicated by medical records. It turned out that those with higher hope and curiosity were less likely to develop high blood pressure, diabetes, and respiratory infections
   [Reference: Richman, L. S., Kubzansky, L., Maselko, J., & Kawachi, I. (2005). Positive emotion and health: Going beyond the negative. *Health Psychology, 24*, 422–429.]
   - In another study, "three hundred thirty-four healthy volunteers aged 18–54 years were assessed for their tendency to experience positive emotions such as happy, pleased, and relaxed; and for negative emotions such as anxious, hostile, and depressed. Subsequently, they were given nasal drops containing one of two rhinoviruses and monitored in quarantine for the development of a common cold (illness in the presence of verified infection). For both viruses, increased positive emotional style (PES) was associated (in a dose–response manner) with lower risk of developing a cold. This relationship was maintained after controlling for pre-challenge virus-specific antibody, virus-type, age, sex, education, race, body mass, and season.... Negative emotional style (NES) was not associated with colds and the association of positive style and colds was independent of negative style. Although PES was associated with lower levels of endocrine hormones and better health practices, these differences could not account for different risks for illness. In separate analyses, NES was associated with reporting more unfounded (independent of objective markers of disease) symptoms, and PES with reporting fewer."
   [Source: Cohen, S., Doyle, W. J., Turner, R. B., Alper, C. M., & Skoner, D. P. (2003). Emotional style and susceptibility to the common cold. *Psychosomatic Medicine, 65*, 652–657.]
   - Stress-prone personality traits are seen in people who have a tendency to try to ignore stressors rather than deal with them, to perceive stressors as long-term, catastrophic threats that they brought on themselves, and who are pessimistic about their ability to overcome stressors.

6. Coping resources and skills

   - Money
   - Flexible schedule
   - Supportive family and friends
   - Experience at handling similar situations
   - Optimistic cognitive style
   - Opportunity and facilities to engage in physical exercise
   - The physical and psychological responses you experience if your car breaks down tend to be more negative if you are broke and pressed for time than if you have the money for repairs and the freedom to take a day off from work.
   - Here are examples of problem-focused and emotion-focused coping skills identified in the Ways of Coping Scale:

Problem-focused	
Confronting	"I stood my ground and fought for what I wanted"
Seeking social support	"I talked to someone to find out more about the situation"
Planful problem solving	"I made a plan of action, and I followed it"
Emotion-focused	
Self-controlling	"I tried to keep my feelings to myself"
Distancing	"I didn't let it get to me; I tried not to think about it too much"
Positive reappraisal	"I changed my mind about myself"
Accepting responsibility	"I realized I brought the problem on myself"
Escape/avoidance (wishful thinking)	"I wished that the situation would go away or somehow be over with"

[Table adapted from Folkman, S., & Lazarus, R. (1988). *Manual for the ways of coping questionnaire.* Palo Alto, CA: Consulting Psychologists Press and from Folkman, S., Lazarus, R., Dunkel-Shetter, C., DeLongis, A., & Gruen, R. (1986). Dynamics of a stressful encounter: Cognitive appraisal, coping, and encounter outcomes. *Journal of Personality and Social Psychology, 50,* 992–1003.]

- Another example of identifying coping skills is provided by the Brief COPE scale, which asks respondents to think about current stressors and then to rate how often they have been using each of 28 possible ways of coping with each of them. The scale looks like this, and as you can see, it includes both problem-focused and emotion-focused coping methods:

Try to rate each item separately in your mind from the others. Make your answers as true FOR YOU as you can.

   1 = I haven't been doing this at all
   2 = I've been doing this a little bit

3 = I've been doing this a medium amount
4 = I've been doing this a lot

1. I've been turning to work or other activities to take my mind off things.
2. I've been concentrating my efforts on doing something about the situation I'm in.
3. I've been saying to myself "this isn't real."
4. I've been using alcohol or other drugs to make myself feel better.
5. I've been getting emotional support from others.
6. I've been giving up trying to deal with it.
7. I've been taking action to try to make the situation better.
8. I've been refusing to believe that it has happened.
9. I've been saying things to let my unpleasant feelings escape.
10. I've been getting help and advice from other people.
11. I've been using alcohol or other drugs to help me get through it.
12. I've been trying to see it in a different light, to make it seem more positive.
13. I've been criticizing myself.
14. I've been trying to come up with a strategy about what to do.
15. I've been getting comfort and understanding from someone.
16. I've been giving up the attempt to cope.
17. I've been looking for something good in what is happening.
18. I've been making jokes about it.
19. I've been doing something to think about it less, such as going to movies, watching TV, reading, daydreaming, sleeping, or shopping.
20. I've been accepting the reality of the fact that it has happened.
21. I've been expressing my negative feelings.
22. I've been trying to find comfort in my religion or spiritual beliefs.
23. I've been trying to get advice or help from other people about what to do.
24. I've been learning to live with it.
25. I've been thinking hard about what steps to take.
26. I've been blaming myself for things that happened.
27. I've been praying or meditating.
28. I've been making fun of the situation.
[Source: Carver, C. S. (1997). You want to measure coping but your protocol's too long: Consider the Brief COPE. *International Journal of Behavioral Medicine, 4*, 92–100.]

Burnout

1. Case example: "Mr. A., 50 years old, married, technician in telecommunications, working for a telephone company for 28 years. His problems started ten years ago after successive administrative changes: he was transferred from his unit twice and took over, without previous consultation, a management position

that increased his responsibilities, while personnel were being reduced. His new tasks included firing employees. To learn his new job, he started working late on weekends. He started feeling physically exhausted, anxious, tense and insomniac. After the company was privatized, a process of productive restructuring was installed, including mass dismissals and service expansion. New employees were not sufficiently qualified for their jobs, which demanded greater effort in supervising them. There were successive 'changes in guidelines' ('they told us to do it in one way, and on the following day that was no longer used, all the work was thrown away') besides dismissal threats, employees' demoralization and increasingly higher demands of productivity ('when our goal was not achieved, it's because we were incompetent; when we managed to achieve it, we should have worked harder to go beyond it'). In addition to physical exhaustion, he felt demanded beyond his emotional limit. Thinking about work made him irritated and impatient, in opposition to what he had always been (he considered work as a priority, source of personal satisfaction and pride). He started feeling, besides anxiety, deep sadness, lack of pleasure in activities, difficulty in taking decisions, loss of appetite and weight (around 30 pounds in 7 months), memory 'blanks,' hopelessness, feelings of personal devaluation and a desire to die. After four years, he was relieved of his duties, and started psychiatric treatment that included prescription of numerous antidepressant and anxiolytic medications. After two years of private treatment, he was referred to a state-run psychiatric hospital where treatment continued for another year. He then retired on disability."

[Source: Adapted from Vieira, I., Bucasio, E., Ramos, A., Jardim, S., Martins, D., Benevides-Pereira, A.M., & Figueira, I. (2006). Burnout in psychiatric practice: A case report. *Revista de Psiquiatria do Rio Grande do Sul, 28*, 352–356.]

2. Case Example: "Stephanie was 11 years old, had been participating in gymnastics for 9 years, and had spent the last 4 years competing at a provincial level. She had trained an average of 15 h per week for 11.5 months out of each year. Although she improved during the previous 2 years, she had recently felt fatigued. She admitted that fatigue contributed to a lack of drive, which in turn hindered performance. New challenges Stephanie associated with her competitive environment were contributing to the difficulties she was experiencing. Balancing school and gymnastics had become a challenge. In fact, recently, she felt that most of her energy was being devoted to gymnastics rather than school. Her coaches confirmed that because of her intense training schedule, little time was left for homework. Her dad explained that she has had to miss birthday parties, among other activities with school friends. At the gym, despite opportunities for socializing, Stephanie felt lonely. She added that she felt lonesome particularly at competitions, since she was alone with her coach. Despite her sentiments, her parents and coaches agreed that Stephanie coped well with her challenges of maintaining a balanced lifestyle. Both adult sources believed that the challenge was an opportunity for Stephanie to learn how to organize competing demands and make the necessary choices that would lead to athletic

success. Despite the coping skills described above, Stephanie felt overwhelmed. Feeling as though she had several time constraints, she expressed the need to have a "social life." She had been falling asleep in class and admitted to lacking daily motivation. She reported that she was waking up several times at night and felt that this was related to her gymnastics training. Recently, while struggling through back pain, her gymnastics performance began to decline. Stephanie's parents and coach acknowledged her fatigue and occasional lack of drive. According to Stephanie's mother, this lack of drive also extended to her daughter's academic efforts as Stephanie had recently started hiding school books and blaming gymnastics for unfinished homework.

At the gym, Stephanie admitted becoming frustrated when not successfully performing a skill and that she had been irritable with others. Interestingly, one of her coaches commented that she was not hard on herself and felt that Stephanie lacked intensity and focus. Stephanie's symptoms were consistent with those typically present during the earlier stages of burnout. If unresolved, however, Stephanie predicted that following her current state of fatigue, her performance would decrease, leaving her "grumpy" and unmotivated. Consequently, she thought she would have little choice but to quit gymnastics."

[Source: Dubuc, N.G., Schinke, R.J., Eys, M.A., Battochio, R. & Zaichkowsky, L. (2010). Experiences of burnout among adolescent female gymnasts: Three case studies. *Journal of Clinical Sport Psychology, 4*, 1–18.]

3. Another case study of burnout in a successful female real estate attorney can be found here.

4. The story of Adriana Huffington's approach to combating burnout can be found here. (See other examples of mindfulness-based stress reduction in the chapter on treatment of psychological disorders.)

Posttraumatic Stress Disorder (PTSD)

1. "Philip, a 60-year-old British man, had a road traffic accident on the motorway 3 months before presenting for assessment. The driver of an adjacent car fell asleep and drove into Philip's car from the side. His daughter and grandson were sitting in the back seat. Philip's car spun twice. He tried to look around to see if his daughter and grandson were safe, but he was trapped and could not see them. He thought they were flying about in the car like everything else and that they had died. The car eventually landed on its four wheels. Philip described excruciating pain in his back. He thought that he had broken his back. He could not hear his daughter or grandson and believed they must be dead. However, they had survived. His daughter had a broken arm and his grandson was without injury. When Philip presented for assessment he was having intrusive memories of the accident every day in which he saw the car spinning. He also had intrusive

images of what could have happened and pictured his daughter and grandson dead in the backseat. Philip had flashbacks when he drove his car, which happened several times per week, and he felt hot and sweaty in these situations. He also often woke up with nightmares about the accident. Philip pushed memories of the accident out of his mind, especially at bedtime. He avoided places that reminded him of the trauma, especially motorways and where it happened on the motorway. Whilst he could remember the trauma, he could not remember that the car had rolled twice until he was told by his daughter. Philip had many hyperarousal symptoms. He had difficulty sleeping, felt irritable, had trouble concentrating, and was overly alert. Philip also developed depression after the accident. He was low in mood, tearful, unmotivated, and preferred to stay indoors rather than engage in his previous activities, such as meeting friends for a drink and going out with his wife once a week for a meal."
[Source: Wild, J., & Ehlers, A. (2010). Self-study assisted cognitive therapy for PTSD: A case study. *European Journal of Psychotraumatology, 1*, 1–11.]

2. "Terry, a 42-year-old earthquake survivor, had been experiencing PTSD symptoms for more than eight years. Terry consistently avoided thoughts and images related to witnessing the injuries and deaths of others during the earthquake. Throughout the years, he began spending an increasing amount of time at work and filling his days with hobbies and activities.

By the time he sought treatment, Terry had managed to fill his entire week with various obligations in order to keep his mind occupied and to minimize the possibility that he would think about the traumatic event. He also worked hard to convince others that the earthquake had not affected him. He did this by avoiding people that knew he had gone through this experience and by quickly changing the topic when it came up. However, he found that whenever he had free time, he would have unwanted intrusive thoughts and images about the earthquake. In addition, he was having increasingly distressing nightmares that were causing him to lose several hours of sleep each night. His repeated violent awakenings throughout the night had also disturbed his wife's sleep, resulting in them no longer sharing a bedroom. Terry found that the harder he worked to avoid these thoughts, the more frequent they would become, and that they were getting stronger each day. He feared that if he thought about the memory he would lose control of his emotions and would not be able to cope. He was concerned that the fear and panic that occurred when he was reminded of the trauma would last forever. By avoiding thoughts about the memory, he never allowed himself to test out his predictions. Furthermore, through his repeated avoidance of the trauma memory, his fear continued to grow. Terry eventually sought treatment because his symptoms were significantly impairing his work and family life."
[Source: APA Clinical Practice Guidelines for the Treatment of PTSD. Retrieved here.]

3. "Jill, a 32-year-old Afghanistan war veteran, had been experiencing PTSD symptoms for more than five years. She consistently avoided thoughts and images related to witnessing her fellow service members being hit by an improvised explosive device (IED) while driving a combat supply truck. Over the years, Jill became increasingly depressed and began using alcohol on a daily basis to help assuage her PTSD symptoms. She had difficulties in her employment, missing many days of work, and she reported feeling disconnected and numb around her husband and children. In addition to a range of other PTSD symptoms, Jill had a recurring nightmare of the event in which she was the leader of a convoy and her lead truck broke down. She waved the second truck forward, the truck that hit the IED, while she and her fellow service members on the first truck worked feverishly to repair it. Consistent with the traumatic event, her nightmare included images of her and the service members on the first truck smiling and waving at those on the second truck, and the service members on the second truck making fun of the broken truck and their efforts to fix it—'Look at that piece of junk truck—good luck getting that clunker fixed.'"
[Source: APA Clinical Practice Guidelines for the Treatment of PTSD. Retrieved here.]

Other Stress-Related Mental Health Problems

1. A recent example of the association of workplace stressors and mental health problems comes from a review and meta-analysis of 13 studies representing about 130,000 participants. It found psychosocial stressors at work to be associated with an elevated risk of sickness absence due to a diagnosed mental disorder. The risk was up to 76% higher among workers exposed to these work stressors compared with nonexposed workers. Here are the details of the study and its results.
[Reference: Duchaine CS, Aubé K, Gilbert-Ouimet M, et al. (2020). Psychosocial stressors at work and the risk of sickness absence due to a diagnosed mental disorder: A systematic review and meta-analysis. *JAMA Psychiatry, 77*(8), 842–851.]

Health Promotion and Disease Prevention

1. Examples of programs:
   - Promoting breastfeeding
   - Promoting child and family nutrition
   - Sudden Infant Death Syndrome prevention and education

- Injury prevention
- Promoting physical activity
- Smoking cessation programs such as 'quit' activities and 'brief interventions'
- Promoting early literacy
- Oral health education
- Child safety education
- Vaccination programs
- Programs to promote eating a healthy diet

2. Examples of bygone advertising that promoted *unhealthy* behavior:

- Search online for "vintage ads for cigarettes," "vintage ads for alcohol," and "vintage ads for unhealthy food." Clicking the "images" option at the top of the page will provide many examples that will help students understand the cultural sea change that has taken place over the last century as health promotion and disease prevention initiatives took hold.

Personality   11

The examples provided in this chapter are designed to help illustrate concepts associated with various personality theories that might not be fully fleshed out in textbooks. We hope that using some of them will stimulate class discussions about further examples and provide opportunities to point out linkages between theories, thus promoting engagement with material that many students tend to perceive as little more than a laundry list of unrelated concepts. We hope some of these examples will also help to debunk certain myths about personality, such as that people fall into only one of a small number of types.

Freudian/Psychodynamic Personality Structures

1. *Behaviors associated with id functioning on the basis of the pleasure principle*

    - A baby crying when hungry or thirsty.
    - A toddler grabbing a toy from another toddler.
    - Hunger leads you to start eating your lunch before others at the restaurant table have been served.
    - Cutting into a ticket line instead of waiting your turn.
    - In a traffic jam, pointlessly blowing the horn and yelling for other blocked drivers to move.
    - Screaming at a store clerk who tells you the item you are seeking is no longer in stock.
    - Punching someone who accidentally bumped into you in a crowd.
    - Shaking a baby who has been crying nonstop.
    - Stealing a car that you want, but cannot afford to buy.
    - Keeping a lost wallet containing cash, but also information about the owner.

2. *Behaviors associated with ego functioning on the basis of the reality principle*

   - An eight-year-old waits her turn to play a computer game.
   - You haven't eaten all day, but when you find you have to wait in line at a fast-food restaurant, you spend the time looking at the menu and thinking about what you will order.
   - You use your time while stuck in a traffic jam to check your email and update your status on social media.
   - When you find that the item you want is not in stock, you ask the clerk if it might be available online or at another store location.
   - When someone accidentally bumps into in a crowd, you step back to make another collision less likely.
   - When you cannot get the baby to stop crying, you try to contact someone to help you deal with the situation.
   - You decide to get a second job to help you save enough money for the down payment on the car you want.
   - You call the owner of a wallet you found and ask how to return it (perhaps hoping for a cash reward).

3. *Behaviors and emotions suggesting the operation of the superego*

   - Feeling guilty because you saw an old person struggling to cross a busy street and you did not stop to help.
   - Going to your child's piano recital even though it meant missing the Superbowl because you know this is what a good parent should do.
   - Donating to worthy charities.
   - Paying off a stranger's layaway account at Christmas, even though no one will ever know that it was you who did it.
   - Feeling anxiety because someone might discover it was you who stole money from the tip jar at the coffee shop where you work.
   - Feeling ashamed when you are actually identified as a thief or fraudster.

4. *Behaviors and emotions suggesting superego is not operating*

   - Cheating, stealing, assault, murder, fraud, bigamy, and other crimes and misdemeanors that do not cause the perpetrator to feel guilt, anxiety, or shame (typically associated with psychopathy or antisocial personality disorder).

Ego Defense Mechanisms

1. *Repression*

   - A person has no memory of the funeral of a loved one.
   - A woman has no memory of being in the car accident that killed her parents when she was six.
   - A man had no memory of being abused by a scout leader until it was triggered by seeing his son in a scout uniform. [Be aware that the recovery of repressed childhood memories in adulthood is highly controversial and should not be presented without including discussion of the psychological science surrounding this alleged phenomenon.]

2. *Rationalization*

   - A parent who never really wanted children says "I spank my kids because it is good for them."
   - A person who embezzles from his employer tells himself that the employer is making a fortune, won't miss the money, and anyway, deserves it because she doesn't treat him with enough respect.
   - A woman who fails to get a promotion at work shrugs it off by saying that she didn't really want the extra responsibilities and longer hours.
   - A man who controls his romantic partner to the point that she is not allowed to work or leave the house alone says it is because he worries about her safety.
   - A woman who is afraid of doctors claims she doesn't have annual physical exams because she does not want to add to her doctor's burden of patients who use the local health care system.
   - A woman who is in love with a man who is not interested in her claims that he has not called her back because he is very busy with his work at the moment.
   - A woman who doesn't like her mother-in-law and doesn't really want to visit her, claims that her work leaves her no time to make family visits.

3. *Projection*

   - A person who resents the success of his next-door neighbor says that the neighbor is very unfriendly and competitive.
   - A married man who fantasizes about having extramarital affairs is insanely jealous of his wife and constantly worries that she might be cheating on him.
   - A woman who often picks fights with her partner complains to friends that the partner is "impossible to get along with".

- A man who is slightly overweight is always complaining about all the obese people he sees in restaurants and shopping malls, saying that they really ought to do something about themselves.
- A woman who is very judgmental about others experiences anxiety in social situations because she is sure that other people don't like her.
- A man who tries to resist his intense attraction to pornography complains that all his male friends "can't stop talking about sex!"
- People may assume that others share the same social or political or religious views, and so feel free to state them forcefully—even to strangers—without concern for the possibility that they may be creating socially awkward situations.
- You love to talk, and when someone interrupts your long monologues, you think of the other person as not being a good listener.
- The laziest person in your work group complains that others in the group are not doing their share.

4. *Reaction formation*

- You are strongly attracted to a married co-worker, but you express strong dislike for the person instead.
- A person has an intense dislike for someone but goes to great lengths to treat the person with extreme kindness and respect.
- A gay man who is uncomfortable about his sexual orientation and wants to conceal it engages in lots of promiscuous heterosexual affairs, opposes gay marriage, and is constantly making anti-gay comments and telling homophobic jokes.
- A woman who gives birth to an unwanted child becomes a smothering, overprotective mother who is constantly worried that something bad might happen to the child.
- An activist deeply engaged in efforts to end sexual violence against minors is actually having sex with underage children and has child pornography on his computer that features prepubescent children. (This is a real case.)
- A woman who has always harbored hatred and resentment toward her elderly mother becomes heroically devoted to her when she becomes ill.
- A person whose hidden desires to fulfill unconventional sexual fantasies, physically attack disliked people, and take advantage of other people's goodness to steal from them chooses to become a minister, priest, imam, or rabbi.
- Someone who hates members of a minority group becomes an advocate for tolerance of ethnic differences and the rights and dignity of that group.
- A person with an alcohol, drug, or smoking problem becomes a vocal advocate of laws against drugs, drunk driving, underage drinking, and smoking in public, and is constantly preaching about the benefits of abstinence.

- A person who fears being rejected in romantic relationships and is sure that true love will never come along becomes completely cynical about romance, claiming that falling in love is overrated, never lasts, eventually leads to disappointment, and that, as the song says "Only fools fall in love."
- Tenderness expressed towards a younger brother or sister may cover an intense jealousy of that sibling.
- A woman who is always cleaning and says she can't stand dirtiness may actually be attracted to disorder and the dirt that she comes in contact with while cleaning.

5. *Sublimation* [Be sure to note that not everyone who engages in the following activities does so because of sublimation.]

- A person who harbors strong aggressive impulses joins a boxing club, plays contact sports such as football or rugby, or seeks to join an elite special operations military unit.
- Someone with strong, unconventional, but unexpressed sexual interests or desires spends time creating erotic paintings or sculpture, and maybe even becomes a full-time artist.
- A woman who is unable to recognize her own sexual needs becomes an avid horseback rider.
- A person who has a strong need to feel superior to other people becomes the head of a company, the dean of a college, or the principal of a high school.
- Someone whose need to prove self-worth is frustrated by lack of appreciation at work decides to quit and create a new start-up company in the same field.
- A man who cannot recognize the anger he feels toward his wife's indifferent attitude toward him spends every weekend cleaning every inch of the house, re-organizing the garage, or waxing his car.
- Rather than becoming angry or developing symptoms of depression, a person whose lover has broken off the relationship begins to write lyrical, romantic poetry.
- Someone who was bullied as a child and harbors deep anger and aggressive impulses toward people in general becomes a dentist or a surgeon or gets a job at a meat packing plant.

6. *Displacement*

- You feel unappreciated by your spouse and children and you take it out on your employees by being unreasonably demanding and rude.
- You have been rejected by the person you had hoped to marry, so you take up a relationship with—and ultimately marry—someone who reminds you of your loved one but is actually so different that the new relationship has no emotional foundation.

- After being abused by a partner whose aggressiveness terrifies you, you find yourself spanking your children for small transgressions and hitting the dog for no reason at all.
- A man cannot handle the guilt he feels because of sexual attraction to his partner's best friend, and soon begins asking his partner to wear dark green lingerie, the same dark green that just "happens" to be the color the best friend usually wears to parties and dinners.
- A man loses his job during an economic downturn and hates to admit that his mediocre skills don't make it easy to find employment, but he blames his situation on minority groups and immigrants who are getting unfair advantages or "stealing" American jobs.
- A child who is bullied at school may bully his younger siblings at home.
- Here is a Dilbert cartoon to illustrate displacement.

7. *Compensation*

- A man who was small for his age in grade school and was bullied as a result, seeks to make up for unconscious feelings of inferiority by being hyper-competitive and obsessed with displaying superiority in his academic or athletic or occupational or sexual pursuits ("Napolean complex").
- A high school student whose disappointment at failing to make the cheerleading squad or the soccer team devotes herself to working on the school newspaper, participating in the drama club, and running for class president.
- A man who was a popular and successful "jock" in high school develops unconscious worries about losing his youthful appearance and sexual capacities as middle age approaches, so he becomes obsessed with covering his grey hair, trades his "sensible" sedan for a flaming red Porsche, and starts hanging out in bars where he is likely to encounter younger women with whom to have exciting, but brief, meaningless, and perhaps extramarital sexual affairs. [Click here to hear Jerry Lee Lewis singing "Middle Age Crazy."].
- A woman whose mother's critical comments in childhood left her with feelings of embarrassment about her appearance spends all her spare time helping others—volunteering at nursing homes and children's hospitals, collecting donations for the local food bank and doing other things that allow her to feel satisfaction with her life despite not having a husband or partner.

8. *Denial*

- A bisexual woman is always finding opportunities to tell anyone who will listen that she has never had the slightest sexual interest in other women.
- In Shakespeare's *Hamlet,* the title character, along with his mother, Queen Gertrude, and his uncle Claudius are watching a play that Hamlet has written. In the play a queen makes an overly dramatic and obviously insincere

promise that she would never remarry if her husband were to die. At this point, Hamlet asks his mother what she thinks of the play. Gertrude, whose husband (Hamlet's father) had indeed died and who had later remarried answers by saying "The lady doth protest too much, methinks." In other words, overemphasizing your feelings might be a sign that those feelings might not be genuine.

- A smoker who finds it impossible to quit claims that smoking is not as unhealthy as everyone says it is.
- A woman whose husband or partner has been cheating on her fails to acknowledge the signs of his infidelity, even when friends or relatives try to point them out to her. "There must be a logical explanation," she might say, and when urged to confront the problem might claim that "He could never do that to me, and he would be so hurt if I asked him to explain these receipts from hotels and restaurants that I have never been to."
- A man has been experiencing cardiac symptoms or toothaches and knows that he might have a medical or dental problem, but rather than seeing a doctor or dentist, he simply ignores the symptoms in the hope that they will go away.
- A person with an alcohol or drug addiction will claim that there is really no problem because things are going fine at work, and that, in any case, "I can quit whenever I want to, but I just don't want to."
- A person who is overspending to the point of risking bankruptcy refuses to admit that he or she has a problem with money and that, "things will work out, they always do."

9. *Regression*

- A newly married young woman returns to the security of her parents' home after her first fight with her husband.
- A child begins to suck his thumb or wet the bed as the time draws near to enter first grade.
- A man who is insecure about his attractiveness tends to behave like an immature teenager whenever he goes out with someone new.
- A person who is facing a major life crisis, such as a divorce or a job loss, suddenly becomes unable to make decisions and begins depending entirely on others for advice about what to do.

Psychosexual Stages

1. *Behaviors indicative of being in the oral stage or of being fixated at that stage later in life:*

   - Infants put everything they touch into their mouths, including their feet.
   - Overeating.
   - Smoking.
   - Excessive drinking.
   - Using "biting" sarcasm.
   - Being excessively talkative, and/or being prone to sudden oral outbursts.
   - Nail-biting.
   - Thumb-sucking.
   - Excessive obsession with female breasts or performing oral sex.
   - Constantly chewing gum or one's long hair; gnawing on pencils.
   - Pica (pronounced "pike-ah"; ingestion of non-food items such as clay, dirt, paint, paper, crayons, etc.)
   - Excessive dependency on others, acting helpless, or manipulating people into doing things for you. [See the chapter on psychological disorders for examples of dependent personality disorder.].

2. *Behaviors indicative of being in the anal stage of psychosexual development or of being fixated at that stage later in life.* (Note that the first 16 examples suggest anal retentiveness, and that the last 7 of those are real readers' responses to blogger Matt Cutts' request for examples of anal-retentive behaviors. The last 5 are examples of anal expulsiveness):

   - Being excessively neat and meticulously organized about even the smallest details. [When taken to extreme, this pattern may be diagnosed as obsessive–compulsive disorder (OCD, or as one wag has suggested, the alphabetically-ordered version, C.D.O.)]
   - You organize your kitchen spices in alphabetical order.
   - You hang your clothes in the closet by color.
   - You arrange the bills in your wallet by denomination.
   - You keep shopping discount coupons in a wallet or folder—arranged by store —so that you always have them with you.
   - When resetting clocks after a power failure or daylight savings time changes, you assure that each clock agrees precisely with all of the others.
   - You check that every item in your credit card statement has a corresponding receipt of same amount and then you add up all the purchase amounts to confirm the card company's total.
   - You have a system for loading the dishwasher and don't allow anyone else to do it.

- You write your grocery shopping list to match each item's location in the store so that you do not have to back-track.
- "At the Dunkin' counter you order 'iced-medium-2 sugars-1 cream' as opposed to 'medium iced coffee, 1 cream and 2 sugars' because when the server hears medium he immediately reaches for the medium HOT cup and when he hears ICED next— it jars him for a sec as he's gotta back-peddle to put the cup back and restart. His next move is for the sugar so if you tell him cream first again it jars him. All to save saying 1 word, 'coffee' and maybe 2 s."
- "I guess the fact that I fold up take-out food wrappers and neatly place them in the bag and THEN neatly fold the bag before throwing it in the trash is yet another example of this "anal-retentive" behavior of which you speak."
- "I organize my fast-food tray into six divisions. I separate burger, drink, napkins, fries, disposed packets of condiments and unspoiled condiments respectively in a zigzag format."
- "I have almost every non-spam piece of email sent to me since 1985. Some on 5 1/4 inch floppy, for which I don't even have a working drive anymore, and some on cartridge tape for which I also no longer have any working drives."
- "You have one sock drawer for colored socks and one for white socks and you do not let your significant other to put your clothes away."
- "I can't sleep with dirty dishes in the sink. I always, always put two ice cubes in my glass of water—not one, not three or more. But in glasses of iced tea/soda etc. I don't mind if there are more than two ice cubes. I often find myself re-folding tee shirts for no real reason…I just thought of this, because I did it yesterday…and I had folded and put laundry away the day before. I clean out/organize my wallet weekly, often every day."
- (In response to the item above about grocery shopping lists) "When the Kroger where I shop re-arranged all of the food items in all of the aisles, I personally 'escorted' the store manager through all of the store, citing logical reasons why (to me) this was not a good arrangement. He did not agree with me and avoids me whenever possible now."
- There is a wonderful cartoon illustrating anal retentive characteristics. It shows a man on the phone with the romantic partner who left him a good-bye note that obviously mentioned problems in the relationship. Outraged at being abandoned, he says "How can you just walk out on me like this? And by the way, 'nit-picking' has a hyphen!"
- Being excessively messy and disorganized.
- Being prone to emotional outbursts.
- Being attracted to sexual activities involving the anus and excrement.
- Being excessively generous.
- Being rebellious against the constraints of society's rules.

3. *Behaviors indicative of being in the phallic stage of psychosexual development or of being fixated at that stage later in life:*

- Boastfulness
- Excessive self-assuredness
- Vanity and narcissism
- Compulsive and promiscuous sexual behavior
- Competitiveness
- Aggressiveness
- Exhibitionism (drawing attention to oneself)

Erickson's Psychosocial Stages of Development

1. Here is an example of a tabular summary of Erikson's stages that you can use to contrast with Freud's. [Note: You might want to point out to your students that these stages are not independent; the way in which one crisis is resolved tends to affect the way in which later crises are resolved.]

Age	Central psychological issue or crisis
First year	**Trust versus mistrust** Infants learn to trust that their needs will be met by the world, especially by the mother—or they learn to mistrust the world
Second year	**Autonomy versus shame and doubt** Children learn to exercise their wills, make choices, and control themselves—or they become uncertain and doubt that they can do things by themselves
Third to fifth year	**Initiative versus guilt** Children learn to initiate activities and enjoy their accomplishments, acquiring direction and purpose—or, if they are not allowed to take initiative, they feel guilty for their attempts at becoming independent
Sixth year through puberty	**Industry versus inferiority** Children develop a sense of industry and curiosity and are eager to learn—or they feel inferior and lose interest in the tasks before them
Adolescence	**Identity versus role confusion** Adolescents come to see themselves as unique and integrated people with an ideology—or they become confused about what they want out of life
Early adulthood	**Intimacy versus isolation** Young people become able to commit themselves to another person—or they develop a sense of isolation and feel they have no one in the world but themselves
Middle age	**Generativity versus stagnation** Adults are willing to have and care for children and to devote themselves to their work and to others—or they become self-centered and inactive

(continued)

Erickson's Psychosocial Stages of Development

(continued)

Age	Central psychological issue or crisis
Old age	**Integrity versus despair** Older people enter a period of reflection, becoming assured that their lives have been meaningful and becoming ready to face death with acceptance and dignity—or they are in despair about their unaccomplished goals, failures, and ill-spent lives

2. Examples of differing resolutions of the *trust versus mistrust* and *autonomy versus shame and doubt* stages can be found in the variations in attachment that appear in the Strange Situation test presented in the chapter on development.
3. Examples of different resolutions of the *initiative versus guilt* stage can be seen in the case of (a) children who are not afraid to try new things (such as to start typing on a computer keyboard or drawing pictures or attempting to join into older children's games) versus (b) those who are reluctant to approach—and perhaps display fear of—new situations and opportunities. Children in the latter group have to be coaxed into exploring the world and testing their abilities; they are ready to stop if, say, the computer makes a sudden sound they did not expect or if they encounter any sort of difficulty. Further, they may feel guilty about having tried something new, especially if they failed at it.
4. Examples of differences in resolving the *industry versus inferiority* stage can be seen in children who are (a) curious about the world, eager to learn, and who persist at tasks even if they do not at first succeed versus (b) those who are not very curious about the world and have to be pushed to learn, especially in school. Those in the latter group are far more likely to lose interest in learning, especially once they have had failure experiences, and are more likely than other children to drop out of school. (Other examples of these motivational differences can be found in the chapter on motivation and emotion.)
5. Examples of differences in resolving the *identity versus role confusion* stage can be seen in youngsters whose infancy, childhood, and early adolescence brought trust, autonomy, initiative, and industry, as compared to those whose infancy and childhood created feelings of mistrust, shame, guilt, and inferiority. Those in the former group are more likely to resolve the identity crisis positively and develop feelings of self-confidence and competence. Those in the latter group are more likely to be confused about their identity and goals.

- Efforts to resolve the identity crisis are particularly clear in late adolescence, when many young people try out various alternative identities—such as that of the rebel, the scholar, or the bored and detached observer—as they seek to answer for themselves questions about sexuality, self-worth, industriousness, and independence.

6. Differences in how the identity crisis is resolved can affect resolution of the issues that arise in the *intimacy versus isolation* stage.

    - For example, those who came through the identity crisis with a clear sense of who they are and what they want in life typically begin to focus on forming mature relationships based on sexual intimacy, friendship, or mutual intellectual stimulation. They may marry or form some other kind of committed relationship. Especially if their early attachment history was a secure one, they tend to feel valued and worthy of support and affection; they develop closeness easily. Their relationships are characterized by joy, trust, and commitment.
    - People who failed to address and resolve identity issues because they unthinkingly accepted the identity their parents set for them may eventually experience problems with anxiety, depression, or substance abuse if they later discover that their life choices (e.g., to marry, have children, and pursue particular kinds of education and employment) were guided more by the expectations of their family and peers than by their own genuine preferences.
    - People who never really dealt with their identity crisis may experience different problems if they remain uncommitted and lacking in direction. This is particularly true for those with an insecure attachment history. They may be aloof and unable to trust or to commit themselves to a partner; they may be more prone than others to infidelity. Yet they also tend to be preoccupied with relationships and may feel misunderstood, underappreciated, and worried about being abandoned. In short, their relationships are often negative, obsessive, and jealous.

7. The ways in which children and adolescents resolve issues in these first five stages may be affected by the parenting styles described in the chapter on development. For example, children who are not allowed or encouraged to exercise their wills or start their own activities are more likely to be uncertain about doing things for themselves and guilty about seeking independence.
8. According to Erikson, successful resolution of the *generativity versus stagnation* stage is exemplified in people who:

    - enjoy the years of middle adulthood, spending their time in building careers or engaging in other activities (including guiding the development of their children) that will result in valuable things that will make the world a better place and will remain when they themselves are gone. These characteristics have been associated with successful resolution of the industry versus inferiority stage in childhood.
    [Reference: Slater, C. L. (2003). Generativity versus stagnation: An elaboration of Erikson's adult stage of human development. *Journal of Adult Development, 10*, 53–65.]
    - take pride in their accomplishments, including in the roles they play in their immediate and extended family.

9. Those with a history of less successful resolution of previous psychosocial crises are more likely than others to stagnate in this stage, as exemplified by people who:

- take little or no interest or pride in their work (they "work to live" rather than "live to work")
- make little or no effort at self-improvement
- place their own needs above those of others
- have stormy interpersonal relationships
- feel bitter about their lives
- blame others for their lack of success
- feel jealous of those whose lives seem better
- feel little sense of control over their lives

10. In the final, integrity versus despair stage of Erikson's theory of psychosocial development, people confront their mortality. It is in this stage that older adults look back on their lives (Erikson called it a "life review") and, depending on how previous crises have been resolved, how they have spent their time, and how successfully they have aged (e.g., in terms of remaining healthy and mentally and physically active and engaged), they come to see their lives and accomplishments as meaningful or meaningless. Those in the former group experience a sense of integrity and fulfillment, as exemplified by feelings of:

- contentment
- peace
- lack of regret
- satisfaction
- treasuring a small number of close social relationships
- acceptance of death and, in some cases, a desire to peacefully end one's life on one's own terms at a time of one's choosing

People in the latter group tend to feel:

- many regrets about failures, missed opportunities, and bad decisions
- guilt over past behaviors
- alienation from others
- anger and bitterness
- a sense that their lives have been wasted
- intense fear of death
- despair that may lead to violent suicide

Trait Theories of Personality

[Note: Examples in this section may be especially helpful for debunking myths about people falling into one of only a small number of discrete personality types, including astrological types.]

1. On January 31, 1931, the Psychograph, a device consisting of a helmet and movable rods designed so that measurements could be made at 32 points on the skull, made its public debut at the Twin City Auto Show in Minneapolis-St. Paul, Minnesota. The device was an excursion into automated phrenology. You can see a bit of an explanation, and witness one in action at the Quackery Gallery.
2. Here are some other examples of phrenology machines, and personality results.
3. Contemporary examples of the everyday application of trait theories are provided by the following personality sketches and excerpts from letters of recommendation (traits are in italics):

   - He's a really *caring* person, and very *outgoing*. He's *generous* with his time, and he *works very hard* at everything he does. Yet sometimes I think he also *lacks self-confidence*. He always *gives in* to other people's demands because he *wants to be accepted* by them.
   - It's my pleasure to provide this letter of recommendation for Charlie, who worked as a server at Solera Restaurant for the past two summers. As Charlie's direct manager who worked closely with him throughout his time here, I was impressed with his *work ethic, friendly* personality, and *ability to work well under pressure*.
   - Charlie demonstrated superlative customer service. Our clientele is a mix of long-term patrons and visiting tourists, and Charlie was *personable* and *professional* toward all. Even when things got hectic during peak business hours, Charlie kept up his *energy level* and *attention to detail*. I recall one instance when the kitchen was backed up and a table complained about how long they had to wait for their food. Charlie listened to their concerns and offered them free desserts to ensure that they left feeling positive about their dining experience. Charlie is *thorough, friendly*, and *helpful*, all qualities that made him an excellent addition to our staff.
   - Alex impressed me with her *warmth, wisdom*, and *kindness* online, over the phone, and in person. She is *capable, confident*, and *committed* to our mission of extraordinary support.
   - Adam is *self-motivated, attentive to detail*, and skilled at both independent and collaborative work. Adam left a mark with his *open, thoughtful* personality.

- Alice is *not afraid to take risks* and often suggests new directions to explore. She's *committed to quality*, growth, and progress, and she *inspires* her team members to strive for the same. In short, Alice is a *person with vision*.
- Jerry impressed me with his *intellectual curiosity, passion* for global cultures, and *adventurous spirit*. He's *hard-working, thoughtful, charismatic*, and *open-minded*.

Big Five Personality Dimensions

[Be sure to explain to your students that though you are describing the characteristics associated with each of these dimensions, they should not be viewed in isolation, but in combination in a particular individual.]

1. Openness

    - Daredevils provide some of the most obvious examples of people who would score high on the Big Five dimension of openness. Here you can find brief stories about some of them—including Harry Houdini, Sam Patch (the 'Jersey Jumper'), Annie Edson Taylor (the first person to go over Niagara Falls in a barrel), and Bessie Coleman (who, in 1922, became the first African-American woman to become a licensed pilot).
    - You might also want to show segments of an 11-min video of famous daredevils in action. It is available here.
    - Other famous people who have clearly displayed the intellectual curiosity, creativity, and sensitivity to beauty associated with high levels of openness include (Google any of them for details about those who might be less familiar to students): Steve Jobs, Elon Musk, Georgia O'Keeffe, Frida Kahlo, Louise Bourgeois, Thomas Edison, Francis Crick, James Watson, Bill Gates, Cynthia Kenyon, Jennifer Doudna, Nina Tandon, and Barbara McClintock.
    - There is a great cartoon illustrating the fact that a complete view of a person from the perspective of the Big Five model requires taking all five dimensions into account, not just one. It shows the foreman of a jury delivering the following verdict: "We find the defendant guilty on all charges, Your Honor. On the positive side, we really liked his openness and energy."

2. Conscientiousness

Here are examples of real and fictional people who displayed the self-discipline, dutifulness, and striving for achievement against the odds that are associated with high scores on the Big Five dimension of conscientiousness:

- Jesus
- Socrates
- Nathan Hale
- Mahatma Gandhi
- Nelson Mandela
- Martin Luther King, Jr.
- Joan of Arc
- Mother Teresa
- Captain Kirk (*Star Trek*)
- Colonel Sherman Potter (*M*A*S*H*)

Some people who score high on conscientiousness can also be hyperattentive to detail and orderliness, rigid, overly controlled, stubborn, and even obsessive–compulsive, as exemplified by TV and movie characters such as:

- Alan Harper (*Two and a Half Men*)
- Melvin Udall (*As Good as It Gets*)
- Felix Unger (*The Odd Couple*)
- Fraser Crain (*Cheers*)
- Emma Pillsbury (*Glee*)
- Monica Geller (*Friends*)
- Sheldon Cooper (*Big Bang Theory*)
- Gregory House (*House*)

People high on conscientiousness can also be very reliable, honest, industrious, academically diligent, and socially responsible. There is a wonderful cartoon that provides an example of taking conscientiousness about recycling or school rules to an extreme. It shows a man holding out a bag to the medieval axman who is about to execute him. The caption says "I brought my own bag."

Another one about rules shows a schoolboy standing beside a teacher in the principal's office. The caption reads: "You're a very good hall monitor, Billy, but we don't detain teachers."

People who score *low* on conscientiousness may display the sloppiness, unreliability, impulsiveness, disregard for rules, and even law-breaking that is associated with such fictional characters and real-life criminals as:

- Bernie Madoff
- Charles Ponzi
- Frank Abagnale, Jr. (*Catch Me If You Can* is a movie about his life)
- Ted Bundy
- Jeffrey Dahmer
- Aileen Wuornos
- Oscar Madison (*The Odd Couple*)
- Saul Goodman (*Breaking Bad/Better Call Saul*)

- Ilana Wexler (*Broad City*)
- Max Blum (*Happy Endings*)
- Alex Forrest (*Fatal Attraction*)

3. Extraversion

As exemplified by the following real and fictional people, those who score high on the Big Five dimension of extraversion display enjoyment of social interaction and the social spotlight, high energy and activity levels, enthusiasm, talkativeness, and assertiveness:

- Robin Williams
- Oprah Winfrey
- Jim Carrey
- Donald Trump
- Judge Judy
- Margaret Thatcher
- Bill Clinton
- Muhammad Ali
- Magic Johnson
- Charlie Harper (*Two and a Half Men*)
- Cosmo Kramer (*Seinfeld*)
- Kelly Bundy (*Married with Children*)
- Ned Flanders (*The Simpsons*)

People who score *low* on extraversion tend to prefer less social interaction, do not seek the spotlight, are more low-key, thoughtful, and quiet in social situations, enjoy time alone or in quiet pursuits, as exemplified by the following real and fictional people:

- Bill Gates
- Warren Buffett
- Albert Einstein
- Meryl Streep
- Greta Garbo
- Rosa Parks
- Steven Spielberg
- Clint Eastwood
- Mark Zuckerberg
- Abraham Lincoln
- J.K. Rowling
- Larry David (*Curb Your Enthusiasm*)
- Rajesh 'Raj' Koothrapalli (*Big Bang Theory*)
- Walter White (*Breaking Bad*)
- Wilson W. Wilson, Jr. (*Home Improvement*)

- Dexter Morgan (*Dexter*)
- Arya Stark (*Game of Thrones*)
- A cartoon illustrates a person who is low on extraversion. It shows "a woman named Molly saying "Happy New Year" to herself in a bathroom mirror while people at the party in the living room nearby say the same to each other (and one asks "Where's Molly?")."

4. Agreeableness

High scores on the agreeableness dimension in the Big Five model are associated with getting along with others, being warm, friendly, and tactful, kind and considerate, optimistic, generous, trusting, helpful, and willing to put other people's interests ahead of one's own, as exemplified by these real and fictional people:

- Laura Bush
- Barbara Bush
- George H.W. Bush
- Mr. Rogers
- Sheriff Andy Taylor (*The Andy Griffith Show*)
- Aunt Bee (*The Andy Griffith Show*)
- June Cleaver (*Leave it to Beaver*)
- Atticus Finch (*To Kill a Mockingbird*)
- Wayne Campbell and Garth Algar (*Wayne's World*)
- Melanie Hamilton (*Gone with the Wind*)
- Forrest Gump (*Forrest Gump*)
- Radar O'Reilly (*M*A*S*H*)

As exemplified by the following real and fictional people, *low scores* on agreeableness tend to be associated with being unfriendly, uncooperative, and sometimes argumentative and suspicious, placing competitiveness and self-interest above social harmony, showing little concern for others' well-being, and an unwillingness to exert much effort to help them:

- Harvey Weinstein
- Phil Spector
- Jeffrey Epstein
- Leona Helmsley
- Gordon Ramsey
- Simon Cowell
- Mariah Carey
- Anna Wintour
- Gordon Gekko (*Wall Street*)
- Miranda Priestly (*The Devil Wears Prada*)
- Nurse Ratched (*One Flew Over the Cuckoo's Nest*)

- Regina George (*Mean Girls*)
- Kathryn Merteuil (*Cruel Intentions*)
- Calvin Candie (*Django Unchained*)
- Miss Trunchbull (*Matilda*)
- Madison Morgan (*The DUFF*)
- Christy Masters (*Romy & Michelle's High School Reunion*)
- A cartoon illustrates *low* agreeableness. It shows a doctor telling the wife of a man in an intensive care unit that "We managed to resuscitate him, but he's still very critical." Use of the word "critical" is the joke because you can see through the ICU window that the man is screaming insults.

5. Neuroticism

Here are examples of real and fictional people who display the tendency toward negative emotions such as anxiety, depression, and pessimism, and toward strong emotional reactivity to stress that are associated with high scores on the Big Five dimension of neuroticism:

- Woody Allen
- Howie Mandel
- Brian Wilson
- Barbra Streisand
- Robin Williams
- Marilyn Monroe
- Kate Spade
- Bobby Wiley (*What about Bob?*)
- Niles Crane (*Frasier*)
- George Costanza (*Seinfeld*)
- Alan Harper (*Two and a Half Men*)
- Frank Burns (*M*A*S*H*)
- Clay Jenson (*13 Reasons Why*)
- Fleabag (*Fleabag*)
- Gretchen Cutler (*You're the Worst*)
- Dr. Lisa Hudson (*Being Mary Jane*)

People who score *low* on neuroticism tend to be calm and relatively free of negative emotions; they are more emotionally stable, less reactive to stressors, and less easily upset by life events, as exemplified by these real and fictional people:

- Winston Churchill
- Dwight D. Eisenhower
- Robert E. Lee
- Clint Eastwood

- Jack Welsh (former General Electric CEO)
- Sir Richard Branson
- Indra Nooyi (former PepsiCo CEO)
- Satya Nadella (Microsoft CEO)
- Colonel Sherman Potter (*M*A*S*H*)
- Captain Kirk (*Star Trek*)
- Vito Corleone (*The Godfather*)
- Nameless getaway car driver (*Driver*)
- Tom Reagan (*Miller's Crossing*)
- William Munny (*Unforgiven*)
- Walt Kowalski (*Grand Torino*)

Humanistic Theories of Personality

1. Examples of Carl Rogers' concept of conditions of worth

   - A mother tells her 5-year-old that he is "a bad boy" when he finger paints on the living room wall.
   - A father tells his 10-year-old that she is "stupid" for still liking to watch Peppa Pig.
   - A mother tells her 6-year-old that he is a "sissy" for playing with dolls.
   - A 12-year-old's friends make fun of her weight.
   - Parents tell their children that they have to get straight A's in school in order to uphold the honor of the family.
   - A physician tells his college-age child that he will be ashamed and humiliated if the child does not get into medical school.
   - A wife makes snide remarks about the fact that her husband's income is less than that of some of their friends.
   - A husband tells his wife that she looks "ugly" whenever she wears clothes that he doesn't like.
   - A woman withholds affection from her partner whenever the partner disagrees with her social or political views.
   - A cartoon provides an example of conditions of worth created by parents. It shows a father telling his young baseball-playing son "Just remember, son, it doesn't matter if you win or lose—unless you want Daddy's love."
   - Another cartoon exemplifies a child apparently unaffected by conditions of worth. It shows a mother reading her child's report card while the child says "May I remind you that my core worth as a human being remains constant, and isn't tied to external validation."

- A cartoon provides a nice graphic summary of the conditions of worth concept. It shows a pair of adult hands holding a heart-shaped platform from which dangle the strings that control a child-puppet.

2. Here are some examples of what Maslow called a deficiency orientation that leads to unhappiness and dissatisfaction with life:

[Note: Examples of Maslow's hierarchy of needs are presented in the chapter on motivation and emotion].

- When you buy your first new car, you are thrilled and enjoy driving it every day. It makes you happy and you feel special, perhaps even superior to those who drive lesser quality cars. But after a few months, your exciting new car becomes just your car, and after a couple of years, you begin thinking about the features it doesn't have, about the cool features of some of the latest models, and about how much you could get for your car on a trade for an even nicer one. If you make a trade, the same cycle of happiness, loss of happiness, and dissatisfaction will repeat itself.
- You win the lottery and can now afford to buy whatever you want, and for a couple of years you just love your new life but, eventually, buying new things becomes so routine that the pleasure of doing so lasts for shorter and shorter periods and you end up buying and traveling simply to relieve your boredom with the things you have that you once thought would bring you permanent satisfaction and happiness.
- In the months and weeks leading up to your wedding, you feel excitement, anticipation, and a sense of being special—especially compared to your friends. But after the wedding and the honeymoon are over and you face all the big and little problems of everyday life, you may feel a sense of disappointment and dissatisfaction with the marriage that you had been so eager to enter.
- You move into a new house or apartment that is much better than where you had been living, and even though it is also more expensive, you feel great satisfaction at being able to afford it and at having and using all its high-end amenities. After some months, though, as with a new car, the features of your new dwelling lose their novelty and become your new normal. Over a period of years, you may start paying attention to the things your place doesn't have, and start shopping for a new and even better place to rent or buy.
- You get a big promotion at work, and it comes with more money, a nicer workspace, and more responsibility, including the supervision of several lower-level employees. You bask in the congratulations of your friends and family, and for the first year you enjoy the new job. Eventually, though, the higher salary begins to seem less than adequate (especially in light of the extra workload and because your increased spending leaves you in about the same financial position as before the promotion), so you begin thinking about

strategies that will put you in line for a further promotion, more money, and more responsibility.
- You enter into a new intimate relationship and you and your partner are so compatible that you are sure you will be happy with this person for the rest of your life. After some time, however, little things that your partner says and does begin to annoy you. The excitement of being together fades, and instead of focusing on the positive aspects of the relationship, you find yourself making unfavorable comparisons between your partner and other potential partners in terms of appearance, sexiness, and personality. Eventually, your dissatisfaction with a partner who had seemed perfect leads you to break up and seek a new "perfect partner."

3. Here are some examples of what Maslow called a growth orientation that nourishes self-actualization and life satisfaction. They all involve appreciating and savoring the relationships, things, opportunities, and circumstances that we have rather than all that we do not have.

- President Harry S. Truman grew up in a house in Independence, Missouri, and after he left office in 1953, he returned to that same house, where he and his wife lived mainly on his Army pension. He turned down lucrative offers to serve on corporate boards and to endorse commercial products. In other words, despite having the opportunity to enrich himself as most presidents before and since had/have done, he chose to enjoy what he had, namely a peaceful, though not prosperous, life in a familiar and satisfying place.
- In 2008, billionaire investment guru Warren Buffett took less than $200,000 in salary from his company (Berkshire Hathaway), and was living in the same house in Omaha, Nebraska that he bought in 1958 for $31,500. He drives his own car, though he could easily afford a limousine and driver. In 2013, he used an old Nokia flip phone, finally upgrading to an iPhone 11 in 2020. When an interviewer asked why he had no interest in moving into a bigger, better house, he said, "I'm happy there. I'd move if I thought I'd be happier someplace else."
- Halle Berry has been quoted as saying "I am very thankful for my good fortune, but one of my biggest fears is that I could lose it all." Although one of the highest-paid actresses in Hollywood, she uses public transportation and shops for her own groceries with her child.
- Kate Middleton, the Duchess of Cambridge, prefers to wear simple, non-designer dresses, including at social events, making her one of the first celebrities who started wearing mass-market clothes, and has been seen wearing the same dress more than once.
- Keanu Reeves has been quoted as saying that "Money is the last thing I think about. I could live on what I have already made for the next few centuries." He often uses public transportation, buys clothes on sale, and can sometimes be seen relaxing on public park benches.

- IKEA founder Ingvar Kamprad is among the world's richest people, but travels on economy class flights, buys secondhand clothes, and drives a 1993 Volvo. Some people call him "Mr. Scrooge," but he considers the need to buy expensive things to be a bad habit.

Social Cognitive Theory

1. *Statements, thoughts, or actions indicative of high self-efficacy:*

   - You have enrolled in a course that everyone says is tough because the teacher is very demanding, but you tell your friends that you are sure you can get an A.
   - You enter your psychology classroom for the midterm exam and tell yourself that "I have done all the reading, I have studied everything, and I can ace this test."
   - You have just been hired as a junior reporter on a local newspaper, and though you have never written news stories before you tell yourself "I have always gotten good grades on my term papers, and so I know I can write well. All I need to do is work hard and learn from any mistakes I make, and I will do fine."
   - You realize that you have been gaining weight and not exercising as much as you used to, so you decide to go on a low-carb diet and visit the campus gym three times a week. You miss a session now and then, and sometimes those mashed potatoes look too good to resist, but you focus on your progress and tell yourself that "This new lifestyle is not easy, but I can stick to it in the long run."
   - You have been diagnosed with a serious illness but you tell yourself that "Many people have beaten this disease, and if I take the treatments my doctor prescribed, I am going to be one of them."
   - You have always been afraid of heights, but now your fear is interfering with your desire to work in the construction industry, so you decide to enter a program of cognitive behavior therapy. You tell yourself that this approach has a lot of evidence for its effectiveness and that it is going to work for you, too, if you follow the therapist's instructions, take responsibility for doing all the homework she assigns, and not lose hope if you are not immediately successful.
   - Here are three versions of *The Little Engine That Could*:
   The first is available here.

The second is available here.

The third is available here.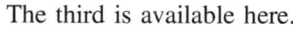

2. *Statements, thoughts, or actions indicative of low self-efficacy*:

   - You would like to act in a local theater company, but after you arrange an audition for the company's next production, you tell yourself that you probably aren't good enough to get a part, so you don't show up for the tryout.
   - You are listening to some fellow students discussing current events, and you disagree with what most of them are saying, but you decide to keep quiet because you don't think your comments would be impressive enough to be taken seriously.
   - You love to watch "Jeopardy!" on television, but you never actually play trivia games because you feel that you won't be able to answer questions fast enough to be successful.
   - Because you think you are "no good" with computers, when your laptop freezes, it never occurs to you to just reboot it, and you waste a lot of time trying to find someone to help you.
   - There is someone you would like to get to know better but you don't try to do so because you feel sure that you would not be able to keep a conversation going.

3. Examples of *reciprocal determinism*:

   - A woman whose parents are prejudiced against a certain minority group came to feel the same way about that group. When she went away to college and began to encounter people from that group, she tended to behave in an unfriendly way toward them (thoughts drive actions). When those people noticed her hostility, they tended to show hostility in return (actions drive changes in the social environment), leading her to tell herself that her parents' views about those people were correct and causing her to become even more unfriendly (environment strengthens thoughts that strengthen behaviors).
   - A child is afraid of going to school because he heard there are lots of bullies there, and so he avoids talking to other children (emotion drives action), but the other children react by teasing him for being "different" (action changes environment), which makes him even more fearful of school (environment drives emotion), so he starts faking illness to avoid going (emotion drives action). Missing school causes him to fall behind in class, to fail tests, and to get negative feedback from his teacher (actions drive changes in environment), which makes the situation even worse.

- A woman is part of a work team charged with creating a new advertising campaign. The team leader asks her to come up with a plan for publicizing the product through social media, but because she knows almost nothing about these media, she is terrified of failing and perhaps losing her job (environment drives emotion). She begins researching other social media campaigns, but she is so anxious about her lack of knowledge that she can't concentrate and ends up missing a lot of important information (emotion drives behavior), which causes the team leader to criticize her poor performance (behavior changes environment), which makes her so sick with worry (environment drives emotion) that she quits her job and is now unemployed (emotion drives action that changes the environment).

4. Examples of statements, thoughts, or actions indicative of internal locus of control:

- Success in life is determined by how hard you work, not who you know.
- You make your own luck.
- When life hands you lemons, make lemonade.
- People fail when they don't try hard enough to succeed.
- If you eat right, exercise, stay away from tobacco, drugs, and excessive drinking you will live a long and healthy life.
- You can make a lot of money in the stock market if you do careful research on companies before you invest in them.

5. Examples of statements, thoughts, or actions indicative of external locus of control:

- It's not what you know, but who you know.
- I'll do well in this course if the teacher likes me.
- If you are meant to succeed, you will. If the odds are against you, you won't.
- Some people just have all the luck.
- The events in our lives are destined by the stars.
- I don't worry about healthy eating because health problems are a matter of bad luck.

Projective Personality Tests

1. An online version of the Rorschach Inkblot Test is available here.

2. An online version of the Thematic Apperception Test (TAT) is available here.

Nonprojective Personality Tests

1. An online version of a Big Five Personality Test is available here.

2. A post alleging to present the first 75 items of the Minnesota Multiphasic Personality Inventory (MMPI-2) is available here. Be very cautious about presenting these items in writing, because if they are in fact real MMPI-2 items, you might be violating a copyright. The comments that follow the post are, in themselves, potentially valuable for generating discussion of the validity and usefulness of the MMPI-2.

3. Here is an example of research that can stimulate discussion of the need to assure that personality (and other mental) tests are supported by scientific research on reliability and validity:

   - Experimenters gave half the students in a psychology class the actual results of the personality test they completed but gave the other half results that were unrelated to their test responses. An equal number of students in both conditions reported that the results described them well. This study was a follow up of an earlier one in which students filled out a personality test and were then all given the *same* personality sketch allegedly based on the test. All students considered the sketches to be highly accurate. Results like these are said to illustrate the "Aunt Fanny effect." This label reflects the fact that if the results of a personality test provide only vague generalizations they could apply to anyone (including "my Aunt Fanny") and thus can seem more valid than they are. This effect is also called the "Barnum Effect" in honor of P.T. Barnum, the impresario who said that "there's a sucker born every minute." [References: Dies, R. R. (1972). Personal gullibility or pseudodiagnosis: A further test of the "fallacy of personal validation." *Journal of Clinical Psychology, 28,* 47–50.
   Forer, B. R. (1949). The fallacy of personal validation: A classroom demonstration of gullibility. *The Journal of Abnormal and Social Psychology, 44* (1), 118–123. https://doi.org/10.1037/h0059240.]

Psychological Disorders 12

Teaching about psychological disorders can be rewarding because these are topics that most students are eager to study, so classroom boredom is seldom a problem. There are challenges, too, because the range of disorders is wide, as is the range of factors that can help explain them, so whether you are teaching about disorders in just one unit in introductory psychology or in a course devoted to abnormal psychology, you will have to decide which topics to include during class and what to assign students to explore on their own. Teaching this material also provides the opportunity to debunk myths about psychological disorders, such as that they are caused by poor life choices, are intensified when the moon is full, that people with disorders are usually dangerous, and that schizophrenia involves "split personality." Finally, it is important to keep in mind that some of your students and/or their families and friends are being affected, or may have been affected, by one or more of the disorders being studied. So you not only have to present the material in a sensitive way, but also remind everyone that although some of the disorders you discuss might seem "weird" or even funny, they are in fact conditions that can have serious, disabling, and even tragic consequences for those affected—possibly including some of their classmates.

Defining Abnormality

1. Examples of subclinical norm violation abound in Candid Camera clips, including a 5-min clip on invasion of personal space.
   [Many other *Candid Camera* clips related to norms and norm violations are cited in the chapter on social psychology.]

© Springer Nature Switzerland AG 2022
E. L. Cameron and D. A. Bernstein, *Illustrating Concepts and Phenomena in Psychology*, Springer Texts in Education,
https://doi.org/10.1007/978-3-030-85650-2_12

2. There are also numerous videos by high school and college psychology students demonstrating the impact on other people of norm-violating behavior in public, including this 2-min one. (See more examples in the chapter on social psychology.)

Diagnostic Manuals

1. *Diagnostic and Statistical Manual of the American Psychiatric Association (DSM-5)*

    - Here you can find the homepage.

    - There are fact sheets that cover changes in the new edition, updated disorders, and general information about the DSM-5.

    - Here is a summary of DSM-5 organization, a bit of history, and some criticisms.

2. *International Classification of Diseases, 11th edition; ICD-11 of the World Health Organization*

    - Here is the homepage.

    - Here is a good summary and history of ICD-11.

3. *Psychodynamic Diagnostic Manual (PDM-2)*

    - This classification system describes psychopathology in terms of psychodynamic concepts such as ego strength, defense style, mental representation of the self, and the like. Its advocates claim that it has diagnostic utility and that it promotes deeper diagnostic assessment than more traditional systems.
    - The PDM-2 is organized along three axes:

    Personality Syndromes (P Axis) include variations in *personality functioning* (ranging from healthy, through neurotic and borderline, to psychotic) and in personality style or pattern.
    Profile of Mental Functioning (M Axis), which includes a detailed description of overall mental functioning (ranging from psychological health to pathology) focusing on capacities such as information processing, impulse control, awareness of self and others, forming and maintaining social relationships, experiencing, expressing, and understanding emotions, regulating self-esteem, use of coping strategies and defenses, adaptability and resiliency, forming internal standards, and giving coherence and meaning to personal experience.

Symptom Patterns: The *Subjective Experience* (S Axis) includes traditional DSM and ICD categories, but focuses heavily on the affective states, cognitive processes, somatic experiences, and relational patterns most often associated with each. This axis includes descriptions of psychological experiences (e.g., conditions related to gender identity, sexual orientation, and minority status) that may require clinical attention.
[Reference: Lingiardi, V., & McWilliams, N. (2015). The psychodynamic diagnostic manual–2nd edition (PDM-2). *World Psychiatry, 14*(2), 237.]

4. *Example of a positive psychology approach to diagnosis:*

   - Here is a summary of the Values in Action Classification of Character Strengths.

5. *The National Institute of Mental Health's Research Domain Criteria (RDoC) framework*

   - A summary is available here.
     You can use this example to help students see that disorders might best be understood not by classifying them by symptoms, but by identifying the dimensions underlying them, including:
   - neurodevelopment, which is thought to be involved to some extent in all forms of disorder. Just as height and weight growth charts provide norms that make it easier to identify deviations from typical dimensions of children's physical development, research on neurodevelopmental processes may provide guidelines that promote earlier identification of deviations from typical developmental trajectories in children's thinking, language, emotion, and behavior.
   - environmental experiences, such as significant stressors or trauma
   - brain processes that coordinate responses to aversive situations, which in the DSM might be labeled as anxiety disorders
   - brain processes that activate and coordinate reward-seeking and response to rewards, which in the DSM might be labeled as motivational problems or substance use disorders
   - brain processes that activate and coordinate mental functions such as attention, perception, memory, language, and cognition, which in the DSM might be labeled as attention deficit disorders, depressive disorders, or schizophrenia
   - brain processes that underlie social behavior, which in the DSM might be labeled as attachment disorders, autism spectrum disorders, or antisocial personality disorder
   - brain processes that underlie physiological arousal, bodily rhythms, and sleep–wake cycles, which in DSM might be labeled as insomnia disorder, narcolepsy, or sleep apnea

So, for example, many anxiety disorders such as panic disorder, may reflect overactivity of brain-based threat systems, whereas many substance use disorders may reflect disruption in brain-based reward systems.

- The RDoC promotes research on each of these domains at 7 levels of analysis, including genes, molecules, cells, brain circuits, physiology, behavior, and self-reports.
- The RDoC approach exemplifies the assumption that, once research at all these levels allows identification and understanding of the processes and dimensions underlying all disorders—*without deciding in advance what those disorders should be called*—a classification system will create itself. For example, it will be clear that when disturbances in processes A, B, and C occur together, they create a set of disorders that are related, even if their outward symptoms are not the same. Similarly, when disturbances in processes X, Y, and Z occur together, they create a different set of disorders that, again despite differing appearances, belong together. And so on.
- The number of disorders discovered would depend on the outcome of this research rather than on decision-making based on symptoms.
- Ideally, because of similarities in underlying causal processes, related disorders will respond to the same types and amounts of psychological and medical treatments.

6. *The Hierarchical Taxonomy of Psychopathology (HiTOP)*.

- A good summary is available here.
- Its advocates argue that normal and abnormal behavior lie at differing points along a continuous dimension, or spectrum, rather than existing as separate entities. From the HiTOP perspective, mental disorders can be seen as extreme versions of the general personality traits—such as introversion, neuroticism, and impulsivity—that are measured by some of the tests described in the chapter on personality. For example, alcohol-use disorder, formerly called alcoholism, may often appear when high levels of anxiety combine with high levels of impulsivity.
[Reference: Kotov, R., Krueger, R. F., Watson, D., Achenbach, T. M., Althoff, R. R., et al. (2017). The hierarchical taxonomy of psychopathology (HiTOP): A dimensional alternative to traditional nosologies. *Journal of Abnormal Psychology, 126*, 454–477.]

7. *The Power Threat Meaning Framework (PTMF)* is not so much an alternative to the DSM as it is a call to think about psychological disorders in a completely different way, namely as understandable responses to the threats created by oppressive forces in society, including, for example, power differentials between employers and employees, competition for advancement in educational and

occupational settings, physical or psychological trauma, income inequality, poverty, discrimination, and social injustice. Here you can find examples of the application of this model in clinical practice.

8. An article summarizing various alternatives to DSM-5 is available here.

Examples of Psychological Disorders

[*Note*: The examples below focus on disorders commonly covered in an introductory psychology course. If you are teaching abnormal psychology, you will likely have access to examples of a wider range of disorders in the materials that accompany your textbook. Also, be aware that YouTube provides a vast array of interviews showing many forms of psychological disorders.]

Neurodevelopmental Disorders

1. Here is a nice introduction to *autism spectrum disorder* (ASD) along with an illustrative hypothetical case.
2. Here is a description of a case of severe *autism spectrum disorder* and its treatment.
3. Examples of celebrities who are said to be, or to have been, on the autism spectrum include (you may have to explain who some of these people are or were):

- Dan Aykroyd
- Hans Christian Andersen
- Benjamin Banneker
- Susan Boyle
- Tim Burton
- Lewis Carroll
- Charles Darwin
- Emily Dickinson
- Albert Einstein
- Bobby Fischer
- Bill Gates
- Temple Grandin
- Daryl Hannah
- Thomas Jefferson
- Steve Jobs
- James Joyce

- Alfred Kinsey
- Stanley Kubrick
- Barbara McClintock
- Michelangelo
- Wolfgang Amadeus Mozart
- Sir Isaac Newton
- Jerry Seinfeld
- Satoshi Tajiri
- Nikola Tesla
- Andy Warhol
- Ludwig Wittgenstein
- William Butler Yeats

4. Here is a useful 4-min video describing the symptoms and behavioral treatment of tic disorders and *Tourette's syndrome* in children.

5. Here is a case study of drug treatment of *Tourette's syndrome*.

6. Here are several short case studies of *ADHD* in children. [*Note*: The next several examples provide an opportunity to debunk myths about the role of sugar in the etiology of *ADHD*.]

7. Here is an interview with a 12-year-old child with *ADHD*.

8. Here, the 12-year-old's brother, a 9-year-old with *ADHD* and Autism Spectrum Disorder, is interviewed.

9. Here, the mother of the two boys in the two previous examples is interviewed and describes her discovery of her own *ADHD*.

10. Here are two case studies of *ADHD* in adults.

11. Here is an interesting 6-min video in which two six-year-olds, one with *ADHD*, are asked the same questions about themselves, and the viewer is asked to guess which child has been diagnosed.

12. A listing of celebrities said to display ADHD is available here.

13. A 2-min video showing a child with a fetal alcohol spectrum disorder is available here. (Other examples of the impact of teratogens are available in the chapter on development.)

14. Here is a detailed composite diagnostic case report on a 9-year old girl named "Jane," who presents with ADHD as well as fetal alcohol spectrum disorder.

Schizophrenia Spectrum and Other Psychotic Disorders

[*Note:* The examples in this section are particularly helpful for debunking the myth that schizophrenia spectrum disorders involve "split personality."]

1. Here is a video of a 10-min interview with a young man hospitalized with what was at the time (1961) known as catatonic schizophrenia.

2. A 3-min video interview with a young man diagnosed with an unspecified form of schizophrenia is available here.

3. Here is a 9-min interview with a Nationalpark@123 schizophrenia patient about her hallucinations.

4. Here is a somewhat melodramatic 9-min video presented by a young woman with schizophrenia who describes her symptoms and their development.

5. A reenacted 12-min video of a mental status exam with a young man who would probably have been diagnosed—using DSM-IV—as paranoid schizophrenic is available here.

6. Another nonprofessional interview with a woman with schizophrenia was published in *Scientific American* in 2009 and is available here.

7. A case study of an adult male with schizophrenia who was treated with both drugs and ECT is available here.

8. This 9-min video shows four patients with schizophrenia, each with different symptoms, including delusions and hallucinations; the fourth of these shows some of the side effects of antipsychotic medication. The video was made for physicians and includes subtitles

that identify symptoms, offer diagnostic information and criteria, and list medical tests that they might want to order for such patients. If you want to present the first two of these patients separately, slightly longer interviews with them are available here, and, here.

9. First-person accounts of people with schizophrenia can be found on the website of the Schizophrenia Oral History Project.

10. A list of celebrities who are said to display, or to have displayed, schizophrenia spectrum symptoms is available here.

Bipolar and Related Disorders

1. A classic 13-min film from the 1950s shows a woman diagnosed with mania. It is available here.

2. Here is a 7-min interview with a woman diagnosed with rapidly-cycling bipolar disorder (as well as a clip of her participating in a group therapy session).

3. A particularly touching 8-min video showing a man with bipolar disorder becoming depressed is available here.

4. Here is a 15-min interview with a young man with bipolar disorder.

5. A list of celebrities said to have, or to have had, bipolar disorder is available here.

Depressive Disorders

1. A 7-min video showing short clips of military veterans describing their experiences with depressive symptoms and successful treatments (scroll down through the page to find it).

2. Here is a case report of the symptoms and prescription drug treatment of a 60-year-old man with major depressive disorder with mixed features.

3. The account of a case of postpartum depression leading to suicide is available here.

4. Another example of postpartum depression, as described by actress Brooke Shields, is available here.

5. This 14-min video interview with a young woman experiencing depression is available here.

6. A list of celebrities said to display, or to have displayed, depression is available here.

Anxiety Disorders

1. Here are five case examples, along with questions that clinicians should ask clients and themselves in dealing with these cases.

2. Here is an overview and case study of generalized anxiety disorder.

3. Here is a case study of social phobia.

4. Here is a 12-min interview with a young woman experiencing social anxiety.

5. Here is a cognitive-behavior therapy-oriented case study of the symptoms and treatment of anxiety over academic exams. (Other examples of cognitive-behavior therapy are available in the chapter on treatment of psychological disorders.)

6. Here is an extreme case of agoraphobia in a very elderly woman.

7. Here is a one-minute clip from an interview with a woman with severe agoraphobia.

8. Here are very brief case descriptions of generalized anxiety disorder in young children.

9. Research on "nomophobia," the fear of being without a mobile phone or out of mobile phone contact, is described in an article that associates it with poor sleep and daytime fatigue. It is available here.

Obsessive–Compulsive and Related Disorders

1. Here is a short case example involving compulsive washing and cleaning.

2. The case of a 12 year-old boy with OCD symptoms is available here.

3. The case of a 42 year-old woman with a longstanding history of OCD is available for download.

4. Here is a description of an unusual form of OCD (called *scrupulosity*) in a 35-year-old.

5. A case history and treatment program involving a 30 year-old woman with complex OCD is available here.

6. A 3-min video of a man describing his OCD behaviors is available here.

7. A 9-min video about comedian Howie Mandel and his longstanding OCD is available here.

8. The case of reclusive billionaire Howard Hughes is recounted here and here, as well as in *The Aviator*, a feature film starring Leonardi DiCaprio.

Examples of Psychological Disorders

9. There is a 7-min video showing a British journalist's story of OCD. Two more videos follow his efforts to understand the disorder. These can be found here and here.

10. A 5-min dramatization of OCD symptoms is available here.

11. A 4-min video showing a three-year old child with OCD is available here.

Trauma- and Stressor-Related Disorders

1. One to 10-min clips from interviews with military veterans diagnosed with PTSD can be found on YouTube here, as well as here and here.

2. A case study of PTSD in an adolescent survivor of the Parkland school shooting is available here.

3. The case study of a 10 year-old girl with acute stress disorder following a natural disaster is available here.

4. Here is a search results page containing a variety of adjustment disorder case studies. [Note that some of these cases are publicly available while others require library access privileges.]

5. A case of reactive attachment disorder in a 4-year-old boy is available here.

6. A case of reactive attachment disorder in a 14 year-old girl is available here.

7. A tragic case of reactive attachment disorder in an adopted child is available here.

8. A 4-min video of an interview with a young boy with reactive attachment disorder is available here. [Note that the sound level is low, so if you play this video in class, you will probably need to activate the closed captions option.]

9. An 8-min clip from a video interview with the mother of an adopted child with reactive attachment disorder is available here.

Dissociative Disorders

1. Here is a case of dissociative identity disorder in a 55-year-old woman.

2. Two cases of dissociative identity disorder in Korea are available here.

3. Here is a description of a patient with dissociative identity disorders switching identities while in an emergency room.

4. An 11-min video interview with a young woman who claims to have 12 personalities is available here.

5. A 5-min video with a woman who displays some of her 20 personalities is available here.

6. A 3-min video showing a woman with dissociative identity disorder describing how she negotiates with her various alter identities is available here (scroll down the page to find the video).

7. Here is a list of commercial films portraying dissociative identity disorder.

8. A case description of a young man showing symptoms of dissociative amnesia with dissociative fugue is available here.

9. A case of dissociative amnesia in a 64-year-old Filipino woman is available here.

10. Here is a case of dissociative fugue in a 28-year-old medical student in Nigeria.

11. Here is a summary of the world's most famous cases of amnesia. (Other examples of amnesia are described in the chapters on biological aspects of psychology and on memory.)

12. A 5-min video that tells the story of a man in Seattle whose dissociative amnesia is so complete that he does not know his own name or anything about himself is available here.

13. A case report of a 22-year-old man with depersonalization/derealization disorder is available here.

14. A case report of a 42-year-old man with depersonalization disorder is available here.

Somatic Symptom and Related Disorders

1. Here is a description of the case of a 31-year-old man with somatic symptom disorder.

2. A more detailed case of somatic symptom disorder in a 72-year-old man is available here.

3. A case of somatic symptom disorder in a 53-year-old woman who also experienced depression is available here.

4. Here is a description of the symptoms and treatment of a 24 year-old man with somatic symptom disorder and multiple additional problems.

5. A 17-min video presenting interviews with a male child and a female adolescent who have displayed and were successfully treated for somatic symptom disorders is available here.

6. A case in which a 57-year-old woman was misdiagnosed as having somatic symptom disorder when she actually had multiple myeloma is available here.

7. Here is a detailed description of a case of illness anxiety disorder (previously hypochondriasis) in a 39-year-old woman.

8. Here is a case in which a 72-year-old woman showing symptoms of illness anxiety disorder is somewhat surprisingly treated with electroconvulsive shock therapy.

9. A 4-min clip from a Woody Allen movie *(Hannah and Her Sisters)* illustrating illness anxiety disorder is available here.

10. A 5-min video showing the case of a 13 year-old girl with conversion disorder is available here. [The interesting aspect of the case is that there is essentially no examination of the psychological causes of the disorder; it was treated essentially as a temporary physical disability. It also comes off as a bit of a commercial for the rehabilitation facility where the girl was treated.]

11. A 6-min video of a conversion disorder case in a teenage girl is available here.

12. A more extensive written case study of symptoms and treatment of conversion disorder in a 20-year-old woman is available here.

13. Here is the story of an apparently contagious form of conversion disorder among high school students.

Feeding and Eating Disorders

1. Here is a case of anorexia nervosa in a 14-year-old Malaysian girl.

2. Here is a case of anorexia nervosa in a 25 year-old woman in India.

Examples of Psychological Disorders

3. A tragic, long-term case of anorexia nervosa in an English woman is available here.

4. Here is a case of a 14 year-old Iraqi male with anorexia nervosa.

5. A lifelong case of anorexia nervosa in a 66-year-old woman is available here.

6. A somewhat melodramatic 12-min video presenting a case of anorexia nervosa in a young woman is available here.

7. A 4-min video of a near-fatal case of anorexia nervosa in a young woman is available here.

8. A first-person account of a decade of bulimia nervosa in a young woman is available here.

9. A brief case study of bulimia nervosa in a young English woman is available here.

10. A 22-min video in which a young woman presents the story of her bulimia nervosa is available here.

11. The story of Lady Diana's struggle with bulimia, and what fictionalized accounts of it got wrong is summarized here.

12. A very brief case description of binge eating disorder is available here.

Sleep–Wake Disorders

[*Note:* Additional examples of some of these disorders can be found in the consciousness chapter.]

1. A brief description of insomnia disorder is available here.

2. Here is a case of hypersomnolence disorder (also known as Excessive Daytime Sleepiness, or EDS) in a 32-year-old woman.

3. Here is a more extensive case study and 9-min video of hypersomnolence disorder in a young man from Iceland.

4. A description of a case of narcolepsy with cataplexy in an adult male is available here.

5. Here is case study of narcolepsy in a six-year-old girl. Here is another in an 18-year old man.

6. A 4-min video of a young woman with narcolepsy since childhood is available here.

7. A detailed case of obstructive sleep apnea in a 30-year-old Asian man who caused an accident by falling asleep on the job is available here.

8. Here is a shorter case description of obstructive sleep apnea in a 36-year-old man.

9. Here is a case of central sleep apnea in a 51-year-old man.

10. Here is a case of REM sleep behavior disorder in a 23-year-old woman.

11. Here is a case of REM sleep behavior disorder in a 78-year-old man.

12. A case of REM sleep behavior disorder involving violent behavior during sleep in a 60-year-old man is available here.

13. Here is a case of circadian rhythm sleep–wake disorder in a 58-year-old man.

Disruptive, Impulse-Control, and Conduct Disorders

1. Detailed descriptions of oppositional defiant disorder in two young boys is available here.

2. An apparent case of oppositional defiant disorder continuing into adulthood is available here.

3. A 4-min video summarizing and illustrating conduct disorders is available here.

Neurocognitive Disorders

[*Note*: Additional examples of these disorders can be found in the chapter on biological aspects of psychology.]

1. Here is a 5-min diagnostic interview for Alzheimer's disease.

2. A particularly moving 5-min video containing a longitudinal case study of a woman displaying ever-worsening symptoms of early onset dementia is available here.

3. A case of frontotemporal neurological disorder in a 61-year-old woman is available here.

4. A case of delirium in a 68-year-old woman is available here.

5. A case of delirium in a 90 year-old man is available here.

6. A 5-min training video that illustrates delirium in an elderly man is available here.

7. A pair of 5-min videos showing two patients' experience with delirium associated with cardiac surgery is available here as well as here.

Personality Disorders

1. You might want to use some clips from a 48-min video about the characteristics and treatment of borderline personality disorder, with case examples that include interviews with patients and their parents. It is available here.

2. A description of a first interview with a 46-year-old man who displays antisocial personality disorder and a criminal history is available here.

3. A somewhat self-serving autobiographical summary from a young man with antisocial personality disorder is available here. As you might expect, he acknowledges previous wrongdoing, but also tends to blame others for his problems.

4. A less self-serving autobiographical summary from another young person with antisocial personality disorder is available here.

5. A 30-min video interview with a young man with antisocial personality disorder is available here.

6. A 7-min story about and interview with a homicidal man with antisocial personality disorder is available here.

7. Here is the case of a hospitalized 65-year-old man diagnosed as paranoid personality disorder.

8. A treatment interview with a 46-year-old man with paranoid personality disorder is available here.

Examples of Psychological Disorders 379

9. Here is a case description of narcissistic personality disorder in a 43-year-old man.

10. Here is an example of narcissistic personality disorder as portrayed in a 9-minute video from a TV show (*30 Rock*).

11. A 4-min video of an actress portraying a woman with narcissistic personality disorder is available here.

12. A list of celebrities who display marked narcissism, though not necessarily narcissistic personality disorder, can be found here.

13. A first therapy session with a 32-year-old woman with dependent personality disorder is available here.

14. A case description of dependent personality disorder in a 21-year-old woman is available here.

Insanity and Competency to Stand Trial

[*Note:* Examples in this section provide good opportunities to debunk the myth that the insanity plea is frequently used and is usually successful, thus supposedly allowing people to literally "get away with murder."].

1. Andrea Yates admitted to drowning her five children in the bathtub of her Houston, Texas, home in 2001. She had twice tried to kill herself in previous years, and she was reportedly depressed at the time of the murders. Accordingly, she pleaded not guilty by reason of insanity. The first legal step in deciding her fate was to confine her in a mental institution to assess her mental competency to stand trial. Following the testimony of psychologists who examined her, she was found competent and ultimately sentenced to life in prison. Her conviction was overturned on appeal, though, and at a second trial in 2006, she was found not guilty by reason of insanity and committed to a Texas state mental hospital, where she remains.

2. A 2-min video summarizing the Yates case in images and subtitles is available here.

3. In a similar case from 2014, Ebony Wilkerson, tried to kill her three children by driving her car into the ocean at Daytona Beach, Florida. She pleaded not guilty by reason of insanity in a non-jury trial, and the judge accepted the plea. After several years of confinement in a mental institution and supervised community release, she was eventually freed and allowed to return to live with her family in South Carolina. A brief summary of her story is available here.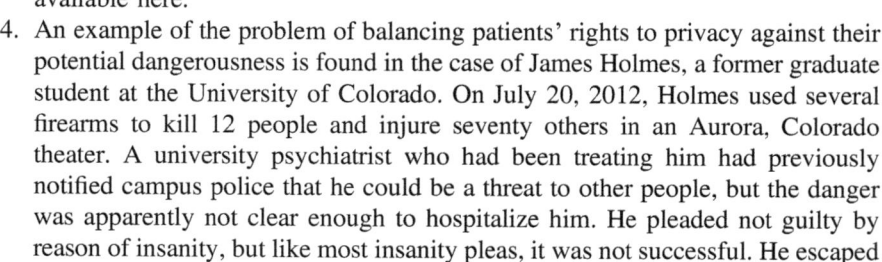

4. An example of the problem of balancing patients' rights to privacy against their potential dangerousness is found in the case of James Holmes, a former graduate student at the University of Colorado. On July 20, 2012, Holmes used several firearms to kill 12 people and injure seventy others in an Aurora, Colorado theater. A university psychiatrist who had been treating him had previously notified campus police that he could be a threat to other people, but the danger was apparently not clear enough to hospitalize him. He pleaded not guilty by reason of insanity, but like most insanity pleas, it was not successful. He escaped the death penalty but was sentenced to 12 life sentences plus 3,318 years in jail, where he remains.

This 1-min video gives a quick summary of the case and includes an interview with Holmes, who says that he would kill again if given the chance. [This interview could be an excellent jumping off point for a class discussion about whether the jury should have found him not guilty by reason of insanity.]

5. The Tarasoff case is the primary example of the origin of duty to warn laws that allow psychiatrists and clinical psychologists to breach confidentiality. In 1969, Prosenjit Poddar, a student at the University of California–Berkeley, sought therapy through the student mental health services center. During a therapy session, he told his psychotherapist, Dr. Lawrence Moore, that he intended to kill a young woman, Tatiana Tarasoff, who had rejected his attempts to have a romantic relationship. The therapist informed his superior, Dr. Harvey Powelson, of this threat. The campus police were called and were also asked, in writing, to confine the client. They did so briefly, but then released him after concluding that he was rational, and they believed his promise that he would stay away from the Tarasoff's home. He did not do so. After terminating his relationship with his therapist, Poddar killed Ms. Tarasoff. He was later convicted of murder. No one had warned the woman or her parents of the threat. In fact, Dr. Powelson had asked the police to return Dr. Moore's letter and ordered that all copies of the letter and Dr. Moore's therapy notes be destroyed. Ms. Tarasoff's parents sued the University of California–Berkeley, the psychologists involved in the case, and the campus police to recover damages for the murder of their daughter. Ultimately, the Supreme Court of California found in favor of the parents.

The case is described in much more detail in an article available here.

6. Here is a recent example in which the process of determining a criminal suspect's competency to stand trial took so long that the time he spent in jail awaiting trial exceeded the length of his ultimate prison sentence. It also exemplifies the fact that clinical judgments about competency and sanity can be flawed, in this case with tragic consequences.

"Kenneth R. Tannassee, 29, was arrested and charged with second-degree murder on August 21, 2020, after an unidentified homeless woman was found dead inside her vehicle at a Home Depot parking lot. Tannassee had been in trouble before. He had been charged with burglary on three occasions in 2018 and 2019, and his behavior was such that a judge signed an order appointing an expert to conduct a competency evaluation of Tannassee before the latest burglary case could be tried. Proceedings stalled for several months, during which time multiple psychiatric and psychological evaluations concluded Tannassee was incompetent to stand trial but did not meet the criteria for commitment to a state hospital (i.e., was not a danger to himself or others). The judge confirmed that status on December 20th 2019 and Tannassee was ordered housed at the Collier County Florida Jail to receive competency restoration treatment provided by staff from a behavioral health agency. By April, 2020, an expert appointed to conduct re-evaluation of competency found Tannassee competent, stating that he spoke clearly, engaged easily, was cooperative and did not present any unusual behaviors. The expert wrote that Tannassee earned a post competency training test score of 98.8%, had dramatically improved since competency training began, and was compliant with medication. At a hearing at the end of July, 2020, Tannassee pleaded no contest to the charges in the latest burglary case and the judge sentenced him to 18 months in state prison. However, because he was given credit for the 21 months he had been in jail since his arrest, he was released. Seventeen days later, he killed the homeless woman." [Source: Allen, J. (2020). Suspect in East Naples homicide released from jail 17 days before incident. *Naples Daily News*, August 29, p. 8A.]

7. Many people are concerned that the insanity defense can allow guilty, responsible defendants to "get away with murder" or other crimes, and that they exploit insanity laws to minimize punishment. This defense is rarely successful, but critics still point, for example, to cases like that of Jarrod Ramos, who killed five employees of the *Capital Gazette* newspaper in Annapolis, Maryland in 2018. After his arrest, Ramos told a psychiatrist that he had resigned himself to pleading guilty and spending the rest of his life in prison until he realized that he might have more access to computers and the Internet in a psychiatric hospital than in a prison. Accordingly, after studying the DSM-5, Ramos chose to plead not criminally responsible (Maryland's version of the insanity plea), an option that he described to the psychiatrist as being "useful." You can access this aspect of the case here.

Treatment of Psychological Disorders 13

The examples provided in this chapter are meant to illustrate various treatment methods, not to evaluate them. Although research on the outcome of psychological and medical treatments does suggest that certain approaches are more efficacious than others for particular kinds of disorders, we have chosen not to include examples of that research. Our goal is simply to provide examples that characterize various treatments, while leaving it to you to decide how and when to describe and discuss what clinical psychological scientists have discovered about empirically supported therapies, the relative value of empirical and clinical evidence, and the need to take into account clients' personal backgrounds, preferences, and values. As is the case when teaching about psychological disorders, presenting examples of treatments for those disorders requires sensitivity to the fact that some of your students and/or their families and friends have been, or may now be, participating in one of those treatments. With that in mind, we recommend that—except in the case of techniques that have been clearly identified as harmful—it is best to describe therapies in a way that does not appear to invalidate any particular approach or set of methods. At the same time, it is important to debunk the myth that the success of psychotherapy depends on exploring the events of early childhood.

Psychoanalytic/Psychodynamic Therapy

Free Association

1. During a psychoanalytic therapy session, Lena (not her real name) described her reaction to a man she met at a weekend continuing education course. "He was a jerk. I guess he thought he was hot stuff. I wondered if he was coming on to me, but I think he was like that with several women. Shameless. Greasy. I don't know why he bothered me so, I didn't even really get to know him." After a few

moments of silence, she said, "I don't know why I thought of this, but I just remembered standing in our bathroom when I was growing up, holding my father's comb."

The fact that thoughts about meeting a man at a medical course led to memories about holding her father's comb could have significance. It could mean that the characteristics of the man she met there reminded her of her father (e.g., greasy black hair, inappropriately flirtatious with women). The therapist asks Lena to consider the possible connections by engaging in further free association about the man, the comb, and her father.

[Source: Bernstein, D.A., Teachman, B.A., Olatunji, B.O., & Lilienfeld, S.O. (2021). *Introduction to clinical psychology: Bridging science and practice* (9th ed.) Cambridge: Cambridge University Press.]

2. A transcript of free association by an actual client is available here.

Analysis of Everyday Behavior

1. Here is one of Freud's first published examples of a parapraxis, or slip of the tongue:

   Freud wrote about a case of a young man who misquoted a Latin phrase to him. It was from *The Aeneid*, when a character cries out for vengeance. The actual line is "Exoriare aliquis nostris ex ossibus ultor," which translates as "Let someone arise as an avenger from my bones," but the young man said, "Exoriare ex nostris ossibus ultor," or "Let an avenger arise from my bones."

   Freud felt that the suppression of the "aliquis," was significant; the man must have some bad association with it. He asked the man to free associate to the word, and got a string of words starting with relics and liquid, meandering through different saints, and then finally ending with a saint Januarius, whose blood, kept in a vial, was supposed to turn to liquid once every year. The man then confessed that his girlfriend had missed her period. Freud concluded that he had blocked out the word, associated with saints, calendars, and blood, that reminded him of the pregnancy scare.

   [Example retrieved here.]

2. In 1991, Senator Ted Kennedy included an infamous slip-up in a televised speech. "Our national interest ought to be to encourage the breast," he paused, then corrected himself, "the best and the brightest." The fact that his hands were suggestively cupping the air as he spoke made the error especially ripe for consideration as a "Freudian slip." (The moment is included in one of the video links listed below.)
3. Other contemporary examples of "Freudian" slips of the tongue, are available here.

4. Several other parapraxes are available here, but be aware that many of them are quite explicitly sexual in nature.

5. Very short videos of examples of funny parapraxes by politicians, sportscasters, and other media figures are available here, here, and here.

Dream Analysis

1. Lisa, a student, shares a dream with her therapist in which she is in the back seat of a moving car that has no driver. The stoplight ahead turns red, and she is unable stop the car. The therapist helps Lisa break down the manifest content into the following symbols: moving car, back seat, red light, and loss of brakes. Through the process of free association, Lisa shares whatever comes to mind when thinking about each symbol. The therapist interprets these associations and offers potential meanings. Lisa and her therapist decide that the dream represents the unconscious conflict she has felt about choosing a career. She reveals that her parents want her to study medicine and that she has not yet told them she wants to become a writer. The therapist suggests that the runaway car is on a path to a future she does not desire. Until she gets into the driver's seat, she will not be able to stop it. This interpretation fits for Lisa, and she decides to tell her parents about her career aspirations.

   [Example retrieved here.]

2. This dream, presented by Freud, illustrates the fact that interpretation cannot depend on the content of a dream alone.

   > The following [is the] dream of a Munich physician in the year 1910. I select it because it goes to show how impossible of understanding a dream generally is before the dreamer has given us what information he has about it. I suspect that at bottom you consider the ideal dream interpretation that in which one simply inserts the meaning of the symbols, and would like to lay aside the technique of free association to the dream elements. I wish to disabuse your minds of this harmful error.

On July 13, 1910, toward morning, I dreamed that I was bicycling down a street in Tübingen, when a brown Dachshund tore after me and caught me by the heel. A bit further on I get off, seat myself on a step, and begin to beat the beast, which has clenched its teeth tight. (I feel no discomfort from the biting or the whole scene.) Two elderly ladies are sitting opposite me and watching me with grins on their faces. Then I wake up and, as so often happens to me, the whole dream becomes perfectly clear to me in this moment of transition to the waking state.

Symbols are of little use in this case. The dreamer, however, informs us, 'I lately fell in love with a girl, just from seeing her on the street, but had no means of becoming acquainted with her. The most pleasant means might have been the Dachshund, since I am a great lover of animals, and also felt that the girl was in sympathy with this characteristic.' He also adds that he repeatedly interfered in the fights of scuffling dogs with great dexterity and frequently to the great amazement of the spectators. Thus we learn that the girl, who pleased him, was always accompanied by this particular dog. This girl, however, was disregarded in the manifest dream, and there remained only the dog which he associates with her. Perhaps the elderly ladies who simpered at him took the place of the girl. The remainder of what he tells us is not enough to explain this point. Riding a bicycle in the dream is a direct repetition of the remembered situation. He had never met the girl with the dog except when he was on his bicycle.
[Example retrieved here.]

3. Descriptions of dreams and how they might be interpreted by Freudian psychoanalysts are available here and here.

4. A case study of brief psychodynamic therapy with a 54 year-old woman is available here.

5. A case study of the use of insight-oriented psychodynamic therapy with a 28 year-old graduate student is available for free download here.

Behavior Therapy

Functional Analysis of Behavior

1. Pretreatment assessment using the SORC approach (stimulus, organism, response, consequence).

Area assessed	General examples	Specific examples for a client diagnosed with bulimia (binging/purging type)
Stimulus	Antecedent conditions and environmental triggers that elicit behavior	Watching commercials about food, selecting clothing, walking by the refrigerator, smelling chocolate, hearing her parents arguing
Organism (person)	Internal physiological responses, emotions, and cognitions	Sensation of hunger, anxiety, concern about weight, worry about being fat, anger over being deprived, fears she might lose control
Response	Overt behavior engaged in by the person	Avoidance of food for a few hours (adding to feeling of deprivation), followed by binging
Consequences	What happens as a result of the behavior	Satiation, increase in guilt and anxiety about weight gain, and renewed plans to restrict eating

[Source: Bernstein, D.A., Teachman, B.A., Olatunji, B.O., & Lilienfeld S.O. (2021). *Introduction to clinical psychology: Bridging science and practice.* (9th ed.) Cambridge: Cambridge University Press.]

2. Pretreatment assessment using ABC approach (antecedent, behavior, consequences):

Antecedent	Behavior	Short-term consequences	Long-term consequences
Argument with spouse	Meet friend at a local bar, drink to excess	Forget for a while about marital problems and unemployment	Was hung over so didn't look for a job the next day, wasted more money, and spouse is now even more angry

[Example based on Bernstein, D.A., Teachman, B.A., Olatunji, B.O., & Lilienfeld, S.O. (2021). *Introduction to clinical psychology: Bridging science and practice.* (9th ed.) Cambridge: Cambridge University Press.]

Exposure Treatment of Anxiety: Systematic Desensitization

1. A 15-min video presenting an example of the progressive relaxation training used in systematic desensitization is available here.

2. A 3-min video example of progressive relaxation-style methods is available here.

3. Five- to six-minute videos of virtual reality desensitization/exposure for fear of flying and for panic disorder are available here and here.

4. A case example of using virtual reality desensitization to treat fear of sharks is available here.
   From the abstract:

   Self-report "... psychometric instruments exhibited a discernable reduction in fear toward sharks. Such gains were maintained at a 12-month follow-up.... This initial study revealed the potential of VR for the treatment of marine biota phobia and its potential to recreate diverse situations for exposure therapy."
   [*Note:* You might want to use this case example to stimulate discussion of the appropriateness of helping people not to fear being in the water with a potentially dangerous animal.]

Exposure Treatment of Anxiety: Graded Exposure In Vivo, with or without Therapist Modeling

1. Hierarchy of activities for a client with a fear of driving, arranged from most to least anxiety-provoking (client would start with the least distressing activity):

Anticipated fear level (1–10)	Exposure activity
10	Merge on and off busy highways alone during rush hour (with no GPS)
9	Drive alone across a busy bridge
8	Drive alone on the highway to a new destination (following GPS)
7	Drive on the highway to a new destination (following GPS) with a friend to help navigate
7	Drive alone to a new destination (following GPS)—no highway driving

(continued)

(continued)

Anticipated fear level (1–10)	Exposure activity
6	Drive to a new destination (following GPS) with a friend to help navigate—no highway driving
5	Drive alone down a suburban street during the morning commute
4	Drive down a suburban street during the morning commute with a friend
4	Drive alone down a quiet suburban street at night
3	Drive down a quiet suburban street at night with a close friend in the car

[Example based on Bernstein, D.A., Teachman, B.A., Olatunji, B.O., & Lilienfeld, S.O. (2021). *Introduction to clinical psychology: Bridging science and practice*. (9th ed.) Cambridge: Cambridge University Press.]

2. Hierarchy of activities for a client with a fear of negative social evaluation, arranged from most to least anxiety-provoking (client would start at the lowest level):

Anticipated fear level (1–10)	Exposure activity
10	Spill a drink on your shirt while talking to a new person
9	Ask X (a potential romantic interest) out for coffee
7	Go to a party where you only know a few people
7	Raise your hand in a class discussion to offer an opinion that could be controversial
6	Ask Y (an acquaintance from psychology class) out for coffee
5	Raise your hand in class when you feel mostly but not totally sure of the answer to a question
4	Go out to dinner with friends
3	Say hello to a person who sits nearby in history class (don't know the person's name)
3	Say hello to a stranger at the bus stop

[Example based on Bernstein, D.A., Teachman, B.A., Olatunji, B.O., & Lilienfeld, S.O. (2021). *Introduction to clinical psychology: Bridging science and practice*. (9th ed.) Cambridge: Cambridge University Press.]

3. Hierarchy of activities for a client with panic disorder, arranged from most to least anxiety-provoking (client would start at the lowest level):

Anticipated fear level (1–10)	Exposure activity
10	Doing the full grocery shopping alone
9	Driving alone more than an hour from home
8	Driving more than an hour from home with your sons (who the client feels are too young to be much help in case of a panic attack)

(continued)

(continued)

Anticipated fear level (1–10)	Exposure activity
7	Driving more than an hour from home with your oldest daughter
7	Driving alone to a familiar destination (other than work)
6	Doing the full grocery shopping with your oldest daughter
5	Going to work all day with no benzodiazepine pills
4	Picking up one item from the grocery store alone
3	Picking up one item from the grocery store with your oldest daughter
3	Going to a meeting at work without benzodiazepine pills in hand

[Example based on Bernstein, D.A., Teachman, B.A., Olatunji, B.O., & Lilienfeld, S.O. (2021). *Introduction to clinical psychology: Bridging science and practice.* (9th ed.) Cambridge: Cambridge University Press.]

Exposure Treatment of Anxiety: Graduated, Extended Exposure and Flooding, with or without Therapist Modeling

1. A 12-min video showing graduated, but extended exposure treatment for a woman with snake phobia is available here.

2. A 5-min video showing graduated, but extended exposure treatment for a woman with a feather phobia is available here.

3. A 4-min video showing an extended exposure session with a client with claustrophobia is available here.

4. Here is an example of a flooding session with a client whose obsessive–compulsive disorder is focused on cleaning due to fear of contamination:

THERAPIST: (Outside the office.) There it is, behind the car. Let's go and touch the curb and street next to it. I don't think that you need to touch it directly because it's a bit smelly, but I want you to step next to it, then touch the sole of your shoe.

CLIENT: Yuck! It's really dead. It's gross!

T: Yeah, it is a bit gross, but it's also just a dead cat if you think about it plainly. What harm can it cause?
C: I don't know. Suppose I get germs on my hand?
T: What sort of germs?

C: Dead cat germs.
T: What kind are they?
C: I don't know. Just germs.
T: Like the bathroom germs that we've already handled?
C: Sort of. People don't go around touching dead cats.
T: They also don't go running home to shower or alcohol the inside of their car. It's time to get over this. Now, come on over and I'll do it first. (Client follows.) OK. Touch the curb and the street. Here's a stone you can carry with you and a piece of paper from under its tail. Go ahead, take it.
C: (Looking quite uncomfortable) Ugh!
T: We'll both hold them. Now, touch it to your front and your skirt, and your face and hair. Like this. That's good. What's your anxiety level?
C: Ugh! 99. I'd say 100, but it's just short of panic. If you weren't here, it'd be 100.
T: You know from past experience that this will be much easier in a while. Just stay with it and we'll wait here. You're doing fine.
C: (A few minutes pass in which she looks very upset.) Would you do this if it weren't for me?
T: Yes, if this were my car and I dropped my keys here, I'd just pick them up and go on.
C: You wouldn't have to wash them?
T: No. Dead animals aren't delightful, but they're part of the world we live in. What are the odds that we'll get ill from this?
C: Very small, I guess... I feel a little bit better than at first. It's about 90 now.
T: Good! Just stay with it now.

The session continues for another 45 min as the client recognizes that she can tolerate the distress and that the feared outcomes do not occur. During this period, conversation focuses generally on the feared situation and the client's reactions to it. The therapist inquires about the client's anxiety level approximately every 10 min.

T: How do you feel now?
C: Well, it is easier, but I sure don't feel great.
T: Can you put a number on it?
C: About 55 or 60, I'd say.
T: You worked hard today. You must be tired. Let's stop now. I want you to take this stick and pebble with you so that you continue to be contaminated. You can keep them in your pocket and touch them frequently during the day.
I want you to contaminate your office at work and your apartment with them. Touch them to everything around, including everything in the kitchen, chairs,

your bed, and the clothes in your dresser. Oh, also, I'd like you to drive your car past this spot on your way to and from work. Can you do that?

C: I suppose so. The trouble is going home with all of this dirt.

T: Why don't you call your husband and plan to get home after he does, so he can be around to help you. Remember, you can always call me if you have any trouble.

C: Yeah. That's a good idea. I'll just leave work after he does. See you tomorrow.

[Example adapted from Franklin, M. E., & Foa, E. B. (2014). Obsessive–compulsive disorder. In D. H. Barlow (Ed.), *Clinical handbook of psychological disorders: A step-by-step treatment manual*. New York, NY: Guilford Press.]

Operant Conditioning Treatment Methods

(*Note*: More general examples of the use of operant conditioning are presented in the chapter on learning.)

1. This website includes 3–4 min videos that provide summaries of the background and use of applied behavior analysis (mainly positive reinforcement) in the treatment of various kinds of behavior problems.
2. A 6-min video showing the use of token reinforcement systems with children with autism spectrum disorder is available here and another (3-min) video is available here.

3. This 4-min video shows therapists using a "bug in the ear" device to provide parents with live guidance in using positive reinforcement to strengthen their children's appropriate behavior.

4. A 90-s video showing the use of a classroom token economy system to support appropriate student behavior is available here.

5. An example of research on the value of a token economy system for improving the negative symptoms of schizophrenia in hospitalized patients is available here.

6. An example of shaping to develop desirable behavior in a young boy with autism spectrum disorder is available here.

7. A very interesting 10-min video shows the use of shaping in helping patients who have had a stroke or brain injury to regain movement.

8. Examples of the principles and procedures involved in using time-out to decrease inappropriate behavior in children are available here.

9. Some basic examples of how punishment and aversive conditioning have been used to decrease undesirable behavior are available here.

10. An example of the controversies associated with the use of punishment to alter the behavior of seriously disordered clients is available here.

Cognitive and Cognitive-Behavior Therapy

Cognitive Distortions and Self-defeating Thoughts

1. Examples of maladaptive automatic thoughts

Cognitive distortion category	Examples of automatic thoughts
Dichotomous (all-or-none) thinking	If I can't be famous, I'll be a total failure
Overgeneralization	He unfriended me—that shows that no one likes me
Catastrophizing	They didn't hire me—I'll never get a decent job and I'll never be happy
Personalization	Everyone thinks it's my fault that we lost
Selective Abstraction (magnification, minimization, disqualifying the positive)	I got one "needs improvement" and ten "goods" in that evaluation—I'm failing
Jumping to conclusions	When she said, "some people are just clueless," she was referring to me
Mind reading	He hated my presentation
Fortune-telling error	I know I'm going to blow the test next week
Emotional reasoning	I feel guilty—I must be a bad person I'm scared of airplanes—it must be dangerous to fly
Unrealistic expectations	Everyone should like me

(continued)

(continued)

Cognitive distortion category	Examples of automatic thoughts
"Should" and "must" statements	I should act happy all the time
Labeling	I'm a loser
	She's an idiot

[Source: Bernstein, D.A., Teachman, B.A., Olatunji, B.O., & Lilienfeld, S.O. (2021). *Introduction to clinical psychology: Bridging science and practice*. (9th ed.) Cambridge: Cambridge University Press.]

2. Examples of attributional tendencies of depressed people and cognitive restructuring to create more adaptive attributions:

Event	Internal, stable, global (maladaptive) attributions characteristic of depressed people	Examples of more adaptive attributions characteristic of nondepressed people
I was home all weekend and no one called me	It's because of me, it's because I'm not likeable, I never will be likeable, and this will affect all my relationships	People are busy right before the holidays (external attribution) I often work on weekends, and my friends know this; that's why they didn't call (unstable attribution) I have a few close friends, so clearly some people like me (specific attribution)
I got a bad grade on my math test	I'm dumb and no good at things	The test was unfairly difficult (external attribution) I didn't study much for this test (unstable attribution) I'm not so hot in math, but I'm good in other subjects (specific attribution)

[Source: Bernstein, D.A., Teachman, B.A., Olatunji, B.O., & Lilienfeld, S.O. (2021). *Introduction to clinical psychology: Bridging science and practice*. (9th ed.) Cambridge: Cambridge University Press.]

3. Worksheets of the kind that cognitive-behavior therapists use in guiding clients to identify maladaptive core beliefs, to generate thoughts to challenges those beliefs, and to engage in cognitive restructuring are available for download here and here.

4. A summary case study of using cognitive behavior therapy with a 32 year-old female combat veteran is available here.

5. A very short transcript of a CBT therapist helping a client to identify automatic thoughts is available here.

6. An elaborate case study of the use of CBT with a 9 year-old boy is available here.

7. A 6-min video of Aaron Beck summarizing his cognitive restructuring efforts with a depressed man is available here.

8. A quick summary of the basics of cognitive-behavior therapy and the goals of cognitive restructuring is available here but be aware that the speaker brings in a number of other concepts that are not fully explained in the clip.

9. A 2-min video illustrating the use of behavioral activation as part of cognitive therapy for depression is available here.

10. A 9-min interview with Albert Ellis provides a basic introduction to Rational Emotive Behavior Therapy (REBT) here.

11. The following transcript from 2006 contains a bit of profanity but provides an excellent example of how Albert Ellis conducted REBT sessions, in this case with a woman who suffered from panic attacks. She has just said "I'm a very anxious person—I have difficulty getting on subways, because I'm afraid of them, I can't sleep at night because of panic attacks, I have a lot of anxiety about being alone in a small room."

Ellis: What are you telling yourself to make yourself panicked?
Client: I feel as if I'm telling myself I am in some sort of danger.
Ellis: What's the danger? I used to travel all the time on the subway and never got hurt once.
Client: I think the danger is very much in my head. When I get on the subway, if someone looks at me funny, I feel they are out to get me.
Ellis: You're inventing danger. Now, what is the real danger of being in the subway? Which millions of people do every day.
Client: I can't get out—if something does happen, I can't get out of that subway.
Ellis: If something happens, what will then happen? Suppose something happens—will you die? What will happen?
Client: I'm more afraid that someone's going to start shooting up the place, and I'm gonna be dead. These thoughts go through my head a lot.

Ellis: So you'll be dead! Then you'll have nothing to worry about! What can you tell yourself not to be afraid of the subway, or anything that's closed like that?

Client: I think I can tell myself that my fear is irrational, because there is evidence that NY City has one of the safest subway systems in the country, and if something were to happen, the likelihood of me getting hurt is not very high.

Ellis: It's very, very low. How do the rest of us survive? You have to prove to yourself over and over that nothing terrible happens. Nothing. And it's very, very unlikely that something will happen, statistically. Right.

Client: What about when I'm in my bed at night, sleeping alone? It's a really small room, when I lie there alone at night, I have racing thoughts, and before I know it, I'm in the middle of a panic attack, and am unable to bring myself out of it.

Ellis: Because you are telling yourself what?

Client: Sometimes I feel like I'm going to die in there, and no one will find out about it.

Ellis: How come you haven't died yet?

Client: Because I'm healthy.

Ellis: Yeah—but if you say, "I'm gonna die! I'm gonna die! How terrible!", then you'll bring on panic. And then you'll get panicked about your panic. And then you're gone. So, tell yourself, "If I die, I'll die! Fuck it! I'll rest in peace!" Then you won't worry about anything. Let's give you Rational Emotive Imagery. Close your eyes and imagine the worst. You panic in the subway—you panic, panic, panic, and everybody sees that you panic and they think you're no good. So, can you imagine that?

Client: Yes.

Ellis: And how do you feel?

Client: I feel as if they can see my weakness. They can see that I'm afraid.

Ellis: So, let's suppose they all see you trembling; they all see you're very afraid. Then what?

Client: Then, they can figure out that I'm vulnerable and easy to hurt.

Ellis: Suppose they figure out that you're vulnerable. Then, what are they gonna do?

Client: I have a bizarre fear of being raped, as well.

Ellis: How many people get raped in a crowded subway?

Client: You have a very good way to dispute my beliefs. That is true. Not many.

Ellis: What can you tell yourself to be displeased and sorry if anything happens, but not panicked? What can you tell you?

Client: That I am over-reacting.

Ellis: Right.

Client: That I am being irrational.

Ellis: Right.

Client: That I need to realize that there is evidence against my thoughts.

Ellis: Right.
Client: My thoughts are actually wrong.
[Source: REBT Network, retrieved here.]

12. A classic 30-min video from 1965 is part of the famous "Gloria" sessions. This one shows Albert Ellis demonstrating Rational Emotive Behavior Therapy (see the section below on humanistic approaches to treatment for links to interviews by Carl Rogers and Fritz Perls; the entire set of three videos is available here and a quite valuable 9-minute comparison of the three is available here).

13. A more contemporary 4-min video example of REBT, this time with a woman dealing with guilt related to the suicide of a loved one, is available here.

14. An extensive case study using Acceptance and Commitment Therapy (ACT) with a 16 year-old African–American client with sickle cell anemia is available here.

15. Transcripts from an ACT session and a Behavioral Activation treatment session, both for depression in young women, is available here.

16. A 3-min video showing ACT techniques is available here.

17. This 10-min video role-play shows a therapist explaining the basic principles of ACT to a client using an effective physical analogy.

18. A series of 1–3-min videos illustrating Dialectical Behavior Therapy techniques is available here. These techniques, which include reducing body temperature, intense exercise, paced breathing, muscle relaxation and other methods aimed at meeting the goals of emotional regulation, are an important part of DBT. Somewhat longer videos on the site demonstrate techniques for distress tolerance and crisis survival skills.

19. An article here provides a straightforward comparison of the similarities and differences between cognitive behavior therapy and mindfulness-based cognitive therapy, and includes this helpful chart (CBT is in the left-hand column):

Focused on new ways to look at stressful situations	Focused on new ways of being with stressful situations
Focused on negative thoughts and beliefs	Recognises negative thoughts but focused on paying attention to present
Carefully mentally reframing thoughts	Noticing thoughts and accepting them
Pushing out negative thoughts	Letting negative thoughts drift through the mind without judgement or attachment
Working to disprove and decrease the power of negative thoughts	Noticing thoughts and feelings without trying to fix them
Charting and analysing reactions	Breathing through reactions
Analysing thoughts	Experiencing thoughts
Way of thinking	Way of being with one's thoughts
I am [angry, upset]	I am having the thought [that I am angry, upset]
Constantly noticing thoughts	Constantly noticing what is around you in the now moment

20. This 9-min video summarizes the goals of mindfulness-based cognitive therapy and then, at about the 3-min mark, asks the viewer to engage in an exercise in which they use mindfulness-based methods to deal with worry about current events (it was shot during the Covid-19 pandemic). This exercise might help your students experience first-hand what mindfulness-based cognitive therapy involves but be sure to warn them about what the video entails so that anyone who might begin worrying about some especially serious or traumatic source of anxiety has the opportunity to opt out.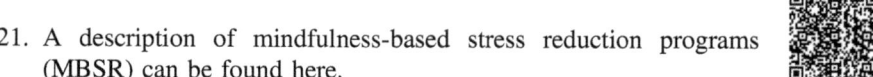

21. A description of mindfulness-based stress reduction programs (MBSR) can be found here.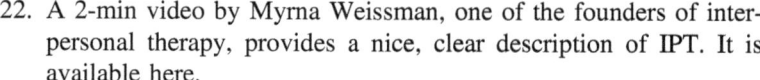

22. A 2-min video by Myrna Weissman, one of the founders of interpersonal therapy, provides a nice, clear description of IPT. It is available here.

23. An extensive case example of the use of interpersonal therapy for irritability, sleep disturbance, and interpersonal conflicts is available here. Here is the abstract of the article:

Interpersonal Psychotherapy (IPT), a time-limited, evidence-based treatment, has shown efficacy in treating major depressive disorder and other psychiatric conditions. Interpersonal Psychotherapy focuses on the patient's current life events and social and interpersonal functioning for understanding and treating symptoms. This case report demonstrates the novel use of IPT as treatment for posttraumatic stress disorder (PTSD). Preliminary evidence suggests IPT may relieve PTSD symptoms without focusing on exposure to trauma reminders. Thus IPT may offer an alternative for patients who refuse (or do not respond to) exposure-based approaches. Interpersonal Psychotherapy focuses on two problem areas that specifically affect patients with PTSD: interpersonal difficulties and affect dysregulation. This case report describes a pilot participant from a study comparing 14 weekly sessions of IPT to treatment with two other psychotherapies. We describe the session-by-session IPT protocol, illustrating how to formulate the case, help the patient identify and address problematic affects and interpersonal functioning, and to monitor treatment response.

[Reference: Rafaeli, A. K., & Markowitz, J. C. (2011). Interpersonal psychotherapy (IPT) for PTSD: a case study. American Journal of Psychotherapy, 65(3), 205–223.]

24. This 2-min video provides an example of how an interpersonal therapist works with a client with depression. You might want to draw your students' attention to the fact that the therapist's interviewing and rapport-building methods reflect those of Carl Rogers.

Social Skills Training

1. Examples of assertive communications are available here.

2. A good overview of the basics of assertiveness is presented here.

3. An example of the positive effects of social skills training for social anxiety disorder in adults is available here.

4. An example of the positive effects of social skills training for social anxiety disorder in adolescents can be found here.

5. An example of using social skills training to develop life skills in schizophrenia patients is available here.

Humanistic Therapy

Client-Centered (Person-Centered) Therapy

1. This 2-min video shows Carl Rogers explaining in simple terms the basics of his therapy approach.

2. An extensive example of client-centered therapy methods in an interview with a young man faced with questions about his career is presented here.

3. A classic 45-min video presents Carl Rogers interviewing "Gloria" to illustrate client centered therapy.

4. This 9-min video, recorded in 1960, is from Carl Rogers's archive of pioneering films of actual treatment sessions. It illustrates his basic methods and shows how those methods lead to a client discovering things for herself rather than being told what to consider. The video is black-and-white and a bit grainy, the soundtrack synchronization is not perfect, and there are Spanish subtitles for some reason, but it has genuine historical value and is far superior to most of the role-played examples available on the Internet.

Gestalt Therapy

1. A classic 30-min video presents Fritz Perls interviewing "Gloria" to illustrate Gestalt therapy. The video is notable when compared to the interviews of this same client by Carl Rogers and Albert Ellis because it is the only one in which she appears to show aspects of her genuine self.

2. A series of transcripts from sessions of Gestalt therapy for various kinds of couple communication problems is available here. They illustrate a wide variety of Gestalt methods, including role-playing and the empty chair technique.

Motivational Interviewing

1. This 9-min video illustrates the basics of motivational interviewing with a woman who feels she is starting to drink too much alcohol.

Humanistic Therapy

2. A 5-min video example of motivational interviewing is available here. This one provides a voice-over narrative describing what the interviewer is trying to do during the session. The last two minutes of the video shows the interviewer discussing with a colleague the goals of motivational interviewing procedures.

Medical Treatments

Psychoactive Drugs

1. An example of the use of ketamine to treat a case of depression in a 27 year-old man is available here.

2. Seventeen examples of the use of high doses of baclofen (a muscle relaxant) for the treatment of alcohol use disorder are presented here.

3. A case study example of the pros and cons of combining medication (anti-anxiety and antidepressant drugs) with psychotherapy for panic attacks is presented here.

4. An example of the use of SSRIs for the treatment of depression in a 77 year-old man with dementia is presented here.

5. A 3-min video of a young woman describing her experiences with antidepressant medication and psychotherapy is available here. You will want to ask your students to listen carefully because the woman speaks softly, and with an English accent. For example, when she mentions having CFS (chronic fatigue syndrome) as well as depression, her words are hard to understand. You should probably watch the video a couple of times in order to familiarize yourself with it before playing it in class.

6. A 2-min video showing clients discussing the pros and cons of taking antidepressant medications is available here.

7. Here is an example of the use of ketamine for anxiety presented as part of a more general discussion of the drug and its applications.

8. An example of the use of cannabidiol (CBD) versus placebo in the treatment of social anxiety disorder in teenage clients is presented here.

9. A 14-min video in which a young woman describes her extensive experience with many kinds of psychotropic medications is available here. It is likely to stimulate a lively classroom discussion.

10. A detailed case study of the use of various antipsychotic medications for a 31 year-old African American woman with violent tendencies, and the complexities involved in managing these medications over time is presented here.

11. Similar complexities involved with switching antipsychotic medications are described for a fictional schizophrenia patient here.

12. A summary of potential side effects of antipsychotic medications is presented here.

13. Short (1-min or less) videos of various movement disorders associated with antipsychotic drugs in certain patients are available here. Scroll down through the web page for the videos.

Electroconvulsive Shock

1. An example of the successful use of electroconvulsive shock therapy (ECT) in the case of Kitty Dukakis is described here.

2. Here is a 4-min video with a young woman whose depression did not respond to drugs but was greatly improved following ECT.

3. This 6-min video clip shows two depressed patients' experiences with ECT. One of them focuses on the treatment's benefits while the other, while improved, focuses on statistics about relatively rare negative side effects.

4. A 6-min proprietary video promoting the value of ECT and presenting endorsements by patients who benefitted from it is available here.

5. A case example in which a 33 year-old woman with depression developed symptoms of mania following ECT is available here.

Medical Treatments

6. A 2-min video comparing induction of seizures via ECT and magnetic seizure therapy (MST) is available here.

Brain Stimulation

1. An example of the use of transcranial magnetic stimulation (TMS) for depression in a 31 year-old man is described in detail here.

2. Six case examples of the use of repetitive transcranial magnetic stimulation (rTMS) to reduce relapse following electroconvulsive shock therapy for depression are presented here.

3. A woman describes the benefits she received from TMS in a 3-min video available here.

4. A 2-min video showing the TMS treatment of a depressed adult woman as part of a research study is available here.

5. A set of 4-min videos describing the TMS treatment of a depressed, suicidal man and a 59 year-old woman is available here. Be aware that these and other similar videos are created by medical facilities that offer TMS for profit.

Psychosurgery

1. Stories about the early history of lobotomies are available here in an NPR piece.

Other Physical Treatments

1. Multiple case examples of the use of Reduced Environmental Stimulation Therapy (REST), which involves flotation in salt water, are described here.

Social Psychology

14

Because human beings are inherently social, the first things that students of any foreign language are taught is how to say "hello," "how are you?," and "goodbye." It is no wonder, then, that social psychology is a subfield that has high interest for students. They are especially eager to learn about such topics as first impressions, prejudice and discrimination, interpersonal attraction, conformity/compliance/obedience, and aggression. The examples in this chapter are meant to illuminate these and other topics in social psychology while also providing targets for class discussions about the reliability, validity, generalizability, and replicability of the research results that have long defined this field. For additional examples and other material that will enhance your social psychology course or the social psychology unit of introductory psychology, we recommend a visit to the Social Psychology Network here.

Identity Theory

1. To help your students recognize examples of personal identity versus social identity, ask them to fill in the blank in the following sentence: I am a(n) ___.

    - Responses such as "good athlete" or "honor student," or "psychology major" or "responsible person" would be examples of personal identity because they focus on the person's individuality.
    - Responses such as "father" or "Hispanic American" or "Republican" or "social justice warrior" would be examples of social identity.

2. Examples of the strength of social identity in altering attitudes and actions with respect to ingroups and outgroups can be seen in the sections below on stereotypes, prejudice, and discrimination.
3. Examples of the strength of social identity in altering behavior can be seen in:
    - sports bars, where fans display devotion to "their" team by wearing team-related clothing and cheering wildly while watching the team on TV and taunting fans of opposing teams.
    - the time, money, or effort that people spend to help family members, friends, fellow citizens, or just fellow humans in times of trouble, need, or natural disaster.
    - conflicts in which people who identify with different countries, ethnic groups, or religions seek to kill each other in declared or undeclared wars.

First Impressions

1. A company president was having lunch with a man being considered for an executive position. When the man salted his food without first tasting it, the president decided not to hire him. The reason, she explained, was that the company had no room for a person who acted before collecting all relevant information.
2. This Dilbert cartoon illustrates the fact that first impressions may not always be accurate.

Self-fulfilling Prophecies

1. If a teacher inadvertently spends less time helping children who at first seemed "dull," those children may not learn as much, thus fulfilling the teacher's impression.
2. Conversely, teachers and coaches and parents who communicate high expectations for academic or athletic performance from youngsters often find that performance rises to meet those expectations.
3. If someone starts a false rumor that the bank is about to close for lack of funds, customers are likely to panic, and they will all want to withdraw all their money at the same time before the bank runs out of money. When this highly abnormal "run on the bank" occurs, the bank may not have enough cash on hand to cover all the withdrawals, and thus actually does fail. In this case, a false belief led to its own fulfillment.

4. A jealous partner in a romantic relationship may bombard the other partner with accusations of infidelity until the relationship becomes so unpleasant for that partner that he or she—though previously faithful—now starts cheating and thus fulfills the prophesy.
5. If people who hold ethnic or racial or religious prejudices expect, say, unpleasant or aggressive behavior from people in the disliked groups, they may behave in defensive, hostile ways toward members of those groups, thus eliciting correspondingly negative reactions that fulfill the prejudice-driven prophesy.
6. Many people with depression hold beliefs that, for example, they are worthless and that others don't like them. These thoughts may lead them to behave in ways that other people find unattractive, thus causing them to avoid the depressed person and therefore fulfill that person's prophesy about what others think of them.
7. A job candidate who expects that there is little chance of being hired may behave in sufficiently unimpressive ways as to bring about the predicted result.
8. In an experiment, men and women in adjoining rooms participated in "get acquainted" conversations over an intercom system. Before the conversations took place, the men were shown a photograph of the woman who was supposedly going to be their conversation partner. Some saw a photo of an obese woman while others saw a woman of normal weight, but none of the photos actually depicted the women in the next room. Independent judges who had not seen any of the research participants listened to recordings of the conversations and made ratings of the women's behavior and personality traits. The women who had talked to men who thought they were of normal weight were rated as more articulate, lively, interesting, exciting, and fun to be with than were the women whose conversation partner thought they were obese. These results suggested that when men thought they were talking to a woman of normal weight, they were more friendly and engaging than when talking to a woman who they thought was obese, and that these differences in the men's behavior drew correspondingly different behavior from the women.
[Reference: Snyder, M., & Haugen, J. A. (1995). Why does behavioral confirmation occur? A functional perspective on the role of the target. *Personality and Social Psychology Bulletin, 21*, 963–974.]

Attribution and Attributional Errors

Internal Versus External Attribution

1. Your friend borrows a jacket but fails to return it in time for you to wear it to an important event. You get angry because you think your friend is irresponsible and inconsiderate (internal attribution), or you worry that something bad must have happened to keep your friend from returning the jacket (external attribution).
2. You failed an exam and feel angry at yourself because you know you didn't study enough (internal attribution), or you are furious at the professor for writing such difficult questions (external attribution).
3. Your romantic partner forgot your birthday and you are sure it is because he or she doesn't love you anymore (internal attribution), or you realize that your partner is dealing with a lot of family stress right now and was too distracted (external attribution).
4. A co-worker does not invite you to her wedding and you decide it's because she doesn't like you (internal attribution), or you realize that her budget is tight and she is only inviting family members (external attribution).
5. When your friend's business failed, you tell yourself that this was predictable because your friend is too disorganized to do well in business (internal attribution), or that the failure was one of thousands during a major economic downturn (external attribution).

Fundamental Attribution Error

1. You get an e-mail message full of errors in spelling and grammar and you assume that the sender is uneducated or careless (internal attribution) without considering any possible external factors, such as not being a native English-speaker (external attribution).
2. A fellow student makes a mess of an in-class presentation and you see the student as incompetent, careless, and unmotivated (internal attribution) without considering external factors that might have disrupted the presentation or prevented adequate preparation (external attribution).
3. A group of customers at a nearby restaurant table gets into a shouting match with their server over an incorrect order and you tell yourself that their behavior is characteristic of people from their racial or ethnic group (internal attribution) rather than considering the possibility that they had been badly mistreated by the server (external attribution).
4. You see someone driving recklessly and assume that the driver is hyperaggressive and obnoxious (internal attribution), without considering the possibility that that driver is trying to get to a hospital as fast as possible with an injured person or a woman in labor (external attribution).

5. Your neighbor's unlocked car was stolen last night, and you assume that the neighbor had it coming for being so careless (internal attribution), but you don't consider that he might have forgotten to lock the car because he was rushing home after hearing that his wife had suddenly taken ill (external attribution).
6. You read about a person being mugged at 3 am in a bad neighborhood and you assume that the victim is not smart enough to avoid being in a dangerous place in the middle of the night (internal attribution), without considering the possibility that the person was on his way to the only all-night pharmacy where medicine for a sick child was available (external attribution).
7. A psychologist and his friends were riding a Washington State ferry boat to one of the San Juan islands, when they noticed a man standing at the stern of the vessel looking out at the water with his arms extended over his head. The psychologist conjectured that the man might be delusional, and maybe thinks he is Jesus (internal attribution). This impressed the psychologist's friends until a flock of seagulls gathered to take the bits of bread the man was offering in his outstretched hands (external attribution).
8. A survey found that the strongest predictor of negative attitudes towards obesity is whether people see the condition as due to overeating and lack of exercise (internal attribution) rather than to genetics (external attribution).
[Reference: Hansson, L.M. & Rasmussen, F. (2014). Attitudes towards obesity in the Swedish general population: The role of one's own body size, weight satisfaction, and controllability beliefs about obesity. *Body Image, 11*, 43–50.]

Ultimate Attribution Error

1. You read a news article about a person of color who graduated from college with top honors despite having grown up in poverty and you say to yourself, Sure, look at all the special help available to 'them' (external attribution), but when a person from the same group is arrested, you assume the person—or perhaps everyone in the person's group—is just dishonest (internal attribution).
2. When asked to explain why students from certain immigrant groups were doing poorly in school, teachers in Germany made internal attributions (e.g., lack of intelligence) for the academic problems of disliked students (from Turkey), but not for students they liked (from Italy).
[Reference: Froehlich, L., Martiny, S. E., Deaux, K., & Mok, S. Y. (2016). "It's their responsibility, not ours": Stereotypes about competence and causal attributions for immigrants' academic underperformance. *Social Psychology, 47*(2), 74–86.]
3. Success by males at traditionally masculine tasks (e.g., target-shooting, math problems) may be attributed to ability (internal attribution), while failure is seen as the result of bad luck or lack of effort (external attribution). Success at such tasks by females may be attributed to luck (external attribution), while failure is attributed to lack of ability (internal attribution).
[Reference: Swim, J. K., & Sanna, L. J. (1996). He's skilled, she's lucky: A meta-analysis of observers' attributions for women's and men's successes and failures. *Personality and Social Psychology Bulletin, 22*(5), 507–519.]

4. A study found that when Hindus observed negative behaviors being displayed by other Hindus, they attributed those behaviors to external factors (such as being provoked), but they attributed the cause of those same behaviors among Muslims to character flaws (internal attribution). Muslims drew the same set of attributions when they observed the behavior of Hindus. That is, when Muslims observed negative behaviors being displayed by other Muslims, they attributed those behaviors to external factors (such as being provoked), but they attributed the cause of those same behaviors among Hindus to character flaws (internal attribution).
[Reference: Taylor, D.M. & Jaggi, V. (1974). Ethnocentrism and causal attribution in a South Indian context. *Journal of Cross-Cultural Psychology, 5,* 162–171.]
5. Seeing someone from your own racial group driving a fancy car, you wonder how the person earned the money to buy it, but seeing a person from a disliked outgroup driving the same kind of car, you wonder where the person stole it.

Actor-Observer Effect

1. When Australian students were asked why they sometimes drive too fast, they blamed circumstances, such as being late (external attribution), but saw other people's dangerous driving as a sign of aggressiveness or immaturity (internal attribution).
[Reference: Harré, N., Brandt, T., & Houkamau, C. (2004). An examination of the actor-observer effect in young drivers' attributions for their own and their friends' risky driving. *Journal of Applied Social Psychology, 34,* 806–824.]
2. When you're driving too slowly, it's because you are looking for an unfamiliar address (external attribution), not because you are a big loser like that overcautious jerk who crawled along in front of you yesterday (internal attribution).
3. Your doctor tells you that your cholesterol levels are too high, and you decide that the problem is caused by genetic factors (external attribution), but when a friend tells you that his cholesterol is too high, you tell him he should start exercising and eating a healthier diet (internal attribution).
4. You and your best friend both failed your last physics test. Thinking back, you recall that the testing room was hot and crowded, your pen was running out of ink, and someone nearby was driving you crazy with their coughing (external attributions). You are sure, however, that your friend failed because she is always skipping class, takes terrible notes, and only studies at the last minute (internal attribution).
5. A psychology professor got lousy ratings from her students this semester and so did one of her colleagues. She knows her colleague deserved those ratings because he is arrogant and a boring lecturer (internal attribution), but she is sure that her ratings were retaliation by unmotivated students who were mad at her for being demanding (external attribution).

Self-serving Bias

1. When you do well on an exam, you take personal credit for being smart and studious (internal attribution), but you blame your low scores on lack of study time or a bad teacher (external attribution).
2. If you win a big tennis match, you enjoy knowing that it was because you played better than your opponent (internal attribution), but if you lose you are sure it was because of bad calls by the umpire (external attribution).
3. You have just had a car accident. You know that it was caused by the other driver's carelessness (external attribution) because you are a good driver (internal attribution). The other driver says the same, except that, despite *his* careful driving, it was you who caused the accident through *your* carelessness.
4. If you get the great new job you interviewed for, you see it as confirmation of your stellar abilities and personal charm (internal attribution), but if you don't get the job, you see it as an obvious example of an employer who doesn't know how to choose the best people or who is biased against people like you (external attribution).
5. The manager of a clothing store takes personal credit for the store's record profits this quarter (internal attribution) but blames next quarter's losses on his unmotivated sales force (external attribution).
6. An example of reversed self-serving bias in people with depression: They may attribute their successes to luck or to people feeling sorry for them (external attribution) and their failures to negative characteristics such as lack of intelligence, unattractiveness, or the like (internal attribution).
7. This cartoon provides a nice illustration of self-serving bias. It shows a college student telling his professor that "I only failed the exam because you didn't cover the material while I was paying attention."
8. A Peanuts cartoon shows Linus asking Lucy "Why are you always so anxious to criticize me?," to which she replies, "I just think I have a knack for seeing other people's faults." Linus then asks, "But what about your own faults?!" and Lucy says, "I have a knack for overlooking them."

Cognitive Dissonance

1. You believe that texting while driving can be dangerous, but because you also know that you text while you drive, your attitude toward texting changes such that you do not see it as all that dangerous, especially for someone as careful as you are.
2. You believe that smoking can be harmful to health, but you also know that you smoke, so your attitude toward smoking changes such that you do not see it as all that dangerous for your own health because you don't smoke enough to cause harm.

3. You believe that it is not right to cheat on a romantic partner, but you also know that you occasionally cheat on your own romantic partner, so your attitude toward cheating changes such that you see it as a way of stabilizing the main relationship by providing needed sexual variety in your life.
4. You believe that lying is wrong, but you also know that you often tell lies when it suits your purpose, so your attitude toward lying changes such that you see it as a necessary evil that must be employed in order to succeed.
5. You believe that it is important to reduce air pollution and energy consumption, but you just bought a gasoline-powered, low fuel efficiency car, so your attitude toward being environmentally responsible changes such that you see the car one drives as being less impactful on the environment than one's home's energy efficiency or the number of children one has.
6. You believe that it is wrong to kill animals, but you enjoy eating beef and chicken, so your attitude toward the food processing system changes such that you focus on its vital role in supporting the economy and keeping millions of people employed.
7. You believe that for the good of the planet you should always recycle paper and plastic, but you know that you often don't bother to do so, so your attitude toward recycling changes such that you come to believe that others are recycling enough that your failure to do so doesn't really matter.
8. During the Covid-19 pandemic, you believed that the virus was a threat to everyone's health, but you didn't always wear a mask in public, so your attitude toward the virus changed such that you began to see it as no more dangerous than the flu.
9. You believe that being overweight is potentially dangerous for one's health, but you also know that you are significantly overweight, so your attitude toward being overweight changes such that you come to believe that health outcomes are based more on genetic factors than on eating habits.
10. You believe that a particular local cause is unworthy and stupid, but your romantic partner is an active member of a campaign for that cause and, after marching for the cause with your partner, your attitude toward the campaign becomes more positive.
11. A Dilbert cartoon provides a workplace example of how cognitive dissonance can alter one's attitudes. In it, after Dogbert highlights all the bad aspects of an employee's job, the employee searches for a reason why he works there and concludes "I love this job."

Ingroups and Outgroups

1. An example of the human readiness to negatively evaluate outgroups, even if grouping is not based on personal characteristics, is provided by a study of five-year-old children who were placed into two groups at random. Despite having no information regarding the relative status of the groups or any

competitive context, the children showed preferences for their own group and negative attitudes about and expectations of the other group. The children also systematically distorted incoming information by preferentially recalling positive information about in-group members as compared to outgroup members.
[Source: Dunham, Y, Baron, A.S., & Carey, S. (2011). Consequences of "minimal" group affiliations in children. *Child Development, 82,* 793–811.]
2. Results similar to the one above can be found here: Yee, M.D., & Brown, R. (1992). Self-evaluations and intergroup attitudes in children aged three to nine. *Child Development, 63,* 619–629.]
3. The famous blue-eyes brown-eyes story is described here.

4. In another illustration of the same minimal group bias effect with adults, research participants were told that they were assigned to one of two groups based only on their preferences for different types of photographs. In fact, the group assignments were random, but when the participants were asked to rate their own group and the other group on 19 personality traits (e.g., flexibility, kindness, and fairness), they rated their own group as significantly more positive than the other group.
[Source: Doise, W., Csepeli, G., Dann, H.D., Gouge, C., Larsen, K., & Ostell, A. (1972). An experimental investigation into the formation of intergroup representations. *European Journal of Social Psychology, 2,* 202–204.]
5. A 9-min video detailing the experimental procedures used in creating and measuring the consequences of minimal groups can be found here (an account is required for full access).

6. A drawing illustrates ingroup and outgroup perceptions of people living on opposite sides of a river. The positive characteristics of their group (e.g., "our great religion," "our noble populace") are described by the other group as negative ("their primitive superstition" and "their backward savages").

Stereotypes, Prejudice, and Discrimination

[*Note*: Examples of implicit prejudice and methods for assessing it are presented in the chapter on consciousness.]

1. Example of the impact of racial stereotypes: When photos of white or black men holding difficult-to-identify objects were briefly flashed on a video screen, research participants using video game "weapons" were supposed to "shoot" them, but only if they appeared to be armed. Stereotypes about whether white men or black men are more likely to be armed significantly affected the errors made by participants in firing their "weapons." Similar results appeared in a sample of police officers, although they were not as quick as civilians were to "shoot" an unarmed black man.

[References: Correll, J., Hudson, S. M., Guillermo, S., & Ma, D. S. (2014). The police officer's dilemma: A decade of research on racial bias in the decision to shoot. *Social and Personality Psychology Compass, 8*(5), 201–213.
Correll, J., Park, B., Judd, C. M., Wittenbrink, B., et al. (2007). Across the thin blue line: Police officers and racial bias in the decision to shoot. *Journal of Personality and Social Psychology, 92*, 1006–1023.]
2. The impact of racial stereotypes about potential criminal intent is exemplified in a news story about two black men being arrested at a Starbucks store for no apparent reason. It can be found here.
3. The learning of stereotypes. A study of the most popular TV shows in the United States found that members of racial and ethnic minority groups are underrepresented in the casts of these shows. When they do appear, they are often depicted in ways that are consistent with racial or ethnic stereotypes.
[Reference: Tukachinsky, R., Mastro, D., & Yarchi, M. (2015). Documenting portrayals of race/ethnicity on primetime television over a 20-year span and their association with national–level racial ethnic attitudes. *Journal of Social Issues, 71*, 17–38.]
4. An example of fair discrimination would be when a football team keeps only those players who are the best performers, or when a company hires on the basis of candidates' ability to safely drive a truck or perform other job-relevant tasks. Unfair discrimination occurs when a job candidate is rejected by an employer solely because of the candidate's race or any other characteristic that is not relevant to the candidate's ability to perform the job effectively.

Interpersonal Attraction

The Mere Exposure Effect and Attraction

1. Research participants were shown nonsense words or foreign language characters a varying number of times. The more times they saw these stimuli, the more they liked them, even though the words and characters had no meaning to them.
[Reference: Zajonc, R. B. (1968). Attitudinal effects of mere exposure. *Journal of Personality and Social Psychology, 9*(2, Pt.2), 1–27.]
2. Researchers arranged for three women of similar appearance to attend a college class even though they were not enrolled in that class. They merely sat in the room; none of them ever interacted with other students. One woman attended five times, one attended ten times, and the third attended fifteen times. At the end of the semester, the class saw pictures of each of the three women, as well as of a fourth woman who was of similar appearance to the others but had never attended the class. Then the students were asked to rate all four women on attributes such as physical attractiveness, intelligence, honesty, warmth, and popularity. Despite never having interacted with these women, the students'

ratings of each of them were more positive the more often each had attended the class. The woman who never attended got the lowest ratings, the one who attended 15 times was rated highest, and the other two were rated in between the extremes.
[Reference: Moreland, R. L., & Beach, S. R. (1992). Exposure effects in the classroom: The development of affinity among students. *Journal of Experimental Social Psychology, 28*(3), 255–276.]

3. Advertisers and political candidates seek to take advantage of the mere exposure effect by repeating their commercials or campaign ads many times each day, but if repeated too often in too short a time, the result can be viewer ambivalence or dislike.

4. We tend to stick with products and services that we are familiar with rather than switching to new and unfamiliar products and services. This tendency creates a challenge for companies trying to break into a market, especially if that market is in a different country where local brands are well established.

5. The more often we make contact with someone—as neighbors, classmates, or coworkers, for example—the more we tend to like that person.
[Reference: Preciado, P., Snijders, T. B., Burk, W. J., Stattin, H., & Kerr, M. (2012). Does proximity matter? Distance dependence of adolescent friendships. *Social Networks, 34,* 18–31.]

6. Academics are likely to give more credence to articles published in familiar scholarly journals than to those published in unfamiliar ones.
[Reference: Serenko, A. & Bontis, N. (2011). What's familiar is excellent: The impact of exposure effect on perceived journal quality. *Journal of Informetrics, 5,* 219–223.]

Similarity and Attraction

[*Note:* Examples in this section may be helpful in debunking the myth that "opposites always attract."]

1. In general, we tend to like others who are, or whom we perceive to be, similar to ourselves on dimensions such as appearance, age, religious affiliation, drug and alcohol use, and the like, but in romantic relationships this tendency appears strongest when the partners are committed to each other. When there is less commitment in the relationship, partners tend to like each other more if they perceive each other as different on various dimensions.
[Reference: Amodio, D.M., & Showers, C.J. (2005). 'Similarity breeds liking' revisited: The moderating role of commitment. *Journal of Social and Personal Relationships, 22*(6), 817–836.]

2. An analysis of the authors cited by social scientists in their own publications found that these scientists tended to more often cite authors from their own religious group than from other religious groups, presumably because, consciously or not, they liked, or trusted those authors more.

[Reference: Greenwald, A. G., & Schuh, E. S. (1994). An ethnic bias in scientific citations. *European Journal of Social Psychology, 24*(6), 623–639.]

3. An example of the influence of even trivial similarities comes from a study in which a researcher mailed out surveys to college students and asked them to complete and return them. The name of the person sending the survey was sometimes similar to that of the recipient and sometimes showed no similarity. When there was no similarity the survey return rate was about 20% but was almost 40% when the sender's name bore some similarity to the recipient's. The same results appeared when the surveys were sent to faculty members; this time the return rate was 30% in the non-similar name condition and 56% in the similar name condition. The implication is that people are more likely to do something for someone they like than for someone toward whom they feel neutral.
[Reference: Garner, R. (2005). What's in a name? Persuasion perhaps. *Journal of Consumer Psychology, 15,* 108–116.]

4. Other studies have found results similar to those above. People who were led to believe that they shared the same birthday, the same name, or similar classes of fingerprints with another person were more likely to do a favor for that person than if they were dissimilar on these variables.
[Reference: Burger, J.M., Messian, N., Patel, S., del Prado, A., & Anderson, C. (2004). What a coincidence! The effects of incidental similarity on compliance. *Personality and Social Psychology Bulletin, 30,* 35–43.]

5. An example of the similarity-liking link at age three is found in a study in which 114 children were randomly paired into 57 same-sex dyads and observed during 3 laboratory visits over a 1-month period. Previously, information about the children's temperament and attachment to their mothers was collected. The quality of interactions during each visit was measured in terms of ratings of dyadic coordination, social play complexity, and shared positive affect. Results showed that child pairs who were similar to each other in attachment security and temperament displayed more rapid increases in positive interaction across the 3 visits.
[Reference: McElwain, N. L., Ogolsky, B. G., Engle, J. M., Holland, A. S., & Mitchell, E. T. (2016). Child–child similarity on attachment and temperament as predictors of positive interaction during acquaintanceship at age 3. *Developmental Psychology, 52*(9), 1394–1408.]

6. Another example of the similarity-liking link appears in a study showing that when people were in situations where they could decide where to sit, they tended to choose seats closest to people who were similar to themselves in terms of wearing/not wearing glasses, hair length, hair color, gender, and race.
[Reference: Mackinnon, S. P., Jordan, C. H., & Wilson, A. E. (2011). Birds of a feather sit together: Physical similarity predicts seating choice. *Personality and Social Psychology Bulletin, 37*(7), 879–892.]

7. An example of the similarity-liking link when similarity is based on personal opinions: Undergraduate students were told that they were about to engage in a group discussion with other students whose views about the fairness of the

criminal justice system were either similar to their own or differed to varying degrees from their own. Measures of the students' liking increased for students whose opinions were similar to their own, and those students' opinions were seen as more correct. The more dissimilar the other students' opinions were, the less the participants liked those other students and the less correct their views were perceived to be.
[Reference: Hensley, V., & Duval, S. (1976). Some perceptual determinants of perceived similarity, liking, and correctness. *Journal of Personality and Social Psychology, 34*(2), 159–168.]

8. A study of speed dating found that couples with similar speaking styles were three times more likely to want to see each other again than did couples whose speaking styles were different. Further, 76.7% of couples with similar speaking styles were still dating three months later compared to only 53.5% of couples with dissimilar styles.
[Reference: Ireland, M. E., Slatcher, R. B., Eastwick, P. W., Scissors, L. E., Finkel, E. J., & Pennebaker, J. W. (2011). Language style matching predicts relationship initiation and stability. *Psychological Science, 22*(1), 39–44.]

9. Examples of promoting liking by adjusting speaking style to match others can be found in politicians who, consciously or not, tend to change their style to use words or intonations that match what they perceive to be the stereotypical speaking style of particular audiences (a process called "code-switching").

10. A 3-min video focusing on Hillary Clinton's changing accent, but mentioning other politicians, too, is available here.

11. An NPR interview with Deborah Tannen contains a number of audio clips exemplifying the same phenomenon. You can find it here.

12. A 3-min video presenting a summary of code-switching in political and non-political situations is available here (requires a subscription for access).

Physical Appearance and Attraction

1. An example of research on the relationship between physical appearance and attraction is provided by a study in which heterosexual college students were first given either flattering or neutral feedback on their own attractiveness to members of the opposite sex, and were then asked to rate photographs of same-sex peers who were physically very attractive, moderately attractive, or unattractive. They were to rate these peers in terms of whether they would like to date each of them, how well matched they thought they would be, whether each of the peers would be interested in dating them, and the like. Results indicated that participants who had received flattering evaluations tended to choose and feel better matched to more attractive peers than did those who had received neutral feedback. The results were interpreted to support the idea that, though most people would prefer to form intimate relationships with the most

physically attractive partners, self-awareness of their own attractiveness leads them to seek partners who are about equal to themselves in attractiveness. [Reference: Kavanagh, P. S., Robins, S. C., & Ellis, B. J. (2010). The mating sociometer: A regulatory mechanism for mating aspirations. *Journal of Personality and Social Psychology, 99,* 120–132.]

Social Norms

Descriptive and Injunctive Norms

1. Culturally learned descriptive norms tell us how to behave in public, even when there are no official rules or signs. For example, this Google search shows photos of people forming orderly lines in public places in some countries and less orderly ones other countries.
2. The following Google search shows photos exemplifying clothing norms that stem from cultural background rather than just from location.
3. Examples of descriptive norms, such as those related to clothing, changing over time can be seen in photos of U.S. College students in the 1950s, the 1970s, the 1990s, and today.
4. Examples of injunctive norms include signs or verbal or nonverbal instructions about how you should or should not behave in particular situations (e.g., "do not enter," "no drones," "all visitors must sign in," a cigarette with a red slash through it to indicate no smoking) can be found here.
5. An example of the difference between descriptive and injunctive norms can be seen in college students' perceptions of how much alcohol their peers drink (descriptive norm) and the extent to which that much drinking is approved on campus (injunctive norm). Because students may overestimate the level of both of these norms, they may drink too much. Therefore, some efforts aimed at reducing students' alcohol consumption focus on providing more realistic normative information.

[Here is a reference to research on this "social norms" approach to moderation: Borsari, B., & Carey, K. B. (2003). Descriptive and injunctive norms in college drinking: A meta-analytic integration. *Journal of Studies on Alcohol, 64*(3), 331–341.]

6. An experiment illustrated the differing effects of descriptive versus injunctive norms: The participants were people who walked through a parking lot just after being handed an advertising leaflet. The experimenters arranged for the participants to see another person either toss a paper bag on the ground or pick

one up from the ground. On half the trials of this experiment, the parking lot was littered with paper; on the other half, the lot was clean. When both a descriptive norm (communicated by a littered parking lot) and an injunctive norm (communicated by the sight of someone discarding paper in the parking lot) were consistent with littering, 30% of the people crossing the parking lot also littered. When the sight of someone picking up a bag in the parking lot created an injunctive norm against littering, fewer than 10% of people littered, whether or not the lot was littered.
[Reference: Reno, R. R., Cialdini, R. B., & Kallgren, C. A. (1993). The transsituational influence of social norms. *Journal of Personality and Social Psychology, 64,* 104–112.]

7. A more recent series of five field experiments in The Netherlands available here supported the Broken Window Theory, which suggests that when descriptive norms clearly violate injunctive norms, a sense of disorder is created that leads people to violate norms in general.
The researchers found, for example, that people who saw graffiti painted on a wall next to a "no graffiti" sign or saw bicycles chained to a fence next to a sign that said "do not chain bicycles to this fence," were far more likely than people who saw no such violations to violate other norms in the situation. Specifically, 69% of people who saw the "no-graffiti" norm violated proceeded to drop litter in the area compared to 33% of those who did not see that norm violated. And 82% of people who saw the "no bicycles" norm violated walked through a gap in the fence despite the presence of a sign saying "do not enter." Only 27% passed through the gap if there were no bikes chained to the fence.
[Reference: Keizer, K., Lindenberg, S. & Steg, L. (2008). The spreading of disorder. *Science, 12,* 1681–1685.]

8. An example of how descriptive and injunctive norms can combine to alter behavior can be found in a survey study that is available here. It found that consumers' intentions to purchase electric cars appear to be driven more strongly by perceptions of what others are doing and what one should do than by how people feel about the electric car technology itself.
[Reference: Bobeth, S., & Kastner, I. (2020). Buying an electric car: A rational choice or a norm-directed behavior? *Transportation Research Part F: Traffic Psychology and Behaviour, 73,* 236–258.]

9. An example of how norms can be activated by the mere presence of other people is provided by a study in which 77% of women in a public restroom washed their hands after using toilet facilities if another person was present, while only 40% did so when they were alone.
[Reference: Munger, K., & Harris, S. J. (1989). Effects of an observer on handwashing in a public restroom. *Perceptual and Motor Skills, 69,* 733–734.]

10. An example of how norms can be activated by the mere suggestion of being observed can be found in a study that presented a written message to 354 women as they entered a public restroom. It reminded them that hand washing

protects against the spread of pathogens. If a pair of human eyes appeared above the message, about 83% of the women washed their hands after using the toilet facilities; if three stars appeared above the message, only about 72% did so.
[Reference: Pfattheicher, S., Strauch, C., Diefenbacher, S., & Schnuerch, R. (2018). A field study on watching eyes and hand hygiene compliance in a public restroom. *Journal of Applied Social Psychology, 48*(4), 188–194.]

11. Another experiment used a sequential design to evaluate the impact of feeling observed on following social norms. It took place in a coffee break room at an English university. Instructions about paying for each cup of coffee or tea were posted prominently on a cabinet, but each week the banner just above the instructions was alternated between an image of flowers or of human eyes. People were nearly three times more likely to pay for their drinks in the presence of eyes than of flowers.
[Reference: Bateson, M., Nettle, D., & Roberts, G. (2006). Cues of being watched enhance cooperation in a real-world setting. *Biology Letters, 2*(3), 412–414.]

12. Individual differences in the impact of social norms governing politeness and privacy can be seen in a 5-min Candid Camera video showing some men studiously avoiding the opportunity to look up a woman's skirt and others taking full advantage. The same variability is seen when women are given the opportunity to look under a man's kilt.

Descriptive and Injunctive Gender Role Norms

1. Gender role norms conveyed by advertising, past and present. Vintage ads are available at several websites, including this one and this one. Still others like them can be found by Googling "gender roles of the 50s."

2. Traditional gender role norms being conveyed by truly amazing "training films" can be found here, here, and here.

3. This 3-min Candid Camera video from 1963 shows the reaction of airline passengers when discovering that their pilot would be a woman in command of her first flight (there were no female commercial pilots at that time).
4. An example of children today retaining traditional gender role stereotypes in the workplace despite widespread efforts to dilute them can be seen in a 2-min video here.

Cultural Norms for Greetings and Personal Space

1. Friends and family: In the USA, Canada, and the UK, for example, females typically greet familiar females or males with a hug and perhaps a kiss on one cheek. Males typically greet familiar males by shaking hands unless they are beloved relatives or very close friends, in which case they will hug briefly; kisses on one cheek occur but are uncommon. Males will typically hug familiar females and kiss them on one cheek.
2. In France, Spain, Italy, and Brazil, for example, hugs and kisses on both cheeks are standard. In the Netherlands, three kisses, on the left, right, and left cheek, are the norm.
3. Strangers: In the USA, Canada, and the UK, for example, greetings are typically restricted to handshakes, and doing more than that is likely to be seen as inappropriately forward. Indeed, in unfamiliar male–female pairs, even handshakes may not occur unless the woman proffers her hand first.
4. In France, hugging is not normal, but a kiss on each cheek is expected. We know an American man who, when he first lived in France, was surprised and shocked when friends of his wife (but unknown to him) arrived at a dinner with their pre-teenage daughters and the girls immediately approached to kiss him.
5. Personal space norms: A study of what almost 9000 people in 42 countries considered to be comfortable distances for conversation with strangers, friends, and intimates found significant differences across countries. A graphic showing those differences can be found in this article:
Sorokowska, A., Scrokowski, P., Hilpert, P., Cantarero, K., Frackowiak, T., Ahmadi, K., ... Pierce, J. D. (2017). Preferred interpersonal distances: A global comparison. *Journal of Cross-Cultural Psychology, 48*(4), 577–592.
6. A 4-min Candid Camera video illustrating Americans' aversion to invasion of personal space in a restaurant can be found here. [The table arrangement shown is standard in most European countries, where it would cause little or no obvious discomfort.]

The Reciprocity Norm

1. Direct-mail sales companies may include a calendar, a sheet of return address labels, a fridge magnet, or some other little gift in their envelopes in the hope that the recipient will feel a certain amount of obligation to buy the sender's product, or at least read the sales material.

2. Promoters of vacation time-share plans often offer potential customers a weekend trip to the time-share location, including free travel, hotel rooms, and meals, in exchange for the opportunity to take the customers on a tour of the facility. Though there is no official obligation to sign a sales contract, accepting this extensive "gift" from the promoters—who are very nice to the potential customer during the visit—tends to create a strong sense of obligation to buy into a time-share arrangement, certainly a stronger sense of obligation than would have occurred had the customer just read an advertisement for the facility.
3. To help activate the reciprocity norm, servers in restaurants often include a little gift of candy along with the bill at the end of a meal. The idea is to increase the customer's sense of obligation to give a good tip, not only for the meal service (which is the server's job) but as a thank-you for the gift. Researchers have found that, indeed, customers who received even one small piece of chocolate along with the check gave higher-percentage tips (about 18%) than did customers who received no candy (about 15%), and that the more candy given, and the way it was given, also was followed by higher tip percentages. Tips averaged 21% after two pieces of candy were delivered but rose to nearly 23% when the server first gave one piece of candy with the bill (which a customer could assume was just standard procedure), but then—showing a personal decision—returned to deliver a second piece of candy.
[Reference: Strohmetz, D. B., Rind, B., Fisher, R., & Lynn, M. (2002). Sweetening the till: The use of candy to increase restaurant tipping. *Journal of Applied Social Psychology, 32,* 300–309.]
4. An example of how the reciprocity norm can operate differently in different cultures is found in a study that asked employees in Thailand how they felt about taking a bribe to do something that they shouldn't do. Many of them said that taking the bribe was not a crime, but rather just returning of a favor after receiving free money.
[Reference: Ariyabuddhiphongs, V., & Hongladarom, C. (2014). Bribe taking acceptability and bribe payment among Thai organizational employees: The mediating effect of reciprocity obligation. *International Perspectives in Psychology: Research, Practice, Consultation, 3* (3), 184–196.]
5. We know of a case in which a salesman was trying to sell a grocery store owner an extended warranty program that would cover all his refrigeration equipment. The owner was reluctant to sign up, but during the conversation mentioned that his refrigerator at home was not working properly. After leaving, the salesman had one of his company's repair technicians go to the owner's house and provide free repair service on the refrigerator. The next day, the owner signed the extended warranty contract.
6. Some publishers offer free face-to-face or online seminars on topics that are of value to potential adopters of their textbooks in the hope that receiving free information (and perhaps lunch, too) will create a sense of obligation to choose, or at least carefully examine, the publisher's products.

Norms Supporting Antisocial Behavior: Deindividuation

1. Normally mild-mannered adults may join with others to throw rocks at police or store windows during political protests or post-game rioting, and normally law-abiding people may commit crimes when in a group whose members provide a descriptive norm for such behavior.
2. Street gangs provide another example of a social groups whose descriptive and injunctive norms create an environment in which members commit crimes as part of the gang that they might not engage in on their own.
3. An example of how deindividuation is amplified when people feel anonymous and thus less personally responsible can be seen in Ku Klux Klan members who wear hoods and robes to hide their identity while committing hate crimes.
4. Another example of the impact of reduced sense of responsibility can be seen in a study of lynch mobs in Georgia whose results showed that the larger the groups, the higher the level of violence in the lynchings.
[References:
Ritchey, A. J., & Ruback, R. B. (2018). Predicting lynching atrocity: The situational norms of lynchings in Georgia. *Personality and Social Psychology Bulletin, 44*(5), 619–637.
Mullen, B. (1986). Atrocity as a function of lynch mob composition: A self-attention perspective. *Personality and Social Psychology Bulletin, 12*, 187–197.]
5. Yet another example from across cultures is a study showing that in about 92% of highly aggressive tribes (e g., head-hunters and those who torture captives), warriors disguised themselves in paint or masks before battle whereas warriors in only about 30% of low-aggression tribes did so.
[Reference: Watson, R. I. (1973). Investigation into deindividuation using a cross-cultural survey technique. *Journal of Personality and Social Psychology, 25*(3), 342–345.]
6. A study has found that darkness, too, can enhance deindividuation effects; when someone is threatening to commit suicide by jumping off a bridge or a building, crowds of onlookers are more likely to encourage the person to jump if the incident occurs at night than during the day.
[Reference: Mann, L. (1981). The baiting crowd in episodes of threatened suicide. *Journal of Personality and Social Psychology, 41*, 703–709.]
7. An example of how one does not have to be in a group to be affected by deindividuation can be seen in high levels of aggressiveness and incivility displayed when people communicate anonymously online, saying things to each other that they would not likely say in person.
[Reference: Zimmerman, A. C., & Ybarra, G. J. (2016). Online aggression: The influences of anonymity and social modeling. *Psychology of Popular Media Culture, 5*(2), 181–193.]

Social Loafing

1. One of the first examples of social loafing appeared when agricultural engineer Max Ringelmann conducted a series of experiments in 1913 showing that individuals working alone exerted more effort while pulling a rope or a two-wheeled cart than did individuals working in a team of two or more.
   [Reference: Kravitz, D. A., & Martin, B. (1986). Ringelmann rediscovered: The original article. *Journal of Personality and Social Psychology, 50,* 936–941.]
2. Students on a team or committee whose task is to organize a class presentation or plan a social event may attend the meetings and state their intention to do their part of the task, but may not follow through, leaving most of the work to be done by one or two members, but still getting their share of credit for being in the group.
3. Other examples of social loafing on physical tasks can be seen when groups of people are asked to clap and cheer as loud as possible, engage in a tug-of-war rope game, swim in a relay race, and operate a manually-activated air pump.
   [Reference: Sheppard, J.A. (1993). Productivity loss in performance groups: A motivation analysis. *Psychological Bulletin, 113,* 67–81.]
4. Examples of social loafing on cognitive tasks include reduced performance by individuals when working in a group (compared to when working alone) to evaluate a poem, engage in a visual vigilance task, solve mazes, and generate creative uses for objects.
   [Reference: Sheppard, J.A. (1993). Productivity loss in performance groups: A motivation analysis. *Psychological Bulletin, 113,* 67–81.]

Social Facilitation and Interference

Social Facilitation

1. An 1898 paper by Norman Triplett of Indiana University provided early experimental evidence for the positive impact on performance of the presence of others (later called social facilitation). While examining the records from the Racing Board of the League of American Wheelmen, Triplett noticed that the times turned in by bicyclists who completed a particular course were somewhat faster when another rider was present, either in competition or just to set a pace, compared to when they were riding alone. He conducted additional research with children who performed a reel-winding task, either alone or in competition with another child, and noticed the same thing—competition was associated with faster performance.
   [Reference: Triplett, N. (1898). The dynamogenic factors in pacemaking and competition. *American Journal of Psychology, 9,* 507–533. See also an interesting article that provides broader perspective on what Triplett did and did not find: Strube, M. (2005). What did Triplett really find? A contemporary analysis

of the first experiment in social psychology. *The American Journal of Psychology, 118*(2), 271–286.]
2. You can find more details about this research, and a drawing of the competition machine here.

3. Other experiments in the 1920s and 1930s found that the mere presence of one or more people facilitated performance on multiplication problems, eye-hand coordination tasks, and word association response times.
[References: Allport, F.H. (1924). *Social psychology.* Boston: Houghton Mifflin.
Dashiell, J. F. (1935). Experimental studies of the influence of social situations on the behavior of individual human adults. In *A handbook of social psychology* (pp. 1097–1158). Clark University Press.
Travis, L. E. (1925). The effect of a small audience upon eye-hand coordination. *The Journal of Abnormal and Social Psychology, 20*(2), 142–146.]
4. An eating example: People tend to eat more when in the company of others than when they are alone.
[Reference: Herman, C. P., Roth, D. A., & Polivy, J. (2003). Effects of the presence of others on food intake: A normative interpretation. *Psychological Bulletin, 129*(6), 873–886.]
5. Examples of social facilitation in nonhuman species: Chickens peck at food more quickly when other chickens are pecking nearby; rats press a response key faster in the presence of other rats; cockroaches run with greater speed when running alongside other cockroaches.
[Reference: Clayton, D.A (1978). Socially facilitated behavior. *The Quarterly Review of Biology, 53,* 373–92.]

Social Interference

1. If you have just learned a new dance, a new piece of music, or a new language, you are not as likely to perform it as well in front of an audience as when you are practicing alone.
2. If you are trying to unscramble letters to form words, you will probably have more trouble doing so if you are being watched.
3. You are trying to follow a complicated new recipe while your partner stands nearby, watching. As you struggle to understand and perform some of the more exotic procedures, even though your partner has said nothing, you finally blurt out "Will you please go and find something else to do?"
4. In the presence of lights, cameras, and an audience of millions, contestants on TV quiz shows such as *Jeopardy* and *Who Wants to be a Millionaire* (now cancelled) may have no trouble coming up with the correct response to easy questions but may have an increasingly difficult time with harder ones even though those questions might seem easy to viewers calmly watching at home.

Social Facilitation Versus Social interference

1. Social facilitation is likely to occur if you have been riding a bike for years and know how to do it so well that it is extremely easy. So, you will probably be able to ride smoothly and safely no matter how many people are watching. In fact, their presence may motivate you to ride faster, or otherwise "show off." Social interference is likely to occur if you are just learning to ride a bike because the task will be more difficult and take more concentrated effort to stay balanced. The presence of an audience may create enough emotional arousal to interfere with your ability to perform well, or as well as you would if no one were watching (see the chapter on motivation and emotion for more examples of the effects of arousal on performance).
2. Social facilitation is likely to occur if you are playing a difficult piano piece, but one that you have practiced a lot and that is now familiar. Here, the presence of an audience is likely to enhance your performance because it gives you a chance to showcase your skills. Social interference is likely to occur if you are playing an unfamiliar piano piece. Here, the presence of an audience may create enough emotional arousal to interfere with your ability to perform the piece, even if it is fairly easy, perhaps because of worry over appearing to be less skilled than you really are.
3. If years of practice have made it easy and familiar, you are likely to be able to speak French fluently, even if you have to make a presentation to a large audience of French speakers. The arousal that might be created by the situation will enhance your tendency to perform the behaviors that have become habitual, the ones you know well, and the result will be a good presentation. If you just started learning French and find yourself in a situation where you have to try to speak to a group of French people, then the emotional arousal you are likely to experience will bring out your tendency to say your most habitual words, which are likely to be English ones. The result will be a less fluent performance.
4. Professional athletes like Serena Williams or Patrick Mahomes, perform at their best even when large crowds are present. In fact, the crowds probably help them do well because the presence of others tends to increase arousal, which enhances the performance of their familiar and well-learned skills, such as hitting a tennis ball or throwing a football. However, that same arousal created by an audience tends to interfere with their ability to perform less familiar and poorly developed skills. This is one reason why famous athletes often freeze up or blow their lines in front of a small production crew when trying for the first time to tape a TV ad or a public service announcement.
5. An observational study found that skilled pool players played better when others were watching than when alone, while relatively unskilled players played worse in front of an audience than when playing alone.
[Reference: Michaels, J.W., Blommel, J.M., Brocato, R.M., Linkous, R.A., & Rowe, J.S. (1982). Social facilitation and inhibition in a natural setting. *Replications in Social Psychology, 2*, 21–24.]

6. The same effect appeared in a study of basketball players' success at making free-throws.
   [Reference: Kotzer, R. D. (2007). The social facilitation effect in basketball: Shooting free throws. *The Huron University College Journal of Learning and Motivation, 45,* Issue. 1, Article 8. Available at: http://ir.lib.uwo.ca/hucjlm/vol45/iss1/8.]
7. Here is a laboratory example of the role of task familiarity in determining whether the presence of other people will facilitate or interfere with performance. The study measured how long it took male college students to put on or take off their shoes and clothing, either alone, in the presence of another male who was present but not watching, or in the presence of another male who was watching. The students were told: "In this experiment you will be part of a group that will perform a task together. It is important that the members of each group have a uniform appearance. To make you as much alike as possible, I'd like you to take off your shoes, put these socks over your own socks, and then put on these shoes. They might be a little large, but we need to have a size that fits everyone. Also, put on this lab coat—it ties in the back—over your own clothes." Later, the students had to remove these clothing items.
   Some of the dressing and undressing tasks were simple and familiar (e.g., putting on shoes or removing them), while others were more complicated and less familiar (e.g., putting on and taking off the large, long, lab coat that had to be tied in the back). Compared to the *alone* condition, both *social* conditions (attentive or inattentive audience) enhanced performance of familiar and well-learned aspects of the task, namely taking off and putting on their own shoes and socks, but having others present hindered performance on the more complex and unfamiliar tasks.
   [Reference: Markus, H. (1978). The effect of mere presence on social facilitation: An unobtrusive test. *Journal of Experimental Social Psychology, 14,* 389–397.]
8. Studies from the 1920s found that when asked to say as many words as possible in response to a given word, 93% of participants produced more words in the presence of another person than alone. However, when the study was replicated with individuals who stuttered when they spoke (making the task more difficult), 80% of the participants produced more words when alone rather than in the presence of another person.
   [References:
   Allport, F.H. (1920). The influence of the group upon association and thought. *Journal of Experimental Psychology, 3,* 159–182.
   Travis, L.E. (1928). The influence of the group upon the stutterer's speed in free association. *Journal of Abnormal and Social Psychology, 23*(1), 45–51.]
9. Even in non-humans, task difficulty and the presence of others combine to create either social facilitation or social interference, as exemplified by a study in which cockroaches ran a maze whose walls were glass (allowing a view of other cockroaches) or opaque (creating a solitary environment). The cockroaches

completed easy mazes faster if they could see other cockroaches but when attempting more difficult mazes, they did better if they were alone.
[Reference: Zajonc, R. B., Heingartner, A., & Herman, E. M. (1969). Social enhancement and impairment of performance in the cockroach. *Journal of Personality and Social Psychology, 13*(2), 83–92.]

Conformity

1. At the end of a play, everyone around you stands to applaud the performance, but you thought it was not very good. You find yourself standing as well, though no one told you to do so; the group's behavior created a silent but influential pressure to follow suit.
2. When you get to the driver's license bureau, there are many people ahead of you, but even though you are in a hurry, you take a number and sit in the waiting room as you see others do.
3. You are at a sports arena when the crowd begins doing "the wave." You think this is silly, but when the wave of people who stand and then sit reaches your section, you join in.
4. You are at dinner at the house of a friend whose family is very religious, so you are not surprised when your friend's father says a prayer before the meal. You are not religious, but you bow your head when everyone else does.
5. Even if you do not particularly like the latest trends in clothing or hairstyles or tattooing or body piercing, you find yourself looking a lot like your peers even though none of them said you should. [You might want to point out that this tendency occurs in every generation, as shown in the photos of college students of various eras mentioned earlier.]
6. An example of how unspoken social pressure for conformity can affect reports about personal experiences is provided by a study in which research participants were shown a number of objects. Later, the same objects were shown again, along with some new ones, and the participants were asked to say whether they had seen each object in the previous display. When tested alone, the participants' memories were quite accurate, but if they first heard another participant's opinion, they tended to agree with it, even if the other participant wrongly reported that a new item had been shown before. [You might want to use this example in addition to or even instead of the classic Asch conformity studies.]
[Reference: Hoffman, H.G., Granhag, P.A., Kwong See, S.T., & Loftus, E.F. (2001). Social influences on reality-monitoring decisions. *Memory and Cognition, 29*, 394–404.]
7. Another example of conforming with the false perceptions of others can be seen in this 2-min Candid Camera video. Notice that once a person "sees" what others see, the person may act to convince others to see the same nonexistent thing.

8. A 2-min video showing conformity to norm-violating behavior in an elevator is available here.

9. The classic 1962 version of the same demonstration from Candid Camera is no longer available, but a summary of it can be found here.

10. This 6-min video shows a recent example of people who conform to the actions of others even when it makes no sense to do so.

11. This 2-min video shows that people may conform to the behavior of others, even if the others are ignoring a potentially dangerous situation.

Compliance

1. You step aside when someone says, "Excuse me, I would like to get by."
2. You push the appropriate elevator button when someone running toward you says, "Please hold the elevator."
3. You choose the appropriate entrance line at a museum in response to a sign that says, "Ticket holders to the left; Purchase tickets to the right."
4. You open your mouth when the dentist asks you to do so.
5. You strip to your underwear when asked to do so by a physician's assistant.
6. You drive at the speed limit that is posted on roadside signs.
7. You stop asking questions of another person when the person says "I'd rather not talk about it."
8. You wash the dishes when asked to do so.
9. You show your ID card when the liquor store clerk asks to see it.
10. You sign forms when asked to do so at a medical office, car dealership, or in many other business situations. A 4-min Candid Camera video shows just how compliant people will be even when the number of forms is excessive.
11. A 90s clip from another Candid Camera video shows people in a shoe repair shop whose floor is made up of black and white tiles, complying with a sign that says "Walk on black tiles only."
12. Another 4-min Candid Camera video shows three out of four people (all females, by the way) complying with an airport screener's request that they lie down on the baggage belt to go through x-ray.
13. You can create an example of personal compliance in the classroom by telling your students that you would like to conduct a little experiment. Then, ask them to do something silly and/or pointless, such as to think of a

number from one to ten, then to stand on one foot (the right if they are left-handed, and the left if they are right-handed) and hop on that foot for the same number of times as the number they chose. Or have them stand and turn in a complete circle (to the left if they are right-handed, to the right if they are left-handed) and then sit down. Or ask them to switch seats with one another. You might even ask the students to give you a standing ovation, complete with whistles and cheers (it takes several tries before the desired level of enthusiasm is reached, but with encouragement, the results are rather gratifying).

When the task or tasks are completed, explain that the only purpose of the "experiment" was to illustrate the power of compliance, and ask the students why they did what you asked them to do. The ensuing discussion will surely make the point that people routinely do what they are asked to do when the request comes from a legitimate authority. Doing the demonstration with the entire class rather than with one volunteer makes it impossible for anyone to dismiss the power of pressure for compliance by thinking that "I wouldn't have done that."

[*Note:* You might want to point out that you merely asked the students to perform a silly task; you did not demand it. Making this distinction can lead into your discussion of the differences between compliance and obedience.]

14. You might invite students to try something similar with a friend by asking the friend to do something silly or pointless, such as performing five push-ups. The friend will probably ask "Why?", but if the student says, "it's an experiment," the friend will probably comply because the word "experiment" tends to create a social role (research participant) in which compliance is legitimate and expected.

15. An experimental example of gaining compliance through the "foot in the door" strategy was provided by a study in which homeowners were asked to either allow a large, unattractive "Drive Carefully" sign to be placed on their front lawns, or simply to agree to sign a petition favoring stronger laws to prevent traffic accidents. Only about 17% of the people who were asked to accept the big sign agreed to do so, but of those who first agreed to sign the petition, 55% complied with a later request to accept the sign.

[Reference: Freedman, J. L., & Fraser, S. C. (1966). Compliance without pressure: The foot-in-the-door technique. *Journal of Personality and Social Psychology, 4,* 195–202.]

16. Another experimental example of "foot in the door" compliance was provided by a study in which a woman asked strangers to keep an eye on her shopping bag while she stepped away for a few minutes. The strangers were twice as likely to agree to do this favor if they had first answered the woman's smaller request to tell her what time it was.

[Reference: Dolinski, D. (2012). The nature of the first small request as a decisive factor in the effectiveness of the foot-in-the-door technique. *Applied Psychology: An International Review, 61*(3), 437–453.]

17. In sales situations, the "foot in the door" may take the form of a request that potential customers merely answer some questions about their problems and needs. The request to buy something comes later, and the sales pitch is tailored

to address the problems and needs revealed in the customer's responses to the earlier questions.

18. The "door-in-the-face" approach to gaining compliance is exemplified by teenagers who influence parents to comply with many kinds of requests. After asking to stay out overnight, a youngster whose curfew is normally 11 P.M. might be allowed to stay out until 1 A.M.—a "compromise" that was actually the original goal.

19. An experiment demonstrating the door-in-the-face technique involved first asking students walking on a college campus if they would be willing to volunteer as chaperones for a group of juvenile delinquents on a two-hour tour of the local zoo. It was not surprising that only 17% of the students agreed. The researcher then asked other student passersby if they would be willing to act as volunteer counselors to juvenile delinquents for two hours a week for the next two years. All of these students refused that request, but about 50% of them then agreed to act as volunteers for the zoo trip.
    [Reference: Cialdini, R.B., Vincent, J.E., Lewis, S.K., Catalan, J., Wheeler, D. & Darby, B.L. (1975). Reciprocal concessions procedure for inducing compliance: The door-in-the-face technique. *Journal of Personality and Social Psychology, 31*(2), 206–215.]

20. Door in the face methods are at the heart of negotiations between labor and management, job candidates and employers, buyers and sellers, politicians of different parties, and even couples. One side asks for a pay raise, a starting salary, a sale price, or features of a new law that the requester knows will not be accepted, and when it is refused, it is moderated so as to seem to be an acceptable compromise.

21. A little-known example of door in the face is described by Robert Cialdini in his book called *Influence*. He tells of a television producer in the 1970s trying to get a racy line included in a TV show called *Laverne and Shirley* (note that your students will not likely know this show, but the example works regardless). One of the characters is rushing off to see a girl in the apartment upstairs and the script called for him to say to another character "…hurry up before I lose my lust," but the producers knew the censors would cut that line. Instead, they sent the censors a script that said "…before I lose my erection," and when that was cut, they offered to "tone it down" to "lose my lust" and the censors agreed.
    [Reference: Cialdini, R. B. (2001). *Influence: Science and practice* (4th ed.). Boston: Allyn & Bacon.]

22. Gaining compliance through the "low ball" method was exemplified by a college student we know who was living at home and needed a ride to campus every morning because she did not like to take the bus. She asked a fellow student who lived nearby if he would provide that ride, but it was only after he agreed to do so that she told him that her first class each day was at 8am. His first class was not until 11am, but by now he felt obligated to follow through on his commitment, even though doing so bore a higher cost than he anticipated.

23. One of the most common examples of gaining compliance through "low ball" comes from cases in which, after a customer commits to buying a certain car at a certain price, the cost of fulfilling the commitment is increased, often because of an "error" in computing the car's price, or the need to include "standard" document or dealer preparation fees, special undercoating, paint sealant, and so on.
24. Low ball methods are also used by sellers of mobile phone plans, cosmetics, streaming video services, or other products. Their advertisement of ridiculously low prices, or even "free" products may cause consumers to buy without reading the fine print. As a result, they may be bound to long-term contracts, required to pay monthly fees and hidden charges not mentioned in the original offer, or must accept new products each month at prices much higher than the promotional items that were so inexpensive.
25. A heating and air-conditioning company in Florida was recently taken to court by hundreds of customers who had been told that they could get new central air-conditioning systems for little or no out-of-pocket cost. However, getting this good deal involved not only agreeing to buy the equipment, but also signing up for a government-sponsored energy-saving loan program that allowed the company to dramatically overcharge for providing and installing the air-conditioning systems. The program also resulting in the placement of a lien on the customers' property and an increase in their property taxes that put some customers in danger of losing their homes.

[Reference: Retrieved here.]
26. Examples of lowball methods being used in the service of more positive compliance goals are found in two studies aimed at promoting energy conservation. In these studies, homeowners were first given tips for energy conservation and asked to try to reduce their consumption. All agreed to try, but none actually did. A comparable group of homeowners were given the same tips and request to save energy, but were also promised that the names of those who agreed to conserve would be published in the newspaper as public-spirited citizens. Within a month, these homeowners had substantially decreased their energy use and they continued to do so even after they were informed that it would not in fact be possible to have their names in the paper. In other words, like a customer who discovers that a promised feature will not be included in the price of a car, these homeowners fulfilled their commitment to save energy. [You might want to point out that the promise of publicity might have driven the initial compliance, but that the compliance was also supported by lower energy bills, and a sense of being a good citizen.]

[Reference: Pallak, M. S., Cook, D. A., & Sullivan, J. J. (1980). Commitment and energy conservation. *Applied Social Psychology Annual, 1,* 235–253.]

Obedience

1. You are standing in the aisle of an aircraft in flight when the captain instructs everyone to return to their seats and fasten their seat belts. You do so immediately.
2. Your boss tells you that you will have to stay late tonight to finish a report for a committee meeting the next morning, so you do.
3. During an active shooter drill, the principal of a high school orders everyone to shelter in place and the whole school immediately goes on lockdown.
4. A military commander orders troops to attack an enemy position, and in spite of the danger, the troops obey the order.
5. A mother tells her daughter to stop hitting the dog with a plastic noodle and the daughter stops doing so.
6. Your professor informs the class that everyone's outline for this semester's term paper must be turned in by next Monday, so you meet the deadline.
7. Examples of the importance of having legitimate authority in generating obedience is seen in the failure to obey when an obviously deranged person on a city street demands that passersby pay him a $1 toll to use the sidewalk, or when a stranger approaches you in a restaurant and demands to see your driver's license.
8. Tourists seeking a parking space in many Brazilian cities will encounter men in the street wearing yellow reflective vests who identify a space, guide drivers into that space, and then ask for money. The vests create the impression that these men have some authority, but even though this is not true, most tourists obey the men's directions and also pay them. (Locals do the same, even though they know the men are not city workers, because they also know that bad things could happen to their cars while they are gone if they refuse to pay.)
9. A Candid Camera clip shows a man backing up a stranger's false claim that they were working together the night before. The question of whether this lying for a stranger who held no legitimate authority over the man illustrates obedience or compliance, or a little of both, could make for an interesting class discussion.
10. A hilarious example of obedience is found in a 5-min video showing unsuspecting people who agree to be a witness at a wedding, but then obey the officiant by repeating wedding vows that would render them married to a complete stranger.
11. Examples of people obeying an ambiguously authoritative figure by doing things ranging from silly to potentially dangerous are seen in a 4-min video from the UK.
    It also shows disobedience when the aura of authority is removed.
12. A trailer for a one-hour Netflix show called The Push describes an elaborate hoax in which social pressure for obedience is applied in an attempt to discover if it can cause someone to commit a murder. The target of the hoax shown in the video does not do so, but the show's presenter claims that three others did. This video should provide plenty of material for discussion about obedience as well as about reality shows.

Aggression

[*Note:* The examples in this section illustrate that aggression is influenced by many factors, thus providing an opportunity for you to debunk the myth that psychological profiling alone can reliably guide law enforcement officials in their search for serial killers and other criminals.]

1. The role of genetic influences on aggression comes from inbreeding studies with animals, such as one in which the most aggressive members of a large group of mice were interbred, and then the most aggressive of their offspring were interbred. After this procedure was followed for twenty-five generations, the resulting animals would immediately attack any mouse put in their cage. Continuous inbreeding of the least aggressive members of the original group produced animals that were so nonaggressive that they would refuse to fight even when attacked.
   [Reference: Lagerspetz, K. M. J., & Lagerspetz, K. Y. H. (1983). Genes and aggression. In E. C. Simmel, M. E. Hahn, & J. K. Walters (Eds.), *Aggressive behavior: Genetic and neural approaches*. Hillsdale, NJ: Erlbaum.]
2. An example of the role of genetics in human aggression is suggested by twin studies in which pairs of siblings showed similar degrees of aggressiveness, even if they were raised in differing environments.
   [Reference: Hudziak, J. J., van Beijsterveldt, C. E. M., Bartels, M., Rietveld, M. J. H., Rettew, D. C., Derks, E. M., et al. (2003). Individual differences in aggression: Genetic analyses by age, gender, and informant in 3-, 7-, and 10-year-old Dutch twins. *Behavior Genetics, 33,* 575–589.]
3. It may be that inheritance of certain aspects of temperament or brain chemistry, not aggressive tendencies themselves, that make people aggressive. For example, two studies have found that an inherited tendency to be hypersensitive to social rejection, including just to the word "No," may make people more likely to display aggression.
   [References:
   Eisenberger, N. I., Way, B. M., Taylor, S. E., Welch, W. T., & Lieberman, M. D. (2007). Understanding genetic risk for aggression: Clues from the brain's response to social exclusion. *Biological Psychiatry, 61*(9), 1100–1108.
   Alia-Klein, N., Goldstein, R. Z., Tomasi, D., Woicik, P. A., et al. (2009). Neural mechanisms of anger regulation as a function of genetic risk for violence. *Emotion, 9,* 385–396.]
4. Examples of the role of testosterone in aggression are found in studies showing that aggressive behavior increases or decreases dramatically with the amount of testosterone in the human bloodstream, that criminals who commit violent crimes have higher levels of testosterone than those whose crimes are nonviolent, and that murderers with higher levels of testosterone are more likely than others to have planned their crimes.

[References:
Nguyen, T.-V., McCracken, J.T., Albaugh, M.D., Botteron, K.N., Hudziak, J.J., & Ducharme, S. (2016). A testosterone-related structural brain phenotype predicts aggressive behavior from childhood to adulthood. *Psychoneuroendocrinology, 63*, 109–118.
Montoya, E.R., Terburg, D., Bos, P.A., & Van Honk, J. (2012). Testosterone, cortisol, and serotonin as key regulators of social aggression: A review and theoretical perspective. *Motivation and Emotion, 36*, 65–73.
Schiltz, K. K., Witzel, J. G., & Bogerts, B. B. (2011). Neurobiological and clinical aspects of violent offenders. *Minerva Psichiatrica, 52*(4), 187–203.
Dabbs, J. M., Jr., Riad, J. K., & Chance, S. E. (2001). Testosterone and ruthless homicide. *Personality and Individual Differences, 31*, 599–603.]

5. Examples of the prenatal impact of testosterone on aggression-related brain development are found in two studies. The first focused on pregnant women who took testosterone to prevent miscarriage. The children of these pregnancies later displayed more aggressiveness than their same-sex siblings who had not been exposed to testosterone during prenatal development. A second study found that men who had been exposed to high levels of testosterone before birth were more likely than other men to be aggressive toward female partners.
[References:
Reinisch, J. M., Ziemba-Davis, M., & Sanders, S. A. (1991). Hormonal contributions to sexually dimorphic behavioral development in humans. *Psychoneuroendocrinology, 16*, 213–278.
Cousins, A. J., Fugère, M. A., & Franklin, M. (2009). Digit ratio (2D:4D), mate guarding, and physical aggression in dating couples. *Personality and Individual Differences, 46*, 709–713.]

6. Environmental factors in triggering aggression are exemplified by research showing that rapes, murders and other violent crimes are most likely to occur during the hottest months of the year, that athletes tend to behave more aggressively in hotter weather, and that even hearing words associated with high temperatures—such as "boiling" or "roasting"—is associated with increased aggressiveness.
[References:
Anderson, C. A., & DeLisi, M. (2011). Implications of global climate change for violence in developed and developing countries. In J. P. Forgas, A. W. Kruglanski, & K. D. Williams (Eds.), *The psychology of social conflict and aggression* (pp. 249–265). New York: Psychology Press.
Bushman, B. J., Wang, M. C., & Anderson, C. A. (2005). Is the curve relating temperature to aggression linear or curvilinear? Assaults and temperature in Minneapolis reexamined. *Journal of Personality and Social Psychology, 89*, 62–66.
DeWall C. N., & Bushman, B. J. (2009). Hot under the collar in a lukewarm environment: Words associated with hot temperature increase aggressive thoughts and hostile perceptions *Journal of Experimental Social Psychology, 45*, 1045–1047.

Larrick, R. P., Timmerman, T. A., Carton, A. M., & Abrevaya, J. (2011). Temper, temperature, and temptation: Heat—related retaliation in baseball. *Psychological Science, 22*(4), 423–428.]

7. Another example of environmental influences on aggressiveness is found in studies showing that aggressiveness is associated with unpredictable and irregular noise, and with living in crowded and unpleasant conditions.
[References:
Geen, R.G. & McCown, E.J. (1984). Effects of noise and attack on aggression and physiological arousal. *Motivation and Emotion, 8*, 231–241.
Yuma, Y. (2010). The effect of prison crowding on prisoners' violence in Japan: Testing with cointegration regressions and error correction models. *Japanese Journal of Psychology, 81*, 218–225.]

Helping

[*Note:* Examples in this section should be helpful in debunking the myth that one is more likely to be helped in an emergency when there are many other people around.]

1. On March 3, 2000, at about 7 a.m., a 62-year-old woman in Darby, Pennsylvania was walking to the grocery store when she was pushed from behind by an attacker. She fended him off and then went on to do her shopping. It was only when she got home, and her daughter saw the handle of a knife protruding from her back that she realized that the assailant had stabbed her. No one in the grocery store said anything to her about the knife, let alone offered to help, presumably because the woman did nothing to suggest that assistance was necessary.
[Source: Associated Press, 2000, retrieved here.]

2. A study showing the importance of asking for help in a situation where diffusion of responsibility typically leads to the bystander effect was conducted with undergraduate students. While waiting alone in a room in a campus building, they saw what appeared to be an accident involving a window-washer (the "accident" was actually staged by the experimenters). The man screamed as he and his ladder fell to the ground. All the students looked out a window to see what had happened, but if the man merely clutched his ankle and groaned in pain only 29% of them did anything to help. However, in cases where the man also said he was hurt and needed help, more than 80% of the participants came to his aid.
[Reference: Yakimovich, D., & Saltz, E. (1971). Helping behavior: The cry for help. *Psychonomic Science, 23*, 427–428.]

3. A clear example of the role of diffusion of responsibility in creating a bystander effect in an artificial lab situation is provided by a 5-min video here.
4. A 7-min video showing examples of the bystander effect in a staged situation in a public place can be found here. This one also shows the impact of the needy person's social class and gender on the strength of the effect. Note also that, in one case, the person actually asks for help but is ignored, which according to research like the Yakimovitz and Saltz study above, is not supposed to happen.
5. This 4-min video of a staged event on a college campus provides further illustration of the bystander effect, but also contains interviews with people who stopped to help a young woman lying on the ground. It is available here.
6. An impressive illustration of the impact of group size on the bystander effect in a university library is available on a 4-min video here. This one involves bystanders who see someone steal another person's mobile device.
7. How about situations where there is no doubt about danger and need for help? A dramatic illustration of the bystander effect is contained in an 8-min video here. It shows people passing by a locked car on a hot day containing what appears to be a crying baby alone inside (it is actually a doll whose "crying" comes from a recorded soundtrack). The reactions of passersby vary. Some ignore the child while others stop and help. It is particularly interesting to see the short interviews with those who walked by without stopping and those who stopped and called the police, and those who reacted with anger and outrage when the "mother" returns to the car.
8. An example of young children already having a desire to help others is seen in a 4-min video here.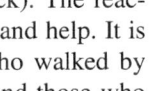

9. An example of the impact of physical attractiveness on the probability of being helped is provided by a study in which male passersby near a university health center were approached by a female student who asked for money to pay for a tetanus injection after being bitten by a rat in the lab where she worked. In one condition, she was wearing an attractive outfit and her hair was nicely arranged, whereas in the other condition she wore an unattractive wig and makeup and mismatched clothing. In the high-severity condition, her hand was bandaged and apparently bloody, while in the low severity condition she was gripping one hand with the other but showed no other evidence of injury. Of the 60 passersby studied, 47 donated some money—20 under the low emergency condition and 27 under the high emergency condition. Of those 27, only slightly more (15 vs. 12) agreed to donate to the more attractive vs. less attractive woman, but they donated nearly *twice as much* money to the more attractive woman.

[Reference: West, S.G. & Brown, T.J. (1975). Physical attractiveness, the severity of the emergency and helping: A field experiment and interpersonal simulation. *Journal of Experimental Social Psychology, 11*, 531–538.]

10. The impact of attractiveness and race were assessed in another decades-old, but interesting experiment with 442 male and 162 female white adults who entered public phone booths in a large metropolitan airport. In the booth they found a completed graduate school application form, a photograph of the applicant, and a stamped envelope addressed to the graduate school where the application was meant to go. Overall, 41% of the people helped the stranger by mailing the application to its destination, but they were significantly more likely to do so if the stranger's photo showed an attractive rather than unattractive person (47 vs. 35%), and if the stranger was white versus black (45 vs. 37%). There was no gender difference.
[Reference: Benson, P.L., Karabenick, S.A., & Lerner, R.M. (1976). Pretty pleases: The effects of physical attractiveness, race, and sex on receiving help. *Journal of Experimental Social Psychology, 12*, 409–415.]

11. An analysis of the biological underpinnings of the bystander effect is presented in an article available here.

12. A dramatic counterexample of the bystander effect is shown in an 8-min video here. It captures the moment when a man named Lenny Skutnik ignored his own safety and jumped into the freezing Potomac river to rescue one of only five survivors of a plane crash on January 13, 1982. The woman was too weak to hold onto a life ring from a helicopter and surely would have died if not for his actions. He had been standing in a crowd of onlookers on the riverbank, but he was the only one who took action.

Industrial/Organizational Psychology 15

The field of industrial/organizational psychology is often given little attention in introductory psychology courses (and textbooks), but it has great importance in the lives of anyone who has a job or wants one. The examples presented in this chapter are designed to help illustrate the relevance of I/O psychology in the daily lives of introductory psychology students as well as to provide teachers of I/O courses with additional illustrative material to attract the attention and interest of their students.

Job Analysis

1. Examples of Position Analysis Questionnaires can be found by Googling "Position Analysis Questionnaire Examples" and clicking on one of the many links that will open a pdf showing various versions of a PAQ.
2. The U.S. Department of Labor maintains an O*Net website that includes the knowledge, skill, ability, and other personal characteristics (KSAOs) necessary for more than 1000 occupational groups.

Testing Employee Characteristics

Tests of job-related knowledge

1. Many of the tests used to screen potential new employees include the cognitive ability and personality tests mentioned in the chapters on thinking and cognitive abilities and personality. More specific tests of the knowledge needed to perform particular jobs include those which assess a candidate's familiarity with things such as (See O*Net online for more examples):

- the principles of accounting,
- computer programming methods,
- real estate procedures and laws,
- county building codes,
- features of office equipment,
- the rules of casino gambling, or
- the proper procedures for baking bread.

Tests of job-related physical and behavioral abilities

1. These are exemplified by tests that evaluate the ability to:

- carry heavy loads,
- climb a rope ladder,
- deal cards,
- wrap packages,
- operate a backhoe,
- press a garment,
- mix cocktails,
- make a sales presentation,
- teach a class,
- cut and style hair,
- draw blood,
- install a floor, or
- pilot a boat or airplane.

Tests of honesty and integrity

1. These are exemplified by forms such as The Reid Report that ask questions such as:

- Do you think that you are too honest to take something that is not yours?
- How much do you dislike doing what someone tells you to do?
- Do you think it is stealing to take small items home from work?
- Do you believe that taking paper or pens without permission from a place where you work is stealing?
- Do you believe most employers take advantage of the people who work for them?
- True or False: I like to take chances.
- Do you believe people should have the same values at work that they do at home?

- What would you do if your boss told you to do something that violates company policy?
- Have you ever explained an incident in a way that made it sound better than it really was?
- Is it OK to take for your own personal use samples intended for customers or clients?
- How upset do you get when you are asked to do something that you don't find is a good use of your time?
- How much time is OK to take out of your workday for non-work tasks, such as internet browsing, online shopping, or daydreaming?

2. These tests may also ask job candidates to choose the statement that describes them best, such as these items regarding rules and honesty:

- I always try to follow the rules.
- I mostly try to follow the rules.
- I may or may not try to follow the rules.
- I rarely try to follow the rules.
- I almost never try to follow the rules.
- I always tell the truth.
- I tell the truth when it won't hurt someone else.
- I will try to tell the truth.
- I don't always tell the truth.
- I don't think it is important to tell the truth.

3. An example of a test of integrity and work ethics is available online, but its teaching value is mainly to illustrate the kinds of overt and covert items used in such tests. The test takes about one hour to complete, may not be valid, and asks the test-taker to pay for a full interpretation of the results.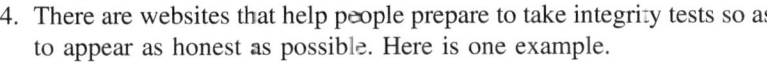
4. There are websites that help people prepare to take integrity tests so as to appear as honest as possible. Here is one example.

Tests of situational judgment

1. Situational judgment tests include asking job candidates to read about or watch videos of simulated workplace situations, such as a conflict between coworkers, and then rate which of several responses would be best or describe what they would do in a similar situation. The candidates' performance is typically rated on dimensions such as:

- Ability to communicate with and influence other people
- Ability to plan, organize, and focus on goals
- Critical, analytical thinking skills

- Decision-making skills
- Ability to cope with challenging situations
- Maintaining a customer service orientation
- Ability to work in a team

- A 5-min video illustrating situational judgment questions and guidance in choosing the best options is available here. The same site also offers four scenarios and response alternatives that students can choose for themselves.

Employee Assessment Interviews

1. Examples of questions typically asked in structured job interviews include:

   - How you would handle [a common job challenge, such as an employee's excessive absenteeism]?
   - Give me an example of a time you had to [perform an important job skill, such as listen to an employee's complaint about working conditions].
   - Who is the best example of a [position the person is applying for, such as office manager] you've worked with? Why is that person such a good example?
   - Which other companies do you admire in [the industry in which the person wants to work]? Why do you admire those companies?
   - What is the most challenging thing about [the position the person is applying for]?
   - What is your favorite thing about [the position the person is applying for]?
   - What do you think will be your biggest challenges if you are hired as [the position the person is applying for]?
   - Tell me about a time you had to explain a difficult concept to a team member.
   - Tell me about a time you failed at a project (or situation or task). How did you try to avoid failure? What did that experience teach you?
   - What do you know about our products and services? Have you used them before?
   - What makes you want to work here?
   - What is our company's mission?
   - Tell me about a time you had to deliver bad news to a manager or team member. How did you do it? What was the other person's reaction?
   - Tell me about a time you had to deal with a difficult colleague. What did you do to communicate properly?
   - Tell me about a time when you had a conflict with a coworker. What did you do?
   - How would you explain [an industry term] to someone from a different industry?

- If you discovered your supervisor was breaking the company's code of conduct, what would you do?
- Tell me about a time you struggled with work-life balance. What did you do? Did you manage to solve the problem, and if so, how?
- Imagine you're assigned an important task, but your team members keep interrupting you with questions. How would you manage the situation?
- Tell me about a time you had an idea that improved your company in some way. How did you make sure it was implemented?
- Tell me about a time someone criticized your work. How did you respond and what did you learn?
- What was the last training you attended? How did you use your new knowledge in practice?

2. Here is an example of a specific interview question and a system for scoring it:

Lead Question: Describe a situation in which you dealt with individuals who were difficult, hostile, or distressed. Probing (Follow-up) Questions: Who was involved? What specific actions did you take? What was the outcome?

Sample Rating Scale

Proficiency level	1- Low	2	3-Average	4	5-Outstanding
Behavioral Examples of Each Proficiency Level	Refers employees to the appropriate staff member	Works with others on a cross-functional team	Establishes cooperative working relationships with managers	Facilitates an open forum to discuss employee concerns	Diffuses an emotionally charged meeting with external stake-holders

3. A summary of structured interviewing, the soft skills that employers typically want to assess during those interviews, and the specific questions used to assess them is available here.

4. This website includes a 90-s video that provides a somewhat stilted but still instructive example of structured interviewing using the STAR format (Situation, Task, Action, Result).

5. A 5-min video designed to help job seekers perform well during unstructured job interviews is available here.

Assessment Centers

1. An example of an assessment center task that simulates various aspects of a manager's job is the *in-basket* exercise. The job candidate is seated at what is described as a "previous manager's" desk and given access to a computer whose files contain emails, memos, phone messages, and the like. The items might include things like this:

   - The boss wants you to correct a presentation within an hour.
   - A customer demands an urgent response to a complaint.
   - A supplier requires feedback on an offer.
   - Your doctor asks that you come to today's appointment an hour earlier than planned.

   The candidate is usually given an hour to go through all this material and enter a comment on each item as to what action should be taken to deal with it and when, including whether to take action oneself or to delegate it to someone else. Throughout the hour, the candidate is subjected to phone calls and other interruptions by people playing the role of co-workers. The employer then interviews the candidate to inquire as to why various actions were taken, or not taken, and assigns an appropriateness score to each action. Candidates who prioritize and delegate items according to importance receive higher scores than those who just deal them in the order in which they were seen or who try to do everything themselves.

2. Another assessment center exercise requires the job candidate to play the role of an employee in the job for which the candidate is applying. For example:

   "You are our sales manager and you are told that a customer called to say that he is extremely unhappy with the home security system he bought, that he has had lousy customer service, and that now he is so angry that he is threatening to tell his story to the State Attorney's office and the local newspaper. Your objective is to resolve the problem with minimum damage to the company's finances and reputation. Plan your response and prepare to call the customer."

   Each candidate is given a score on the knowledge, skills, abilities, and other job-relevant characteristics (KSAOs) displayed during the role-play.

3. A third assessment center task is to measure the candidate's knowledge of the business or industry where the person wishes to work by giving the candidate 30-min to prepare a presentation about some aspect of a political or economic development that has implications for the company. These might include, say, the United Kingdom's exit from the European Union, the rise of electric or self-driving car technology, or trade tensions between the USA and China. After the presentation, the candidate is usually asked questions about it. The candidate is typically rated on dimensions such as:

- Organization skills
- Clarity of communication
- Topic knowledge and ability to analyze and synthesize that knowledge
- Quality of suggested problem solutions or action recommendations
- Public speaking ability
- Confidence and ability to stay calm under pressure

4. Assessment centers may also involve putting candidates into groups of four to six and giving them a job-related topic to discuss or a problem to solve. They might also be asked to prepare and deliver a group presentation about the topic or problem. The groups are observed by the employer and the candidates' social and leadership skills are rated on dimensions such as:
   - Teamworking abilities, leadership potential and the ability to influence others
   - Quality of ideas and ability to consider different perspectives
   - Ability to communicate, to listen, and to mediate conflict
   - Self-confidence
   - Problem solving abilities
   - Critical thinking ability
   - Decisiveness

5. If a *case study exercise* is included in an assessment center, a candidate—or a small group of candidates—will be asked to consider a problem faced by employees in the job for which the candidate(s) is/are applying, and to come up with a specific plan of action to solve it. Here are two examples of such case studies:

   - A publisher is interested in expanding by buying another publishing company. It has identified a target company and approached a number of investment banks for their views on the merits of a potential deal and a target price per share. You work for one of these banks, and you are going to make a bid to be the one to be the publisher's advisor. You need to analyze the financial performance figures provided, review the marketplace, analyze the strengths and weaknesses and synergy potential of the publisher and the target company, prepare a five-minute presentation in which you recommend whether the publisher should proceed with the acquisition, do so under certain conditions, or back away. You must also explain the basis for your recommendation.
   - You work in the marketing department at Yummy Foods, a company that sells snack food throughout the USA. Business has expanded rapidly over the past five years, and the company is launching new products and entering new areas, such as sponsoring racing cars and golf tournaments. Now, just as the company is about to launch a massive marketing campaign for its latest candy bar, a national newspaper reports that Yummy Foods is underpaying

its production line employees and making them work in unsafe conditions. The story goes viral on social media, and there are calls for a boycott of the company's products. What would you do to deal with this situation?

6. A 6-min video shows the procedures involved in the course of a one-day assessment center in the European Union, but there are only labels of each segment, no dialogue.

Assessing Job Performance

1. Examples of unstructured job performance narratives provided by supervisors:

"John is a self-motivated team member and a pleasure to work with. He demonstrates superior technical ability and produces work of exceptional quality. John takes the time to fully understand the scope of projects and displays a keen attention to detail, but often at the expense of effective time management."

"Jessica demonstrates a practical and data-driven approach to problem-solving. She actively seeks different perspectives and creative solutions from her teammates and is continuously experimenting to drive results."

"Lisa recently moved into her position in our product team. Despite the steep learning curve associated with a shift in career direction, Lisa is already showing great potential in her new role. She displays an ability to learn rapidly and a determination to broaden her skill set."

"Kate still needs to focus on her level of accountability and willingness to take ownership when projects fall short of expectations. When faced with difficult situations, she has a tendency to become defensive and divert blame away from herself."

"Monica shows little engagement during meetings and team-building activities, as well as a lack of commitment to her own professional development. Over the next three months, we'd like Monica to focus on setting more aggressive personal goals. I will also work with her directly to identify learning opportunities to further her career growth. Our hope is that these steps will motivate her to develop the skills necessary to allow for upward movement within the organization."

2. Here is an example of a *graphic rating form* that supervisors might use to quantify their personal experience with an employee, including their subjective impressions of the employee's work.

Rate employee on each dimension on the left by checking the appropriate box corresponding to the level of performance for the past year.

Dimension

Customer service	☐ Poor	☐ Fair	☐ Satisfactory	☐ Above satisfactory	☐ Outstanding
Management of time	☐ Poor	☐ Fair	☐ Satisfactory	☐ Above satisfactory	☐ Outstanding
Professional appearance	☐ Poor	☐ Fair	☐ Satisfactory	☐ Above satisfactory	☐ Outstanding
Teamwork	☐ Poor	☐ Fair	☐ Satisfactory	☐ Above satisfactory	☐ Outstanding
Work quality	☐ Poor	☐ Fair	☐ Satisfactory	☐ Above satisfactory	☐ Outstanding
Work quantity	☐ Poor	☐ Fair	☐ Satisfactory	☐ Above satisfactory	☐ Outstanding

2. A 90-s video shows an example of a *behavioral rating scale* being used at Auburn University. It is available here and nicely illustrates the characteristics of behaviorally-based performance assessment.
3. Here is an example of a *behaviorally-anchored rating scale (BARS)* for assessing employee performance at oral communication:

Oral Communication:
Organizes thoughts and expresses them in a clear and logical manner, quickly comprehends another's meaning, uses appropriate vocabulary, correct grammar, and appropriate non-verbal communication

9	Expresses ideas clearly and concisely
8	Answers questions completely and precisely. Speaks with a voice that exhibits an appropriate command presence
7	Relates thoughts in an organized manner. Gives concise answers to questions. Demonstrates effective active listening behaviors (e.g. leans forward, nods in agreement, repeats statements back, verbalizes understanding)
6	Clearly enunciates words Attentively leans forward
5	Voices ideas randomly or several at a time
4	Interrupts others inappropriately Excessive use of filler words, phrases (umm, like I said, etc.)
3	Fails to listen to questions Uses incorrect words or grammar in responding to questions
2	Talks too long without making a point
1	Uses profanity

4. Other examples of BARS are available here.

5. A light-hearted video available here presents the BARS approach for supervisors who don't really want to use it.

6. Here is an example of a one-page behavioral rating form that also allows for open-ended comments to justify the ratings:

RATING IDENTIFICATION

O—Outstanding—Performance is exceptional in all areas and is recognizable as being far superior to others.

V—Very Good—Results clearly exceed most position requirements. Performance is of high quality and is achieved on a consistent basis.

G—Good—Competent and dependable level of performance. Meets performance standards of the job.

I—Improvement Needed—Performance is deficient in certain areas. Improvement is necessary.

U—Unsatisfactory—Results are generally unacceptable and require immediate improvement. No merit increase should be granted to individuals with this rating.

N—Not Rated—Not applicable or too soon to rate.

GENERAL FACTORS	RATING SCALE	SUPPORTIVE DETAILS OR COMMENTS
1. **Quality**—The accuracy, thoroughness, and acceptability of work performed.	O ☐ 100–90 V ☐ 90–80 G ☐ 80–70 I ☐ 70–60 U ☐ below 60	Points ☐
2. **Productivity**—The quantity and efficiency of work produced in a specified period of time.	O ☐ 100–90 V ☐ 90–80 G ☐ 80–70 I ☐ 70–60 U ☐ below 60	Points ☐
3. **Job Knowledge**—The practical/technical skills and information used on the job.	O ☐ 100–90 V ☐ 90–80 G ☐ 80–70 I ☐ 70–60 U ☐ below 60	Points ☐
4. **Reliability**—The extent to which an employee can be relied upon regarding task completion and follow-up.	O ☐ 100–90 V ☐ 90–80 G ☐ 80–70 I ☐ 70–60 U ☐ below 60	Points ☐
5. **Availability**—The extent to which an employee is punctual, observes prescribed work break/meal periods, and the overall attendance record.	O ☐ 100–90 V ☐ 90–80 G ☐ 80–70 I ☐ 70–60 U ☐ below 60	Points ☐

7. Here are examples of *critical incidents* that may be included in behavioral rating forms to illustrate levels of job performance ranging from "extremely effective" to "extremely ineffective":

- listens patiently
- tries to reach a compromise
- coldly states store policy
- angrily demands that complaining customers leave

Assessing Job Performance 449

8. Here is an example of a behavioral rating form for use in assessing performance in groups:

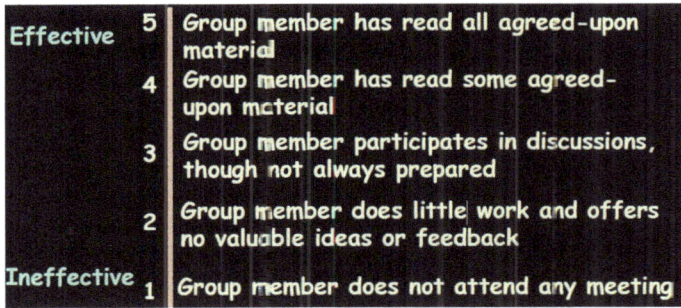

7. This Dilbert cartoon provides an example of how *not* to construct behavioral rating forms.

Recruiting Employees

1. An example of job-posting options for employers on Monster.com is available here.

2. Here is a webpage from *Indeed*, where employers post jobs and where candidates can search for them:

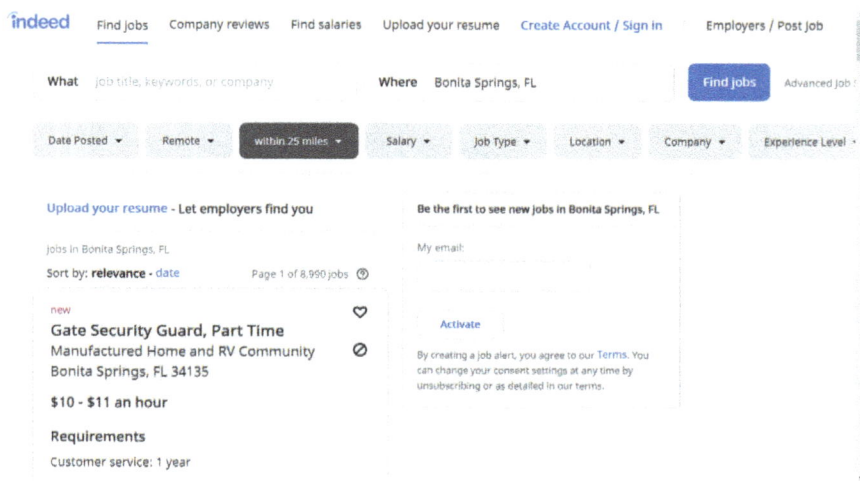

3. Designed to prevent unfair discrimination in hiring and promotion practices, the Federal Equal Employment Opportunity Commission maintains Uniform Guidelines on Employee Selection Procedures. They are available here.

Training Employees

1. Examples of the characteristics of high-quality training programs employ many of the principles described in the chapter on learning and on thinking and cognitive abilities, including *training for generalization* (promoting transfer or application of skills learned in training to the workplace), *providing early feedback* (positive reinforcement, shaping), using *optimal training schedules* (arranging for distributed rather than massed learning/practice sessions), creating employee *engagement* with the training (active learning), providing opportunities for *overlearning* (arranging for enough practice that employees can perform new skills more or less automatically).
2. Evaluation of training outcomes using *training-level criteria* typically involve asking trainees to answer the following questions at the end of training:

    - Did you feel that the training was worth your time?
    - Did you think that it was successful?
    - What were the greatest strengths and weaknesses of the training?
    - What are the three most important things that you learned from this training?
    - From what you learned, what do you plan to apply in your job?
    - What support might you need to apply what you learned?

- What barriers do you anticipate you might encounter as you attempt to put these new skills into practice?
- What ideas do you have for overcoming the barriers you mentioned?

Trainees might also be asked to rate their agreement with the following statements on a 1–5 scale at the end of a training program:

- I understood the learning objectives.
- I was able to relate each of the learning objectives to the learning I achieved.
- I was appropriately challenged by the material.
- I will be able to immediately apply what I learned.
- My learning was enhanced by the knowledge of the facilitator.
- My learning was enhanced by the experiences shared by the facilitator.
- I was well engaged during the session.
- It was easy for me to get actively involved during the session.
- I was comfortable with the pace of the program.
- I was comfortable with the duration of the session.
- I was given ample opportunity to get answers to my questions.
- I was given ample opportunity to practice the skills I was asked to learn.
- I was given ample opportunity to demonstrate my knowledge.
- I was given ample opportunity to demonstrate my skills.
- I found the room atmosphere to be comfortable.
- I was pleased with the room set-up.
- I experienced minimal distractions during the session.
- I anticipate that I will eventually see positive results as a result of my efforts.
- I am clear about what is expected of me as a result of going through this training.

3. Evaluation of training using *trainee-learning criteria* requires either comparing trainees' knowledge, abilities, skills, and attitudes before and after training, or simply using post-training tests to assess the extent to which the trainees are now able to meet the learning objectives of the training.
4. Evaluation of training using *performance-level criteria* involves observation of changes in the on-the-job attitudes and behaviors of employees after they have completed training. An example of successful and unsuccessful training on performance-level criteria is provided by a professional trainer named Jim Kirkpatrick, who tells of the time he was in a hotel lobby where a man was washing tall windows using a sponge on a long pole. When he asked the man what his job entails, the man didn't stop or turn his head, but simply said "I am a window washer." When Kirkpatrick asked the same question to an employee who was doing the same job at a different hotel, the man stopped what he was doing, made eye contact, smiled, and said "I am helping to make for a memorable experience for my hotel's guests!"

[Kurt, S. (2016). Kirkpatrick model: Four levels of learning evaluation. *Educational Technology*, October 24. Retrieved here.]

5. This nearly 4-min video summarizes the four levels of training evaluation contained in the Kirkpatrick Model, provides examples of each, and describes the pros and cons of using it.

Employee Motivation

Examples of the main sources and theories of human motivation are to be found in the chapter on motivation and emotion. Here we provide examples of concepts and theories that are specific to the workplace:

1. Motivation affects the *direction* of work-related behavior in that it shapes people's decisions about whether to work and what kind of job to seek.
2. Motivation affects the *intensity* of work, determining how often an employee is absent or late, or chooses to work overtime, or goes beyond the call of duty.
3. Motivation is also reflected in workers' *persistence* at a task, as shown by giving up as soon as difficulties arise, or continuing to try, using every strategy possible until their efforts are successful.
4. Applying *ERG (existence, relatedness, growth) theory* to management decisions would be exemplified when a company promotes employees' job-related growth needs by offering flex-time work schedules that improve work-life balance, including allowing employees with children to better satisfy their relatedness needs (e.g., care for a sick relative or enable coordinated day-care drop-off or pickup).
5. A 2-min video from Dell Computers illustrates how flex-time and telecommuting has become an integral part of the modern workplace, especially in information technology. In fact, as illustrated in this article, some employees who began telecommuting during the Covid-19 pandemic, are no longer motivated to return to the office.

6. An example of an ERG-based prediction would be that employees whose job-related growth needs are frustrated by lack of opportunity for skill development or advancement would start to spend more time socializing on the job (reflecting relatedness needs) or perhaps overeating or sleeping at work (reflecting existence needs).
7. Examples of what employers can do to satisfy employees' existence needs on the job include providing comfortable break rooms, facilities for exercise and other recreational activities, high-quality cafeterias, making visible efforts to meet workplace safety standards, and dealing with cases of interpersonal

conflict, harassment, or bullying in ways that communicate a commitment to maintain a psychologically safe workplace.

8. Efforts to satisfy existence needs can also take the form of giving employees a sense of job security by avoiding capricious firing decisions. And even when layoffs are necessary, as during the recent Covid-19 pandemic, some companies do everything possible to limit the number of employees affected.
9. You can find examples of the layout of modern workplaces that aim to satisfy employees' existence needs by Googling "modern workplaces" and choosing "images" at the top of the page.
10. An example of employer efforts to promote employees' job-related growth needs is structuring annual performance reviews so that, in addition to evaluating past performance, they include discussion of plans for further training that will qualify the employee to expand responsibilities, take on more complex jobs, and be eligible for promotion, better pay, and more benefits.
11. A general example of applying an *expectancy theory* of motivation in the workplace: Predicting that employees will put in extra effort when they (a) expect a bonus for doing so, and (b) the bonus is valuable enough to be worth the effort.
12. A more specific example: An information technology expert put in long extra hours to improve the company's procedures for capturing business data, all with the expectation that her supervisor will recognize and reward her with a cash bonus or a more flexible work schedule.
13. The importance of individual differences in applying expectancy theory in the workplace is exemplified when the prospect of a cash bonus for extra effort has no effect on the performance of some employees because they don't believe that a supervisor will actually provide the bonus.
14. Another example of the importance of individual differences among employees appears when extra pay for extra work has little or no effect on those who are less focused on money than they are on, say, the challenge of solving a difficult problem or having more time to spend with their families.
15. Applying expectancy theory in a way that recognizes individual differences is exemplified by a system of rewards in which a high-performing employee who has a long commute to and from work would be given a day working from home, whereas a high-performing employee who is eager for more responsibility would be given an opportunity to lead the next small-team project.
16. This Dilbert cartoon provides a humorous take on expectancy theory.
17. The application of *goal-setting theory* of motivation in the workplace is seen, for example, when employers give employees a chance to set their own short- and long-term goals, such as increasing sales by 10% this quarter, or to earn promotion to a higher position in the company within a year.

18. Examples of the most motivating goals are those that are:
    - clearly stated (e.g., reduce emergency room wait times to no more than 30 min)
    - chosen in consultation with the employees who will work toward them
    - difficult enough to be challenging (e.g., re-write the code for a user interface to make it more intuitive), but not so difficult as to be impossible (e.g., have the new code ready by tomorrow afternoon)
    - specific enough (e.g., "reduce customer complaints by one-third" or "increase our website's subscriber base by 20%") to allow employees to keep track of their progress and know when they have succeeded
    - achievable given the employees' skill sets (you would not ask your company's air-conditioner service technicians to develop a new customer billing system)
19. An 11-min video about SMART goals (Specific, Measurable, Attainable, Relevant, Timely) is available here.
20. Examples of applying both expectancy and goal-setting theory in the workplace are provided when companies not only provide rewards to employees who meet short-term goals, but also hold end-of-year ceremonies to honor and reward (e.g., with significant cash bonuses, plaques, or vacation trips) employees, or groups of employees who have been especially productive and/or have met long-term goals that benefit them and the company.
21. Examples of the most motivating systems for recognizing and rewarding good performance are those that
    - provide larger rewards for higher levels of performance (e.g., the top salesperson of the month should be given a larger bonus or nicer gift than the one who came in second, third, and so on).
    - recognize the contributions of each member of a high-performing group (e.g., rather than identifying "shipping department at the Chicago factory" as having been the most efficient in the country, the announcement would list the names of all employees who work in that department).
22. This Dilbert cartoon provides a humorous example of the fact that employee motivation is not maximized when the goals of employer and employees are not in synch.
23. Examples of employer behaviors and employment situations and incentives that tend to reduce employee motivation are summarized here and here.

Job Satisfaction

1. An early example of measuring general job satisfaction (the global approach) is Kunin's *Faces Scale*, which asks workers to put a check mark under the face that best expresses the workers' view of their job:

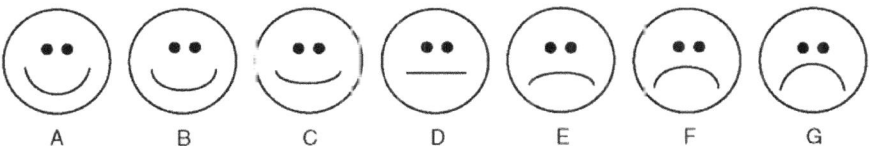

[Source: Kunin, T. (1955). The construction of a new type of attitude measure. *Personnel Psychology, 8,* 65–77. You can also find the image here.]

2. A more contemporary example of the global approach to job satisfaction measurement is the *Job in General Scale*, which asks workers to rate the extent to which each of the following 18 adjectives correctly describe their job:

- Pleasant
- Bad
- Ideal
- Waste of time
- Good
- Undesirable
- Worthwhile
- Worse than most
- Acceptable
- Superior
- Better than most
- Disagreeable
- Makes me content
- Inadequate
- Excellent
- Rotten
- Enjoyable
- Poor

[Source: Ironson, G. H., Smith, P. C., Brannick, M. T., Gibson, W. M., & Paul, K. B. (1989). Construction of a Job in General Scale: A comparison of global, composite, and specific measures. *Journal of Applied Psychology, 74,* 193–200.]

3. An abridged version of the Job in General Scale is designed to be used by researchers and practitioners in I/O psychology. Its 8 adjectives are:

- Good
- Undesirable
- Better than most
- Disagreeable
- Makes me content
- Excellent
- Enjoyable
- Poor

[Source: Russell, S. S., Spitzmüller, C., Lin, L. F., Stanton, J. M., Smith, P. C., & Ironson, G. H. (2004). Shorter can also be better: The abridged Job in General Scale. *Educational and Psychological Measurement, 64*(5), 878–893.]

4. An example of measuring various factors underlying job satisfaction (the facet approach) is the *Job Descriptive Index*, which asks employees to say "Yes," "No," or "Cannot decide" about whether each of several adjectives accurately describe:

- Coworkers (e.g., stimulating, boring, slow, helpful, likeable, lazy).
- Current work (e.g., fascinating, routine, boring, repetitive, creative).
- Pay (e.g., fair, bad, enough to live on, underpaid, well paid).
- Opportunities for promotion (e.g., good, somewhat limited, dead-end, regular, fairly good).
- Supervision (e.g., supportive, hard to please, tactful, annoying, intelligent, bad, has favorites).

[Source: Smith, P. C., Kendall, L. M., & Hulin, C. L. (1969). *The measurement of satisfaction in work and retirement*. Chicago: Rand McNally. (You can download the actual Job Descriptive Index and Job in General Scale forms by registering for free.)]

5. Another example of the facet approach to measuring job satisfaction is the *Job Satisfaction Survey*, which asks employees to rate their agreement with 4 statements about each of 9 facets of their jobs, including Pay, Promotion, Supervision, Fringe Benefits, Performance-based Rewards, Rules and Procedures, Coworkers, Nature of Work, and Communication. The four items from the Pay facet are presented below:

Please circle the one number for each question that comes closest to reflecting your opinion about it.	1 Disagree very much 2 Disagree moderately 3 Disagree slightly	4 Agree slightly 5 Agree moderately 6 Agree very much

1. I feel I am being paid a fair amount for the work I do.

       1   2   3   4   5   6

2. Raises are too few and far between.

       1   2   3   4   5   6

3. I feel unappreciated by the organization when I think about what they pay me.

       1   2   3   4   5   6

4. I feel satisfied with my chances for salary increases.

       1   2   3   4   5   6

[Source: Spector, P. (1985). Measurement of human service staff satisfaction: Development of the Job Satisfaction Survey. *American Journal of Community Psychology, 13*, 693–713.]

6. Examples of factors affecting job satisfaction include:

- Complexity of the job
- How interesting and challenging the job is
- How much control the employee feels
- Pay
- Amount of work-family conflict the job creates
- Amount of physical or psychological stress the job creates

7. Examples of behaviors associated with job satisfaction include:

- Organizational citizenship behavior (going beyond the job's formal requirements)
- Loyalty to the company (not seeking to work elsewhere)

8. Examples of behaviors associated with job dissatisfaction include:

- Seeking employment elsewhere (if other jobs are available)
- Workplace aggression (bullying, harassment, threats of or actual violence)

- Counterproductive workplace behavior (theft, sabotage, industrial spying, obstruction of other employees' progress, purposely slow or incorrect work, drug or alcohol use at work)
- Absenteeism or chronic lateness

9. This Dilbert cartoon offers a humorous example of counterproductive workplace behavior.

Occupational Health Psychology

[*Note:* Many examples of material in this area, including the impact of physical and psychological stressors, stress responses, and mediating factors that affect physical and psychological health are presented in the chapter on health, stress, and coping. Additional examples of the impact of changing work shifts on circadian rhythms are included in the chapter on consciousness.]

1. Examples of physical stressors in the workplace that can result in physical disorders or injuries include:

    - Repetitive strain (such as repeatedly twisting or cutting or typing) can create or worsen repetitive strain injuries such as carpal tunnel syndrome.
    - Taking improper working postures or positions when performing tasks such as lifting heavy objects can contribute to musculoskeletal disorders (e.g., back injury).
    - Working for long periods while holding the same position (static load) can result in low back pain and muscle aches.
    - Excessive force impact, particularly from heavy weights can result in excessive fatigue and the risk of various musculoskeletal disorders.
    - When hard or sharp objects repeatedly run against the skin, abrasions and other injuries to soft tissue can result.
    - Operating vibrating equipment can cause hand-arm vibration syndrome (HAVS), as well as specific diseases such as "white finger" or Raynaud's syndrome, carpel tunnel syndrome and tendonitis.
    - Inadequate lighting can cause fatigue, eye strain, headache, and higher risk of accidents.
    - Screen glare caused by overbright computer screens or light reflected from nearby windows, or looking at a computer screen against an overbright background can cause eye strain and fatigue.
    - Working in extreme temperatures or in the presence of loud sounds can cause discomfort or permanent hearing loss.

Occupational Health Psychology

2. Three-to-5 min videos showing examples of correct and incorrect methods of interacting with workplace equipment and loads are available here.

3. Mayo Clinic offers a good overview of carpal tunnel syndrome.

4. A 2-min video illustrates a quick test to diagnose carpal tunnel syndrome.

5. This Dilbert cartoon shows a humorous example of once-common corporate lack of concern about employee health.

6. Some examples of how human factors psychologists (engineering psychologists) help industrial designers to create ergonomic workplace equipment that minimizes repetitive strain and other injuries can be found here and here.
A 90-s video at the bottom of the webpage shows the features of an ergonomically designed bio-laboratory workstation.

7. Here is a "top ten" list of ergonomically designed office equipment.

8 An example of how workplace performance can be impaired by disruption of employees' circadian rhythms is seen in jet-lagged jewelry company employees who arrive in Hong Kong from around the world and set up displays at Asia's largest jewelry show. Then they try to wait on customers while keeping track of their treasures. Jewel thieves take advantage of the inattentiveness that can be caused by jet lag to steal millions of dollars' worth of merchandise at every show. (See also the chapter on consciousness.)
[Source: Fowler, G.A. (2004, March 4). Calling all jewel thieves. *Wall Street Journal*, p. B1.]

9. An example of the symptoms, correlates, and impact of *shiftwork disorders* on workplace performance is described in the 7-min video available here.

10. Examples of simple procedures that can help to prevent shiftwork disorders are available here.

11. Examples of the benefits of psychologists' research on the negative impact of extended work shifts include corporate and government rules requiring rest breaks at fixed intervals for commercial airline pilots, long-haul bus and truck drivers, and others whose jobs require constant attention to complex tasks and systems. The rules also limit the total number of hours these employees can work in any twenty-four-hour period.

12. Examples of major industrial accidents in which sleepiness and/or shiftwork disorder may have played a part:
    - The Three Mile Island nuclear power plant incident, which occurred at 4:00 a.m. Overnight shift workers failed to respond quickly and appropriately to a mechanical problem that caused a near meltdown.
    - Sleepiness is thought to be partly to blame for the nuclear plant disaster at Chernobyl, which took place at 1:30 a.m.
    - The Exxon Valdez oil tanker spill
    - The Space Shuttle Challenger accident (where managers at the flight control center were known to be working irregular hours on very little sleep).
    - Thirty-two passengers were injured on March 24, 2014, when a Chicago Transit Authority train slammed into a station at the end of the line because the train operator had fallen asleep. She had been overtired after working a lot of overtime. (Details of the accident can be found here.)
    - On February 12, 2009 a Continental airlines flight made a routine takeoff from Liberty Airport in Newark, New Jersey, but as it neared its destination in Buffalo, New York, the plane stalled, then crashed, killing everyone on board. The pilots had failed to properly respond to cockpit warnings that the plane was moving too slowly through the air, and in fact, the Captain actually raised the plane's nose, slowing it even further. The accident report said that ahead of the flight, both pilots had long commutes and slept in the crew lounge instead of a hotel. Tiredness was cited as one of the factors in the crew's failure to respond quickly and appropriately to the aircraft's loss of speed.

13. Details of railroad accidents caused in part by sleepiness are available here.

14. A study evaluated the effects of having employees wear blue-light filtering glasses in an effort to improve sleep, workplace engagement, and organizational citizenship behavior, and to decrease counterproductive workplace behavior. The apparently positive effects, as

well as the controversy surrounding the value of blue-light filtering, allow you to use this study to promote a critical-thinking-based discussion of the research design.

[Source: Guarana, C. L., Barnes, C. M., & Ong, W. J. (2020). The effects of blue-light filtration on sleep and work outcomes. *Journal of Applied Psychology, 106*(5), 784–796. https://doi.org/10.1037/apl0000806.]

Work Groups and Work Teams

1. An example of the difference between a work group and a work team: The four servers waiting on customers during the dinner shift at a restaurant is a work group. The entire staff on duty during the restaurant's dinner shift would be considered a work team. All members of the team are working on the same task with the same goal in mind—namely, to successfully serve customers as quickly and efficiently as possible. Further, each team member has a specialized role: greeters seat customers, servers take orders and deliver the food prepared by the cooks, and managers monitor progress, direct employees, and fill in at various tasks as needed.
   Another example of a work team is the doctors, nurses, and technicians who join forces to perform surgery. Everyone on the surgical team is devoted to the same goal of completing a successful operation, but each performs a somewhat different task in a coordinated way under the direction of the surgeon, who acts as the team leader.
2. An example of self-managed work teams can be seen at the Durham, North Carolina GE plant that makes jet engines. There are nine production teams of people whose only supervision comes in the form of the date on which their next engine must be ready. The team members themselves make all other decisions, including who does what tasks, how training sessions, vacations, and overtime are scheduled, as well as how to improve the efficiency of the manufacturing process, and how to handle members who are underperforming. This plant has no time clock. Workers decide among themselves how to arrange for members to take time off to go to their kids' band concerts, Little League games, and the like. Here you can read more about the plant.
3. Examples of other companies that have adopted some version of self-managed work teams include Zappos.com, Gore-Tex, Valve, Spotify, Electronic Arts, and GitHub.
4. Here is the story of Zappos' adoption of self-managed work teams.

5. A 3-min video provides an example of why self-managed work teams can be superior to standard management practices using the analogy of managing traffic passing through a busy intersection.

6. A 3-min video appearing well down the page describes the ways in which a European company allows workers to decide how and when to get feedback from "sparring partners" to facilitate their development on the job, and how this feedback-request system takes the place of annual performance evaluations.

Leadership

1. Examples of relationship-oriented leader behavior (high on consideration):

   - Engaging in two-way communication
   - Expressing concern for subordinates
   - Emphasizing employee comfort and satisfaction
   - Leaning towards subordinates during conversation
   - Maintaining eye contact
   - Displaying positive facial expressions
   - Being friendly, appreciative, responsive, and willing to listen

2. Examples of task-oriented leader behavior (high on initiating structure):

   - Letting group members know what is expected of them
   - Maintaining definite standards of performance
   - Scheduling the work to be done
   - Checking that group members follow standard rules and regulations
   - Providing direction
   - Solving problems

3. Examples of charismatic/transformational leaders (those who inspire followers to embrace a vision of success and make extraordinary efforts to achieve things they would not have done on their own):

   - Adolph Hitler
   - Winston Churchill
   - Margaret Thatcher
   - Steve Jobs
   - Elon Musk
   - Donald Trump
   - Barak Obama
   - Mahatma Ghandi
   - Dr. Martin Luther King, Jr.
   - John F. Kennedy

Leadership

4. An example of efforts to teach leaders to become more charismatic is described in a study that evaluated a charisma training program delivered by I/O psychologists at a large Canadian bank. The managers of 20 bank branches were randomly assigned to either a charisma training group or a no-training control group. Two weeks before training and five months afterward, the people who worked for each manager filled out a questionnaire, which included rating their manager's charisma as well as their own level of job satisfaction. Charisma training was delivered in five sessions over three-months. At the first day-long training session, managers met as a group to learn about the behaviors that make charismatic leaders charismatic and to practice those behaviors in order to increase their own charisma. In the next four sessions, managers worked individually with one of the researchers, receiving additional training, getting feedback on performance, and setting goals for further progress. The results indicated that the training program had a positive impact on managers' charisma, as measured by their employees' ratings. Untrained managers' charisma ratings showed a small decline. Employees who worked for the trained managers also reported higher levels of job satisfaction after the training was over than did those who worked for the untrained managers. In addition, the financial performance of the trained managers' branches increased, whereas that of the untrained group decreased somewhat.

[*Note*: You might want to ask students to think critically about these results, given the design of the study. Specifically, the changes seen in the trained managers might have been due to positive expectations and other nonspecific (placebo) effects associated with participating in any kind of special program, not necessarily the training itself. Even the improved financial performance could have been the result of expectation-driven efforts by managers and employees to do better, efforts that had nothing to do with the training itself. If you ask students to redesign the study, they might well point out that it would have been better had the untrained managers participated in some sort of placebo program that, like the charisma training, would have raised their expectations and those of their employees. They might also realize that, even if the training had a specific effect, it would be important to know whether that effect would last beyond the five-month follow-up period.]

[Source: Barling, J., Weber, T., & Kelloway, E. K. (1996). Effects of transformational leadership training on attitudinal and financial outcomes: A field experiment. *Journal of Applied Psychology, 81*, 827–832.]

5. Two Dilbert cartoons here and here provide funny takes on the idea of learning to be charismatic.

Index

A
Abulia, 52
Acalculia, 38
Acceptance and Commitment Therapy (ACT), 397
Accommodation, 302
Achievement motivation, 282
Achromatopsia, 65
Acronyms, 173
Acrostics, 173
Actor-observer effect, 410
Acute stress disorder, 371
Adaptation, 103
Addison's disease, 78
Addisonian crisis, 78
Adenoma, 79
ADHD, 366
Adrenal insufficiency, 78
Adrenocorticotropic hormone, 77
Afferent baroreflex failure, 75
Age regression, 264
Aggression, 273, 434
Agnosias, 100
Agoraphobia, 369
Agreeableness, 352, 353
Akinetic mutism, 52
Akinetopsia, 46
Akira Haraguchi, 177
Albert Ellis, 400
Alcoholism, 364
Alcohol-use disorder, 364, 401
Alexia without agraphia, 37
Algorithms, 205, 206, 218
Alice in Wonderland syndrome, 66
Alien hand syndrome, 67
Allochiria, 66
Alternative Uses Test, 212
Alzheimer's, 56
Alzheimer's disease, 69, 377

Ambiguous figures, 104
American College Testing (ACT), 234
Amnesia, 373
Amnestic disorders, 57
Amusica, 100
Amyloid plaque, 69
Anal expulsiveness, 342
Anal-retentive, 342
Anal stage, 342
Analysis of everyday behavior, 384
Anchoring Effect/Anchoring Heuristic, The, 207
Androgens, 77
Angular gyrus, 38
Animal communication, 308
Anorexia nervosa, 374
Anosagnosia, 55
Anosognosia, 48, 60
Anterograde amnesia, 57, 192
Anticipatory nausea, 127
Antisocial personality disorder, 378
Anxiety disorders, 364, 369
Apgar, 298
Apperceptivevisual agnosia, 100
Applications of classical conditioning, 131
Applications of operant conditioning, 148
Applied behavior analysis, 392
Apraxia, 67
Arousal and performance, 274
Arousal Theory, 273
Assertiveness, 399
Assessing job performance, 446
Assessment center, 444, 445
Assessment center exercise, 444
Assimilation, 301
Associative visual agnosias, 100
Astatikopsia, 47
Attachment, 312
Attachment styles, 312

© Springer Nature Switzerland AG 2022
E. L. Cameron and D. A. Bernstein, *Illustrating Concepts and Phenomena in Psychology*, Springer Texts in Education,
https://doi.org/10.1007/978-3-030-85650-2

Attention and perception, 114
Attribution, 408
Attributional errors, 408
Auditory agnosia, 65
Auditory illusions, 102, 104
Auguste Deter, 69
Aunt Fanny effect, 360
Authoritarian parenting, 315
Authoritative parenting, 314
Autism spectrum disorder, 365, 366, 392
Autonomic Nervous System (ANS), 74
Autonomic neuropathy, 74
Autonomy vs. shame and doubt, 345
Availability heuristic, The, 208
Aversive conditioning, 393

B
Babbling, 310
Baclofen, 401
Barnum effect, 360
Beck Depression Inventory, 25
Behavioral activation, 395, 397
Behaviorally-anchored rating scale, 447
Behavioral rating scale, 447
Behavioral Stress responses, 322
Behaviors associated with job dissatisfaction, 457
Behaviors associated with job satisfaction, 457
Behavior therapy, 387
Belongingness and love needs, 277
Biases and flaws in decision making, 230
Bias in perceiving gains, 230
Big five personality dimensions, 349
Big Five Personality Test, 360
Binge eating disorder, 375
Biological bases of behavior, 35
Biological bases of memory, 192
Biological motion, 112
Biological rhythms, 245
Biology of emotion, The, 293
Bipolar and related disorders, 368
Bipolar disorder, 368
Blindsight, 47, 119, 243
Blue-eyes brown eyes, 413
Borderline personality disorder, 378
Bottom-up perceptual processes, 119
Bottom-up processing, 101
Brain stimulation, 403
Brainstorming, 212
Brief COPE scale, 328
Broca's aphasia, 42, 54
Broken Window Theory, 419
Bug in the ear, 392
Bulimia nervosa, 375

Burnout, 329
Bystander effect, 436–438

C
Cannabidiol, 402
Capacity of working memory, 159
Capgras syndrome, 64
Capsaicin, 88
Carl Rogers, 399, 400
Carpal tunnel syndrome, 458, 459
Case studies, 20
Case study exercise, 445
Catatonia, 367
Categorical clustering, 172
Categories, 203
Central nervous system, 36
Change blindness, 116
Charismatic/transformational leaders, 462
Charisma training, 463
Child-rearing and parenting styles, 313
Chorea, 72
Chronic fatigue syndrome, 401
Chronic Traumatic Encephalopathy (CTE), 45
Chronotypes, 245
Chunks, 162
Circadian, 245
Circadian rhythms, 459
Circadian rhythm sleep-wake disorder, 377
Circle of thought, The, 196
Classical conditioning, 125, 161
Client-centered (person-centered) therapy, 400
Client-centered therapy, 400
Cognitive abilities, 232
Cognitive and cognitive-behavior therapy, 393
Cognitive appraisal of stressors, 325
Cognitive cycles, 246
Cognitive development, 300
Cognitive dissonance, 411
Cognitive distortions, 393
Cognitive maps, 204
Cognitive restructuring, 394
Coma, 59
Compensation, 340
Competency to stand trial, 379
Compliance, 429
Compound emotional expressions, 292
Computerized cognitive training, 69
Concepts, 202
Concurrent (convergent) validity, 33
Conditioned stimuli (CS), 128
Conditions of worth, 354
Conduct disorders, 377
Confabulation, 59
Configural superiority effect, 198

Confirmation bias, 225
Conformity, 428
Confounding variables, 15
Conscientiousness, 349, 350
Consequences Test, The, 212
Conservation, 301
Consideration, 462
Consolidation, 162
Constructive memory, 191
Construct validity, 31
Content validity, 32
Context, 197
Context-dependent retrieval, 181
Context reinstatement effect, 181
Continuous reinforcement, 141
Contrast sensitivity, 90
Control group, 12
Convenience sample, 17
Convergent thinking, 211
Conversion disorder, 374
Cooing, 310
Coping resources and skills, 328
Corpus callosum, 53
Correlational research, 22
Correlation coefficient, 23
Cortisol, 77
Counterproductive workplace behavior, 460
Creativity, 212
Crimes of passion, 270
Critical incidents, 448
Critical period, 295
Critical/sensitive periods, 295
Critical thinking, 4
Cross-modal sensory effects, 86
Cross sectional research, 26
Crystalized intelligence, 233
Cued recall, 179
Cultural norms, 421
Cushing's syndrome, 79

D

Daily Hassles Scale, 320
Daily Hassles Scale-Revised, 320
Dark adaptation, 99
Decision making, 229
Deep coding, 167
Deficiency orientation, 355
Defining abnormality, 361
Delayed gratification, 304
Delirium, 60, 377
Dementia, 68, 401
Denial, 340
Dependent and independent variables, 12
Dependent personality disorder, 379

Dependent variable, 9
Depersonalization/derealization disorder, 373
Depression, 401–403, 407
Depressive disorders, 368
Descriptive and injunctive norms, 418
Descriptive norms, 418
Descriptive vs. injunctive norms, 418
Detection/Absolute Thresholds, 90
Developmental proscpagnosia, 64
Development of Depth Perception, 111
Diabetes, 77
Diagnostic manuals, 362
Dialectical Behavior Therapy, 397
Difference Thresholds/Just Noticeable
    Difference (JND), 93
Diffusion of responsibility, 436, 437
Disconnection syndromes, 37
Discriminant (divergent) validity, 33
Discriminative stimuli, 144
Dishabituation, 152
Disorders of consciousness, 59
Disorders of movement, 67
Disorders of Sensory Systems, 89
Displacement, 339
Disruptive, impulse-control, and conduct
    disorders, 377
Dissociating eye movements and attention, 115
Dissociative amnesia, 373
Dissociative disorders, 372
Dissociative fugue, 373
Dissociative identity disorder, 372
Divergent thinking, 212
Divided attention, 114
Door in the face, 431
Double-blind designs, 17
Dream analysis, 385
Dream engineering, 262
Dreams and dreaming, 261
DSM-5, 362
Duty to warn, 380
Dysmetropsia, 66
Dystonia, 72

E

Early-onset Alzheimer's, 69
Early onset dementia, 377
Eating behavior, 283
Echoic (auditory) memory, 157
Echolalia, 52
Echopraxia, 52
Ego, 336
Egocentrism, 301
Ego defense mechanisms, 337
Eidetic (photographic) memory, 177

Elaborative rehearsal (deep processing), 170
Electroconvulsive shock, 402
Electroconvulsive shock therapy, 403
Emotional and Social Competence Inventory (ESCI), 237
Emotional intelligence, 233
Employee assessment interviews, 442
Employee motivation, 452
Encoding, 167
Encoding specificity principle, 174
Encoding Through Rehearsal, 169
Endocrine system, 77
Engineering psychologists, 459
Enuresis, 131
Epilepsy, 46
Episodic memories, 58
Equilibrium and disequilibrium, 302
Equilibrium/Vestibular system, 88
Ergonomic workplace, 459
Erickson's psychosocial stages of development, 344
Esteem needs, 277
Estimated Daily Intake Scale for Sugar, 25
Estrogen, 77
Evolutionary psychology, 272
Examples Contrasting Sensation and Perception, 100
Examples of free-range parenting, 315
Examples of helicopter parenting/overparenting, 316
Examples of indifferent-uninvolved, 315
Examples of Informal/Inductive Reasoning, 205
Examples of over-regularization errors, 311
Examples of Positive Reinforcement (Reward), 135
Examples of psychological disorders, 365
Examples of sensory memory, 156
Examples of sensory registers, 156
Exceptional autobiographical memories, 176
Exceptional memory, 175
Excessive Daytime Sleepiness, 376
Exemplars, 203
Existence,Rrelatedness, Growth (ERG) theory, 452
Expectancy theory, 453
Expected value, 230
Experiment, 9, 10
Experimental and control groups, 11
Experimental design, 9
Experimental group, 12
Explicit (declarative) memory: episodic, 161

Explicit (declarative) memory: semantic, 161
Exposure treatment, 387, 388
Expressive aprosodia, 56
External locus of control, 359
Extinction, 129, 145
Extrapolation bias, 211
Extrapyramidal motor system, 293
Extraversion, 351
Extrinsic motivation, 279
Eyewitness testimony, 185

F

Face blindness, 100
Faces Scale, 455
Facet approach, 456
Face validity, 31
Facial expressions of emotion, 291
Factors affecting job satisfaction, 457
Failures of attention, 116
Failures of perception, 102
Fair discrimination, 414
False memory, 187
Familial dysautonomia, 75
Familial narcolepsy, 247
Feature detectors, 115, 119
Feeding and eating disorders, 374
Fetal alcohol spectrum disorder, 367
Fetal Alcohol Syndrome, 299
Fight-flight response, 77
Fight or Flight, 321
First impressions, 406
Fixated, 342, 344
Flashbulb memories, 173
Flooding, 390
Fluid intelligence, 232
Foot in the door, 430
Formal concepts, 202
Formal/Logical/Deductive reasoning, 205
Franco Magnani, 177
Free association, 383, 385
Free recall, 178
Fregoli delusion, 65
Freudian/psychodynamic personality structures, 335
Freudian slip, 384
Fritz Perls, 400
Frontal lobe, 51
Frontotemporal degeneration, 56, 72
Frontotemporal dementia, 72
Frontotemporal neurological disorder, 377
Functional analysis of behavior, 387
Functional fixedness, 223

Functions of thinking, 195
Fundamental attribution error, 408

G
Gabor patches, 90
Gambler's fallacy, 230
Gate-control theory, 87
Gender role, 420
General Adaptation Syndrome, 321
Generalized anxiety disorder, 15, 369
Generalized Anxiety Disorder-7, 25
Generativity vs. stagnation, 346
Genie, 297
Gestalt Laws of perceptual organization, 105
Gestalt therapy, 400
Gestures, 309
Gigantism, 79
Glial cells, 45
Global approach, 455
Goal-setting theory, 453
Graded exposure in Vivo, 388
Graduated, extended exposure, 390
Graduate Record Examinations (GRE), 235
Graphic rating form, 446
Graves' dermopathy, 78
Graves' disease, 78
Graves' ophthalmopathy, 78
Growth orientation, 356
Guillain-Barre syndrome, 75

H
Habituation, 152
Hallucinations, 367
Halstead-Reitan Battery, 73
Hamilton Anxiety Rating Scale, 25
Haptic (touch) memory, 158
Health promotion and disease prevention, 333
Heinz dilemma, 318
Helping, 436
Helplessness, 325
Hemineglect, 48
Hemiparesis, 61
Hemiplegia, 61
Hemispheric lateralization, 53
Heuristics, 206
Hierarchical Taxonomy of Psychopathology (HiTOP), 364
Highly Superior Autobiographical Memory (HSAM), 176
Holographic speech, 310
Honesty and integrity, 440
Human and Non-Human Auditory Systems, 83
Human and Non-Human Gustatory (Taste) Systems, 85
Human and Non-Human Olfactory Systems, 84
Human and Non-Human Tactile (Touch) Systems, 86
Human and Non-Human Visual Systems, 83
Human communication, 305
Human factors, 459
Humanistic theories of personality, 354
Humanistic therapy, 400
Huntington's disease, 72
Hypergraphia, 50
Hypersomnolence disorder, 376
Hyperthymesia, 176
Hyperthyroidism, 78
Hypnotic phenomena and applications, 263
Hypochondriasis, 374
Hypoglycemia, 78
Hypotheses, 6
Hypothesis testing, 18
Hypothyroidism, 78

I
ICD-11, 362
Iconic (visual) memory, 156
Ideational apraxia, 68
Identity theory, 405
Identity vs. role confusion, 345
Ideomotor apraxia, 67
Ignoring negative evidence, 227
Ill-defined problems, 215
Illness anxiety disorder, 374
Illusions of motion, 103
Implicit Association Test (IAT), 245
Implicit bias, 244
Implicit (non-declarative) memory, 161
Implicit prejudice, 244, 413
Impossible figures, 103
Imprinting, 296, 297
Inattentional blindness, 116
In-basket exercise, 444
Incentives, 279
Independent variable, 9
Indulgent or permissive parenting, 315
Industry vs. inferiority, 345
Infant-directed speech, 309
Infradian rhythms, 246
Ingroups and outgroups, 412
Initiating structure, 462
Initiative vs. guilt, 345
Injunctive norms, 418
Insanity and competency to stand trial, 379

Insight problems, 218
Insomnia disorder, 375
Instinct Theory: Fixed- or modal-action patterns, 272
Instinct theory of complex human behavior, 272
Integrity tests, 441
Integrity vs. despair, 347
Internal locus of control, 359
Internal vs external attribution, 408
International Personality Item Pool Representation of the NEO (IPIP-NEO), 25
Interpersonal attraction, 414
Interpersonal therapy, 398
Interrater reliability, 30
Intimacy vs. isolation, 346
Intraparietal sulcus, 38
Intrinsic motivation, 278
Introspection, 240

J
Job analysis, 439
Job Descriptive Index, 456
Job in General Scale, 455, 456
Job-related knowledge, 439
Job satisfaction, 455
Job Satisfaction Survey, 456

K
Kaufman Assessment Battery for Children (K-ABC-II), 236
Kaufman Test of Educational Achievement (K-TEA-3), The, 235
Ketamine, 401
Kinesthesia, 76, 88
Kirkpatrick model, 452
Knowledge affects perception, 115
Knowledge, Skills, Abilities, and Other job-relevant characteristics (KSAOs), 439, 444
Kohlberg's Stages of Moral Development, 318

L
Language, 305
Language development/acquisition, 309
Latent learning, 151
Law of effect, 133
Law School Admission Test (LSAT), 235
Leadership, 462
Learned helplessness, 146
Learning styles, 8
Left cerebral hemisphere, 54

Leiter International Performance Scale, The, 237
Levels of processing, 167, 168
Lie detectors, 294
Life review, 347
Limbic system, 77
Limitations of expertise, 227
Linguistic structure, 306
Links between motivation and emotion, 286
Lobotomies, 403
Localization of function, 41
Logopenic PPA, 56
Longitudinal research design, 26
Long-term memory, 160
Lou Gehrig's disease, 72
Low ball, 431, 432
Lucid dreaming, 262
Luria-Nebraska Neuropsychological Battery, 73

M
Macropsia, 66
Magnetic seizure therapy, 403
Maintenance rehearsal (shallow encoding), 169
Major neurocognitive disorder, 68
Mania, 368, 402
Manifest content, 385
Marshmallow Test, The, 304
Maslow, 355
Maslow's hierarchy of needs, 275, 355
Maturation, 299
Maximization Scale, 231
Maximizers vs. Satisficers, 231
Mayer-Salovey-Caruso Emotional Intelligence Test (MSCEIT), 237
Means-ends analysis (decomposition), 219
Medical College Admission Test (MCAT), 235
Medical treatments, 401
Medium encoding, 167
Melodic intonation therapy, 54
Memory failure and its consequences, 183
Memory palace, 172
Memory storage, 155
Mental representations, 202
Mental set, 222, 227
Mental status exam, 367
Mere exposure effect, 414, 415
Meta-analysis, 27
Metacognition, 214
Metacognitive Awareness Inventory, 215
Method of loci, 173
Micropsia, 66
Mild cognitive impairment, 68

Mild neurocognitive disorder, 68
Mindfulness-based cognitive therapy, 398
Mindfulness-based stress reduction, 393
Mind palace (method of loci), 172
Miscellaneous examples related to parenting and child-rearing, 316
Mixed emotions, 290
Mnemonic devices, 172
Mnemonists, 176
Modularity, 37
Modules, 37
Monocular depth cues, 106
Mood dependent retrieval, 183
Moral development, 318
Morphemes, 307
Motherese, 309
Motion aftereffect, 103
Motivational conflict, 287
Motivational interviewing, 400
Multiple sclerosis, 44
Myasthenia gravis, 76
Myelin, 44
Myths and intuitions, 1

N
Naglieri Nonverbal Ability Test, 237
Naïve realism, 104
Narcolepsy, 246, 376
National Health and Social Life Survey, 286
Natural/abstract concepts, 202
Naturalistic observation, 20
Nature of consciousness, 239
Nature of emotion, The, 289
Negative emotions, 289
Negative punishment, 139
Negative reinforcement, 138
NEO PI-R, 25
Networks, 37
Neural plasticity, 39
Neurocognitive disorders, 377
Neurodevelopmental disorders, 365
Neurofibrillary tangles, 69
Neuropathic pain, 46
Neuropsychological disorders, 47, 73
Neuroticism, 353
Newborn reflexes, 298
Nightmares and night terror disorder, 352
Non-associative learning, 152
Nonconscious, 241
Nonprojective personality tests, 360
Nonreactive measures, 22

Norms supporting antisocial behavior: deindividuation, 423
Not guilty by reason of insanity, 379
Null hypothesis, 18
Number Reduction Task, The, 218, 222

O
Obedience, 433
Obesity, 283
Object permanence, 300
Observational learning, 150
Observational study, 10
Obsessive-compulsive and related disorders, 370
Obsessive-Compulsive Disorder (OCD), 342
Obstacles to problem solving, 222
Obstructive sleep apnea, 376
Occam's Razor, 6
Occipital lobe, 47
Occupational health psychology, 458
Oculomotor cues to depth: accommodation, 110
Oculomotor cues to depth: convergence, 110
Odor Awareness Scale, 25
O*Net, 439
One-word stage, 310
Openness, 349
Operant conditioning, 133
Operant conditioning treatment methods, 392
Operational definitions, 13
Oppositional defiant disorder, 377
Optimal level of arousal, 274
Oral stage, 342
Organizational citizenship behavior, 460
Orthostatic hypotension, 74
Osteoporosis, 78
Other Race Effect, 95, 186
Other stress-related mental health problems, 333
Overjustification effect, 136, 281

P
Pain, 87
Pain control, 87
Palinacousis, 50, 89
Palinopsia, 48
Panic attacks, 401
Paranoid personality disorder, 378
Paraplegia, 43
Parapraxis, 384
Parenting styles, 346

Parietal lobe, 48
Parkinson's dementia, 72
Parkinson's disease, 72
Parosmia, 89
Parsimony, 5
Partial reinforcement: fixed-interval, 142
Partial reinforcement: fixed ratio, 143
Partial reinforcement: variable interval, 142
Patient Health Questionnaire, 25
Pavlov's experiments, 125
Peabody Picture Vocabulary Test–Revised, The, 237
Pegwords, 172
Pelli Robson contrast sensitivity chart, 90
Pelopsia, 66
Perception without sensation, 120
Perceptual constancies, 105
Performance-level criteria, 451
Peripheral nervous system, 74
Perseveration, 52
Persistent vegetative state, 59
Personal identity, 405
Personality disorders, 378
Person Object Action system, 171
Person schemas, 301
Phallic stage, 344
Phantosmia, 89
Phineas Gage, 51
Phoneme restoration effect, 199
Phonemes, 306
Phrenology, 1, 41
Physical appearance and attraction, 417
Physical stressors, 319
Physical stress responses, 321
Physiological needs, 278
Piaget, 300
Piagetian stages, 300
Piaget's Mountain task, 301
Placebo effects, 16
Pleasure principle, 335
Polygraph, 294
Position Analysis Questionnaires, 439
Positive emotions, 289
Positive psychology, 363
Positive punishment, 138
Positive reinforcement, 392
Positive reinforcers, 134
Postpartum depression, 369
Postprandial hypotension, 74
Posttraumatic stress disorder, 331
Power Threat Meaning Framework (PTMF), 364
Praxis, 67
Preconscious, 240

Predictability, 323
Predictive validity, 33
Preferential-looking technique, 300
Primacy effects, 166
Primary negative reinforcers, 135
Primary progressive aphasia, 55
Priming, 161, 200, 243
Princess Card Trick, 184
Proactive interference, 163
Problem solving, 215
Procedural memory, 161
Progressive relaxation training, 387
Projection, 337
Projective personality tests, 359
Proprioception, 76
Proprioceptive systems, 88
Prosody, 56
Prosopagnosia, 42, 63, 100
Prospective memory, 168, 180
Prototypes, 203
Psychoactive drugs, 401
Psychodynamic Diagnostic Manual (PDM-2), 362
Psychodynamic therapy, 383
Psychological/emotional stressors, 320
Psychological/emotional stress responses, 322
Psychophysical measurements, 90
Psychosexual stages, 342
Psychosurgery, 403
PTSD, 371
Punishment, 138, 393
Pure autonomic failure, 74
Pyramidal motor system, 293

Q

Quadriplegia, 44
Quasi-experiments, 11

R

Racial stereotypes, 413
Rajan Mahadevan, 176
Random assignment, 17
Random dot stereograms, 111
Random sampling, 17
Rational Emotive Behavior Therapy, 395, 397
Rationalization, 337
Raven's Progressive Matrices, The, 236
Reaction formation, 338
Reactive attachment disorder, 372
Reality principle, 336
Recall, 178
Recency effects, 166
Receptive aprosodia, 56
Receptive field, 115

Index

Reciprocal determinism, 358
Reciprocity norm, The, 421
Recognition, 179
Recognition heuristic, 206
Recruiting employees, 449
Reduced Environmental Stimulation Therapy, 403
Reflexive behavior, 43
Regression, 341
Reid Report, The, 440
Reinforcers, 134
Relationship-oriented leader, 462
Release from proactive interference, 164, 165
Reliability, 29
Reliability vs. Validity, 34
REM behavior disorder, 251
Remote Associates Test, 213
REM sleep behavior disorder, 376
Repetitive Transcranial Magnetic Stimulation (rTMS), 403
Representativeness heuristic, The, 210
Repression, 337
Research Domain Criteria (RDoC), 363
Research measures, 28
Reticular activating system, 59
Retinal/binocular disparity, 110
Retrieval, 163, 178
Retroactive interference, 166
Retrograde amnesia, 58, 192
Right cerebral hemisphere, 56
Risk/loss aversion, 230
Risky decisions, 229
Rorschach Inkblot Test, 359

S

Safety needs, 277
Sample, 17
Samples/sampling, 17
Scaffolding, 302
Scales of measurement, 28
Schedules of reinforcement, 141
Schemas, 190, 301
Schizophrenia, 399, 402
Schizophrenia oral history project, 368
Schizophrenia spectrum and other psychotic disorders, 367
Scholastic Aptitude Test (SAT), 234
Science vs. Pseudoscience, 1
Scientific method, 3
Scripts, 301
Secondary negative reinforcers, 135
Seizure disorders, 46
Selective attention, 114
Self-Actualization Scale, 276

Self-defeating thoughts, 393
Self-determination theory, 278
Self-efficacy, 357, 358
Self-fulfilling prophecies, 406
Self-managed work teams, 461
Self-reference effect, 170
Self-serving bias, 411
Semantic coding, 164
Semantic memory, 58
Semantic paraphasias, 55
Semantics, 308
Sense of control, 325
Sensitization, 152
Sensory Adaptation/Habituation, 98
Sensory systems, 81
Serial position effect, 166
Serial recall, 178
Sexual behavior, 285
Shading, 109
Shallow encoding, 167
Shape from shading, 109
Shaping, 144, 392
Shass Pollak, 177
Shiftwork disorders, 459, 460
Short-term (working) memory, 158
Signal Detection Theory (SDT), 95
Similarity and attraction, 415
Simple Examples of Conditioned responses (CR), 129
Simultagnosia, 101
Simultanagnosia, 48, 62
Situational judgment, 441
Situational judgment tests, 441
Skinner's air crib, 316
Sleep apnea, 257
Sleep deprivation, 260
Sleep disorders, 246
Sleep-Wake disorders, 375
Sleepwalking, 248
Slip of the tongue, 384
Smoking during pregnancy, 300
Snowy Pictures Task, 96
Social anxiety disorder, 399, 402
Social cognitive theory, 357
Social development, 312
Social facilitation, 424, 426
Social facilitation and interference, 424
Social facilitation vs. social interference, 426
Social identity, 405, 406
Social interference, 425, 426
Social loafing, 424
Social norms, 418
Social phobia, 369
Social readjustment rating scale, 320

Social referencing, 292
Social schemas/scripts, 301
Social skills training, 399
Social support, 326
Soft skills, 443
Somatic nervous system, 75
Somatic neuropathy, 75
Somatic symptom and related disorders, 373
Somatoparaphrenia, 67
Somatosensory agnosia, 65
Somatosensory allochiria, 66
Sources of motivation, 269
Specific sources of motivation, 269
Split-half reliability (internal consistency), 30
Spontaneous recovery, 130
Spurious correlations, 24
SSRIs, 401
Standardized Measures of Achievement, 235
Standardized Measures of Aptitude, 234
Standardized Measures of Intellectual Functioning (Intelligence), 235
Stanford-Binet Intelligence Scales (SB5), 235
STAR format, 443
State dependent retrieval, 182
Statistical vs. Practical/clinical significance, 19
Stephen Wiltshire, 177
Stereopsis, 111
Stereotypes, prejudice, and discrimination, 413
Still faceprocedure, 312
Stimulus control, 144
Stimulus discrimination, 130
Stimulus generalization, 131
Storing Long-Term Memories, 162
Strange Situation, 312
Stress-hardy, 327
Stressors, 319
Stressors in the workplace, 458
Stress-prone, 327
Stress response mediators, 323
Stress responses, 321
Stroboscopic phenomenon, 246
Structured interviewing, 443
Studying consciousness, 239, 240
Subconscious/unconscious, 242
Subjective well-being, 277
Sublimation, 339
Subliminal messaging, 118
Subliminal perception, 118
Substance use disorders, 364
Summarizing parenting styles, 313
Superego, 336
Superstitious behaviors, 137
Supertasters, 85
Survey and questionnaire research, 24

Surveys about sexual behavior, 286
S.V. Shereshevsky, 176
Syndromes of neuropsychological disorder, 57
Syntax, 307
Systematic desensitization, 387

T

Tactile agnosia, 65
Tarasoff case, 380
Task-oriented leader, 462
Telegraphic/2-word speech, 311
Teleopsia, 66
Temperament, 317
Temporal lobe, 49
Temporal lobe epilepsy, 50
Teratogens, 299
Testing employee characteristics, 439
Testosterone, 77, 434
Test-retest reliability, 29
Tests of cognitive abilities, 234
Tests of emotional intelligence, 237
Thalidomide, 299
Thalidomide babies, 299
Thematic Apperception Test (TAT), 359
Theories, 8
Theories of motivation, 272
Thinking and reasoning, 205
Tic disorders, 366
Time-out, 393
Todd's syndrome, 66
Token economies, 148
Token economy system, 392
Top-down influences on perception, 120, 197
Top-down processing, 101, 115
Touch Sensitivity, 86
Touch threshold, 92
Tourette's syndrome, 366
Trainee-learning criteria, 451
Training employees, 450
Training-level criteria, 450
Trait theories of personality, 348
Transcranial magnetic stimulation, 38, 403
Trauma- and stressor-related disorders, 371
Trigeminal neuralgia, 76
Trolley car moral dilemma, 318
Trust vs. mistrust, 345
Two-point discrimination thresholds, 92
Type I and II errors, 18

U

Ultimate attribution error, 409
Ultradian rhythms, 246
Unconditioned Responses (UR), 128
Unconditioned Stimuli (US), 128

Unfair discrimination, 414
Uniform Guidelines on Employee Selection Procedures, 450
Unobtrusive meaasures, 22
Unstructured job interviews, 443
Unstructured job performance narratives, 446
Using analogies, 219
Utility, 230

V

Validity, 31
Values in Action Classification of Character Strengths, 363
Variable ratio, 143
Vascular dementia, 71
Virtual reality, 262
Virtual reality desensitization/exposure, 388
Visual agnosia, 50, 62
Visual cliff, 111
Visual illusions, 102
Visual persistence, 156
Visual search, 113
Vygotsky, 302

W

Wada procedure, 42

Ways of Coping Scale, 328
Weak critical periods, 296
Weber's Law, 94
Wechsler Adult Intelligence Scale (WAIS-IV), The, 235
Wechsler Individual Achievement Test (WIAT-III), The, 235
Wechsler Intelligence Scale for Children (WISC-V), The, 236
Well-defined problems, 216
Wernicke's aphasia, 55
Wernicke's area, 55
Where's Wally/Waldo pictures, 113
Wide Range Achievement Test (WRAT5), The, 235
Wild boy of Aveyron, 296
Woodcock-Johnson Tests of Achievement IV, The, 235
Work group, 461
Working backwards, 220
Work Preference Inventory, 281
Work team, 461

Z

Zones of Proximal Development, 302

GPSR Compliance
The European Union's (EU) General Product Safety Regulation (GPSR) is a set of rules that requires consumer products to be safe and our obligations to ensure this.

If you have any concerns about our products, you can contact us on

ProductSafety@springernature.com

In case Publisher is established outside the EU, the EU authorized representative is:

Springer Nature Customer Service Center GmbH
Europaplatz 3
69115 Heidelberg, Germany

www.ingramcontent.com/pod-product-compliance
Ingram Content Group UK Ltd.
Pitfield, Milton Keynes, MK11 3LW, UK
UKHW021255180426
11947UKWH00010B/792